ADVANCE PRAISE

"Stephen Rue's book is truly game-changing. It provides a powerful roadmap for anyone seeking to unlock their potential and transform their lives. With profound insights and practical strategies, this book will inspire you to embrace your journey of self-discovery and become the person you were meant to be."

—Jack Canfield, coauthor of the Chicken Soup for the Soul® series and The Success Principles™: How to Get from Where You Are to Where You Want to Be

"This is a practical, hard-hitting book that shows you how to unlock your hidden potential to achieve any goal you can set for yourself. It teaches you how to become on the inside whatever you really want to be, have, or do on the outside."

—Brian Tracy, motivational speaker and author of over eighty bestselling books

"Stephen Rue's Must is a powerful guide to personal transformation and resilience. Through compelling storytelling and practical wisdom, Rue shows us how to turn life's challenges into opportunities for growth. This book provides a roadmap for anyone seeking to unlock their full potential and live a life of purpose. Must is not just inspirational; it's a call to action for those ready to become the person they were meant to be."
—Loren Lahav, international speaker, bestselling author of *Stay True: Own Your Badass and Beautiful Life*, and Life and Wealth Mastery Facilitator for Tony Robbins Companies

"Stephen Rue's Must is a personal testament to the power of resilience and purpose. Through his raw and inspiring story of triumph over adversity, masterfully weaving scientific insights, wisdom from global thought leaders, and proven success strategies, this book provides you with a powerful tool kit to dismantle your self-limiting beliefs and build the exceptional life you're destined to live. This extraordinary work will ignite a fire within you. Must is an awakening for anyone ready to rewrite their story!"
—Les Brown, world-renowned motivational speaker and bestselling author of books including *Live Your Dreams* and *It's Not Over Until You Win*

MUST

Must

BECOMING THE
PERSON YOU ARE
MEANT TO BE

=

STEPHEN RUE

HOUNDSTOOTH
PRESS

COPYRIGHT © 2025 STEPHEN RUE
All rights reserved.

MUST
Becoming the Person You Are Meant to Be

FIRST EDITION

ISBN 978-1-5445-4827-2 *Hardcover*
        978-1-5445-4826-5 *Paperback*
        978-1-5445-4828-9 *Ebook*

To my beloved family—my mother, Jeannie Rue Pearson, whose unwavering love and resilience have been the guiding light and inspiration for this book; my uncle, J. Robert Ates, who stepped into my life as a guiding father figure, mentor, and steadfast supporter; my sister, Elizabeth Rue Brennan, whose courage in adversity and devotion as a mother to Brooke and Ashley Brennan continually inspire me; and to Elizabeth Herberg, the love of my life, whose encouragement and partnership have sustained me through every challenge. I also honor all my family members, past and present, whose love and legacy have shaped the person I am today.

The love, lessons, and strength I have received from my family inspire me to dedicate this book to a wider circle: to all who yearn for a more fulfilled and meaningful life, who are committed to expressing love through service to others, and who strive each day to rise above perceived emotional, psychological, physical, or mental limitations. This book is for those searching for hope, a new direction, and a path to living an extraordinary life while uplifting others, regardless of where they begin.

We are bound together by a shared journey of challenge, growth, and transformation. May these pages offer you inspiration, guidance, and the courage to become the person you are truly meant to be—and to help others do the same.

Contents

INTRODUCTION 11

PART ONE: EXPLORATION
1. MY JOURNEY 21
2. MUST MINDSET 39
3. MUST CORE BELIEFS 61
4. MUST CORE VALUES 95
5. OUR MUST PERSONAL NARRATIVE 135
6. MUST STANDARDS 157
7. MUST PURPOSE 185

PART TWO: IMPLEMENTATION
8. MUST ACTIONS 209
9. THE MUST ZONE 221
10. GOAL SETTING 237
11. TIME MANAGEMENT AND PRODUCTIVITY 269
12. MUST HABITS 289
13. TENACITY AND PERSEVERANCE 311

PART THREE: INTEGRATION: TRANSCENDENCE, TRANSFORMATION, AND THE FULLNESS OF LIFE
14. SUFFERING: THE DARKNESS BEFORE THE LIGHT 331
15. TRANSFORMING SUFFERING INTO PURPOSE 375
16. BLESSINGS, GRATITUDE, AND GRACE 395
17. ON LOVE AND SELF-LOVE 421

CONCLUSION 457
ACKNOWLEDGMENTS 463
ABOUT THE AUTHOR 467
HOW TO STAY IN TOUCH WITH ME 469
BIBLIOGRAPHY 471

Introduction

OUR JOURNEY TOGETHER

Have you ever felt the stirring of greatness within you, a whisper of the extraordinary person you were meant to become? If so, you're not alone. Each of us carries within us the seeds of greatness, waiting to be nurtured and brought to life. Welcome to *Must: Becoming the Person You Are Meant to Be*, a transformative journey that will guide you from where you are to where you've always dreamed of being.

This book is your roadmap to unlocking your true potential and embracing the life you were destined to live. As you read these pages, you'll embark on a profound exploration of personal growth and self-discovery. We'll delve into the core principles that shape our lives, from the power of mindset to the importance of values and beliefs. You'll learn how to harness your inner strength, overcome obstacles, and cultivate the habits that lead to lasting success and fulfillment.

But this book offers more than just theory and concepts. It's filled with real-life stories of triumph over adversity, practical strategies for personal transformation, and actionable insights you can apply immediately to your life. From mastering your mindset to discovering your life's purpose, from setting ambitious goals to developing unshakable habits, each chapter builds upon the last to create a comprehensive framework for becoming your best self. Built on decades of research and mentored knowledge, this book is for individuals who are dedicated to intentionally designing their own extraordinary life.

At the heart of this journey is the concept of *Must*—the driving force that will propel you toward your personal discovery and growth. *Must* is not just a word; it's a mindset, a commitment, and a call to action. It's the voice inside you that says, "I must become the person I was meant to be." Throughout this book, we'll explore how embracing your *must* can transform your life, helping you fulfill your dreams beyond your wildest expectations.

I understand the challenges you face. Perhaps you're feeling stuck, unsure of your direction, or overwhelmed by life's demands. Maybe you've experienced setbacks that have shaken your confidence, or you're struggling to break free from limiting beliefs that hold you back. I've been there too. My journey has been marked by personal tragedies, physical challenges, and moments of deep doubt. But it was through these very struggles that I discovered the transformative power of personal development and the principles I'll share with you in this book.

As I sit here reflecting on the journey that led me to write this book, I'm struck by the profound connection I feel with you. If you've picked up this book, we likely share a common quest for growth, meaning, and becoming the person we were created to be.

I vividly remember the day I realized I wasn't living up to my full potential. It was a crisp autumn morning, and as I looked in the mirror, I saw a man who had weathered storms but was still adrift. The tragedies my family and I had endured—the loss of my stepfather to suicide, abandonment by my biological father, and the physical challenges of my youth—had left their mark. Though not unhappy, I knew deep in my soul there was more to life, more to me than what I was living.

In that moment of clarity, I felt a desperate need for direction. I yearned for a guiding light, a push toward a path of transformation. This led me on several decades-long quests for wisdom and understanding. I immersed myself in personal development books, audio programs, seminars, a law degree, a master's in business, university certification as a trauma-based life coach, certification in leadership at Harvard Law School, and, ultimately, a doctorate curriculum. I devoured and read biographies of individuals who had triumphed over seemingly insurmountable obstacles. For over three decades, I dedicated myself to this pursuit, spending countless hours on research, reflection, and seeking mentorship from extraordinary minds.

This journey of self-discovery became my personal yellow brick road. Each book, each seminar, and each conversation with a mentor was a stepping stone, leading me closer to the person I was meant to become. The collective wisdom I gathered became the compass that guided me through the fog of uncertainty toward my true purpose.

Through this process, I discovered a profound truth: our hardships, pain, and struggles are not mere obstacles but the very forge in which our purpose is shaped. The tragedies that once threatened to define me became the catalyst for my transformation. They instilled in me a burning desire to help others navigate their own paths to self-discovery and growth.

In the vast landscape of self-improvement literature, many books focus on a single aspect of personal development, offering insights into specific areas such as mindset, goal setting, or resilience. However, these works often leave readers without a comprehensive guide to navigate the entire journey of self-discovery from start to finish. This is where *Must: Becoming the Person You Are Meant to Be* stands out. Unlike other self-help books, this transformative guide takes you by the hand from the very beginning of your personal development journey, providing a step-by-step roadmap to unlock your true potential. For many, the journey of self-discovery can be daunting, with no clear starting point or direction. This book addresses that gap by offering a holistic approach, building upon foundational principles to help you develop the essential building blocks of self-improvement.

As you embark on this journey, you will discover a profound and revolutionary transformation in your life. Each chapter is carefully crafted to guide you through the process of personal growth, from understanding your core beliefs and values to setting ambitious goals and cultivating unshakable habits. By following this comprehensive framework, you will not only gain clarity on your life's purpose but also develop the resilience and mindset necessary to overcome obstacles and achieve lasting fulfillment. What sets this book apart is its ability to keep you on track throughout your journey, ensuring you stay focused and motivated as you progress toward becoming the person you were always meant to be. The insights and strategies presented here are not just theoretical; they are actionable and grounded in real-life experiences, making your journey of self-discovery both practical and profoundly impactful.

This book is my outstretched hand, heart, and mind to you, offering insights and principles gathered over years of dedicated study and personal experience. I want you to know I take this responsibility extraordinarily seriously. The wisdom contained in these pages is not my own—it is a carefully curated collection of insights from luminaries and thought leaders, adapted and refined through the lens of my own experiences. It is my gift to you, a roadmap to help you navigate your journey of personal growth and self-discovery.

As we embark on this journey together, remember that each chapter builds upon the last, offering you a step-by-step approach to unlocking your potential and becoming the person you were always meant to be. My purpose, forged in the fires of personal tragedy and triumph, is to be your guide on this transformative path. So if you're ready to take that first step, to begin your journey of self-discovery and growth, know that you're in good company. Together, we'll explore the wisdom of the ages, apply timeless principles to modern challenges, and uncover the extraordinary potential that lies within you.

By the time you finish this book, you will:

- Develop an unshakable growth mindset that empowers you to overcome any obstacle
- Uncover and rewrite the limiting beliefs that have been holding you back
- Discover your unique purpose and align your life with your deepest values
- Master the art of goal setting and develop the habits of highly successful individuals
- Learn to harness the power of your emotions and build unwavering resilience
- Cultivate deep, meaningful relationships and surround yourself with supportive, like-minded individuals
- Unlock your full potential and become the person you were always meant to be

Most importantly, you'll learn to embrace your *must*—that inner drive that will push you to achieve greatness and fulfill your true potential. You'll discover how to tap into this powerful force, using it to overcome obstacles, push through self-doubt, and achieve things you never thought possible.

Whether you're facing personal challenges, seeking professional growth, or simply yearning for a more meaningful existence, *Must* provides the tools and inspiration you need to take that crucial first step toward change. It's about recognizing that you have a choice at every moment—a choice to remain as you are or to become the person you were always meant to be.

THE POWER OF *MUST*: REDEFINING OUR COMMITMENT

The origins of the word *must* are deeply rooted in our language. Etymologically, *must* comes from the Old English word *moste*, meaning "had to," which itself stems from the Proto-Germanic *motan*, conveying necessity or obligation. Traditionally, *must* has been associated with a sense of compulsion or inevitability—something that we are required to do, often without choice.

For many of us, the word *must* might conjure memories of childhood, where authority figures told us what we must do, often accompanied by a sense of reluctance or resistance. It was something imposed upon us—a rule or directive that felt burdensome, something we did not choose but were forced to follow.

However, as we step into our journey of self-discovery and personal growth, it's time to reshape and redefine what *must* means for us. No longer should *must* be seen as a heavy-handed command from external sources.

Must is not a burden; it's a beacon. It's the energetic, exhilarating feeling of living in alignment with who we are meant to be, fully embracing the life that God and the universe have intended for us. *Must* represents our deepest desires and truest aspirations, guiding us toward a life of authenticity and fulfillment.

When we say that we must do something, it's not about being forced into action against our will. It's about recognizing the nonnegotiable aspects of our existence that align with our core beliefs, values, and purpose. *Must* is about being true to ourselves. It's about understanding that to live authentically, we must honor who we are at our core. After all, we must be ourselves, right? There is no greater necessity than the call to exist in a way that is fully aligned with our true nature.

EXPLORING, IMPLEMENTING, AND INTEGRATING THE BUILDING BLOCKS OF PERSONAL GROWTH

As we embark on this transformative journey of self-discovery and growth, it's essential to understand the comprehensive roadmap this book provides. Your transformative journey is divided into three distinct parts, each offering unique insights and challenges that contribute to personal growth and self-discovery.

Part 1 is your Exploration. The first part of the book lays the foundation for transformation by exploring the concept of the Must Mindset. You are introduced to the concept that personal development starts with changing your mindset from a fixed perspective to one of growth and opportunity. Through personal stories, you are encouraged to confront your own limiting beliefs. This section emphasizes the importance of identifying and reshaping core beliefs, highlighting how early experiences and societal influences shape our perceptions of ourselves. This exploration will help you in your journey from self-doubt to empowerment and inspire you to embrace your potential and adopt a mindset of unwavering resilience and determination.

Part 2 is your Implementation phase. The second part delves deeper into actionable strategies for personal transformation. Here you are introduced to practical tools for overcoming obstacles, such as goal setting, time management, and cultivating productive habits. The Must Zone is introduced as the nonnegotiable space where individuals align their imperative actions with their core beliefs, values, standards, and purpose. You are guided to establish meaningful goals that intentionally reflect your deepest aspirations. This section also addresses the role of obstacles as a catalyst for growth, encouraging readers to transform pain into purpose. Through stories of perseverance, tenacity, and grit, you learn how to navigate adversity with grace and emerge stronger.

Part 3 is Integration. The focus shifts to achieving self-actualization and living in alignment with your true self. This section examines how we face and move through life's inevitable suffering and hardships, while also learning to recognize and embrace our blessings, gratitude, grace, love, well-being, and the legacy we leave behind. You are encouraged to reflect deeply on your relationships, spiritual beliefs, and the ways you contribute to the world. True fulfillment, as explored here, arises from embracing authenticity and pursuing a balanced life that nurtures every dimension of your well-being. The book concludes with an invitation to embody the Must Mindset fully, transforming personal growth from an aspiration into a nonnegotiable commitment.

By following this structured approach, you'll not only gain clarity on your life's purpose but also develop the resilience, mindset, and habits necessary to overcome obstacles and achieve lasting fulfillment. Each chapter builds upon the last, providing a step-by-step guide that keeps you on track throughout your journey of self-discovery and growth.

As we journey together through these pages, remember that true transformation is not about becoming someone else; it's about becoming more authentically yourself. It's about peeling away the layers of doubt, fear, and limiting beliefs to reveal the brilliant, capable, and worthy individual that has always existed within you.

This book promises more than just a reading experience; it offers you a profound journey of self-discovery. As you turn these pages, you'll explore vital aspects of existence that most people never take the time to examine, delving into insights that will dramatically transform your view of yourself, the world around you, and your unique purpose in life.

So if you're ready to unlock your potential, live with purpose and passion, and make your unique mark on the world, then let's begin. The path to becoming the person you are meant to be starts here and now. Your extraordinary life awaits. Are you ready to embrace your *must* and claim it?

PART ONE

Exploration

Exploration serves as the foundation for your journey toward self-actualization by guiding you through the process of uncovering your *musts*—the mindset, core beliefs, values, personal narrative, standards, and purpose that define who you are and what truly matters to you. This section is about self-discovery, inviting you to pause, reflect, and examine the inner workings of your life. Through thoughtful exploration, you will identify the personal narrative that has shaped your identity, uncover the values that guide your decisions, and confront the beliefs that either empower or limit you. The goal of this part is to help you gain clarity about what drives you at your core and to align your life with your authentic self.

Exploration is not about finding quick answers but about asking meaningful questions. Who are you at your essence? What do you stand for? What are the nonnegotiables—the *musts* that will serve as your compass moving forward? By delving into these questions, you will lay the groundwork for everything that follows in this book. This is where transformation begins: by understanding yourself deeply and creating a clear vision of the life you are meant to live.

CHAPTER 1

My Journey

"The purpose of life is not to be happy. It is to be useful, to be honorable, to be compassionate, to have it make some difference that you have lived and lived well."

—Ralph Waldo Emerson

On a warm summer Saturday morning, under the bright, clear skies of Camp Lejeune, the marines marched past the red brick hospital. That day radiated with beauty and promise. On that day, remarkable beginnings and poignant endings occurred. Approximately 250,000 people were born, their first cries marking new life and a future yet to be defined, while another 125,000 people died, each individual experience being so personal, so brief, and so definitive.

For my mother and father, this day held a unique and joyous significance—it was the day I was born. I imagine that my father and mother were overjoyed with the birth of their first child. To them, this was a wondrous day of hope and blessings. I also imagine that on that very same day, for another family, that day was a day of tremendous sadness, grief, and pain because of the loss of a loved one or a tragic event that forever changed their world. The beauty and grace of life continue to exist simultaneously with the moments of extreme personal suffering of others. Our time will come for each experience, some more than others.

Please pause for a moment and consider: What is one significant day in your life that shaped your perspective? How do you remember it now?

After my father's military service ended, my father, Robert, my mother, Jeannie, and I moved to New Orleans, the place of our family roots. My sister, Elizabeth, was born two and a half years later. I remember her as a beautiful infant. I can smell the baby powder even today. Do you remember the sights and smells of your youth? It's remarkable the simple things that we remember and the senses that can bring up images of our past. It's also regrettable that we cannot remember many things from our childhood. I have visual images of my father in those formative years. I remember the special occasions like Christmas mornings and Mardi Gras, but I don't remember the sound of his voice. I don't remember his scent. I can't remember statements of love and affection. I don't remember much about my biological father. I do remember the day he moved out. I was six years old. My sister, Elizabeth, was three and a half years old.

What early memories stand out most for you? Are they associated with joy, loss, or something else? How do these memories shape your sense of self today?

My parents got divorced. Last year, as a lawyer, I decided to look for the courthouse records of their divorce. Surprisingly, I found them. The digital image of the yellowed, faded, typed pages unexpectedly stung. I did not expect that those old pleadings filed by my father's lawyer would reference me as a child with some special physical needs. I was a child, and he did not seek custody.

After the divorce, my father took us for a visitation a few times. Soon enough, we got to meet his new girlfriend and their new baby. Soon thereafter, the visitations stopped altogether. Through the years, I received an occasional birthday or Christmas card. But we did not talk, and we did not see him. Soon there was a painful silence. My sister and I were introduced to the demon called abandonment. His absence became a reminder of my lack of significance to him. Little did I know that I'd gotten the first glimpse of the blessing that would make me who I am today.

As you'll discover in later chapters, early experiences often plant the seeds for our core beliefs—about ourselves, our worth, and what's possible. Keep this in mind as you reflect on your story.

My mother, a very beautiful woman, was quite lonely after my father left us. Mom became reacquainted with someone whom she knew from high school. Leonard Rodney Rue came into not only my mother's life but also my sister's and my lives as though he were a miraculous savior. Rodney was a gentle, intelligent, and sensitive man who became an eye surgeon. After his residency and studies at Louisiana State University Medical School, he asked my mother to marry him. She did, and we moved to Atlanta, Georgia, where he started his private medical practice. I cannot remember a happier time. This was our personal Camelot, equipped with a beautiful home and surrounded by hills and pine trees. We finally had a father who loved us and who was not going to leave us. We called our new father Dad. We were happy and loved.

One summer, Dad sent me to camp in the beautiful Great Smoky Mountains in North Carolina. Mom and Dad came to visit me one weekend. As they were leaving the parents' weekend, they got into their car and started to drive away, but the car stopped. My father, Rodney, got out of the car, walked back over to me, and told me how much he loved me. Then he walked to the car and drove away. My mother later told me that as he got into the car and began driving away, tears rolled down his cheeks as he said, "I love Steve so very much."

Two days later, in the quiet twilight of a July evening, Rodney, my stepfather, my beloved dad, retreated to the solitude of his master bedroom closet. There, in the stillness, he held a handgun, its cold steel barrel pressed against the roof of his mouth. In a moment, in unfathomable despair, in a millisecond of time, and with a few ounces of pressure, he pulled the trigger and blew the back of his head off.

My mother and nine-year-old sister found my father in that closet and experienced the unspeakable aftermath that could not be unseen.

The repercussions of that single last act reached far beyond the physical confines of that closet; they echoed through the souls of those he left behind. Our dad, Rodney, was thirty-six years old. My mother, thirty-four. For years, I often pondered the depths of his suffering, trying to grasp what led him to that irreversible decision.

I was spared this visual torment, being away at summer camp, but the news of my father's departure abruptly ended my childhood.

Have you experienced a loss or event that changed your life's direction? How did you respond at the time, and how do you see it now?

In the wake of this tragedy, although I was a child, I felt the need to be responsible, telling myself that as the sole son, I must be the strength of my family. I must be the "man of the house." I refused to cry. My grief was my silent burden. At the funeral home, I found a moment alone in the room with my father in the coffin, and I reached out hesitantly to touch the face that once held smiles, warmth, and expressions of love, now cold and still. Everything became hauntingly real. At the funeral, the minister recited the words of Psalm 23:4, as I heard, "I walk through the valley of the shadow of death." I did not hear any other part of the pastor's message. All I knew was that my family and I were in that "shadow of death."

Adding to our anguish over the death of my stepfather, my biological father, Robert, remained distant, failing to provide any comfort or support that we desperately needed. Our personal journey through despair was an intimate encounter with loss, and the profound pain engulfing our family had just begun. This pain was a relentless force, inescapable and all-consuming. Our cries for relief seemed to vanish into the void, unanswered. In this darkness, I sought solace in prayer, yearning for divine intervention to alleviate our suffering. I felt I had been abandoned by my first father, by my second father, and now by God.

I know, without a doubt, my mother suffered her own form of a nervous breakdown and darkest depression after the love of her life killed himself. Yet I learned the meaning of what one must do in life through the willpower and actions of my mother. Despite her immense pain, she had a singular purpose of taking care of my sister and me.

This experience planted the seeds for my understanding of resilience—a theme we'll revisit when we explore the Must Mindset and the role of adversity in shaping our character. When have you had to be strong for others? What did you learn about yourself?

My path, sculpted by my mother's teachings and example, led me to higher education. Degrees in law and business were milestones, yet my true calling has been adding the element of trauma-based life coaching. Loyola Law School and later Harvard Law School's training in leadership beckoned and led me to doctoral studies in organizational leadership. In the heart of New Orleans, I became more than an attorney; I was a healer of wounds unseen, a guide to help others through trauma and self-doubt.

I had known my purpose for a while and started pursuing my *musts*, yet I had not been healed. This journey led me back to my inner child, the eleven-year-old "man of the house" trapped within me. At a personal development event, I confronted and embraced this part of my past, finding peace and wholeness. In a dark room, I lay on the floor and was asked to go find that earlier self, that young child, Steve, who had been hurt, and who had to be the strong "man of the house." Going toward this hurt space, I, the adult Stephen—tempered by years of self-improvement and introspection—reached back through the mists of time, deep within my soul, to that eleven-year-old Steve. I whispered to him, "I am you now." I assured him, "You are safe, you are loved, and I am here to heal and embrace you. You have excelled in your role and shown incredible strength as the 'man of the house.'"

At that moment, I hugged my inner child in an embrace of acceptance and love. It was a profound merger of past and present, a dissolution of old wounds into the healing light of now. As I opened my eyes, tears, the first in many years, were a testament to the liberation I felt. For the first time in a long while, I was whole. That hurt little boy, once trapped in a past of pain and responsibility, was now part of my present, his pain purified and transformed. In its place, I found an unshakable calm and peace, a serenity that has never left me. This moment marked my escape from my self-imposed torment in my mind, setting me free to assist others, including you, toward healing, toward realizing that within each of us is a resilient spirit waiting to be acknowledged, loved, and integrated into the wholeness of our being. I rose from that great inner battle of my mind and soul that had tormented me for years. I turned to my God and thanked Him.

Just when I thought I had a good grasp on healing, I found myself with one more hurdle—my biological father, to whom I had not spoken, except just once, since I was a child. Was there an avenue for reconciliation and healing?

The answer came one night with a phone call. It was my half sister, whom I had not seen since she was that little baby I saw during one of my last visits with my father. She was now in her fifties. She called to tell me our father had died. In my father's obituary, his latest wife did not mention my sister or me as being his daughter and son. Yet my adult half sisters welcomed my sister and me to the funeral. I decided to go.

Prior to the funeral, I met my half sisters, and we were tasked to find a container to bury my father's ashes in later that day. Once we found a container, my sister took his bag of ashes out of her trunk and, without thinking, placed it in my arms. I immediately started crying as that was the first time since I was six years old that I had held my father. It was a bag of his ashes, but it was the closest I ever got. I was holding the remains of a man who abandoned my sister and me and whom I had hated and who I was hurt by for decades. My half sister then took the ashes and poured them into the burial container. Some of the ashes were suspended in the air. God whispered in my ear, "Stephen, you cannot be angry at ashes." This was a revelation of freedom.

Is there someone in your past you need to forgive—not for their sake, but for your own freedom? What would letting go of that pain make possible for you?

I cannot be angry at ashes!

How long had I carried that pain and anger within me, when it did not affect anyone else but me? The anger and pain were self-maintained in my own internal battle in my mind. I was finally freed. I forgave my father and my stepfather.

Forgiveness—of others and ourselves—is a recurring theme in personal transformation. We'll revisit this concept in later chapters as we examine how beliefs and values shape our journey.

FINDING THE COURAGE TO BE VULNERABLE

As you can see, my journey was not a linear path, but a winding road filled with moments of triumph and periods of deep introspection. Each step forward required me to confront my fears, doubts, and ingrained beliefs about my capabilities.

What is one area of your life where you feel called to be more vulnerable? What might you gain by sharing your story or asking for support?

I vividly remember a time when I truly challenged my perceived limitations. It was during my law school years, a period marked by intense academic pressure and self-doubt. There were nights when I sat at my desk, surrounded by towering stacks of legal textbooks, feeling overwhelmed and questioning my ability to succeed. The voice of my childhood insecurities whispered that I wasn't smart enough, that my prior life's challenges had somehow made me less capable.

But in those moments of doubt, I made a conscious decision to push back against those limiting beliefs. I began a practice of daily affirmations, each morning declaring, "I am capable. I am worthy. I can overcome any challenge, and I will be successful." At first these words felt hollow, almost laughable. But as days turned into weeks, and weeks into months, I internalized those affirmations.

This practice of self-reflection extended beyond mere positive thinking. I kept an informal journal, documenting not just my struggles but also my small victories. I wrote about the day I successfully argued in a mock trial at law school, the moment I received praise from a professor I admired, and when that shift came when I started to excel and helped fellow students understand complex legal concepts. These entries became a tangible record of my growth and a reminder that I was constantly evolving and improving.

Journaling and affirmations are tools we'll return to in the Must Habits and Goal Setting chapters. They are not just for reflection but for rewiring your beliefs and building momentum.

As I expanded my vision of what was possible, I took on challenges I would have previously deemed impossible. I remember the day I decided to run my first marathon. The idea seemed absurd at first. How could someone who had once worn steel leg braces possibly run 26.2 miles? But I approached this challenge with the same mindset of growth and self-reflection I had developed.

Training for the marathon became a metaphor for my entire journey of personal growth. Each long run was an opportunity to push my limits, to prove to myself that I was capable of more than I had ever imagined. There were days when my legs ached and my lungs burned, but I kept going, driven by the knowledge that I was becoming stronger with each step.

The day of my first marathon was a profound experience. As I crossed the finish line, tears streaming down my face, I realized I had not just completed a race—I had shattered the limitations I had placed on myself for so long. This achievement became a powerful reminder that I could keep evolving and there was no fixed ceiling to my potential.

What is your marathon? Is it a goal that seems beyond reach but might be possible with a new mindset? How would your life change if you achieved it?

This mindset of continual growth extended into my professional life as well. I took on complex cases that challenged me intellectually and emotionally. Each case became an opportunity to learn, to grow, and to develop litigation abilities that would make a material difference in others' lives. I remember late nights, poring over legal precedents, driven by the belief that I could find a way to help my clients, no matter how difficult their situations seemed.

Throughout this journey, I learned the importance of vulnerability. I realized that true strength comes not from pretending to be invincible, but from acknowledging our weaknesses and working to overcome them. I shared my story more openly, speaking about my childhood challenges and the journey I had undertaken. This vulnerability not only helped me connect more deeply with others, but it also allowed me to receive support and encouragement from unexpected sources.

Research on vulnerability, which we'll explore in Chapter 2 "Must Mindset," shows that sharing our struggles is often the first step toward building authentic relationships and lasting change.

As we explore the profound nature of *musts* and the leaps of faith they require, it's essential to recognize the courage it takes to embrace vulnerability in this process. Brené Brown delves deeply into this concept in her powerful book *Daring Greatly*. Brown's work is a testament to the idea that vulnerability, far from being a weakness, is a source of great strength. When we dare to step into our *musts* we are, in essence, choosing to live vulnerably, to expose our deepest selves to the world, and to take risks in pursuit of our truest calling.

Brown's inspiration for *Daring Greatly* comes from a famous speech by Theodore Roosevelt, often referred to as "The Man in the Arena." In this speech, Roosevelt eloquently captures the essence of what it means to take bold action, to step into the arena of life, fully aware of the risks but driven by the desire to live authentically and purposefully. Here is the full quote from Roosevelt's speech, which serves as a powerful reminder of the importance of daring greatly:

> It is not the critic who counts; not the man who points out how the strong man stumbles, or where the doer of deeds could have done them better. The credit belongs to the man who is actually in the arena, whose face is marred by dust and sweat and blood; who strives valiantly; who errs, who comes short again and again, because there is no effort without

error and shortcoming; but who does actually strive to do the deeds; who knows great enthusiasms, the great devotions; who spends himself in a worthy cause; who at the best knows in the end the triumph of high achievement, and who at the worst, if he fails, at least fails while daring greatly, so that his place shall never be with those cold and timid souls who neither know victory nor defeat.

This powerful passage from Roosevelt's speech is more than just an eloquent expression of courage—it is a clarion call to those who wish to live a life of meaning and purpose. To step into your *musts* is to enter the arena and embrace the possibility of stumbling, facing criticism, and experiencing setbacks. But it is also to engage fully with life, to strive valiantly in the pursuit of something greater than yourself, and to commit to a cause that is worthy of your devotion.

Where in your life are you being called to "step into the arena"? What is one risk you are willing to take in pursuit of your *must*?

Brown argues it is in this space of vulnerability, where we expose ourselves to potential failure, that we find our greatest strength. When you commit to your *musts*, you are not just making practical decisions—you are daring greatly. You are choosing to live with the knowledge that true fulfillment comes not from avoiding risks, but from embracing them with an open heart. This act of daring is where real growth occurs, where you push beyond the boundaries of comfort and into the expansive realm of possibility.

Roosevelt's words and Brown's insights converge to reinforce the idea that embracing your *musts* is an act of profound bravery. It is about choosing to live authentically, even when the outcome is uncertain, and understanding that the value lies not just in the victories you may achieve, but in the courage it takes to step into the arena in the first place.

Recognize that by daring greatly, by stepping into the arena of life and embracing your *musts* with all their inherent risks, you engage in the truest form of self-expression. You are living in a way that honors your deepest values and your highest potential, fully aware that while you may stumble, you are doing so in pursuit of something extraordinary.

In the end, the journey toward fulfilling your *musts* is not just about the goals you set or the achievements you attain; it is about the courage to live fully, to embrace vulnerability, and to dare greatly in every aspect of your life. By doing so, you align yourself with the most authentic version of who you are and open the door to a life rich with purpose, meaning, and profound satisfaction.

In the chapters to come, we'll explore how to shift from vulnerability and self-reflection into action—building habits, setting goals, and crafting a life aligned with your deepest values. Keep these reflections close; they are the foundation for your next steps.

THE CIRCLE OF LIFE: A HOLISTIC APPROACH TO WELL-BEING

As we continue this transformative journey of self-discovery and growth, it's essential to have a comprehensive framework for evaluating our lives. This is where the Circle of Life comes into play—a holistic tool that allows us to assess and balance various aspects of our existence. The Circle of Life offers a panoramic view of our existence, inviting us to examine the intricate nature of our lives.

This holistic approach to self-assessment encourages us to evaluate the various domains that contribute to our overall well-being and fulfillment. As we embark on this journey of self-discovery, we map out the terrain of our lives and identify peaks of success and valleys of opportunity.

Drawing upon both ancient wisdom and modern insights, the Circle of Life represents our lives as a dynamic, interconnected whole. Imagine a circle divided into several segments, each representing a different aspect of life. These segments typically include:

1. **Health and Vitality:** Health and vitality are the bedrock of our well-being, serving as the foundation upon which all other aspects of our lives are built.

2. **Relationships:** Relationships are a fundamental pillar of personal growth, deeply rooted in the wisdom of historical teachings on social harmony.
3. **Career and Professional Achievement:** Our career and achievements reflect our pursuit of personal and professional fulfillment.
4. **Financial Well-Being:** Financial stability provides security and freedom, enabling choices that align with personal and professional goals while reducing stress.
5. **Personal Growth and Learning:** Personal growth and continuous learning are the cornerstones of holistic development.
6. **Spirituality, Religion, and Inner Peace:** Inner peace fosters harmony with the self and the transcendent, offering comfort and resilience across religious and secular traditions.
7. **Community and Legacy:** Building connections and leaving a meaningful impact ensures continuity, reflecting the cyclical wisdom of collective existence.

These elements function like the spokes of a wheel, each contributing to the smooth and balanced progression of our life journey. This concept is often attributed to personal development pioneers like Zig Ziglar and Paul J. Meyer in the 1960s. It is widely used today as a self-assessment tool in coaching and personal growth.

One of the most cherished moments in my self-improvement journey occurred years ago when I had the privilege of personally meeting Zig Ziglar during his visit to New Orleans. He was the epitome of authenticity, radiating personal charisma and serving as a beacon of transformational wisdom. Zig Ziglar often proclaimed, "I believe that being successful means having a balance of success stories across the many areas of your life. You can't truly be considered successful in your business life if your home life is in shambles." Ziglar's philosophy is that true success requires balance across various aspects of life, not just excelling in one area while neglecting others.

Take a moment to visualize your own Circle of Life. Which areas—health, relationships, career, finances, personal growth, spirituality, or community and legacy—feel vibrant and fulfilling? Which ones feel neglected or out of balance?

What is one area of your life that, if nurtured, could bring greater harmony and satisfaction to your overall well-being? What small step could you take this week to begin that process?

Success within the Circle of Life is about achieving balance and growth across all these areas, recognizing that each contributes to our overall sense of fulfillment. However, success in one area does not compensate for failure in another; it is the harmonious development of all aspects that leads to a truly successful life.

Throughout this book, we will apply the principles of the Circle of Life to guide our exploration of personal development. By dividing our lives into segments, we can systematically examine each area and identify where we need to focus our efforts. This approach will enable us to achieve a more balanced and fulfilling life, ensuring that no aspect of our well-being is neglected. As we delve into each chapter, we will use the Circle of Life as a lens to integrate the concepts of mindset, core beliefs, values, purpose, and habits, providing a cohesive and practical roadmap for becoming the person we were meant to be.

The true beauty of personal development lies in its boundless potential. You have no limits. The Circle of Life is not a fixed design but a living, breathing reflection of your unique journey—a journey that evolves with you.

You possess the power to create, add, or invent new sections in your Circle of Life that may not have been mentioned here. Perhaps there is an area of your life that sings with special significance, something that resonates in the depths of your soul and demands to be acknowledged. This is your journey, and your Circle of Life should encompass all that is meaningful to you.

Is there a unique aspect of your life, such as creativity, adventure, or service, that deserves its place in your Circle of Life? How might honoring this part of yourself change your daily experience or sense of fulfillment?

The concept of life balance isn't about achieving perfection in every area simultaneously, but rather about creating harmony and alignment with our values and aspirations. As the renowned psychologist Carl Jung once said, "The shoe that fits one person pinches another; there is no recipe for living that suits all cases." This wisdom underscores the importance of personalizing our approach to life balance, recognizing that each individual's ideal "circle" may look different.

What does balance look like for you personally, rather than what others expect? Where do you feel pressure to conform, and how might you redefine balance on your own terms?

As we assess different life areas, from career and relationships to health and personal growth, we often uncover surprising insights about ourselves. It's not uncommon to find that areas we thought were strengths may actually need attention, while hidden talents and passions might emerge in unexpected domains.

Can you identify a life area you thought was a strength but, on reflection, needs attention? What small step could you take this week to nurture it?

This process of self-discovery can be both enlightening and empowering, providing a roadmap for personal development and growth.

Consider what other dimensions of your life deserve their own place in your circle. Does a passion, a calling, or a responsibility define your essence? Perhaps it's your commitment to creativity, adventure, community, environmental stewardship, or something else entirely unique to you. Whatever it may be, honor it by crafting an additional section in your Circle of Life that rings true with your innermost being.

In our quest for balance, we must remember the goal is not perfection but progress. Each small step toward harmony in our lives contributes to a greater sense of fulfillment and purpose. As we nurture the various aspects of our being, we cultivate a resilience that allows us to weather life's storms with grace and emerge stronger on the other side.

THE ROLE OF FEAR

Let's talk about a universal force that often stands behind our self-imposed limitations—fear. Fear is a powerful emotion that can shape our thoughts, actions, and, ultimately, our destiny. We all grapple with it, but understanding its role in our lives can be transformative.

What fear of failure, success, or judgment most often holds you back from pursuing your goals? When did you last notice this fear influencing your choices?

FEAR OF FAILURE

Let's contemplate the fear of failure coming to life when a negative force whispers in your ear, "What if you fail? What if you're not good enough?" These whispers can paralyze you, keeping you from taking steps toward your dreams. How often have you stopped yourself from pursuing a goal because the fear of failing loomed large? William Shakespeare wrote, "Our doubts are traitors, and make us lose the good we oft might win, by fearing to attempt." Think about this in your own life. How many opportunities have you missed because of this fear?

Recall a recent opportunity you passed up because of fear. What might have been possible if you had acted despite your fear? What lesson can you carry forward?

Remember, failure is not the opposite of success; it's part of the success journey. Each time you fail, you've merely found one more way not to achieve your goal. Each misstep is a building block to greatness if you choose to see it that way.

FEAR OF SUCCESS

Surprisingly, fear doesn't just hold us back from failing; it also holds us back from succeeding. The fear of success is subtle but equally debilitating. It makes you question, "What will happen if I do succeed? Will people treat me differently? Will I become someone I don't recognize?" This fear can be as paralyzing as the fear of failure, maybe even more so because it hides in the shadows of your consciousness.

Reflect on your experiences. Have you ever self-sabotaged because the idea of success seemed too overwhelming? Have you addressed these fears? Have you ever noticed yourself pulling back when things were going well? What beliefs about success might be lurking beneath the surface?

Arianna Huffington, founder of *The Huffington Post*, urges, "Fearlessness is like a muscle. I know from my own life that the more I exercise it the more natural it becomes to not let my fears run me."

Embracing success requires acknowledging these fears and understanding that they are part of the journey. By doing so, you can step into your most empowered self, ready to face the challenges and rewards that success brings.

FEAR OF JUDGMENT

Let's address the fear of judgment. This is the voice that says, "What will people think? Will they judge me? Will I be rejected?" This fear can stop you from speaking your truth, pursuing your passions, or even being yourself. Consider how this fear has influenced your decisions. When have you held back your true self because you worried about what others would think? What would it feel like to act authentically, regardless of others?

Bernard M. Baruch, the American financier and political consultant, offers his wisdom, often misattributed to Dr. Seuss: "Be who you are and say what you feel, because those who mind don't matter and those who matter don't mind." Your life is not a popularity contest; it's a journey to become the fullest expression of yourself. Judgment will come whether you play it safe or take risks. Wouldn't you rather be judged for who you truly are than live a life that's a pale imitation of your true self?

Think about how many times you've held back from expressing an idea, pursuing a goal, or even wearing a certain outfit because you were afraid of what others might think. This fear of judgment can stifle your creativity and prevent you from reaching your full potential. Reflect on your life—how often have you let the opinions of others dictate your actions? Remember, the people who judge you are often dealing with their own insecurities and are not as focused on you as you might think. In reality, people spend only a few seconds thinking about you before their thoughts return to their own lives.

As we mature, we realize the opinions of others should not affect who we are to ourselves. It is in this realization that we find true freedom. Aristotle proclaimed, "It is the mark of an educated mind to be able to entertain a thought without accepting it." By shedding the fear of judgment, you liberate yourself to live authentically and pursue your passions without restraint. Your journey is unique, and it deserves to be honored and lived to its fullest without the shadows of others' opinions holding you back.

REDEFINING THE ROLE OF FEAR

The role of fear in our lives is undeniably significant, but we have the power to redefine that role. Will you allow fear to be a roadblock or a springboard? The choice is yours.

How could you use fear as a signal for growth, not a stop sign? What is one courageous action you can take this week to move through fear and toward greater balance in your Circle of Life?

Every time you face your fears, you reclaim a piece of your personal power. You tell the universe, "I am bigger than this fear. I am stronger. I am more capable." And the universe will reply, saying, "I've been waiting for you to realize that. Now let me show you what you can do."

Tony Robbins, a master of personal transformation, encourages us to embrace fear rather than run from it. He says, "The quality of your life is in direct proportion to the amount of uncertainty you can comfortably deal with." I have often heard Tony remind us to "dance with our fear" rather than being paralyzed by it, and this shall open doors to personal growth and success.

Let's recognize fear for what it is—a self-created limitation, a figment of our imagination, a gate that we have closed. And let's be the ones to swing it wide open. Trust in yourself, in the unfolding of your life, and in the masterpiece that only you can create with your unique hues of experience, wisdom, and love.

We should always remember that when we viscerally feel fear, we know that we are alive. We know we are not simply waiting in the wings of life, but we are stepping onto the main stage of our potential and greatness. Each time you choose courage and commitment over fear, you reclaim your power and reinforce your commitment to growth. This act of bravery is what transforms fear from a roadblock into a stepping stone, paving the way for a mindset where personal development is not just possible but nonnegotiable.

CHAPTER 2

Must Mindset

"I am always doing what I cannot do yet, in order to learn how to do it."
—Vincent van Gogh

My mother always told me I was the most beautiful baby who had ever lived and I was destined for greatness. She bathed me in compliments and praise. She loved me so unconditionally, and the truth about what she always told me was not important. What was important was that she instilled in me a sense of self-worth, a sense of being someone special. I was a young child with innate potential. I knew it because my mother told me so. The truth is that most mothers tell their child, and everyone else who will listen, that they have the most beautiful baby on the planet—that their child is special and meant for greatness. This was the beginning of my belief system.

I also had a father for the first six years of my life, and I don't recall any praise from him, pats on the back, or hugs of encouragement. I honestly don't recall a single positive thing he ever said to me in my entire life. In fairness to him, we don't remember too much as infants or very young children, but as I grew into my formative years, I discovered he had a huge disinterest in my existence. I felt unloved by him. Whether we have real memories of our first few years or not, sometimes we fill in the blanks based on experiences we remember. I felt there must be something wrong with me, and that was why he did not care about me. I must be somehow inferior and not the boy he wanted. It must be me. I must be unworthy of his love. This was also the beginning of my belief system.

My mind was full of mixed thoughts about my identity. Was I that child in my mother's eye, or was that child not worthy of the love of his own father? Was I both a gift from God and an irrelevant soul? Did I have potential, or was I destined to live a lackluster life of failure and mediocrity?

My self-esteem and beliefs about myself incrementally evolved with my interactions with other children at school, the kids in the neighborhood, and what other adults had to say.

The tough thing about my young life was compounded because I had some physical hurdles. I was born literally tongue-tied, severely pigeon-toed, with a pronounced concave chest. The things we don't like about ourselves are the things we intensely focus on. My mother would tell me how beautiful my blue eyes were and how wonderful I was as a tall boy for my age, but I focused on my imperfections and shame. My negative views about myself far overshadowed any ego-building positive affirmations my mother told me. I knew I was simply less.

Reflecting on my struggles with self-worth, I found clarity in my search to understand these internal battles are not unique—they are shaped by what is called our mindset.

Our mindset is the lens through which we view our abilities and our potential for growth. It's more than just a belief system; it's a foundational element that shapes our approach to life, our reactions to challenges, and our capacity to evolve.

Are your early memories of life full of happy visions of loving embraces and proclamations of your destiny for success? Did your family and schoolmates make you feel good about yourself and your potential? Do you remember people asking you what you want to be when you grow up? What was your answer? Did you deeply believe in your answer that you would be that person?

Did you also experience darker times when you did not feel good about yourself? Were there times when you thought that you were less? What did others say to you, and what did you say to yourself that made you feel that way? Did you feel you were awkward or ugly, fat or skinny, alone or lonely, slow or stupid? Pick your flavor of self-defining loathing.

Did you have a mixed mindset like I did?

FIXED AND GROWTH MINDSETS

We are blessed that academics, philosophers, and other deep thinkers have explored mindsets and how they shape our lives. One of these extraordinary souls is Carol Dweck, whose groundbreaking research and book *Mindset* venture into this world and give us insight we can use today. Dweck's years of research found that there are fundamentally two types of mindsets: fixed and growth.

A fixed mindset is the belief that intelligence and abilities are static, while a growth mindset is the belief that skills and intelligence can be developed through hard work, learning, and dedication. These distinct mindsets reflect how we view our abilities, approach to challenges, and intelligence.

Carol Dweck's research shows that mindsets are not simply a binary choice or an on/off switch. Instead, our beliefs about our abilities and potential exist on a spectrum, and most people experience a blend of both fixed and growth mindset tendencies depending on the situation. For example, you might approach learning a new language with excitement and perseverance (a growth mindset), while feeling anxious and limited about your athletic abilities (a fixed mindset). Think of an area in your life where you feel you can improve with effort and another where you feel stuck. How might your beliefs differ in each?

Understanding these mindsets is just the beginning. The real transformation comes when we learn how to shift our thinking in daily life.

Dweck emphasizes that our mindset can shift over time and across contexts, sometimes even within the same day, much like riding a roller coaster with its natural ups and downs. Rather than being determined by fate or defaulting to a fixed mindset, we have the capacity to notice our thinking patterns and intentionally nurture a growth mindset through self-awareness and effort. The key is not to eliminate fixed mindset thoughts entirely, but to recognize them and choose to respond with curiosity and resilience.

If you've ever felt like life's coin flips land on "tails" more often than "heads," you're not alone. As described earlier, a fixed mindset can limit your willingness to take on challenges or learn from setbacks, while a growth mindset encourages you to see abilities as improvable through effort and learning. Remember, these perspectives shape how we respond to life's ups and downs. Dweck's work highlights that everyone has moments of self-doubt or limitation, but these do not have to define us. This research mirrors my journey. Understanding science is one thing, but living it is another. My experience brought these ideas to life. For years, I struggled to break free from a fixed mindset, feeling trapped by my past. But as I applied these principles, my perspective—and my life—began to change.

In my youth, I sometimes believed I had no control over my future. Dweck's research reassures us that our mindset is not set in stone: we can learn to see challenges as opportunities, and even if we sometimes slip into a fixed mindset, we can always choose to shift back toward growth.

Do we let people say things that sabotage our belief in ourselves? I truly believe people are innately good in spirit, yet others can be initially and purposely downright cruel, dishonest, and deceitful when they say things to us. I now understand why Mark Twain quipped, "The more I learn about people, the more I like my dog." Do any of those dark thoughts linger in your mind, soul, and spirit, suffocating your beliefs in your potential? Sometimes we let those moments of personal suffering cloud our mindset with doubt and a lack of belief in ourselves. We are just not that winner in life. We settle for what is given to us, for what comes our way.

While it's possible to have confidence in your abilities, holding a fixed mindset—as defined earlier—can actually hinder your success and growth. This perspective can lead to several limitations:

1. **Avoiding challenges:** People with a fixed mindset tend to shy away from difficult tasks that might expose their weaknesses.
2. **Giving up easily:** When faced with obstacles, those with a fixed mindset are more likely to become discouraged and quit.
3. **Ignoring feedback:** Constructive criticism is often seen as a personal attack rather than an opportunity for improvement.
4. **Feeling threatened by others' success:** Instead of finding inspiration in others' achievements, fixed mindset individuals may feel intimidated.
5. **Stunted growth:** By believing abilities are fixed, individuals may not put in the effort to develop their skills further.

Beyond these outward behaviors, a fixed mindset also shapes how we see ourselves on the inside. People with a fixed mindset often find themselves preoccupied with proving their abilities, which can lead to overestimating or underestimating what they're truly capable of. This need to constantly validate their intelligence or talent makes it difficult for them to see themselves clearly. In contrast, those with a growth mindset are more interested in learning and improvement than in defending their self-image. As a result, they become more honest and accurate in assessing their strengths and weaknesses. This self-awareness allows them to identify areas for growth and take meaningful steps forward, turning self-reflection into a powerful tool for personal development.

Remember the other side of the coin with a profile of optimism—heads! Those who embrace a growth mindset believe they can develop through ongoing dedication, hard work, and perseverance.

Even if you have a strong ability in a certain area, adopting a growth mindset is more likely to lead to long-term success. This approach encourages continuous learning, resilience in the face of setbacks, and a willingness to put in the effort required for achievement.

In a growth mindset, effort is much more than just hard work. It's the engine of progress. People who believe their abilities can develop understand that improvement doesn't come from effort alone, but from using effective strategies and a willingness to seek help when needed. Rather than repeating the same approach and hoping for a different outcome, those with a growth mindset actively look for new ways to tackle challenges. They ask questions, learn from others, and adapt their methods, seeing each obstacle as a chance to refine their approach. This openness to learning and collaboration is a hallmark of real growth.

A person with a growth mindset believes that anything is possible. Doors will open; if doors are closed, windows will open; if windows are closed, somehow, some way, at the end of the day, the object of their desire will be achieved. Success is in their grasp. It is inevitable.

People with a growth mindset don't just believe they can get better—they actually handle challenges differently. When they make mistakes or face setbacks, they're more likely to bounce back and try again, showing greater resilience. They see errors as opportunities to learn rather than as signs of failure.

Scientists have found that having a growth mindset changes how our brains react: when people believe they can improve, their brains are more active and engaged when they make a mistake, helping them learn from it more effectively. So a growth mindset doesn't just change how we think—it can also change how our brains work and how we respond to life's obstacles.

Please find a coin. Take one out of your pocket, place it in your hand, and flip it high into the air. Watch as it shimmers, spins, and twirls back to earth until you grab it and cover the coin with your other hand. Don't look! Is it heads or tails for you? Do you have a fixed or growth mindset?

MY SHIFT FROM A FIXED MINDSET TO A GROWTH MINDSET

For years, I felt trapped in a cycle of stagnation, feeling as though I was merely existing rather than truly living. The weight of past tragedies and obstacles seemed to anchor me in place, preventing me from moving forward. I felt I was falling short of my true potential, and this realization gnawed at me relentlessly.

The struggles my family and I faced were numerous and, at times, overwhelming. From the loss of my stepfather to suicide, to the abandonment by my biological father, to the physical challenges I faced as a child, each experience had left its mark. For a long time, I viewed these hardships as insurmountable barriers, defining limitations I couldn't overcome.

I vividly remember a moment from my childhood. When I was ten years old, I failed a math test despite studying. My teacher pulled me aside and said, "It's not about being naturally good at math. It's about continually working hard and practicing." This simple interaction planted the seed of a growth mindset in me, shaping my belief that abilities can be developed through effort. Parenting author Peggy O'Mara tells us, "The way we talk to our children becomes their inner voice."

Despite my stagnation, that inner voice whispered there had to be more.

During a period of introspection, I questioned my fixed mindset. I realized that by viewing my abilities and potential as static, I was limiting myself. I allowed my past to dictate my future, and in doing so, I denied myself the opportunity for growth and change.

This realization was the catalyst for my transformation. I began to seek new perspectives, immersing myself in personal development books, attending seminars, and engaging with mentors who challenged my way of thinking. I saw that my experiences, rather than being roadblocks, could be pathways to a greater purpose.

This shift in perspective was not instantaneous. It required constant effort and self-reflection. I had to consciously challenge my negative self-talk and replace it with affirmations of growth and potential. I had to push myself out of my comfort zone, embracing new challenges as opportunities for learning rather than risks of failure.

As I embraced this growth mindset, I approached life with renewed energy and purpose. The world around me began to look different, full of possibilities rather than limitations. I saw how my unique experiences could be used to help others, to make a difference in the world. This journey led me to my calling as an attorney and advocate for those facing their own struggles. It inspired me to run marathons, proving to myself that the physical limitations of my youth were no match for my determination. It drove me to coauthor a book with Les Brown, sharing the insights I had gained through my transformation.

Looking back, I realize the pain and struggles were indeed catalysts—not for stagnation, but for growth. They were the crucible in which my growth mindset was forged. Today, I continue to embrace this mindset, always seeking new ways to learn, grow, and contribute to the world around me.

My journey from a fixed mindset to a growth mindset taught me that our potential is not set in stone. It's a choice we make every day—a choice to learn, grow, and become the person we were meant to be. And I'm grateful to have made that choice.

HOW YOUR MINDSET IS CREATED

Understanding how your mindset is created is essential for transforming it and unlocking your full potential. Let's explore how your mindset has been shaped over time and how you can actively influence it for tremendous personal growth and success.

Over two centuries ago, an English philosopher and physician, John Locke, sparked controversy with his intellectual contemporaries. This man proclaimed that we, as newborns fresh out of a mother's womb, have a mind tabula rasa, or a blank slate. Locke believed we are a blank canvas born without innate ideas, and from the first light and sound of our environment and experiences, we shape our identity and mindset. Locke wrote, "The little and almost insensible impressions on our tender infancies have very important and lasting consequences."

Our experiences, what we are told, and how we incorporate these beliefs into our definition of ourselves become identity tattoos that are difficult to remove. Our young brains are developing, and the fertilizer in our mental greenhouse determines whether we have a positive mindset, like a cascading cluster of purple wisteria blooms, or a fixed mindset, like limiting invasive, smothering kudzu vines.

In my formative years, my blank canvas was painted by impressionists. Yours was too. My mother, who was an artist and teacher for most of her adult life, painted a picture of me that glistened with the growth mindset that I could do anything, and life was full of beauty like Monet's serene lily ponds. Life was a joyous dance, as seen in Renoir's and Degas's works. My mother and my maternal grandmother, named Memaw, always taught me to embrace the positive essence of life and to "dance in the rain." In this world, anything is possible.

Think back to your early years. Picture yourself in various scenarios: playing in the park, attending school, interacting with family. What messages did you receive from those around you? From your well-intentioned family members to teachers and friends, early influences played a crucial role in shaping your mindset. If you were praised for your effort and encouraged to embrace challenges, you likely developed a growth mindset.

Our mindset is not formed in isolation—it is shaped and reinforced by the messages we receive from those around us. Parents, teachers, coaches, and even the media play powerful roles in influencing how we see our abilities and potential. When we are praised for effort, encouraged to embrace challenges, or shown that mistakes are opportunities to learn, we are more likely to develop a growth mindset. Conversely, when we are labeled or judged solely on outcomes, we may internalize a fixed mindset, believing our qualities are set in stone. The good news is that by becoming aware of these external influences and consciously challenging limiting messages, we can reshape our mindset. Surrounding ourselves with people who support our growth and seeking positive, constructive feedback can help us nurture a mindset that is open to learning and change.

While our early mindsets are shaped by the words and actions of parents, teachers, and the media, we are not powerless to our upbringing or environment. As adults, we can intentionally cultivate a growth mindset environment by surrounding ourselves with people who model growth-oriented thinking, seeking mentors who encourage learning from mistakes, and choosing media that celebrates effort and resilience over innate talent. Practically, this means giving and seeking process-focused praise ("You worked hard and tried new strategies") rather than person-focused praise ("You're so smart"), openly discussing setbacks as learning opportunities, and being mindful of the language we use with ourselves and others. By consciously creating spaces—at home, at work, and in our communities—where growth is valued and mistakes are reframed as stepping stones, we reinforce the belief that abilities can always be developed. In this way, we not only reshape our own mindset but also become positive influences for those around us.

"The influence of each human being on others in this life is a kind of immortality." These words, attributed to John Quincy Adams, emphasize the profound and lasting impact that individuals, especially those we encounter in our formative years, can have on shaping our mindsets and beliefs of what we can accomplish. This highlights the critical role that mentors, parents, and role models play in fostering a growth mindset through their guidance and support.

Another impressionist in my early life was my father, Robert. He was a different kind of painter. He painted with broad strokes, placing his image of me in a corner of limitations. As I previously mentioned, as a young child, I had physical hurdles. My tongue had to be surgically cut to release the bottom part of my tongue so I could learn how to speak normally. I recall countless sessions with a speech therapist, reciting, "She sells seashells by the seashore. The shells she sells are surely seashells. So if she sells shells on the seashore, I'm sure she sells seashore shells."

To deal with the severe inner pronation of my legs while being pigeon-toed, I was fitted and wore steel leg braces—yes, exactly like Forrest Gump. I even slept wearing them. Over time, they gradually helped. Even now, especially when I'm really tired, I may still walk a little pigeon-toed. The difference now is that I don't care. I know I'm perfectly imperfect. So are you.

These physical challenges were compounded by emotional ones, as my father's absence left an indelible mark on my sense of self-worth. His broad strokes painted me as someone confined by limitations rather than possibilities—a belief I carried for years until I redefined myself.

Have you experienced criticism or harsh words from your parents? Were you praised solely for your natural ability and not your potential? If so, you might have developed a fixed mindset. This belief—that your intelligence and talent are static—can lead to a fear of failure and a reluctance to face new challenges. Imagine a child growing up in an environment where success is celebrated only for its outcomes and failures are met with disappointment or ridicule. Such experiences can cement a fixed mindset, where the child may come to believe that their abilities are limited and immutable. As Carl Rogers, a prominent psychologist, wisely noted, "The only person who is educated is the one who has learned how to learn and change." This statement underscores the importance of nurturing a mindset that embraces growth and learning.

Malcolm Gladwell, the bestselling author of *Outliers: The Story of Success*, uses as an illustrative example Tiger Woods's incredible journey, which is a testament to the power of the growth mindset to achieve mastery. Woods's commitment to practice and improvement has driven him to unparalleled heights in his career. Through these experiences, Woods learned to thrive under pressure, turning every challenge into a bridge toward his legendary career.

In the early years of my journey of personal development, I had the privilege of speaking with Earl Woods, Tiger Woods's father. Earl emphasized that "You have to look deep down within yourself to realize your own expectations, set your own goals, and find your own strength to achieve them." Tiger's parents instilled a belief system within that talented young boy that has served him well in life.

Performance psychologist and *New York Times* bestselling author Dr. Jim Loehr has been instrumental in helping professional athletes—such as tennis greats Monica Seles and Andre Agassi, major golf championship winner Mark O'Meara, and quarterback Troy Aikman—gain their mental attitude and discipline for success. Loehr believes in building character and emotional resilience for purpose-driven performance and embraces challenges with a positive personal dialogue with a person seeking continual improvement. He opines, "Tiger Woods embodies the growth mindset through his mental toughness and commitment to excellence. He views challenges as opportunities to grow and improve." When I spoke with Dr. Loehr, he emphasized that an enlightened growth mindset is "one which strengthens moral character and a purpose-driven life."

So how and when were these attributes of a growth mindset formed? Tiger Woods's father, Earl, saw that Tiger, as a young child, had innate extraordinary potential in golf. Earl, a former amateur golfer, started teaching Tiger how to play when he was just a toddler. Tiger first held a golf club at eleven months old, and by age two, he was already appearing on television shows demonstrating his golfing skills. Earl Woods's parental influence played a crucial role in nurturing Tiger's interest in golf. He not only introduced him to the sport but also served as his primary coach and mentor. Earl's dedication to teaching Tiger the game laid a strong foundation for his development.

Tiger Woods's youth was a complex and multifaceted journey, a mixed cocktail of experiences that collectively shaped his growth mindset. From an extraordinarily early age, Tiger had an unwavering supporter in his father, Earl. This early exposure was coupled with a disciplined training regimen that emphasized not just physical skill but mental toughness. Tiger faced the pressures of high expectations and media scrutiny, appearing on television shows and competing in junior tournaments, all while navigating the challenges of racial discrimination and social isolation. The rigorous practice sessions orchestrated by his father, often filled with intentional distractions to build resilience, taught Tiger to view setbacks as opportunities for growth. Balancing his schoolwork with his golfing ambitions, Tiger developed a relentless work ethic and a deep passion for the game. This blend of intense practice, high expectations, early public exposure, and personal challenges forged a resilient growth mindset characterized by a relentless pursuit of excellence and an ability to adapt and overcome obstacles.

A FIXED MINDSET CAN STILL CHANGE

Imagine standing at the edge of a vast, open field. In front of you lies an uncharted path filled with opportunities and obstacles. Your beliefs about your capabilities determine whether you see a treacherous journey or an exhilarating adventure.

The great news is that we can change to create our own growth mindset.

I'd like to introduce you to Patricia Bartell. Patricia crawled, malnourished, on the dusty stone floor of an orphanage in Bolivia. She existed in a third-world country alone and in deep despair. She crawled on the dirt floor as she could not walk. Polio had stolen her mobility and her young spirit. This child had a deep scar that was wrapped like barbed wire around her left ankle. Another scar haloed her right ear as another reminder of the unrecorded abuse and neglect that she had suffered that left her abandoned in the orphanage. Her inner screams of suffering were not heard.

The orphanage had a catalog of the orphaned children residing in the stark building. Each child had a picture and a brief description so that potential adoptive parents could make informed decisions about whom to take home. Everyone had a picture and a narrative, except Patricia. Where a picture should have been was a void space, just like her life had been up to this point. There was no description of the child, only the name "Patricia Mamani." The last name of Mamani was often used by the orphanage when they had no idea what to call the child. It was like using "Jane Doe."

Patricia Bartell was near death. In her young world, hope did not exist. Each breath, each moment, was one of personal strife and solitude. Can we imagine that she had anything but formative experiences that led her to a fixed mindset about her life? Was a growth mindset even possible for a child who was bound to the dirt of the earth by disease and cruelty?

Yet despite this inauspicious beginning, Bartell pulled herself off the dirt floor of the orphanage. One pivotal moment in her life was when she decided to embrace music as a means of self-expression and healing. Initially, she struggled with the physical limitations imposed by polio, but she refused to let these obstacles define her future. Through sheer determination, she practiced relentlessly, honing her skills and mastering the accordion—a symbol of her triumph over adversity. This commitment not only allowed her to excel as a musician but also became the foundation for her growth mindset. Bartell learned that her abilities could evolve through effort and dedication, proving that even the most daunting challenges could be transformed into milestones for success. She is now an internationally acclaimed musician, public speaker, and author. Her book, *From Crutches to Crushing It: A Journey from Pain to Power*, tells the story of how, through perseverance and belief in ourselves, we can thrive in life. Her message to the world is "You're not broken, you don't need fixing, and there is nothing wrong with you!"

When you embrace a growth mindset, challenges become stepping stones rather than stumbling blocks. You see each obstacle as a chance to learn and grow. Carol Dweck asserts, "In a growth mindset, challenges are exciting rather than threatening. So rather than thinking, 'I'm going to reveal my weaknesses,' you say, 'I'm going to challenge myself to grow.'" This shift in perspective is crucial for personal development.

Consider Thomas Edison's growth mindset: "I have not failed. I've just found 10,000 ways that won't work." Picture Edison in his lab, surrounded by failed experiments, yet his eyes gleaming with determination. His approach exemplifies a growth mindset—embracing failures as part of the journey toward eventual success. His perseverance and ability to learn from setbacks transformed him into one of history's most prolific inventors.

I will share with you this right now: transforming to a growth mindset starts with the fundamental recognition that your abilities and intelligence can evolve through dedicated effort, learning, and perseverance. This shift is more than a theoretical concept; it is a practical and actionable change that you can make. By adopting a growth mindset, you open yourself up to continuous personal development and the ability to overcome challenges that once seemed insurmountable.

One of the most profound examples of this transformation is Viktor Frankl's experience, detailed in his seminal work, *Man's Search for Meaning*. Frankl, a Jewish man, was born in Austria. In 1942, he and his beloved family were torn from their lives by German Nazis who threw them into the Theresienstadt ghetto. In this transit camp, they experienced demonizing and demoralizing treatment. Soon they were forcibly separated, never seeing each other again.

In October 1944, Frankl was transferred to Auschwitz, then later moved to several other camps, ultimately being imprisoned in the Kaufering concentration camp in Bavaria, Germany. On April 27, 1945, Viktor Frankl was liberated by American forces.

As time passed, Frankl learned of the devastating fate of his loved ones. The immense devastation, grief, and loss he experienced, along with his realization that the world still was a miraculous place full of blessings, profoundly shaped his mindset to move forward in his life.

Viktor Frankl proclaimed, "Everything can be taken from a man but one thing: the last of the human freedoms—to choose one's attitude in any given set of circumstances, to choose one's own way."

Despite the extreme adversity he faced, Frankl discovered that the human spirit has the power to transcend even the most harrowing conditions. Frankl's insights offer a powerful testament to the potential for growth and resilience in the face of severe hardship.

Frankl's philosophy centers on the idea that while we cannot always control our circumstances, we can control how we respond to them. He famously stated, "When we are no longer able to change a situation, we are challenged to change ourselves." This perspective embodies the essence of a growth mindset: acknowledging our limitations while striving to transform our responses and attitudes.

Frankl's journey reveals a profound truth: even in the face of unimaginable suffering, we possess the freedom to choose our response. His ability to find meaning in his suffering marked a pivotal shift—a realization that while he could not control his circumstances, he could control his attitude and purpose. This moment of clarity became the foundation for his growth mindset, as he chose to transform his pain into a mission to help others discover meaning in their own lives. His story challenges us to ask, "In our darkest moments, how might we also find the strength to redefine our path and embrace growth?"

Stories like these show us what's possible when we nurture a growth mindset. But how do we start making this shift in our own lives? Here are some practical strategies to get started. Shifting to a growth mindset isn't something that happens overnight, but there are practical steps we can take to start the journey. One powerful strategy is to pay attention to our inner dialogue and gently reframe negative self-talk. Instead of thinking, "I can't do this," try adding a simple word: "yet." Saying "I can't do this yet" opens the door to possibility and progress. Another key is to actively seek feedback from others, not as criticism, but as valuable information that can help us improve. When we view feedback as a tool for learning rather than a judgment of our abilities, we become more open to growth. It's important to celebrate effort and persistence, not just the end result. By recognizing the hard work and determination we put into our goals, we reinforce the belief that growth is always possible. These small shifts in how we think and act can make a big difference on the path to developing a true growth mindset.

From a growth mindset perspective, trophies or titles do not measure our view of success or even the final outcome of our efforts. Instead, it is defined by the commitment to give our best, to persist through challenges, and to embrace the learning that comes from every attempt—regardless of whether we win or lose. In a growth mindset, effort is not a consolation prize; it is the very heart of achievement. Each time we stretch ourselves, take risks, and invest genuine effort, we are succeeding—because we are growing. This perspective frees us from the fear of failure and the pressure of perfection, allowing us to find fulfillment and pride in the journey itself. When we celebrate effort and learning, we unlock the door to continual improvement and lasting satisfaction, no matter the outcome.

Now let's turn these strategies inward. How might you begin to recognize and reshape your own mindset?

FINDING OUR OWN GROWTH MINDSET

Henry Ford, the founder of the Ford Motor Company, revolutionized the automobile industry by introducing the assembly line, making cars affordable and accessible to the masses. His innovative mindset and determination transformed not only his own life but also the lives of countless others. Ford famously said, "Whether you think you can, or you think you can't, you're right," highlighting his belief in the power of mindset to shape one's destiny. Despite facing numerous challenges and skepticism, Ford's unwavering commitment to his vision serves as a powerful reminder that with persistence and a growth mindset, extraordinary achievements are possible.

I want you to do something that will constantly remind you that you have a growth mindset. Every time you see the Ford emblem of a car or truck made by the Ford Motor Company, say out loud, "Yes, I can; yes, I have a growth mindset today and for the rest of my beautiful life. If Henry Ford can do it, so can I."

At the beginning of this chapter, I shared with you that my young formative years were filled with competing self-beliefs that I was blessed, loved, and not worthy of love and unwanted by my father. I introduced you to my dear friend Patricia Bartell, whose young life seemed helpless. We later learned the devastating story of Viktor Frankl and the immense tragedies and suffering that he encountered. How is it possible for any of us to have a growth mindset when we encounter shattering experiences that cast us into deep pain and suffering? When our belief systems are numbed by being told that "We are not enough," "We cannot do it," "or "We are destined to be failures," how is it possible to establish a growth mindset for the foundation of our future development and success in life?

First, know this: I believe in you, and I want you to believe in yourself. In my life, I chose to hang on to the belief system urged by my mother that I was, in fact, loved and blessed and had great potential. Success did not happen overnight. Yet years later, my once tongue-tied mouth has become an instrument of powerful change, an advocating voice for others in need. My legs, once tender and confined by steel braces, have become unshackled, carrying me through over a dozen marathons and hundreds of miles on my bike. I have learned that my concave chest holds a heart that yearns to help others heal and grow. Patricia Bartell turned her history into her mission to encourage others that each of us can overcome ourselves and our prior belief systems. Viktor Frankl's message is that regardless of our experiences, we have chosen to live a life of meaning.

So no matter what you have been told about yourself in the past, and no matter what you have experienced, you, my friend, can and will have a life based on the foundation of a growth mindset. I know this because you are reading this book. You would not have chosen this book to read or listen to if you did not possess within you a growth mindset. So let us now use this growth mindset as an initial foundation for our further development to become the person that we were always meant to be.

CHANGING YOUR GROWTH MINDSET INTO A MUST MINDSET

As we've explored in depth the beneficial power of a growth mindset, it's time to elevate this concept to a new, higher level of intentionality and commitment. Please allow me to introduce what I call the Must Mindset—a paradigm shift that represents a more profound dedication to your personal growth and success.

The Must Mindset goes beyond merely believing in your ability to grow and improve. It's a state of unwavering commitment where you view your personal development not just as a possibility but as an absolute necessity. With a Must Mindset, you don't just think you can grow—you know you must grow, and you're willing to do whatever it takes to make that growth happen.

A sense of urgency characterizes this mindset. You approach your goals with immediacy, understanding that time is precious and growth cannot be postponed. It involves a nonnegotiable commitment to making personal development an integral part of your daily life, not something you do when it's convenient.

In the Must Mindset, challenges are not just opportunities for growth, but expected parts of the journey that you're prepared to overcome. You actively seek out opportunities for growth rather than waiting for them to come to you. Most importantly, you hold yourself accountable for your growth, refusing to make excuses or blame external circumstances.

The Must Mindset represents a higher level of intentionality because it transforms personal growth from a choice into a fundamental part of one's identity. It's the difference between saying, "I can do this if I try" and "I must do this because it's who I am."

This shift in perspective can lead to remarkable changes in your life. When growth becomes a *must*, you tap into a deeper well of motivation that can sustain you through challenges. The urgency and commitment of a Must Mindset often lead to accelerated personal development and greater resilience. As you consistently push your boundaries, you'll discover capabilities you never knew you had.

To cultivate a Must Mindset, start by identifying the areas of your life where growth is not just desirable but essential for your success and fulfillment. Ask yourself, "What must I become to achieve my goals and live the life I truly want?" Then commit to making that growth happen, no matter what obstacles you may face.

To truly embrace the power of a Must Mindset, you need to actively engage in practices that reinforce this transformative way of thinking. Begin by identifying your nonnegotiables—those critical areas of your life where growth isn't just a nice-to-have but an absolute necessity for your success and fulfillment. These might be your career aspirations, your health and fitness goals, or your relationships. By pinpointing these essential domains, you create a clear focus for your Must Journey.

What is one area of your life where growth is not just desirable but essential? What would it look like to treat this as a nonnegotiable *must*?

Craft a personal Must Mantra—a powerful, resonant phrase that shows your unwavering commitment to growth. This mantra should be more than just words; it should be a rallying cry that ignites your spirit and propels you forward, especially when you are faced with challenges. Make it a daily ritual to repeat this mantra, letting its energy infuse your thoughts and actions.

Here are three examples of Must Mantras that can help reinforce a growth mindset and drive personal transformation:

1. **"I must embrace challenges as opportunities for growth."** This mantra reminds you to view obstacles not as barriers but as chances to learn and improve. It encourages a shift from avoiding difficulties to actively seeking them out as a means of personal development.
2. **"I must take action today to become who I'm meant to be."** This mantra emphasizes the urgency of personal growth and the importance of consistent, purposeful action. It reinforces the idea that becoming your best self is a daily choice and commitment.
3. **"I must persist in the face of setbacks, for they are part of my journey."** This mantra reframes failures and setbacks as integral

parts of the growth process rather than reasons to give up. It cultivates resilience and determination in pursuing your goals despite obstacles.

These Must Mantras can be powerful tools for reinforcing your commitment to personal growth and keeping you focused on your journey of self-improvement. By repeating them daily, especially when facing challenges, you can strengthen your resolve and maintain a growth-oriented mindset. Whether you're tackling a daunting task or facing a moment of self-doubt, your mantra will serve as a beacon, guiding you back to your *must* path.

A Must Mindset embraces this idea, recognizing that the discomfort of growth is far preferable to the pain of stagnation. By adopting a Must Mindset, you're not just opening yourself up to the possibility of growth—you're making it an integral part of who you are. This powerful shift in perspective can be the key to unlocking your full potential and achieving the extraordinary life you've always dreamed of.

Your Must Mindset supercharges the growth mindset by infusing it with a sense of urgency and unwavering commitment. It aligns personal development with a deeper purpose, fosters a nonnegotiable attitude toward improvement, promotes proactive seeking of growth opportunities, and encourages a holistic integration of growth principles across all aspects of life.

As we move forward, keep this Must Mindset at the forefront of your thoughts. Let it guide your actions and decisions as we delve deeper into understanding and reshaping your core beliefs. With this heightened mindset, you're not just prepared for the journey ahead—you're committed to making it a transformative experience that will redefine who you are and what you're capable of achieving. As my mother would tell you, "You must be your best version of yourself."

CHAPTER 3

Must Core Beliefs

"For as he thinketh in his heart, so is he."
—Proverbs 23:7

"We become what we think about most of the time."
—Earl Nightingale

As a young child, I struggled with the sense that I was not loved by my early father figures and I simply was not "enough" in virtually all aspects of my existence. The unconditional love of my mother, uncle, and little sister could not dissuade me from these beliefs of inadequacy—of being less. This feeling was exacerbated by several physical challenges that significantly impacted my self-image and my beliefs about myself and the world around me. These physical imperfections became the focus of my attention, overshadowing any positive attributes I possessed. I would be bullied each day after school as I walked home. A group of students would push me down a steep embankment as I walked home each day. They laughed and scoffed at me.

As they taunted me, I would find myself lying at the bottom, my books scattered in the dirt. I would fight back tears of shame and confusion. Why me? What made me their chosen target? With trembling hands, I would gather my belongings, each movement a reminder of my perceived worthlessness. The climb back up the hill felt like scaling a mountain of my own inadequacies, each step a struggle against the weight of their scorn and my self-doubt. I felt constant shame and could not understand why they chose me to pick on. I felt the riveting constant reminders of my inadequacies.

I fixated intensely on my perceived flaws. I couldn't shake the belief that I was somehow "less" than others. This core belief became a lens through which I viewed the world and my place in it. Over time, it became a silent force that dictated how I approached challenges, relationships, and opportunities. It wasn't until years later, through deliberate self-reflection and personal growth, that I dismantled these limiting beliefs and replaced them with empowering truths. This transformation wasn't easy or quick, but it was profound. I learned to see my imperfections not as weaknesses but as unique aspects of who I am, capable of shaping my strength and resilience. My past struggles were not proof of inadequacy, but the forge that had tempered my spirit. Those moments of pain and doubt had not diminished me; they had prepared me for a life of empathy, resilience, and purpose.

The beliefs we hold about ourselves shape the actions we take and the outcomes we achieve. Our core beliefs are the deep-seated convictions that form the bedrock of how we understand ourselves and navigate the world.

Core beliefs are fundamental convictions that persist over time, guiding our worldview and self-perception. Imagine them as the internal compass that directs how we interpret our experiences and our role within them. These beliefs are often rigid and resistant to change and are not always grounded in reality or evidence. For instance, someone might perceive themselves as fundamentally unlikable despite having a circle of friends who cherish them.

Take a moment to reflect on your own internal compass. What beliefs guide your daily actions and decisions? Think about a recent situation where you felt strongly. What underlying belief might have influenced your reaction? Core beliefs extend beyond how we view ourselves; they encompass our perspectives on others as well. For example, you might hold a belief that people are generally trustworthy or, conversely, that the world is inherently unfair. Sometimes these beliefs can conflict, creating cognitive dissonance—a state where actions and beliefs are at odds or where contradictory beliefs coexist, leading to inner turmoil. This inner struggle often mirrors the external conflicts we face, illustrating how our beliefs shape our reality.

Imagine your core beliefs as the lens through which you view the world. If this lens is clouded by negativity or fear, it can distort your perception and create unnecessary suffering. By bringing these beliefs into conscious awareness, you empower yourself to choose a different lens—one that aligns with your highest potential and aspirations. This journey of self-discovery is not always easy, but it is profoundly rewarding. By examining and challenging your core beliefs, you can transform the foundation of your reality.

ORIGINS OF OUR CORE BELIEFS

Our beliefs come from the same origins as our mindsets. Understanding the root cause of our beliefs is akin to tracing back the source of a river. As we develop, we make sense of the world around us and the people in it, and we build our views based on these understandings. Early beliefs may not necessarily be founded on fair or well-informed assessments and are often shaped by messages from friends, family, instructors, and the media, including not just TV, but social media as well. They tell us what success looks like, what beauty is, what's valued, and what's not.

And then we have the school of life itself—our personal experiences. Sometimes a single event can be so impactful that it forms a core belief. Maybe you tried something and failed miserably, and that failure led you to believe you would never succeed in that area. Or perhaps you were bullied, belittled, or rejected, and you internalized that experience as a reflection of your worth.

These deeply rooted ideas have a profound effect on our actions and feelings, often reinforcing misconceptions about who we are and how the world works. If our early experiences tell us failure is inevitable or we are unworthy, these beliefs can limit our potential and reinforce a cycle of self-doubt and missed opportunities.

The first step to changing your reality is becoming aware of how it was shaped. Picture this: you're a young child, like a sponge, absorbing the world around you. The voices you hear most often are those of your parents or caregivers, and you take their words as gospel. If those voices convey messages of limitation, whether intentionally or unintentionally, those messages often become imprinted in the blank canvas of your belief system. It's almost as if you've been programmed with a set of rules about what you can or cannot achieve, who you should be, and what is considered acceptable. For example, when I was growing up, my family struggled financially. I often heard my mother say, "Money doesn't grow on trees." While meant to teach frugality, this phrase inadvertently instilled a scarcity mindset in me.

Take a moment to reflect on your life. Can you name specific events or interactions that may have shaped your core beliefs? Perhaps there were moments of praise that instilled a sense of confidence or instances of criticism that planted seeds of self-doubt. By tracing these roots, you can gain a deeper understanding of why you hold certain beliefs and how they influence your present-day actions and emotions.

As you delve into this exploration, remember that core beliefs are not set in stone. Just as a tree can grow new branches and heal old wounds, you, too, can cultivate new beliefs that support your growth and well-being. This process requires patience, self-compassion, and a willingness to confront and challenge long-held assumptions. Embrace this journey with an open heart and mind, knowing each step forward is a step toward a more empowered and fulfilling version of yourself. Your beliefs are the architects of your reality, and by consciously shaping them, you can build a life that reflects your true potential.

HOW DO WE IDENTIFY OUR CORE BELIEFS?

Understanding and identifying your core beliefs is essential for personal growth and transformation. These beliefs shape your reality, guiding how you interpret your experiences and interact with the world.

By bringing your core beliefs into conscious awareness, you can evaluate which beliefs are empowering your growth and which may be limiting your potential. This awareness will empower you to reshape any beliefs that do not serve you well, replacing them with more empowering ones that support your highest aspirations in your growth mindset.

To embark on this journey of self-discovery, you must approach it with intellect, empathy, and a genuine desire to uncover the truths about yourself. The following strategies can help you find your core beliefs.

NOTICING YOUR THOUGHTS

Begin by paying attention to your automatic thoughts—those fleeting, often unnoticed thoughts that pop into your mind throughout the day. These thoughts are windows into your subconscious mind and can reveal recurring themes or patterns that highlight your core beliefs.

Sarah, a marketing professional, often thought, "I'm not creative enough," every time she faced a new project. This recurring thought made her feel inadequate and hesitant to share her ideas. By recognizing this pattern, she uncovered a deeper belief that her contributions were not valuable. Remember what Marcus Aurelius revealed: "The mind is everything. What you think, you become."

KEEPING A JOURNAL

A journal is a powerful tool for self-discovery. Record your thoughts, feelings, and experiences regularly, focusing particularly on moments of intense emotion or stress, such as conflicts or disappointments. By reviewing your entries, you can find patterns and recurring themes in your beliefs.

John kept a journal and noticed his entries often included feelings of frustration and self-doubt after work meetings. By reflecting on these entries, he realized he had a core belief that his colleagues did not respect him, which stemmed from past experiences.

Write down the thoughts and circumstances that reveal your core beliefs. When did these beliefs form? What experiences shaped them? Who influenced their development? What beliefs consistently surface in different situations? And here's the transformative question: Do these beliefs truly serve your highest potential? This reflective process becomes your compass, illuminating where your beliefs originated and guiding you toward more empowering perspectives. As you examine your core beliefs, remember this: Do the best you can until you know better. Then when you know better, do better. If you seek personal growth and fulfillment, you must be willing to evolve your foundational beliefs.

ASKING QUESTIONS

Delve deeper by asking yourself probing questions about your recurring thoughts and behaviors. For instance, if you often worry about being late, ask yourself what it means to you if you are late. Why does it matter? This introspection can uncover deeper core beliefs, such as a need for perfection to feel likable or fear of judgment from others.

Emily constantly worried about making mistakes at work. She asked herself why mistakes bothered her so much and discovered a deeper belief that she needed to be perfect to be accepted by her peers. Aristotle would tell Emily and you that "knowing yourself is the beginning of all wisdom."

CONSIDERING EVIDENCE

As a lawyer who has spent decades in courtrooms, I have learned that the truth is most often found by looking at the evidence. Evaluate your beliefs against the evidence. Look at situations where your beliefs have been challenged or contradicted. For example, if you believe you are unlovable, consider the instances where people have shown you love and kindness. If you find it challenging to alter a belief despite strong contradictory evidence, it might be a core belief.

My friend Michael believed he was not good at public speaking despite receiving positive feedback from colleagues and friends. By objectively reviewing the positive feedback and recognizing the instances where he performed well, he challenged and changed his core beliefs.

Aldous Huxley was a renowned English writer and philosopher, best known for his dystopian novel *Brave New World*, published in 1932. As a prominent intellectual of the twentieth century, writing extensively on a wide range of topics including science, philosophy, religion, and human potential, he concluded that "facts do not cease to exist because they are ignored," emphasizing the importance of acknowledging reality regardless of whether it is convenient or comfortable to do so. This underscores the idea that truth and facts stay constant irrespective of our willingness to recognize them.

It's important not to be disheartened if a thorough and in-depth evaluation of the evidence, after discounting bias, ignorance, incorrect information, and the motivations of others who may have provided input, does not leave you with a positive feeling of hope. True hope lies in the awareness and understanding of your core beliefs, whether they are factual or not. Once you identify these foundational convictions, you gain the power to change them to align with the person you want to become and the life you wish to lead. As Carl Jung, renowned Swiss psychologist, is attributed as wisely saying, "I am not what happened to me; I am what I choose to become." This declaration perfectly suggests the transformative power of understanding and reshaping your core beliefs.

EMBARKING ON THE JOURNEY OF SELF-DISCOVERY

As you engage in these practices, remember to be gentle with yourself. Finding core beliefs is a process that requires patience, honesty, and compassion. Embrace vulnerability and be open to exploring uncomfortable truths about your beliefs, as this strength allows you to connect with your authentic self. Seek support by talking to a trusted friend, mentor, or therapist about your discoveries; sometimes an external perspective can offer valuable insights. Celebrate your progress, no matter how small, recognizing that every step forward is a step toward greater self-awareness and empowerment.

By understanding and finding your core beliefs, you take control of your inner narrative. This self-awareness empowers you to transform limiting beliefs into empowering ones, paving the way for a more fulfilling and authentic life. As you uncover your core beliefs, you will begin to see yourself and the world through a clearer, more compassionate lens, opening new possibilities for growth and connection.

As you explore your core beliefs, which one surprises you the most? How has this belief shaped your choices?

BELIEFS AND THE CIRCLE OF LIFE

Core beliefs can impact all areas of our life—for good and ill. Using the Circle of Life rubric, we'll now explore different areas where we might hold core beliefs, how we might overcome core beliefs that limit us, and the ways others have used core beliefs to shape the world around them.

HEALTH AND VITALITY

In my youth, I was convinced my physical limitations would define my life's boundaries. Born tongue-tied, severely pigeon-toed, and with a pronounced concave chest, I never saw myself as an athlete. These perceived limitations became a part of my identity, a narrative I accepted without question.

In contrast, consider the inspiring story of Dr. Terry Wahls, a renowned physician and researcher who transformed her life and career through her core beliefs about health and vitality. Diagnosed with multiple sclerosis (MS) in 2000, Dr. Wahls was told she would eventually need a wheelchair. However, she chose to believe in her body's ability to heal and adapt, and she began exploring lifestyle changes that could complement her medical treatment.

Dr. Wahls's core belief in the power of nutrition and lifestyle to enhance health led her to develop the Wahls Protocol, a comprehensive approach to managing chronic diseases through diet, exercise, and stress reduction. By applying these principles to her life, she improved her health significantly and regained her mobility.

This transformation not only changed Dr. Wahls's life but also inspired her to help countless others. She has written several books and became a leading advocate for lifestyle-based approaches to health, emphasizing the importance of working with healthcare professionals while also taking proactive steps to enhance one's well-being.

Dr. Wahls's journey embodies a core belief such as "I have the power to make informed choices that support my health and vitality, working in harmony with medical professionals to achieve optimal well-being." Her story shows that by believing in our body's potential for healing and resilience, we not only transform our own lives but also make a profound impact on the lives of others.

This kind of positive core belief can transform your relationship with health and wellness. It encourages you to make conscious choices that support your well-being, such as maintaining a balanced diet, engaging in regular exercise, and practicing mindfulness, all while collaborating with healthcare professionals to ensure comprehensive care. By believing in your body's ability to thrive, you create a self-reinforcing cycle of health and vitality that enhances every aspect of your life.

RELATIONSHIPS

The belief that we are worthy of love is one of the most profound and foundational aspects of our emotional well-being. It shapes not only how we see ourselves but also how we interact with the world around us. If we hold the belief "I am unlovable" or "I am unworthy of love," it can create a barrier to forming deep, meaningful connections with others. These negative beliefs often become self-fulfilling prophecies, causing us to push people away or avoid intimacy, even when we deeply crave it.

Limiting beliefs in this domain can have a devastating impact, leading you to either avoid relationships or settle for less than you deserve. These beliefs often originate from past hurts, societal pressures, or a lack of self-worth.

But what if we challenge these beliefs? What if we embrace the ideas "I am likable" and "I am a loved human being?" Leo Buscaglia, often affectionately known as "Dr. Love," dedicated his life to teaching the power of love and the importance of believing in our own worthiness. He famously said, "You yourself, as much as anybody in the entire universe, deserve your love and affection." This powerful statement reminds us that love begins with self-love—the recognition that we deserve love simply because we exist. Buscaglia believed love is a choice, an action we must take every day, starting with how we treat ourselves: "Too often we underestimate the power of a touch, a smile, a kind word, a listening ear, an honest compliment, or the smallest act of caring, all of which have the potential to turn a life around." This sentiment emphasizes that the love we give and receive starts with the smallest, most genuine expressions of care, and these are available to all of us regardless of our perceived flaws or shortcomings. He encouraged us to see love not as something we must earn but as something inherent to our being.

Imagine the transformation that could occur if we truly believed we were worthy of love. If we embraced Buscaglia's teaching that "love is always bestowed as a gift—freely, willingly, and without expectation. We don't love to be loved; we love to love." By embodying this belief, we allow ourselves to be open to love in all its forms—romantic, platonic, familial, and, most importantly, self-love. This openness to love can heal wounds, build stronger relationships, and create a life filled with more joy and fulfillment.

Believing in our own worthiness of love doesn't just change our interactions with others; it changes how we treat ourselves. It allows us to give ourselves grace, to forgive our mistakes, and to nurture our well-being. So as you reflect on your beliefs about being loved and liked, ask yourself, "Do I believe I am worthy of love? Am I allowing myself to receive the love that is all around me?" As Buscaglia reminds us, "Love yourself. Accept yourself. Forgive yourself, and be good to yourself, because without you, the rest of us are without a source of many wonderful things." This journey of embracing your worthiness of love is not just for your benefit—it's for the benefit of everyone whose life you touch.

Fred Rogers, the beloved host of the children's television series *Mister Rogers' Neighborhood*, exemplifies the profound impact of believing in kindness, acceptance, and being loved and liked. Born in 1928 in Latrobe, Pennsylvania, Rogers grew up feeling somewhat isolated and lonely due to his shy nature and health issues. Despite these early challenges, he deeply believed in the power of kindness and acceptance. Rogers told us, "When I was a boy and I would see scary things in the news, my mother would say to me, 'Look for the helpers. You will always find people who are helping.'"

Rogers pursued a career in television, aiming to create content that nurtured children's emotional and social well-being. His gentle demeanor, genuine concern for others, and unwavering belief in the goodness and lovability of every individual resonated with millions. Fred Rogers's ability to connect deeply with his audience stemmed from his belief that everyone deserves to be loved and accepted just as they are.

As Carl Rogers, a prominent psychologist (no relation to Fred Rogers), noted, "The curious paradox is that when I accept myself just as I am, then I can change." Accepting oneself is the first step toward changing the belief in one's unlikability. Fred Rogers's legacy continues to inspire, reminding us that by believing in our inherent worthiness of love and acceptance, we can build stronger, more meaningful connections with others. His life and work highlight the transformative power of self-acceptance and the belief in being loved and liked.

In 1997, Fred Rogers received the Lifetime Achievement Award at the 24th Annual Daytime Emmy Awards. The actor Tim Robbins presented the award to Mr. Rogers.

> For giving generation upon generation of children to have confidence in themselves for being their friend, for telling them again and again and again they are special, and they have worth it is my honor and on the behalf of everyone here, and on the behalf of the millions of children whose mornings you have brightened with your kindness to present you with this lifetime achievement award.

Fred Rogers walked to the podium and said,

> Oh, it's a beautiful night in this neighborhood. So many have helped me to come to this night. Some of you are here. Some are far away. Some are even in heaven. All of us have special ones who have loved us into being. Would you just take, along with me, ten seconds to think of the people who have helped you become who you are. Those who have cared about you and wanted what was best for you in life. Ten seconds of silence. I'll watch the time. Whomever you have been thinking about, how pleased they must be to know that you've been thinking about the difference you feel they've made in your life.

I wish to reiterate Mr. Rogers's sentiment to you: "How pleased your loved ones must be to know that you've been thinking about the difference you feel that they made in your life." Please remember this always. *You are loved.*

CAREER

Assumptions like "I am intelligent and capable" or "I will succeed if I put in the effort" significantly influence our actions and resilience. A person who believes in their competence is more likely to persevere through challenges and pursue ambitious goals.

In contrast, limiting beliefs about our competence can hold us back from reaching our full potential. Many individuals have overcome such beliefs about their level of competence to achieve extraordinary success, transforming their lives and inspiring others along the way. Their stories illustrate the power of challenging and overcoming self-doubt.

Les Brown's journey is a profound example of overcoming limiting beliefs about competence. Born in Miami, Florida, in 1945, Brown faced significant challenges early in life. Raised in poverty by a single mother, he was labeled as "educable mentally retarded" in school, a term that deeply affected his self-esteem, sense of worth, and belief about his level of competency in life…He recalls, "I was labeled 'educable mentally retarded' in school, and my teachers thought I would never amount to anything. They thought I was not capable of succeeding in life."

Despite this early stigma, Brown was determined to prove himself. His first career efforts were met with skepticism, but he refused to let these limiting beliefs define his potential. He met rejection and doubt but remained steadfast in his belief that he could overcome his past limitations. Reflecting on his struggles, Brown said, "It's not the title that makes you a success; it's how you handle the setbacks. The setbacks are just setups for a comeback."

Brown's breakthrough came when he gained recognition for his dynamic speaking style and inspiring messages. His famous speech "It's Not Over Until You Win" resonated with many, offering encouragement and hope. As he reflected on his journey, he shared, "You are never too old to set another goal or to dream a new dream." His books have reached millions, showing how challenging and overcoming limiting beliefs about competence can lead to remarkable success.

Brown often quotes Norman Vincent Peale, minister, author, and motivational speaker, who said, "Shoot for the moon. Even if you miss it you will land among the stars." This competency growth mindset fueled his relentless pursuit of success despite early doubts from others and himself.

Overcoming limiting beliefs about our competence is crucial for personal and professional growth. To unlock your full potential, it's important to evaluate and reboot any negative or self-doubting beliefs about your competency.

FINANCIAL WELL-BEING

How many times have you caught yourself thinking, "I'll never have a successful business" or "I'll never be wealthy?" These limiting beliefs can stem from your upbringing, societal norms, or personal experiences. The idea that financial abundance is beyond your reach is a narrative that can severely limit your potential. It's crucial to recognize that the universe is abundant, and there is no reason you can't partake in that abundance. Napoleon Hill, a pioneer in personal development, wisely said, "Whatever the mind can conceive and believe, it can achieve." This sentiment underscores the power of belief in shaping our reality. By transforming our beliefs and embracing the possibility of abundance, we open ourselves to opportunities that can lead to financial prosperity.

Let's learn from the story of Daymond John, the founder of FUBU clothing. Growing up in Queens, New York, John faced numerous challenges, including financial struggles and skepticism from others about his business ideas. However, he refused to let these limiting beliefs define his potential. Instead, he believed in his creativity and entrepreneurial spirit.

John's journey began with a simple idea: to create a clothing line that would appeal to young people in urban communities. Despite facing numerous rejections and setbacks, he persevered, driven by his conviction that his product could make a difference. His unwavering belief in his vision and his ability to innovate led him to become a successful entrepreneur and a star on the hit TV show *Shark Tank*.

John's story is a testament to the power of challenging limiting beliefs about financial success. By embracing the idea that abundance is within reach, he transformed his life and created a global brand. His success shows that with the right mindset, anyone can overcome perceived barriers and achieve remarkable financial prosperity.

This kind of transformation is not just about achieving wealth; it's about cultivating a mindset that sees opportunities where others see obstacles. By believing in your own potential and the abundance of the universe, you can unlock doors to financial success and live a more fulfilling life. Daymond John's journey embodies this principle, inspiring us to challenge our own limiting beliefs and strive for greatness.

PERSONAL GROWTH AND LEARNING

Our perceived personal capabilities are the beliefs that make us question our abilities, talents, and worth. Thoughts like "I'm not smart enough" or "I don't have what it takes" can become self-fulfilling prophecies if we let them. These doubts often stem from past failures, criticisms, or comparisons with others. Marianne Williamson, an inspirational author, poignantly said, "Our deepest fear is not that we are inadequate. Our deepest fear is that we are powerful beyond measure." This highlights a profound truth: it is often our boundless potential that terrifies us the most. Yet it is this same potential that holds the promise for extraordinary achievements and happiness. By embracing your inherent capabilities and challenging limiting beliefs, you can unlock a reservoir of talent and possibility within yourself.

Many people tell themselves they have every reason to have a negative view of themselves by struggling with self-doubt and fear. This can be seen in the story of Chris Gardner, who, despite being homeless, developed a belief of his worth and the potential for goodness in the world, ultimately becoming a successful businessman and author of

The Pursuit of Happyness. His life story is a powerful testament to the impact of positive self-belief.

Born in Milwaukee, Wisconsin, Gardner faced a tumultuous childhood marked by poverty, domestic violence, and sexual abuse. As an adult, he struggled with homelessness while raising his young son as a single father. Gardner states, "The future was uncertain, absolutely, and there were many hurdles, twists, and turns to come, but as long as I kept moving forward, one foot in front of the other, the voices of fear and shame, the messages from those who wanted me to believe that I wasn't good enough, would be stilled."

Despite these overwhelming challenges, Gardner believed in his potential and inherent goodness. He pursued a career in finance, eventually securing an internship at a prestigious brokerage firm. Through sheer determination and unwavering self-belief, Gardner rose to become a successful stockbroker and entrepreneur. Gardner urges us forward, saying, "The cavalry ain't coming. You've got to do this yourself." His journey from homelessness to success highlights how positive self-belief can transform one's life and circumstances. Gardner reminds us, "Others may question your credentials, your papers, your degrees. Others may look for all kinds of ways to diminish your worth. But what is inside you no one can take from you or tarnish."

Brené Brown, a research professor and bestselling author, has extensively studied the concepts of worthiness and vulnerability. Her work emphasizes that recognizing we are enough is essential for living a wholehearted life. Brown's research shows that those who believe they are enough are more likely to embrace vulnerability, leading to deeper connections and greater emotional resilience.

In her TED Talk "The Power of Vulnerability," Brown discusses how embracing our imperfections and believing in our worthiness allows us to lead more fulfilling lives. She says, "Because true belonging only happens when we present our authentic, imperfect selves to the world, our sense of belonging can never be greater than our level of self-acceptance." This insight highlights the importance of self-acceptance in achieving a sense of belonging and fulfillment.

When we start believing we are enough, the transformation in our lives can be profound. Consider my client Samantha, who spent years doubting her abilities and worth. She often avoided taking on new challenges, fearing failure and rejection. However, after working with professionals who helped her challenge these negative beliefs, Samantha saw herself differently. She acknowledged her strengths and achievements, no matter how small they seemed.

As Samantha's belief in her own *enoughness* grew, so did her confidence. She took on new opportunities, both personally and professionally, without the paralyzing fear of not being good enough. Her relationships improved as she no longer sought constant validation from others. Instead, she embraced her authenticity, which led to more genuine and fulfilling connections. Samantha's story shows how shifting our core belief to one of inherent worthiness can lead to a more peaceful, joyful, and authentic life.

SPIRITUALITY, RELIGION, AND INNER PEACE

The remarkable journey of Billy Graham, a renowned evangelist, exemplifies the transformative power of spiritual core beliefs. Born in 1918 in Charlotte, North Carolina, Billy Graham grew up in a devout Christian family. His early life was marked by a deep sense of faith and a calling to serve others. Graham's core belief in the power of faith and the importance of spreading God's love guided him throughout his life.

Billy Graham's journey began with a simple yet profound conviction: that every human being is worthy of love and respect due to their divine creation. This belief led him to dedicate his life to sharing the message of hope and redemption with millions around the world. Through his crusades and sermons, Graham emphasized the idea that faith can transform lives and provide inner peace, even in the face of adversity.

Graham's core belief in the transformative power of faith was not just about personal salvation; it was also about inspiring others to find peace and purpose. His message of love and forgiveness resonated with people from all walks of life, transcending denominational boundaries and cultural divides. Billy Graham's legacy is a testament to the impact that one person can have when driven by a strong spiritual core belief.

Graham's story embodies a core belief such as "I am a vessel of divine love, and my purpose is to spread this love to all those I meet." His journey shows that by holding on to positive spiritual core beliefs, we can transform our lives and also make a profound impact on the lives of others. This kind of belief can guide us toward a life of purpose, compassion, and inner peace.

After the devastation of Hurricane Katrina, I was filming a documentary in New Orleans' Ninth Ward—a place where a levee broke, killing many and destroying the lives of thousands. In this desolation, I saw Graham, a figure of calm amidst the chaos, walking with his son, Franklin Graham. They moved through the remnants of the flood. The international media, a buzzing hive of cameras and microphones, swarmed around them, capturing this poignant moment for the world to see. Reverend Graham did not answer any questions and was opening the door to enter his car when I was compelled to ask, "Reverend Graham, what can we learn from this experience?" There was a hush, a collective intake of breath as everyone turned to the venerable pastor. He paused, as if a thoughtful stillness had enveloped him, and then he turned around. In his eyes, there was a depth of understanding, a reservoir of shared grief and compassion. His voice, when he spoke, carried a weight that resonated in the very soul of the Ninth Ward. "In Katrina's aftereffects, if ever a country needs to turn to God, it's now."

Those words, simple yet profound, lingered in the air long after they were spoken. I had long thought that God had forsaken and abandoned me and my family based on several personal tragedies. Yet it was my mother who brought me back to my faith. She told me God did not cause our pain; God delivered us through it and from it. The blessing of life had always been there; even in the darkest times, God was there. God told us our purpose. God gave us our *musts*. We just had to have faith and see them right in front of us, and our blessings had always been there. God gave us our gift. As a man of faith, I believe in God, and I respect others with different beliefs about spirituality and religion. The idea that every human is inherently worthy of love and respect due to their divine creation is a common thread found across several major religions. Throughout time and the world, the following religious belief exists: "You are worthy of love because you are made in the image of God."

COMMUNITY AND LEGACY

Malala Yousafzai, a Pakistani activist for girls' education and the youngest-ever Nobel Prize laureate, exemplifies the strength of believing in the goodness of education and equality. Yousafzai was only eleven years old when she began advocating for girls' education, writing a blog under a pseudonym for the BBC. Yousafzai's purpose is displayed as she says, "I tell my story not because it is unique, but because it is the story of many girls." Her activism drew the ire of the Taliban, and in 2012, she was shot in the head by a Taliban gunman while on a bus returning home from school.

Despite facing grave dangers, Yousafzai's belief in the inherent goodness of education and equality never wavered. The heart of one of her core beliefs is shown in her declaration in her speech at the United Nations in 2013: "One child, one teacher, one book, one pen can change the world." She survived the assassination attempt and continued her advocacy on a global scale. Her conviction empowered her to overcome adversity and inspire millions worldwide. Yousafzai's story underscores the transformative power of believing in one's goodness and the goodness of one's cause. She proclaims to the world, "With guns, you can kill terrorists. With education, you can kill terrorism."

Eleanor Roosevelt, the longest-serving First Lady of the United States and a renowned advocate for human rights, said, "No one can make you feel inferior without your consent." She also exemplifies the power of believing in one's goodness. Born into a wealthy but troubled family, Roosevelt faced numerous personal challenges, including the death of both parents by the time she was ten and a difficult marriage to Franklin D. Roosevelt.

Despite these hardships, Roosevelt believed in her ability to contribute positively to society. She became a vocal advocate for civil rights, women's rights, and social justice. Roosevelt's belief in her own goodness and the goodness of her cause inspired her to make a lasting impact on the world. Eleanor Roosevelt urges us, "The purpose of life is to live it, to taste experience to the utmost, to reach out eagerly and without fear for newer and richer experiences."

Ultimately, our beliefs about whether we are inherently good or bad shape our actions, resilience, and capacity to effect change in our lives and the world around us. No stronger statement can be made about the belief in goodness than this declaration from a sermon by William Lonsdale Watkinson, an English Wesleyan minister: "It is better to light a candle than curse the darkness."

We all face challenges, doubts, and fears, just as Malala Yousafzai and Eleanor Roosevelt did. What sets them apart is not their fame or achievements but their unwavering conviction in the power of action to overcome adversity, inspire others, and create change. This belief is a choice—one that each of us can make in our daily lives.

When we choose to believe in our own goodness, we open ourselves to greater resilience, compassion, and courage. It allows us to face our challenges with confidence, knowing we can rise above them. It encourages us to treat others with kindness, understanding that everyone navigates their own struggles. It empowers us to contribute positively to the world, no matter the scale of our actions.

We are all human beings, capable of both great good and great mistakes. Our belief in goodness is what guides us toward the former. It's what enables us to make a difference, whether in our families, communities, workplaces, or even just within ourselves. Bill Wilson, co-founder of Alcoholics Anonymous (AA), is reported to have said, "To the world you may be one person, but to one person you may be the world." Ordinary people make extraordinary choices fueled by the belief in their own goodness and the goodness of those around them.

Anne Frank wrote, "How wonderful it is that nobody need wait a single moment before starting to improve the world." So how will you let this belief shape your life? How will it influence the way you treat yourself and others? In what ways can you use this belief to create a positive ripple effect in your world? Remember, you don't need to be a Nobel laureate or a public figure to make a difference—you just need to believe in the goodness that lies within you.

LIMITING BELIEFS

"The only limits that exist are the ones you place on yourself."
—LES BROWN

As we examine our core beliefs, it's crucial to recognize that some of these deeply held convictions may be limiting beliefs that no longer serve our best interests. Core beliefs, while fundamental to our worldview, are not inherently positive or beneficial. Some may have formed in response to past experiences or influences that are no longer relevant to our current lives or aspirations.

These negative convictions we hold about ourselves overshadow our feelings and shape our personal narrative, ultimately having the power to thwart our potential unless recognized and transformed. Self-limiting beliefs influence how we see ourselves and what we believe we can achieve, profoundly impacting our growth. As the insightful Carl Jung said, "Until you make the unconscious conscious, it will direct your life, and you will call it fate." It's crucial to recognize how your limiting beliefs are coloring your interactions with others and, more importantly, with yourself.

Understanding and overcoming limiting beliefs is one of the most crucial aspects of personal development and self-improvement. These self-limiting core beliefs can cast a shadow over our emotions, shape our personal narratives in restrictive ways, and ultimately hinder our potential for growth and fulfillment. They often manifest as negative self-perceptions or rigid assumptions about our capabilities and worth. For instance, a core belief like "I'm not creative" or "I don't deserve success" can profoundly impact our choices, behaviors, and the opportunities we allow ourselves to pursue.

The power of these limiting core beliefs lies in their ability to influence how we see ourselves and what we believe we can achieve. They can create self-fulfilling prophecies, causing us to act in ways that reinforce these negative convictions. This cycle can significantly impede our personal and professional growth, preventing us from reaching our full potential.

Recognizing these limiting core beliefs is the first step toward transformation. By identifying which of our core beliefs are holding us back, we can begin the process of challenging and reframing them. This self-awareness allows us to consciously choose more empowering beliefs that align with our true potential and aspirations.

As we progress through this journey of self-discovery and belief evaluation, it's important to approach the process with compassion and patience. Transforming long-held core beliefs takes time and effort, but the resulting personal growth and expanded sense of possibility make it a worthwhile endeavor.

Life has a way of surprising us when we dare to challenge our self-imposed limits. In my late thirties, I was dining at a New Orleans restaurant, and I overheard these athletic men proclaiming their prowess to their accompanying lady companions; they had all just run a marathon together. I remember thinking to myself, "Wow, I would love to be able to do that, but I'm not an athlete, and I'm not even a runner. So much for that fleeting thought." For some reason, I could not get that encounter out of my head. Sometimes when we focus on something, we notice that life's doors open, inviting us to take that once unimaginable path.

At the age of forty, I decided to rewrite my story. I joined a beginner's marathon running group. I laced up a pair of running shoes and set out to prove to myself that my body and mind were capable of more than I had ever imagined. That decision led me to complete fourteen full marathons, including seven New York City Marathons.

With each mile, I chipped away at the belief that I was physically limited, replacing it with a newfound confidence in my mind and body's strength and resilience.

What about you? What core beliefs did you form in your early years that may have held you back? Perhaps you internalized messages about your capabilities, your worth, or your place in the world that no longer serves you. Take a moment to reflect on these beliefs. Can you identify the ones that have limited your potential or happiness? What empowering beliefs could you adopt to replace them? Just as I had to confront and reshape my own limiting beliefs, you, too, have the power to transform yours. Your past experiences may have shaped your initial beliefs, but they don't have to define your present life or future.

MOVING BEYOND THE LIMITING BELIEFS OF OTHERS

Consider the story of Madam C. J. Walker, born Sarah Breedlove. Her early life was profoundly shaped by external forces, poverty, racism, and personal loss, which could have easily cemented limiting beliefs about her worth and potential. Born in 1867 to formerly enslaved parents, Walker faced immense challenges that seemed to define her existence. However, these external hardships also planted the seeds for resilience and determination. After experiencing hair loss due to stress and scalp conditions, Walker created a line of hair care products for African American women. Her success was fueled by her belief that she had the power to rise above her circumstances and create opportunities not only for herself but for others as well.

Walker's journey demonstrates how external forces can shape both limiting and empowering beliefs. Despite the societal barriers she faced, she believed in her ability to overcome adversity and made a positive impact. Her story reminds us that even when external forces attempt to define our limitations, we have the power to rewrite those narratives.

Another example comes from my friend Bruce. After graduating from law school, Bruce encountered rejection after rejection; one hundred résumés sent out resulted in 101 rejection letters (one law firm sent him two). These external forces could have easily shaped a core belief that he was unworthy or incapable of succeeding in his chosen field. Yet Bruce refused to internalize these messages of limitation. Instead, he believed in his ability to create his own path forward.

Bruce's resilience led him to establish a successful law firm, where he has helped thousands of clients over the years. His story illustrates how external forces can attempt to shape our beliefs about ourselves, but it is ultimately our choice whether to accept them or challenge them.

A personal mentor and friend of mine is Jack Canfield. Jack Canfield's journey to publishing *Chicken Soup for the Soul* is a testament to his unwavering perseverance and belief in his work. Despite facing an astounding 144 rejections from publishers, Canfield refused to give up on his vision.

When he finally secured a publisher, he was met with skepticism and limiting beliefs about the book's potential success. The publisher predicted they'd be lucky to sell twenty thousand copies, but Canfield boldly declared his goal of selling 1.5 million copies in the first eighteen months.

This ambitious target was met with laughter and disbelief. However, Canfield's determination and strategic approach paid off spectacularly. The *Chicken Soup for the Soul* series has now sold over 123 million copies in North America alone, with more than 500 million copies in print worldwide. The books have been translated into over forty languages, touching lives across the globe.

Canfield's persistence in the face of numerous rejections and doubts ultimately led to the creation of a global phenomenon, proving that with the right mindset and unwavering commitment, even the most ambitious goals can be achieved.

CHALLENGING OUR LIMITING BELIEFS

Albert Einstein once said, "Insanity is doing the same thing over and over again and expecting different results." If you want a different life, you'll need to replace outdated beliefs.

Cognitive behavioral therapy (CBT), a powerful tool for changing core beliefs, focuses on identifying and challenging negative thought patterns that contribute to emotional distress. By reframing these thoughts, individuals can cultivate a more positive and constructive mindset, ultimately leading to improved emotional well-being and personal growth. CBT works by helping you identify negative thought patterns and replacing them with more positive, realistic ones. But it's not just changing your thoughts—it's actually changing your brain!

A fascinating study published in the journal *Translational Psychiatry* found that CBT produces measurable changes in brain activity. The researchers looked at patients with social anxiety disorder and found that after CBT treatment, there were significant changes in the way different parts of their brains communicated with each other.

Imagine your brain as a vast network of highways. Your thoughts and beliefs are like the traffic patterns on these highways. When you have limiting beliefs, it's as if there's a traffic jam on certain routes. CBT helps to clear these jams and create new, smoother pathways for your thoughts to travel.

When you challenge and reframe your limiting beliefs through CBT, you're not just changing your mind—you're physically rewiring your brain! It's like your brain is forming new, healthier connections. These new connections support more positive thoughts and behaviors, making it easier for you to maintain your new, empowering beliefs.

This process doesn't happen overnight. Just like building muscle through exercise, rewiring your brain takes time and consistent effort. But the more you practice challenging and reframing your beliefs, the stronger these new neural pathways become.

The implications of this research are profound. It means that no matter how long you've held on to limiting beliefs, you have the power to change them. Your brain is not static; it's a dynamic, ever-changing organ that responds to your thoughts and actions. By consciously working to reshape your core beliefs, you're changing your mind—you're physically rewiring your brain for greater resilience, positivity, and personal growth. So the next time you catch yourself in a negative thought pattern, remember that by challenging that thought, you're not just changing your mood in the moment. You're actually reshaping your brain, creating a foundation for lasting change and growth. This is the power of neuroplasticity, and it's a tool that's available to all of us, every day.

Take a moment to reflect on your journey. What limiting beliefs have you held in the past that no longer serve you? Perhaps you once believed you weren't smart enough, talented enough, or deserving of success. How did those beliefs hold you back? More importantly, how did you overcome them? Recognizing the limiting beliefs you've already conquered is a powerful reminder of your capacity for growth and transformation.

But what about the limiting beliefs you may still carry? Are there quiet voices in your mind whispering doubts about your worthiness or abilities? How are these beliefs affecting your life today? How might they be shaping the trajectory of who you are becoming? Take a moment to contemplate these questions. Identifying these beliefs is the first step toward breaking free from their grip. Remember, the path to becoming your best self begins with challenging the narratives that no longer serve you and replacing them with empowering truths that align with your potential.

James Baldwin, writer, essayist, novelist, playwright, and civil rights activist, once said, "The world is before you, and you need not take it or leave it as it was when you came in." You see, you have the power to question the societal norms that have been handed down to you. Just because a belief is widely accepted doesn't make it true. In fact, some of the most transformative figures in history were people who dared to challenge the status quo.

LEARNED HELPLESSNESS

Learned helplessness is a psychological condition that occurs when an individual believes they have no control over the outcomes of their actions, even when opportunities for change are available. It is a state of mind that can severely limit our potential and stifle our growth. Learned helplessness is often the result of repeated exposure to uncontrollable and adverse situations. Over time, individuals internalize the belief that they are powerless to change their circumstances. This mindset can permeate various aspects of life, from personal aspirations to professional endeavors, leading to a pervasive sense of defeat and resignation.

At its core, learned helplessness is a deeply ingrained limiting belief—a conviction that one's efforts are futile and that external forces dictate outcomes. This belief becomes part of an individual's core belief system, shaping how they perceive themselves and their ability to influence their environment. When learned helplessness takes root, it reinforces other limiting beliefs, creating a cycle of self-doubt and inaction that can be difficult to break.

The connection between learned helplessness and core beliefs lies in how these experiences shape our internal narratives. For example, someone who repeatedly faces failure despite their best efforts may internalize the belief "I am incapable of success," which then influences their future actions and decisions. Recognizing this link is crucial for breaking free from the mental constraints of learned helplessness and replacing these limiting beliefs with empowering ones.

The concept of learned helplessness was first named by psychologists Martin Seligman and Steven Maier in 1967. In their pioneering studies with dogs, they discovered that animals subjected to unavoidable shocks eventually stopped trying to escape, even when escape was possible. Subsequent research conducted by Seligman and Donald Hiroto extended these findings to humans. In their study, participants exposed to uncontrollable noise later did not escape the noise when given the opportunity, showing similar patterns of learned helplessness observed in animal studies. These experiments highlight the profound impact of perceived powerlessness on behavior and motivation. Seligman stated, "Learned helplessness is the giving-up reaction, the quitting response that follows from the belief that whatever you do doesn't matter."

A vivid illustration of learned helplessness can be found in the poignant tale of captive elephants, once a common sight in traveling circuses. Picture a young elephant, its leg bound by a heavy chain to a sturdy stake driven deep into the ground. The chain clinks and rattles as the confused calf tugs and pulls, its eyes wide with distress. Day after day, the elephant strains against its bonds, trumpeting in frustration and fear.

As time passes, the elephant's struggles gradually diminish. Its once-determined efforts fade into resigned acceptance. The mighty beast, capable of uprooting trees in the wild, now stands docile, convinced of its own powerlessness. Even when the chain is replaced by a flimsy rope, a tether that the adult elephant could easily snap, it remains tethered by invisible bonds of belief.

This heartbreaking scene displays the essence of learned helplessness. The elephant, having internalized its perceived limitations, no longer attempts to break free. Its captivity becomes a self-fulfilling prophecy, a mental cage far stronger than any physical restraint. The animal's spirit, once as vast as the savanna, is now confined to an area determined by the length of its chain—a poignant reminder of how early experiences can shape lifelong perceptions of possibility and limitation.

Now I invite you to reflect on your life. Are there areas where you feel stuck, powerless, or resigned? Perhaps you've faced repeated failures in your career, leading you to believe that no matter what you do, success is unattainable. This belief might prevent you from seeking new job opportunities or pursuing a promotion. Maybe in your personal life, you've experienced heartbreak and now think that a loving, healthy relationship is out of reach, causing you to shy away from potential connections. We must break free from our own learned helplessness so we may experience the splendor of our present and future potential.

BREAKING FREE FROM LEARNED HELPLESSNESS

Consider the story of my friend Tina, a talented artist who dreamed of showcasing her work in galleries. Early in her career, she faced several rejections from galleries and critics. These repeated setbacks led her to believe her art was not good enough and she would never succeed. Despite having opportunities to improve and showcase her work, Tina felt paralyzed by her past failures. She stopped submitting her art, convinced that her efforts were futile. It was only when a friend encouraged her to try again that she realized the power of her own potential. With renewed determination, Tina's art eventually gained recognition, and she broke free from the chains of learned helplessness.

The journey to overcoming learned helplessness begins with recognizing that perceived barriers are often self-imposed. It requires a shift in mindset and the courage to challenge long-held beliefs about our limitations. Ancient stoic philosopher Epictetus proclaimed, "You can bind up my leg, but not even Zeus has the power to break my freedom of choice." This declaration highlights that while external circumstances may restrict us, our internal choices and responses remain free.

Reflect on the patterns of thought and behavior that show learned helplessness. Where in your life do you feel stuck or powerless? Actively challenge the beliefs that have kept you in a state of helplessness. Are these beliefs based on facts or past experiences that no longer apply? Begin by taking small, manageable steps toward your goals. Each small success can build confidence and reinforce the belief that change is possible. Surround yourself with supportive individuals who can provide encouragement and perspective. Sometimes an external viewpoint can help you see possibilities that you might have overlooked. Acknowledge and celebrate each step forward, no matter how small. Recognizing your progress can help reinforce a positive mindset and build momentum.

It's important to acknowledge that feelings of unworthiness can be deeply entrenched and challenging to overcome. But remember, these feelings don't define your true value. Acknowledging this is the first step toward healing and transformation.

Begin by examining and challenging the negative beliefs you hold about yourself. Ask yourself, "Where do these beliefs come from? Are they based on past experiences, criticisms, or misunderstandings?" Understanding their origins can help you separate these beliefs from your true self-worth.

Start small with acts of self-care and self-compassion. Engage in activities that nourish your soul and reflect on moments when you felt loved or valued, even if they seem minor. As Fred Rogers wisely said, "You are special. You are unique. You are you. And that is a reason to celebrate every day." By celebrating your uniqueness, you affirm your own worthiness.

Surround yourself with positive influences and supportive people who remind you of your value. The people you choose to be around can significantly change how you see yourself. Seek relationships and communities that reflect the kindness and acceptance you want to cultivate in yourself.

Practice self-acceptance and kindness, both to yourself and to others. Rogers observed, "Love isn't a state of perfect caring. It is an active noun like 'struggle.' To love someone is to strive to accept that person exactly as he or she is, right here and now." Extend this compassion to yourself. Understand that it's okay to have flaws and imperfections; they don't diminish your worth.

As you embark on this journey of self-discovery and self-love, remember that change takes time. Be patient with yourself and continue to nurture a belief in your own goodness.

By challenging the beliefs that limit us and embracing our inherent power, we can break free from learned helplessness. Remember, my dear friend, you have the strength within you to overcome any obstacle. Your potential is boundless, and the journey to realizing it begins with the belief that you can.

The limitations we perceive are often just that—perceptions. They're stories we tell ourselves, narratives that can be rewritten at any time. Whether they're physical challenges, age, or any other perceived barriers, remember that these are merely invitations to prove yourself wrong.

So I challenge you, as I challenged myself: What limiting belief are you ready to shatter? What story are you prepared to rewrite? The first step is recognizing that the power to change your narrative lies within you. Your journey of transformation can begin today, right now, with a simple decision to believe in your unlimited potential.

Remember, the only true limitations are the ones we accept. Everything else is an opportunity for growth, for proving our resilience, and for redefining what's possible. Your exceptional life is waiting. As we move forward, let us commit to shedding the mental chains that have held us captive. Embrace the empowerment that comes from recognizing your own agency. All you need to do is believe in it and take that first step toward making it a reality.

Take a moment and imagine holding a jar of your personal core beliefs. The jar contains some empowering and positive core beliefs, yet it is also weighed down with disabling limiting beliefs. The combination of the mixed core beliefs has created the person you believe yourself to be at this very moment. Is this person the individual who you are meant to be, full of possibilities, achievements, wonder, and the extraordinary? To get to this place, let's remove the heavy, negative, limiting beliefs and replace them with empowering Must Core Beliefs.

DEFINING AND EMBRACING YOUR MUST CORE BELIEFS

We are now at the pinnacle section of this chapter, where we take the concepts that have been explored and climb to a higher level of self-actualization and personal transformation. As we explore our core beliefs, it's crucial to recognize that some beliefs are not just beneficial but essential for personal growth and transformation. These are what I call our Must Core Beliefs—the foundational convictions that we must develop and maintain regardless of our current mindset or circumstances. While core beliefs represent the deeply ingrained convictions that shape our worldview and self-perception, Must Core Beliefs elevate this framework to a higher level of intentionality and necessity. Unlike core beliefs, which may be passive or even limiting, Must Core Beliefs are actively chosen and cultivated as nonnegotiable principles that drive us toward growth, resilience, and purpose. They are not merely reflections of our past experiences but deliberate commitments to who we must become to fulfill our potential.

Our Must Core Beliefs are the bedrock upon which we build a meaningful life. They represent a paradigm shift from merely examining our existing beliefs to actively sculpting them into what we must become. This shift is necessary to transcend our limitations and unlock our full potential.

Many self-improvement experts suggest that cultivating Must Core Beliefs can have a profound positive impact on personal development. These experts propose that adopting beliefs such as the following may significantly enhance our growth journey:

1. **Self-Love and Love for Others:** Believing in our inherent worthiness of love and capacity to love others unconditionally
2. **Self-Sufficiency:** Embracing the belief that we are enough as we are while maintaining a drive for continuous growth
3. **Competence and Capability:** Trusting in our ability to learn, adapt, and overcome challenges
4. **Embracing Imperfection:** Recognizing that imperfections contribute to our unique beauty and strength
5. **Positive Worldview:** Maintaining the belief that the world is fundamentally good and filled with opportunities
6. **Significance:** Believing that our existence and actions positively impact others through service and unique talents

I agree with these experts, who argue that adopting such core beliefs can serve as a powerful foundation for personal transformation and fulfillment. Ultimately, the decision to embrace these beliefs and incorporate them into your life is a personal choice that you alone can make.

Developing these Must Core Beliefs requires conscious effort, intention, and practice. It's about choosing to embrace these beliefs even when our past experiences or current circumstances might suggest otherwise. This is where the power of the Must Mindset comes into play—we choose these beliefs because we must, not because they're easy or immediately apparent.

Remember, these beliefs are not about denying reality or ignoring challenges. Instead, they're about creating a mental framework that empowers us to face life's difficulties with resilience, optimism, and purpose.

By adopting these Must Core Beliefs, we open ourselves to extraordinary possibilities. We become more resilient in the face of adversity, more compassionate toward ourselves and others, and more capable of making a positive impact on the world.

As you reflect on your core beliefs, ask yourself, "Which of these Must Core Beliefs do I already hold? Which ones do I need to develop or strengthen? How might my life change if I fully embraced these beliefs?"

Cultivate and reinforce these beliefs in your daily life. Remember, this is not about perfection but about progress. Each step you take toward embodying these beliefs is a step toward becoming the extraordinary person you are meant to be.

CHAPTER 4

Must Core Values

"Values are like fingerprints. Nobody's are the same, but you leave them all over everything you do."

—Elvis Presley

After graduating from law school, I worked for an insurance defense law firm that represented one of the most famous insurance company syndicates in the world. My role was to defend corporations and insurance carriers, often in cases where lives had been irreparably altered. In one case, I was tasked with finding ways to defend an insurance carrier and a barge company after a barge explosion killed a worker. His widow was suing for financial relief for herself and her family. As I reviewed the case files late into the night, I felt a gnawing sense of unease. The idea of defending corporate interests over a grieving widow violated something deep within me—a sense of justice I had not yet fully articulated or understood. I couldn't do it. That moment marked the beginning of my awareness that my career, though successful by societal standards, was misaligned with my core values.

For many years, I unknowingly operated under external expectations—what others thought success should look like. These expectations were rooted in societal norms: climb the corporate ladder, earn prestige, and accumulate wealth. They were also shaped by my need to prove myself—to show I was capable, worthy, and successful despite the challenges of my early life.

As I sat in my law office late one evening, surrounded by case files and the weight of countless legal battles, I found myself at a crossroads. The success I had achieved in my career felt hollow, and I couldn't shake the feeling that something was missing.

I received a call from a woman named Anna. Her voice was a fragile whisper of despair, trembling with the weight of an unspeakable tragedy. I recognized that voice; it was like my mother's when she got up from the floor where she was scrubbing my father's blood out of the carpet. This was a mother who had suffered a seemingly unbearable loss. Her family's children were in a car coming back from a fast-food restaurant when a speeding car collided with the side of the car carrying the children as it was turning into their home driveway. The car with the children was literally split in half. Five children were instantly killed; another child was rushed to intensive care. I felt a profound connection, a shared language of loss and love. It was a realization that in our shared pain, we find an unspoken bond, a silent pact to walk together through the darkest tunnels, holding on to the faint glimmer of hope that lies at the end. I became their attorney and a friend to help guide them through their path of grief.

This experience awakened something profound within me: a recognition that my deepest values revolved around justice, compassion, and using my skills to make a meaningful difference in people's lives.

Yet it wasn't until I embarked on a personal development journey that I truly understood these values and how they could shape my life moving forward. A mentor suggested I take time for stillness and uninterrupted reflection—a concept that initially seemed foreign to me. How could sitting in silence reveal anything meaningful? But as I carved out time for introspection, something remarkable happened.

In those quiet moments, free from the noise of daily life and external expectations, I uncovered layers of myself that had long been buried beneath ambition and obligation. I realized that at my core, I valued integrity above all else—the kind of integrity that meant aligning my actions with what felt right in my heart. I valued connection, the ability to empathize with others' pain and offer them hope. And I valued purpose, the belief that our work should serve something greater than ourselves.

These realizations didn't come all at once; they unfolded gradually as I allowed myself to sit with difficult questions: What truly matters to me? What kind of legacy do I want to leave behind? What am I willing to stand for, even when it's inconvenient or uncomfortable? The answers weren't always easy or clear, but they were transformative.

Looking back now, I see how these moments—rejecting cases that violated my sense of justice, connecting deeply with Anna's family during their darkest hours, and taking time for stillness—were pivotal steps in aligning my life with my values. They marked the shift from living according to external expectations to living authentically and intentionally.

As I continued this practice of reflection, something remarkable happened. My core values emerged from the depths of my consciousness. I saw patterns in my thoughts, feelings, and behaviors that pointed to what truly mattered to me. It was as if a fog was lifting, revealing a clear picture of who I was at my core.

The results of this exercise were truly game-changing. For the first time in my life, I had a clear understanding of my core values. This newfound clarity brought a greater sense of purpose and direction to my life that I had never experienced before. Decisions that once seemed difficult became easier as I now had a solid foundation of values to guide me.

I remember feeling an overwhelming sense of elation and appreciation when I finally identified my core values. It was like discovering a hidden treasure within myself—a treasure that had always been there, waiting to be uncovered. This discovery has profoundly impacted every aspect of my life, from my personal relationships to my professional endeavors.

The essence of a core value is the fundamental principle that anchors one's identity and guides their decisions, actions, and interactions with the world. It is the unwavering beacon that illuminates the path toward personal integrity and fulfillment, reflecting the deepest convictions of one's soul. A core value is not merely an abstract ideal but a living, breathing force that shapes who we are and who we aspire to become. It is the quiet yet powerful voice within that reminds us of what is most meaningful and true, even in the face of adversity. A core value is the heart of our character, the compass that steers our journey through life, ensuring we remain aligned with our highest aspirations and truest selves. Roy E. Disney, Walt Disney's industrious brother, said, "It's not hard to make decisions when you know what your values are."

I invite you now to pause and reflect on your life. Are you living in alignment with your true values, or have you, like I once did, found yourself swept along by the currents of others' expectations? Identifying your core values is not just an exercise in self-discovery; it's a crucial step in becoming the person you are meant to be. As you read this chapter, I encourage you to consider what principles guide your decisions, what ideals you hold most dear, and what legacy you wish to leave behind. Remember, your core values are the compass that will guide you through life's most challenging moments and lead you to your most fulfilling achievements.

DIFFERENTIATING CORE BELIEFS AND CORE VALUES

Though intimately connected, core beliefs and core values represent distinct aspects of our inner framework, each playing a unique role in shaping our lives.

Core beliefs are the deeply ingrained convictions we hold about ourselves, others, and the world around us. They are the silent architects of our perceptions, often formed in early life through our experiences, culture, and upbringing. These beliefs act as the lens through which we interpret reality, influencing our thoughts, emotions, and behaviors in profound ways. Core beliefs can be empowering, driving us toward growth and fulfillment, or limiting, trapping us in cycles of fear and self-doubt. They are the underlying assumptions that, whether we are fully aware of them or not, dictate how we see the world and our place within it.

Core values, on the other hand, are the guiding principles that reflect our highest ideals and deepest commitments. They are the moral compass that directs our actions, choices, and interactions with others. Core values often inform our core beliefs about ourselves and the world. For example, if honesty is a core value, it may reinforce the core belief that "I am a trustworthy person."

Conversely, our core beliefs can shape which values we prioritize. For instance, if someone holds the core belief that "the world is a dangerous place," they may come to value security and caution above all else, making safety and vigilance guiding principles in their life. In this way, the interplay between beliefs and values shapes not only how we see ourselves but also the principles by which we choose to live.

While core beliefs shape our perception of the world, core values shape our response to it. Core beliefs are the foundation of our worldview, often operating in the background, whereas core values are the principles we actively uphold, guiding our journey through life with purpose and intention. Together, they form the bedrock of who we are, influencing everything from our decisions to our destiny.

As we continue this journey of self-discovery together, we will revisit your core beliefs and delve deeply into identifying and understanding your core values. These values will serve as the nucleus of your ongoing personal development, providing you with a sense of direction and purpose as you navigate the complexities of life. These values will become your compass, guiding you with clarity and intention as you move forward. They will help you align your actions with your most deeply held convictions, ensuring your path is authentic and fulfilling.

This process of self-discovery is not a one-time event but an ongoing journey. As you grow and evolve, so will your understanding and application of your core beliefs and values. In the upcoming pages of this book, we will explore how these foundational elements interact, how you can nurture and strengthen them, and how they can be integrated into every aspect of your life.

Remember, this journey of self-discovery is unique to everyone. Your core values may be different from mine or anyone else's, and that's perfectly okay. What matters is that they are authentically yours. So as you embark on this exercise, be patient with yourself, be honest, and be open to what you might discover. The rewards of understanding your core values are immeasurable, and I'm excited for you to experience this transformative process.

CORE VALUES AND GROWTH MINDSET

Core values are not static; they can evolve as we grow and gain new experiences. The process of discovering and refining our core values is an essential aspect of personal development. As we become more aware of our values, we can make more conscious choices that align with our authentic selves, leading to greater fulfillment and self-actualization.

Recent neuroscientific research has shed light on how core values are represented in the brain. Studies using functional magnetic resonance imaging (fMRI) have shown that thinking about core values activates the ventromedial prefrontal cortex (vmPFC), an area associated with self-reflection and decision-making.

This activation suggests that core values are deeply intertwined with our sense of self and play a crucial role in how we process information and make choices.

Psychologists have recognized the significance of core values in shaping human behavior and well-being. Research has demonstrated that individuals who live in alignment with their core values experience greater life satisfaction, resilience, and overall psychological well-being.

By understanding the science behind core values and their relationship to our beliefs, narratives, and mindset, we can more effectively engage in the process of self-discovery and personal growth. This knowledge empowers us to consciously shape our identities and live more authentic, fulfilling lives aligned with our deepest values.

Core values serve as a guiding compass in our lives, providing a sense of purpose and direction that helps us navigate complex decisions and maintain a stable sense of identity even in the face of life's challenges. These values play a crucial role in shaping our mindset, particularly in fostering and maintaining a growth-oriented perspective. When personal growth is itself a core value, it naturally cultivates a growth mindset, encouraging continuous learning and development. Strong core values serve as a wellspring of motivation, enabling us to persist in the face of challenges, a key aspect of the growth mindset. The process of discovering and living by our core values also fosters ongoing self-reflection, which is crucial for maintaining a growth-oriented mindset. This introspective practice allows us to continually assess our progress, adjust our approach, and remain aligned with our fundamental beliefs, thereby reinforcing our commitment to personal development and resilience in the face of obstacles.

DISCOVERING CORE VALUES

While core values are deeply personal, a strategically focused approach can aid in their discovery. In what follows, I'll lead you to examine different areas of your life through the following lenses:

- **Value Sorting Exercises:** Psychological assessments that involve ranking or prioritizing lists of values have been shown to be effective in helping individuals identify their core values. In this chapter, we will explore this value prioritization process in all major areas of life.
- **Guided Introspection:** I will ask you to uncover your core values by examining past decisions and emotional responses.
- **Behavioral Analysis:** Observing patterns in our behavior and

decision-making can reveal underlying values, even those we may not consciously recognize.

As we transition from understanding the dual foundation of personal development through core beliefs and values, it is essential to explore how these elements integrate into the broader context of living a holistic life. Evaluating our core values gains even greater importance when we consider the multiple facets of our existence, each contributing to the overall balance and harmony we seek in life.

Here are instructions for assessing your core values in each area of the Circle of Life to help you identify and prioritize the values that resonate most with your personal development journey.

1. **Select Your Core Values:** Choose three values from each of the provided lists that best describe your core values for each area. Consider which values resonate most deeply with you and align with your goals and aspirations.
2. **Add Personal Values:** If you believe there are important values that are not listed, feel free to add them. Ensure these values are significant to you and play a crucial role in how you approach and experience each area of your life.
3. **Prioritize Your Values:** Once you have selected your values, prioritize them from most important to least important within each area. This helps you understand which values you hold highest and how they influence your decisions and actions.
4. **Reflect on Your Choices:** Take a moment to reflect on why these values are significant to you. Consider how they guide your behavior and decisions in each area of your life.

For those who wish to delve deeper into this process of self-discovery and value alignment, this book has a companion guided journal and workbook that can provide further opportunities for exploration and reflection. You can find more information about these resources at the end of the book.

Remember, the journey of aligning your life with your core values is ongoing. By regularly revisiting and refining your understanding of these values, you can ensure that your actions and decisions consistently reflect what matters most to you.

By examining each segment of the Circle of Life, we gain a deeper appreciation of how our core values intersect with these aspects of our life, guiding us toward a more fulfilling and harmonious existence. This framework encourages us to reflect on the balance between different areas in our lives.

Taking the time to explore and identify your core values is a rare and powerful step in your personal development journey. The insights you gain will bring immeasurable benefits, as you will discover later in this book. Your commitment to understanding and living by these values will guide you toward a life that is vibrant, balanced, and deeply fulfilling. Be sure to write down your answers, as you will use them later in this journey and for the rest of your life.

HEALTH AND VITALITY

Well-being encompasses a comprehensive approach to health, reflecting our commitment to self-care, balance, and mental clarity. Vitality, on the other hand, represents our zest for life and the energy that drives us to engage in activities that enhance our physical fitness and overall wellness.

Ancient wisdom, such as that of Aristotle, emphasized the principle of moderation—advocating for a balanced approach to physical health as essential for a thriving life. Similarly, Ayurvedic traditions from ancient India underscore the importance of maintaining physical vitality to support overall wellness. In this context, the core values of self-discipline and balance are paramount, guiding us to manage our diet, exercise, and overall health with care and moderation.

Reflecting on these values helps us understand how our health practices align with our deeper aspirations and whether we are taking the necessary steps to nurture our bodies and minds. As we consider the values that drive our approach to health, it is essential to ask ourselves whether our practices truly reflect a commitment to well-being and vitality. Are there areas where you could enhance your self-care or embrace a more vibrant approach to life? Reflecting on these questions can help guide you toward a more comprehensive and fulfilling approach to health.

Sample Core Values for Health and Vitality

Below are twenty core values often associated with health:

1. **Well-Being:** Embracing holistic health through physical, mental, and emotional care
2. **Vitality:** Cultivating energy and enthusiasm for life
3. **Resilience:** Building the ability to recover from setbacks
4. **Self-Care:** Prioritizing practices that promote personal health and relaxation
5. **Balance:** Maintaining equilibrium through work, rest, and play
6. **Fitness:** Committing to regular physical activity and exercise
7. **Nutrition:** Focusing on healthy eating habits and proper nutrition
8. **Mindfulness:** Practicing awareness and presence in the moment
9. **Rest:** Ensuring adequate sleep and recovery
10. **Prevention:** Taking proactive measures to avoid illness and injury
11. **Mental Clarity:** Seeking mental sharpness and focus
12. **Stress Management:** Developing strategies to handle stress effectively
13. **Hygiene:** Maintaining personal cleanliness and health standards
14. **Longevity:** Striving for a long, healthy life
15. **Detoxification:** Removing toxins and harmful substances from the body
16. **Self-Discipline:** Exercising control over habits and choices
17. **Physical Strength:** Building and maintaining bodily strength
18. **Flexibility:** Improving physical and mental adaptability

19. **Holistic Wellness:** Integrating all aspects of health for overall well-being
20. **Empowerment:** Taking charge of one's health and wellness journey

As you reflect on your core values for health, take a moment to consider why these values are significant to you. Think about how they guide your behavior and decisions in this crucial area of your life. Which values resonate most deeply with you? How do they align with your goals and aspirations for your health and well-being?

By identifying and prioritizing your core values for health, you're taking control of your well-being and creating a master plan for a healthier, more fulfilling life. These values represent the foundation upon which you'll build the extraordinary life you're meant to live, guiding you toward becoming the person you're destined to be.

Once you've identified your top three Must Core Values for health, consider how you can implement them in your daily life. You might create a daily routine that prioritizes these values, set specific and measurable health goals aligned with them, or regularly reflect on how your health choices align with your core values.

Practical Strategies for Implementing Your Must Core Values in Health

The following tips will help you clarify your values in this area.

1. Create a daily routine that prioritizes your health values.
2. Set specific, measurable health goals aligned with your values.
3. Regularly reflect on how your health choices align with your core values.

Health Values in Action: Scott's Vitality Revolution

In the heart of New Orleans, Scott, a radio personality, transformed his daily life into a vibrant celebration of vitality. Every morning, as the sun peeked over the Mississippi River, he took a brisk walk along the scenic riverfront. The refreshing breeze carried the scent of blooming jasmine, and the distant sound of jazz music filled the air, energizing his spirit. At lunchtime, Scott embraced meal prepping with a Creole twist. His fridge was a colorful display of fresh produce from the local market: bright green okra, plump tomatoes, and sweet bell peppers. The sizzle of shrimp in a garlic-lemon sauce filled his kitchen while the rich aroma of spices danced through the air, making his mouth water. Each bite of his carefully crafted lunches was a burst of flavor, reminding him he was nourishing his body and prioritizing his health amid the vibrant culture of the city.

RELATIONSHIPS

In the realm of relationships, the values of love and trust stand out as foundational. Love speaks to the depth of our emotional bonds and our capacity to form meaningful connections with others. Trust represents the confidence we place in those around us and the reliability we strive to offer in return. Reflecting on these values invites us to consider how well we nurture our relationships—whether we are building a network of support and mutual respect that aligns with our deepest aspirations. Esther Perel, renowned psychotherapist, author, and speaker who specializes in relationships and sexuality, reminds us, "The quality of your relationships is what determines the quality of your life, and the bonds and the connections that we make with other people that we established with them gives us a greater sense of meaning of happiness of well-being than any other human experience."

Confucius championed respect and integrity in human interactions, underscoring the importance of building strong, supportive connections. Similarly, Taoist philosophy highlights empathy and compassion as essential for fostering meaningful relationships, suggesting that these qualities are vital for achieving balance in life. Valuing kindness, respect, and understanding in our relationships reflects these timeless principles, guiding us toward more harmonious and fulfilling connections.

To see how these values can be actively embodied, we can look to the life and work of Brené Brown, a renowned researcher and author who has extensively explored the dynamics of vulnerability, courage, and empathy in relationships. Brown's research underscores the power of love and trust in creating genuine, meaningful connections. She emphasizes the importance of embracing vulnerability as a pathway to authenticity, showing that love and trust are integral to building strong and supportive relationships.

Brown's concept of "braving trust"—an acronym that stands for Boundaries, Reliability, Accountability, Vault (confidentiality), Integrity, Nonjudgment, and Generosity—offers a practical framework for cultivating trust in relationships. She teaches that trust is developed through consistent actions and open communication, highlighting its importance in creating lasting, meaningful bonds. Her words, "Connection is why we're here; it is what gives purpose and meaning to our lives," beautifully capture the significance of love and trust in fostering deep and fulfilling relationships.

Evaluating these values in our lives encourages us to reflect on how well we are fostering love and trust in our relationships. Are we actively nurturing our emotional connections and building a network of support? Are we reliable and trustworthy in our interactions with others? By considering these questions, we can better understand how to strengthen our relationships and ensure they are built on a foundation of love and trust.

As you reflect on your own relationships, consider whether they embody the principles of love and trust. Are there areas where you can deepen your connections or enhance your reliability? Understanding and integrating these values can guide you toward more enriching and supportive relationships.

Sample Core Values for Relationships

Here are several core values often associated with relationships:

1. **Love:** Nurturing deep, affectionate connections with others
2. **Trust:** Building and maintaining reliability and confidence in relationships
3. **Respect:** Valuing and honoring others' boundaries and opinions
4. **Communication:** Engaging in open and honest dialogue
5. **Empathy:** Understanding and sharing the feelings of others
6. **Support:** Offering encouragement and help in times of need
7. **Forgiveness:** Letting go of grudges and past grievances
8. **Kindness:** Demonstrating compassion and goodwill
9. **Loyalty:** Remaining steadfast and supportive in relationships
10. **Commitment:** Investing time and effort into nurturing connections
11. **Understanding:** Seeking to grasp others' perspectives and experiences
12. **Quality Time:** Spending meaningful moments together
13. **Patience:** Exercising tolerance and understanding in interactions
14. **Gratitude:** Appreciating and expressing thanks for others' contributions
15. **Honesty:** Being truthful and transparent in communication
16. **Collaboration:** Working together harmoniously to achieve common goals
17. **Affection:** Showing warmth and care through gestures and words
18. **Boundaries:** Setting and respecting personal limits in relationships
19. **Nurturing:** Providing emotional support and growth opportunities

As you reflect on your core values for relationships, take a moment to consider why these values are significant to you. Think about how they guide your behavior and decisions in this crucial area of your life. Which values resonate most deeply with you? How do they align with your goals and aspirations for your relationships?

By identifying and prioritizing your core values for relationships, you've pinpointed the values you must align with to live authentically and realize your truest potential in this vital area of your life.

Once you've identified your top three Must Core Values for relationships, consider how you can implement them in your daily life. You might create a daily routine that prioritizes these values, set specific and measurable relationship goals aligned with them, or regularly reflect on how your relationship choices align with your core values.

Practical Strategies for Implementing Your Must Core Values in Relationships

Here are tips that have improved my life.

1. Practice active listening to embody values like respect and understanding.
2. Schedule regular quality time with loved ones to prioritize your connection.
3. Communicate your values openly and discuss how to support each other.

Relationship Values in Action: Sheila and Tyrone's Royal Parade of Communication

Sheila, a former Mardi Gras queen of the famous Zulu Social Aid & Pleasure Club, turns her family gatherings into a hive of lively connection and understanding. Sheila and her husband, Tyrone, a former Zulu Mardi Gras king, have their home adorned with colorful Mardi Gras decorations, a welcoming sanctuary where everyone feels welcome. The warm glow of purple, green, and gold lights creates an inviting atmosphere as the sweet scent of beignets wafts through the air. Each person who enters their home is considered family, their voices filled with happiness while the sounds of laughter and the occasional joyful shout echo in each room. Sheila and Tyrone live intentionally, celebrating their life together in their loved community.

CAREER AND PROFESSIONAL ACHIEVEMENT

The ancient Greek concept of *eudaemonia* emphasizes the importance of striving for excellence through virtuous actions, resonating deeply with our aspirations for success and growth. Across cultures, the value of ambition, when balanced with integrity and ethical behavior, has been a cornerstone of meaningful achievement. This balanced approach encourages us to thoughtfully integrate personal growth with our professional ambitions, ensuring that our career paths are both fulfilling and aligned with our deeper values.

In the context of a career, the values of growth and achievement often take center stage. Growth represents a commitment to continuous learning and professional development, pushing us to expand our skills, knowledge, and horizons. Achievement reflects our drive to reach milestones and realize our career goals, turning our ambitions into tangible success. Reflecting on these values allows us to assess our career trajectory and determine whether we are progressing toward both professional ambitions and personal satisfaction.

To illustrate the power of growth and achievement in one's career, we can look to the journey of Satya Nadella, the chairman and CEO of Microsoft. Nadella's career exemplifies the profound impact of these values. His leadership emphasizes continuous learning and innovation, which has driven both his personal success and the transformation of Microsoft. By fostering a growth mindset within the company, Nadella has been instrumental in embracing new opportunities and adapting to the rapidly evolving technology landscape.

Nadella's philosophy is that growth is not just about acquiring new skills but about evolving one's mindset. He encourages viewing challenges as opportunities for learning and development, a perspective that has been pivotal in Microsoft's success. One of his insightful phrases, "The learn-it-all does better than the know-it-all," reflects his belief that a mindset focused on continuous learning leads to greater achievements and career success.

Reflecting on these values in our own careers prompts us to ask ourselves, "Are we actively seeking opportunities to expand our skills and knowledge? Are we setting and striving toward meaningful career goals?" By considering these questions, we can gain a better understanding of our career trajectory and assess whether we are making progress toward our professional ambitions and personal satisfaction.

As you contemplate the values of growth and achievement, consider whether they are guiding your career path. Are there areas where you can pursue further development or set new goals? Embracing these values can help steer you toward a more fulfilling and successful career.

Sample Core Values for Career

Below are twenty core values often associated with career:

1. **Growth:** Committing to continuous learning and professional development
2. **Achievement:** Striving to reach goals and excel in one's career
3. **Ambition:** Setting and pursuing high career goals
4. **Innovation:** Embracing creativity and new ideas in the workplace
5. **Integrity:** Upholding ethical standards and honesty in work
6. **Leadership:** Leading with vision and influencing others positively
7. **Dedication:** Showing commitment and perseverance in one's role
8. **Collaboration:** Working effectively with others to achieve common objectives
9. **Responsibility:** Taking ownership of tasks and duties
10. **Competence:** Demonstrating skill and proficiency in one's field
11. **Initiative:** Proactively seeking opportunities and solving problems
12. **Accountability:** Accepting and managing personal and professional obligations
13. **Creativity:** Applying original thinking to work challenges

14. **Adaptability:** Adjusting to changes and new circumstances in the workplace
15. **Professionalism:** Maintaining a high standard of conduct and performance
16. **Work-Life Balance:** Managing career demands while nurturing personal life
17. **Resilience:** Overcoming setbacks and persisting through difficulties
18. **Networking:** Building and maintaining professional relationships
19. **Vision:** Setting a clear and inspiring direction for one's career
20. **Mentorship:** Guiding and supporting the growth of others in the field

As you reflect on your core values for your career, take a moment to consider why these values are significant to you. Think about how they guide your behavior and decisions in this crucial area of your life. Which values resonate most deeply with you? How do they align with your goals and aspirations for your relationships?

By identifying and prioritizing your core values for career, you've pinpointed those that resonate deeply within you and guide the way you choose to live and work. These are the values you must align with to live authentically and realize your truest potential in this crucial area of your life.

Once you've identified your top three Must Core Values for career, consider how you can implement them in your daily life. You might create a daily routine that prioritizes these values, set specific and measurable career goals aligned with them, or regularly reflect on how your career choices align with your core values.

Practical Strategies for Implementing Your Must Core Values in Career and Professional Achievement

Let these tips improve your clarity of your values.

1. Align your daily actions with your Must Core Values.
2. Create a personal accountability system.
3. Communicate and reinforce your values in the workplace.

Career Values in Action: Isabella Colorfully Capturing the Culture of the Big Easy

In the bustling French Quarter of New Orleans, Isabella's painting career is her passion. In the vibrant French Quarter, Isabella splits her time between New Orleans and France, channeling the city's spirit onto canvas—jazz-filled second lines parading down Royal Street, magnolia trees draped in Mardi Gras beads. Each brushstroke preserves the city's lively culture, her art a celebration of New Orleans's enduring soul.

FINANCIAL WELL-BEING

Financial well-being is a critical aspect of our overall sense of security and freedom, deeply rooted in principles of balance and justice that have been valued across cultures for centuries. The ancient Egyptian principle of *Ma'at*, representing equilibrium and fairness, offers a timeless framework that can be applied to modern financial management. Embracing values of responsible stewardship, ethical practices, and thoughtful resource management reflects these enduring principles, helping us navigate the complexities of our financial lives with wisdom and integrity.

In the realm of finances, the values of security, abundance, and financial freedom are paramount. Security refers to the stability and peace of mind we gain from managing our resources wisely, ensuring that our financial foundation is solid and our future is well planned. Abundance embodies the belief that there is enough wealth and opportunity for everyone, encouraging us to approach financial decisions with a mindset of prosperity rather than scarcity. Financial freedom, however, represents the ultimate goal of achieving independence and self-sufficiency, allowing us to live life on our own terms, free from financial constraints.

To illustrate the power of these values in practice, we can turn to the life of Warren Buffett, the legendary investor and philanthropist. Buffett's approach to finance is a master class in the application of financial security, strategic growth, and, ultimately, financial freedom. His investment philosophy is grounded in the value of financial security—ensuring that investments are sound, risks are carefully managed, and returns are sustainable over the long term.

Buffett's success also reflects his commitment to strategic growth. Known for his meticulous research, long-term investment horizon, and disciplined approach, Buffett has consistently demonstrated how careful planning and informed decision-making can lead to significant financial achievements. His ability to navigate the financial markets with patience and foresight has made him one of the most successful investors in history.

Buffett emphatically suggests, "The best investment you can make is in yourself," underscoring his belief in the importance of financial security, strategic growth, and the pursuit of financial freedom. This belief highlights the idea that investing in one's own knowledge and skills is foundational to achieving long-term financial stability and success.

Reflecting on these values in our own financial practices prompts us to ask essential questions: "Are we making informed and strategic decisions about our investments and savings? Are we planning for long-term financial stability while seeking opportunities for growth? Are we striving for financial freedom, where our resources allow us the independence to pursue our passions and live authentically?" By considering these questions, we can better understand our financial trajectory and assess whether we are on the path to achieving our economic goals and personal fulfillment.

As you reflect on the values of financial security, abundance, and financial freedom, consider whether they are guiding your financial decisions. Are there areas where you can improve your approach to managing and growing your finances? Embracing these values can help you achieve greater financial stability, success, and the freedom to live life on your own terms.

Sample Core Values for Finances

Here are some core values often associated with finances:

1. **Security:** Ensuring financial stability and safety
2. **Abundance:** Embracing a mindset of plenty and opportunity
3. **Financial Freedom:** Achieving independence and self-sufficiency in financial matters
4. **Wealth:** Building and managing financial resources effectively
5. **Responsibility:** Handling money with care and accountability
6. **Savings:** Prioritizing the setting aside of funds for future needs
7. **Investment:** Allocating resources to grow and multiply wealth
8. **Planning:** Creating and following a financial strategy or budget
9. **Generosity:** Sharing financial resources with others in need
10. **Discipline:** Exercising control over spending and financial decisions
11. **Growth:** Seeking opportunities for financial advancement and improvement
12. **Clarity:** Understanding one's financial situation and goals
13. **Ethical Management:** Managing finances with honesty and integrity
14. **Resourcefulness:** Finding creative solutions to financial challenges
15. **Prosperity:** Striving for success and thriving in financial endeavors
16. **Frugality:** Practicing wise spending and avoiding unnecessary expenses
17. **Investment Wisdom:** Making informed decisions about investments
18. **Risk Management:** Assessing and mitigating financial risks

19. **Financial Literacy:** Educating oneself about money management and financial principles
20. **Legacy:** Planning for the future and creating a lasting impact with resources

As you reflect on your core values for your finances, take a moment to consider why these values are significant to you. Think about how they guide your behavior and decisions in this crucial area of your life. Which values resonate most deeply with you? How do they align with your goals and aspirations for your relationships?

By identifying and prioritizing your core values for financial well-being, you've pinpointed those that resonate deeply within you and guide the way you choose to spend and save.

Once you've identified your top three Must Core Values for your finances, consider how you can implement them in your daily life. You might create a daily routine that prioritizes these values, set specific and measurable financial goals aligned with them, or regularly reflect on how your financial choices align with your core values.

Practical Strategies for Implementing Your Must Core Values in Financial Well-Being

Many financial experts suggest these tips.

1. Set up automatic transfers to savings accounts that align with your values (e.g., retirement, travel fund, charitable giving).
2. Use apps or software to track your spending and categorize expenses based on your core values.
3. Create reminders for regular financial check-ins to ensure you're staying true to your values.

Financial Values in Action: Todd Graves—Raising Cane's

Todd Graves, the founder of Baton Rouge–based Raising Cane's Chicken Fingers, exemplifies the value of making money while fostering a supportive corporate culture and championing his beloved LSU athletic teams. His passion for LSU football infuses the spirit of his restaurants, where vibrant decor and game-day events create a sense of community among employees and customers alike. By prioritizing employee well-being and engagement, Todd cultivates a workplace where team members feel valued and motivated, leading to exceptional service and business success. His commitment to both financial growth and community support resonates deeply in Baton Rouge, making Raising Cane's not just a restaurant but a cherished part of the local culture that celebrates the spirit of LSU athletics while ensuring his employees thrive.

PERSONAL GROWTH AND LEARNING

The Buddhist Eightfold Path emphasizes the importance of right effort and mindfulness, supporting the pursuit of self-improvement and awareness. This ancient wisdom aligns seamlessly with the value of ongoing personal development, reminding us that continuous growth and learning are essential throughout our lives.

With personal growth, the values of authenticity and self-discovery are fundamental to leading a fulfilling and meaningful life. Authenticity involves being true to yourself and living in accordance with your core beliefs and values. Self-discovery is about exploring and understanding your potential and purpose. Reflecting on these values encourages us to consider how we are pursuing our personal development and whether we are embracing our true selves while seeking meaningful self-improvement.

A compelling example of how these values can shape our journey of personal development can be found in the life of Elizabeth Gilbert, the bestselling author known for her memoir, *Eat Pray Love*. Gilbert's work and life embody the principles of authenticity and self-discovery. Her memoir details a transformative journey in which she reconnected with her true self after a period of personal crisis. Gilbert's story illustrates how authenticity involves a deep commitment to understanding and expressing our genuine self, free from societal expectations or external pressures. Her courage to explore her inner life and embrace her vulnerabilities resonates with the essence of living authentically.

Self-discovery, as highlighted in Gilbert's writings, involves a quest to explore one's passions, desires, and potential. In *Eat Pray Love*, she embarks on a journey across Italy, India, and Indonesia to find her true self and reclaim her sense of purpose. Her exploration of different cultures, philosophies, and practices serves as a powerful example of how self-discovery can lead to profound personal growth and clarity.

Gilbert's life story reminds us, "You are not a mistake. You are not a problem to be solved. You are a perfect, unrepeatable human being." You are authentically valuable. This notion reflects the importance of accepting and valuing oneself just as one is rather than constantly striving to meet external expectations.

Reflecting on these values prompts us to examine how we are pursuing our personal development. Are we being true to ourselves and our core beliefs? Are we actively exploring our potential and seeking a deeper understanding of who we are? By embracing authenticity and engaging in self-discovery, we can navigate our personal growth journey with greater self-awareness and purpose.

As you consider these values in your life, think about whether they are guiding your personal growth. Are there aspects where you can become more aligned with your true self or delve deeper into your self-discovery process? Embracing these values can lead to a more authentic, meaningful, and fulfilling journey of personal development.

Sample Core Values for Personal Growth

Here are some core values often associated with personal growth:

1. **Authenticity:** Being true to oneself and one's values
2. **Self-Discovery:** Exploring and understanding one's true potential
3. **Curiosity:** Embracing a desire to learn and explore new ideas
4. **Reflection:** Engaging in a thoughtful examination of one's life and actions
5. **Courage:** Facing challenges and fears with bravery
6. **Self-Awareness:** Understanding one's strengths, weaknesses, and motivations
7. **Resilience:** Developing the ability to bounce back from setbacks
8. **Growth Mindset:** Believing in the capacity for development and improvement
9. **Empowerment:** Taking control of one's life and decisions
10. **Adaptability:** Being flexible and open to change
11. **Goal Setting:** Defining and pursuing personal objectives
12. **Learning:** Continually acquiring knowledge and skills
13. **Self-Compassion:** Treating oneself with kindness and understanding
14. **Passion:** Pursuing activities that ignite enthusiasm and drive
15. **Balance:** Maintaining equilibrium between various aspects of life
16. **Mindfulness:** Practicing present-moment awareness and focus
17. **Gratitude:** Recognizing and appreciating the positive aspects of life
18. **Self-Improvement:** Actively seeking ways to enhance oneself
19. **Confidence:** Believing in one's abilities and worth
20. **Vision:** Creating and pursuing a clear sense of purpose and direction

As you reflect on your core values for your personal growth, take a moment to consider why these values are significant to you. Think about how they guide your behavior and decisions in this crucial area of your life. Which values resonate most deeply with you? How do they align with your goals and aspirations for your relationships?

By identifying and prioritizing your core values for personal growth, you've pinpointed those that resonate deeply within you and guide the way you choose to learn and evolve. You must align with these values to live authentically and realize your truest potential in this essential area of your life.

Once you've identified your top three Must Core Values for personal growth, consider how you can implement them in your daily life. You might create a daily routine that prioritizes these values, set specific and measurable learning goals aligned with them, or regularly reflect on how your choices align with your core values.

Practical Strategies for Implementing Your Must Core Values in Personal Growth

I highly recommend these activities to improve your value alignment in personal development.

1. Develop a daily learning habit aligned with your growth values.
2. Seek feedback and opportunities for self-reflection.
3. Set challenging personal goals that propel you into the Must Zone and out of your comfort zone.

Personal Growth Values in Action: Embodying New Orleans's Spirit of Resilience

Wendell Pierce, a renowned actor and activist from New Orleans, embodies the city's spirit of resilience and growth through his personal journey and community involvement. Rooted in the historic African American neighborhood of Pontchartrain Park, Pierce's story is a testament to the power of cultural preservation and community empowerment. From his acting career, where he infuses performances with the rhythms of New Orleans jazz and the flavors of Creole cuisine, to his hands-on involvement in rebuilding efforts after Hurricane Katrina, Pierce consistently demonstrates his commitment to his hometown's values.

Pierce's dedication to personal and community growth extends beyond the entertainment industry. He has been actively involved in educational initiatives, including mentoring young artists at the New Orleans Center for Creative Arts and advocating for improved educational opportunities citywide. His entrepreneurial venture of opening grocery stores in low-income areas to address food deserts further illustrates his innovative approach to community development. Through his ongoing advocacy and presence in local community centers and schools, Wendell Pierce continues to inspire and uplift, showcasing how personal growth can catalyze positive change for an entire community.

SPIRITUALITY, RELIGION, AND INNER PEACE

Spirituality and inner peace are often regarded as the most essential elements in the quest for a balanced and harmonious life. For millions of people throughout millennia, this area of life is seen as the wellspring from which all other aspects flow. It is the foundation upon which everything else is built—the source of strength, wisdom, and purpose that guides us through life's challenges and triumphs. Throughout history, spiritual traditions and religious teachings have emphasized the importance of aligning with higher principles to find peace, purpose, and fulfillment.

This section of the Circle of Life is one of the most personal and, at times, divisive areas of discussion. Spirituality, religion, and inner peace touch upon the deepest parts of our identity, often shaped by cultural, family, and individual experiences. What one person holds sacred may differ vastly from another's beliefs. Yet the beauty of this journey is that it does not matter what others believe. What truly matters here, for the purposes of this book, is being true to yourself and your version of faith, spirituality, and inner peace. This exploration is about connecting with what resonates most deeply within you, whether through organized religion, personal spiritual practices, or a profound connection to the natural world. We will delve further into the rich and diverse landscapes of religion and spirituality in greater detail later in this book, offering deeper insights and reflections.

Throughout history, one of the most profound examples of a life dedicated to spirituality and inner peace is found in the teachings and life of Jesus Christ. Central to Christianity, Jesus's life and teachings emphasize love, compassion, forgiveness, and humility. His message of unconditional love and service to others continues to inspire billions of people around the world. Jesus's teachings often centered on the importance of inner transformation and aligning one's life with the will of God, which he conveyed through parables and direct instruction. In the Gospel of John, Jesus says, "Peace I leave with you; my peace I give to you. I do not give to you as the world gives. Do not let your hearts be troubled, and do not let them be afraid" (John 14:27 King James Version [KJV]). This powerful statement reveals the essence of inner peace that Jesus offered—a peace that transcends worldly troubles and resides deep within the soul.

Jesus's life was marked by profound compassion and a commitment to serving others, especially those who were marginalized and oppressed. His call to love our neighbors as ourselves and to forgive those who have wronged us forms the cornerstone of Christian ethics. His example teaches that true spirituality is not just about personal salvation but also about embodying the principles of love and compassion in everyday life. Jesus's teachings remind us that spirituality is both a personal journey and a call to action, guiding us to live lives of purpose, peace, and profound connection to others.

Another powerful example of spiritual dedication is found in the life of His Holiness the Dalai Lama, a spiritual leader revered worldwide for his unwavering commitment to compassion, wisdom, and peace. The Dalai Lama's life is a testament to the transformative power of these values, which have guided his teachings and actions. Rooted in the principles of Buddhism, his philosophy emphasizes the interconnectedness of all beings and the importance of serving others, reflecting the belief that true spiritual fulfillment comes from acts of kindness and understanding.

The Dalai Lama often speaks of compassion. In his words, "Love and compassion are necessities, not luxuries. Without them, humanity cannot survive." This profound statement underscores his belief that compassion and love are not just virtues to be admired but essential qualities that sustain and nurture human life. Through these values, we can foster inner peace, cultivate deeper connections with others, and contribute to the well-being of the world.

Reflecting on these spiritual values invites us to examine our own beliefs and practices. Are we cultivating compassion, wisdom, and service in our daily lives? Are we seeking inner peace through alignment with our spiritual principles? For those who view spirituality as the central pillar of their Circle of Life, these questions take on even greater significance. By ensuring our spiritual life is in harmony, we create a ripple effect that positively influences every other area of our lives—relationships, careers, finances, health, and personal growth.

As you contemplate these values, consider how they resonate with your own spiritual or religious practices. Are there aspects of your spiritual journey where you can more fully embody these values? Are there areas where you seek greater alignment with your inner self or with a higher purpose? Embracing these values can guide you toward a more fulfilling and peaceful spiritual life and, by extension, a more balanced and harmonious existence overall.

Ultimately, this journey is about being true to yourself and your version of faith, spirituality, and inner peace. It is an exploration that requires honesty, reflection, and a deep commitment to living in alignment with what you hold most sacred.

Sample Core Values for Spiritual and Religious Development

Here are twenty core values often associated with spirituality and religion:

1. **Faith:** Believing in something greater than oneself
2. **Compassion:** Extending kindness and understanding to others
3. **Purpose:** Finding and fulfilling one's true calling or mission in life

4. **Forgiveness:** Letting go of resentment and embracing healing
5. **Gratitude:** Recognizing and appreciating the blessings in life
6. **Mindfulness:** Practicing present-moment awareness and focus
7. **Integrity:** Living in accordance with one's highest principles
8. **Humility:** Acknowledging one's limitations and embracing modesty
9. **Generosity:** Sharing resources and time to help others
10. **Patience:** Cultivating the ability to wait and endure with grace
11. **Wisdom:** Seeking deep understanding and insight
12. **Love:** Embracing unconditional affection and care for all beings
13. **Harmony:** Striving for balance and peace within oneself and with others
14. **Service:** Dedicating oneself to helping and uplifting others
15. **Respect:** Honoring the dignity and worth of all beings
16. **Trust:** Building confidence in one's spiritual path and in others
17. **Devotion:** Committing oneself to spiritual practices and beliefs
18. **Acceptance:** Embracing life's circumstances with peace and understanding
19. **Courage:** Facing spiritual challenges with strength and resolve
20. **Inner Peace:** Cultivating tranquility and calm within the soul

As you reflect on your core values for your spiritual life, take a moment to consider why these values are significant to you. Think about how they guide your behavior and decisions in this crucial area of your life. Which values resonate most deeply with you? How do they align with your goals and aspirations for your relationships?

By identifying and prioritizing your core values for spirituality and religion, you've pinpointed those that resonate deeply within you and guide your spiritual journey. These are the values that you must align with to achieve true inner peace, spiritual fulfillment, and a life that reflects your highest spiritual aspirations. For those who view spirituality as the central pillar of their existence, aligning with these values is not just important—it is essential for living a life that is truly balanced, meaningful, and aligned with the deepest truths of their being.

Once you've identified your top three Must Core Values for spirituality, consider how you can implement them in your daily life. You might create a daily routine that prioritizes these values, set specific and measurable goals aligned with them, or regularly reflect on how your choices align with your core values.

Practical Strategies for Implementing Your Must Core Values in Spirituality, Religion, and Inner Peace

Reflect on these activities to enhance this valuable area of your Circle of Life.

1. Establish a daily spiritual practice (e.g., meditation, prayer, reflection).
2. Seek a community or mentorship that supports your spiritual values.
3. Integrate your spiritual values into your decision-making process.

Religion and Spirituality Values in Action: Gayle Benson—A True Saint

Gayle Benson, a philanthropist, the owner of the New Orleans Saints, and the widow of Tom Benson, embodies the spirit of generosity and faith that New Orleans holds dear. Her journey from interior designer to one of the most influential figures in Louisiana sports and business is a testament to her resilience and commitment to her community. Deeply rooted in her Catholic faith, Benson has consistently demonstrated her values and how religious beliefs can guide one's actions in both personal and professional spheres.

Benson's spiritual convictions have been the cornerstone of her philanthropic efforts. Through the Gayle and Tom Benson Charitable Foundation, she has made significant contributions to Catholic charities, educational institutions, and healthcare initiatives throughout New Orleans and beyond. Her support for the restoration of local churches and the establishment of scholarship programs for underprivileged students reflects her dedication to preserving the city's rich cultural heritage while investing in its future. Gayle Benson's hands-on approach to community service—she is often seen volunteering at local events or visiting hospitals—showcases her belief in the power of personal connection and compassion. Her actions exemplify the true spirit of a "Saint," not just in name but, indeed, as she continues to use her position and resources to uplift those in need, embodying the values of faith, hope, and charity that are central to her religious beliefs and the vibrant culture of New Orleans.

COMMUNITY AND LEGACY

Contribution to our community and leaving a meaningful legacy are the very essence of a life well lived. They are the threads that weave our actions, our words, and our intentions into the fabric of humanity, creating a pattern of light and hope that endures long after we are gone. Across the span of history, these values have been revered, cherished, and celebrated in spiritual traditions and philosophical teachings that call us to rise above the mundane and touch the eternal. Buddhism and Hinduism speak to the virtues of selfless service and compassion, urging us to open our hearts and extend our hands to those in need. Ancient Greek philosophy, too, calls us to leave a mark on the world—a legacy that speaks of our character, our values, and our unwavering commitment to the greater good.

In the realm of contribution, the values of service and legacy are like beacons, guiding us through the storms of life and illuminating the path to purpose and fulfillment. Service is the act of pouring ourselves out for the benefit of others, of giving without expecting anything in return. It is the quiet, uncelebrated acts of kindness that can change the course of a life—the outstretched hand that lifts someone from despair, the comforting word that eases a troubled heart, the generosity that transforms scarcity into abundance. Legacy is the lasting imprint of our lives on the world—the echo of our deeds, our love, and our compassion that reverberates through the corridors of time, inspiring and uplifting those who come after us.

Imagine the power of your contributions. Picture a person teetering on the edge of despair, their world darkened by loneliness and fear. And then, through a simple act of compassion—a call, a visit, a moment of genuine connection—you light a candle in their darkness, illuminating a path. Envision the family, caught in the relentless grip of financial ruin, who, with your help, find the strength to rebuild, to rise from the ashes of their misfortune. See the face of a person who has given up all hope, contemplating the end of their journey, but who, through your words and your presence, finds a reason to keep going, to believe in the possibility of a brighter tomorrow. These are not just acts; they are lifelines, reaching into the depths of despair and pulling someone back into the light.

Your contributions can extend far beyond the immediate, touching the lives of countless others in ways you may never fully see. Picture yourself as a guardian of the earth, working tirelessly to protect the fragile balance of nature to ensure that future generations inherit a world where they can breathe clean air, drink pure water, and marvel at the beauty of the natural world. Imagine the impact of standing against injustice, speaking out for those who have no voice, and fighting for a world where dignity, equality, and peace are not just ideals but realities. These contributions are the seeds of change, planted with intention and nurtured with love, growing into a legacy that will bloom for generations to come.

A living testament to the power of service and legacy is Eliud Kipchoge, the legendary Kenyan marathoner whose life embodies the very essence of these values. Kipchoge's achievements on the global stage are nothing short of extraordinary. He has redefined what the human body can endure and what the human spirit can achieve. But it is not just his athletic prowess that sets him apart; it is his unwavering commitment to using his success as a force for good.

Despite his global fame, Kipchoge remains deeply rooted in his community, dedicating his time, resources, and influence to uplift those around him. He is a beacon of hope for young athletes in Kenya, a supporter of educational initiatives, and a passionate advocate for environmental sustainability. Kipchoge's legacy is not merely the records he has shattered, but the lives he has touched, the dreams he has ignited, and the hope he has instilled in those who look to him as an example of what is possible.

His words, "No human is limited," echo across the world, a rallying cry for those who dare to dream beyond the constraints of their circumstances. Kipchoge's legacy is one of resilience, perseverance, and unwavering belief in the boundless potential of the human spirit. It is a legacy that will continue to inspire long after his final race, a testament to the power of service and the enduring impact of a life lived with purpose.

As you reflect on these values, consider the immense power you hold to shape the world around you. How can you make a difference, not just in the lives of those you touch directly but in the broader arc of history? What legacy do you wish to leave behind? These are not just rhetorical questions; they are calls to action, invitations to step into the fullness of your potential and to contribute in ways that resonate with your deepest values.

Embrace the values of service and legacy, and remember this unparalleled inspiration: William James, American philosopher and psychologist, offered, "The greatest use of a life is to spend it on something that will outlast it." This profound truth displays the essence of a life dedicated to contribution. In giving yourself, you not only change the lives of others but also discover the deepest, most enduring parts of your soul. By living these values, you create a legacy of light, hope, and love that will shine brightly for generations to come.

Reflecting on these values encourages us to assess how we contribute to the greater good and the kind of legacy we wish to create. Are we engaging in acts of service that resonate with our values and make a meaningful difference in the lives of others? Are we actively shaping a legacy through our actions and contributions that align with our deepest aspirations and the values we hold dear? These questions are crucial in guiding us toward a life of purpose, fulfillment, and lasting impact.

As you consider these values in your life, reflect on how you can enhance your contributions and the lasting impact you want to leave behind. How can you integrate the principles of service and legacy into your daily actions? What steps can you take to ensure your life leaves a meaningful and positive mark on the world? Embracing these values can lead to a more fulfilling life, marked by significant contributions and a legacy that inspires and uplifts those who come after you.

Sample Core Values for Community and Legacy

Here are twenty core values often associated with the contribution to community within the Circle of Life:

1. **Service:** Making a positive impact through acts of kindness and support
2. **Legacy:** Creating a lasting influence through one's actions and contributions
3. **Compassion:** Demonstrating empathy and concern for others' well-being
4. **Generosity:** Giving time, resources, or support to those in need
5. **Impact:** Striving to make a meaningful difference in the lives of others
6. **Leadership:** Guiding and inspiring others toward positive change
7. **Volunteerism:** Engaging in activities that support community and social causes
8. **Mentorship:** Offering guidance and support to help others grow
9. **Advocacy:** Championing causes and standing up for what is right
10. **Collaboration:** Working together with others to achieve common goals
11. **Inspiration:** Motivating and encouraging others through example and action

12. **Education:** Sharing knowledge and helping others learn and develop
13. **Philanthropy:** Contributing to charitable causes and organizations
14. **Empowerment:** Enabling others to achieve their own potential and goals
15. **Integrity:** Acting with honesty and strong moral principles in contributions
16. **Responsibility:** Taking ownership of one's role in making a difference
17. **Support:** Providing assistance and encouragement to those in need
18. **Social Justice:** Working toward fairness and equity in society
19. **Creativity:** Using innovative approaches to address social issues and contributions
20. **Sustainability:** Promoting practices that support long-term environmental and social health

As you reflect on your core values for your legacy, take a moment to consider why these values are significant to you. Think about how they guide your behavior and decisions in this crucial area of your life. Which values resonate most deeply with you? How do they align with your goals and aspirations for your relationships?

You have now taken a profound journey inward, reflecting on and identifying the most essential core values that define your sense of contribution and legacy—those that resonate deeply within your soul and guide your actions as you make a meaningful impact on the world. By prioritizing these values, you have uncovered your Must Core Values in the realm of contribution. These are not just guiding principles; they are the very essence of who you are and what you aspire to be. They are the compass that directs your journey, ensuring your life is filled with acts of purpose, generosity, and love.

Once you've identified your top three Must Core Values for spirituality, consider how you can implement them in your daily life. You might create a daily routine that prioritizes these values, set specific and measurable goals aligned with them, or regularly reflect on how your choices align with your core values.

Practical Strategies for Implementing Your Must Core Values in Community and Legacy

Here are tips that help clarify your contribution values.

1. Identify causes that align with your values and volunteer regularly.
2. Mentor others in areas where you have expertise.
3. Consider how your daily actions contribute to the legacy you want to leave.

Community and Legacy Values in Action: Nurturing the Future of Jazz Through Education and Cultural Heritage

Ellis Marsalis Jr. was a pivotal figure in the New Orleans jazz scene, exemplifying core values of education, mentorship, and cultural preservation throughout his life. As a jazz pianist and educator, he dedicated himself to nurturing the next generation of musicians, believing that education was essential for personal growth and the continuation of jazz as an art form. His role as a mentor extended to many young artists, including his sons, who have become prominent figures in the music world. Marsalis instilled in them the importance of understanding jazz history and developing their unique voices, ensuring that the rich traditions of New Orleans would be passed down through generations.

Marsalis's commitment to cultural preservation was evident in his performances and teachings, where he often celebrated the unique blend of musical styles that define New Orleans. He emphasized the significance of local influences, incorporating the rhythms of jazz and the flavors of the city into his work. This dedication to his roots not only enriched his own music but also inspired countless others to embrace and honor their cultural heritage. By fostering a deep appreciation for jazz, he contributed to the broader narrative of New Orleans as a cultural hub, reinforcing the idea that music is a vital part of the city's identity.

Throughout his life, Marsalis exemplified resilience and a growth mindset, adapting to the evolving landscape of jazz while remaining true to his values. His legacy continues through the many musicians he mentored and the cultural impact he made in New Orleans. By prioritizing education, cultural heritage, and community, Ellis Marsalis Jr. not only shaped the jazz scene but also left an indelible mark on the hearts and minds of those who were fortunate enough to learn from him, ensuring that his influence would resonate for years to come.

MUST CORE VALUES

As you align your life with these Must Core Values, you set into motion a powerful ripple effect that extends far beyond your immediate reach. Every action, every word, every gesture of kindness rooted in these values touches the lives of others—both known and unknown—spreading hope, compassion, and inspiration. The impact of your contributions will echo through time, influencing not only the individuals you encounter but also the fabric of our society and the world at large.

It is easy, at times, to feel that our efforts—small and personal as they may seem—make little or no difference in the grand scheme of things. We may wonder if one person's contributions can truly change the world. But this is a profound misunderstanding of the power we each hold. The truth is that helping one person is helping all. The kindness you extend to a single soul may inspire them to do the same, creating a chain reaction of goodwill and positive action that ripples outward, touching countless lives.

Consider the compounding effect when multitudes of people, each driven by their own Must Core Values, come together in their efforts to make a difference. What begins as a single drop of kindness in the vast ocean of humanity grows into a wave—a force of change that can move mountains, transform communities, and change the world. The cumulative contribution from each of us, though it may seem small in isolation, becomes monumental when joined with the efforts of others.

Imagine the world as a vast field, with each person planting a single seed of goodness. One seed may sprout a single tree, but when thousands, millions, or even billions of seeds are planted, a forest grows—strong, resilient, and capable of withstanding any storm. This is the power of collective action, of each of us doing our part, no matter how small it may seem. Together, our contributions create a legacy of compassion, justice, and hope that future generations will inherit.

Embracing these principles will not only enrich your own life with a profound sense of fulfillment and purpose but will also leave an indelible positive mark on the world around you. Your legacy will be one of enduring light, a beacon that continues to inspire and uplift future generations, reminding them of the boundless potential within every human heart to make a difference. In this way, the cumulative effect of our shared humanity becomes the force that shapes a brighter, more compassionate world for all.

As you embrace your Must Core Values in all areas of life, remember Oscar Wilde's words: "Be yourself; everyone else is already taken."

CHAPTER 6

Our Must Personal Narrative

"The first step that leads to our identity in life is usually not 'I know who I am,' but rather 'I know who I'm not.'"
—MATTHEW MCCONAUGHEY, AWARD-WINNING ACTOR AND AUTHOR

"The stories we tell ourselves shape our lives and our world."
—UNKNOWN

At the heart of the Must Framework lies the idea that certain elements of our lives—our beliefs, values, mindset, and even our personal narrative—are not optional but essential for achieving our highest potential. The Must Personal Narrative represents a pivotal step in this journey, as it is the story we choose to tell ourselves about who we are and what we stand for. Unlike a general narrative, which can be shaped passively by external forces or fleeting emotions, a Must Personal Narrative is intentional, empowering, and rooted in our deepest values. It is the guiding story that drives us forward, helping us align our actions with our purpose and aspirations.

What's your story?

We all have a personal narrative—a story we tell ourselves about who we are, where we've been, and what we're capable of. This narrative isn't just a recounting of past events; it's a powerful tool for aligning our lives with our deepest values and becoming the person we are meant to be. These narratives shape our reality, influencing our decisions, relationships, and the very trajectory of our lives.

In the early years of my career, I was primarily focused on my own desires, financial goals, and selfish ambitions. My personal narrative revolved around achieving material success and personal gain. I measured my worth by my financial achievements and the accumulation of wealth. This self-centered approach to life left me feeling unfulfilled and disconnected from my true purpose.

In Chapter 4, I explored how being out of touch with my values led me to operate on autopilot, driven by external expectations rather than internal convictions. That disconnect shaped a personal narrative that was misaligned with who I truly wanted to be. While my lack of introspection about my values created a hollow framework for decision-making, it also reinforced a story I told about myself that prioritized external validation over meaningful contribution. This realization—that the gap between my values and actions was also reflected in the story I told myself—became a pivotal moment in reshaping both my core beliefs and personal narrative.

One day, I experienced a profound realization. I recognized that the life I was living was entirely inconsistent with the man I believed God intended me to be. There was a significant gap between how I honestly described myself and the person I aspired to become. My "I am" statement at that time was far from stellar: "I am looking out for and protecting myself out of fear of feeling unloved by people outside of my immediate family." My "I am" statement was inwardly focused, reflecting a narrative focused on personal gain rather than a meaningful contribution.

Faced with this stark realization, I turned to my faith for guidance. I prayed fervently, asking God to lead me to a different mindset, a new way of being. I sought to become a better person, not just in terms of financial success, but as a holistic human being. This vulnerability marked the beginning of a significant shift in my personal narrative.

As I delved deeper into personal development, my focus underwent a dramatic transformation. Instead of solely pursuing financial success, I prioritized becoming a better person in all aspects of life. This shift was not just about changing my goals or purpose—it was about rewriting the personal narrative that had long defined me. My earlier "I am" statement—centered on self-protection and fear of being unloved—had driven me to seek external validation through material achievements. Financial success became a way to prove my worth, both to myself and to others, as I shielded myself from feelings of inadequacy. However, this narrative left me feeling disconnected and unfulfilled. As I reflected on what truly mattered, I realized my story needed to change. I started to see myself not as someone defined by fear and self-preservation but as someone capable of creating value for others and living with purpose. This realization marked the beginning of a profound transformation in both my narrative and my approach to life.

This change in perspective had a profound impact on me. I found that as I shifted my focus away from myself and directed my energy toward helping others, my prayers were being answered in all aspects of my life. Interestingly, when financial success ceased to be my primary focus, my wealth significantly increased as a natural result of the value I added to others' lives. My journey of personal growth didn't stop there. I learned that personal narratives can continually evolve as we challenge our limitations and strive for further self-actualization. My new "I am" statement is that I am here on this earth to help others overcome the thought processes that hold them back and guide them toward becoming their true potential selves.

Seeing the shift from what it was decades ago to where I am today fills me with hope and excitement for the future. I believe my future "I am" could reach levels I have never even imagined in terms of positively impacting others' lives.

My own story is a powerful reminder that personal narratives are not fixed. They can be reshaped and redefined as we grow and align our lives with our deepest values and aspirations. My journey from a self-centered focus to a life dedicated to helping others illustrates the profound impact that changing our personal narrative can have on both individual fulfillment and the ability to positively influence the world around us.

I share this experience with you as an inspiration, showing that it's possible to dramatically shift one's life focus and find greater purpose and satisfaction in the process. I believe and pray that you can embark on a similar journey of evolution, transforming your personal narrative to create a more meaningful and impactful life.

Take a moment to reflect on your story. What tale have you been telling yourself? Is it one of limitation or possibility? Of victimhood or resilience? Of fear or courage?

Now ask yourself, "Does this story serve me well? Is it consistent with my best being and my highest potential?"

As we journey through life, we craft a narrative that defines who we are, what we stand for, and what we can achieve. This personal narrative, our "I am," is a picture drawn from our experiences, mindset, core beliefs, limiting beliefs, values, and perceptions. It evolves over time, shaped by the triumphs and trials we encounter. Understanding and consciously shaping this narrative is crucial for personal growth and self-empowerment.

As you navigate the complexities of your life journey, remember that you are the architect of your personal narrative. You possess the profound power to revisit, revise, and reframe the chapters that no longer resonate with your current aspirations or values. This process of narrative transformation is both liberating and challenging, as it requires you to confront the stories you've been telling yourself about your life, your abilities, and your potential.

Your Must Personal Narrative often lies hidden beneath layers of outdated narratives—stories that past experiences, societal expectations, or self-doubt may have shaped. By examining and reshaping your personal story, you open yourself to new possibilities and align more closely with your authentic self.

As explored in earlier chapters, your mindset and core beliefs significantly influence the story you tell yourself. Reflect on how you now view your abilities and potential. Do you see setbacks as insurmountable barriers or as opportunities for growth and learning? Shifting to a growth mindset and embracing positive core beliefs can transform your personal narrative from one of limitation to one of evolution and empowerment. Our Must Values influence the events we choose to highlight within our personal narrative, the meaning we assign to our experiences, and the future we envision for ourselves. For instance, if one of your top values is growth, your personal narrative likely emphasizes moments of learning and transformation. If connection is a key value, your story might focus on relationships and community.

I challenge you to explore your narrative, question it, and if necessary, have the courage to rewrite it. Your true story—one of strength, resilience, and unlimited potential—is waiting to be told. As you navigate this journey of self-discovery, remember that every chapter of your life is a pivotal moment toward becoming the person you were meant to be. By embracing your *must* and rewriting your narrative, you are not just changing your story; you are transforming your life.

THE FORMATION OF OUR PERSONAL NARRATIVE

From a young age, we form an internal story about ourselves. This narrative is influenced by various factors, including our upbringing, cultural context, significant life events, and the messages we receive from those around us. These elements come together to form our core beliefs, which act as the foundation of our personal narrative.

Our personal narrative weaves together core beliefs, Must Core Beliefs, core values, and Must Core Values, creating a coherent story that gives meaning and continuity to our life experiences. Each element plays a distinct yet interconnected role in shaping our identity and worldview. Core beliefs serve as the foundational convictions that influence our perceptions and reactions, often operating subconsciously. Must Core Beliefs elevate this foundation by introducing intentional, nonnegotiable principles that drive personal growth and transformation. Similarly, core values represent the guiding principles that shape our decisions and actions, while Must Core Values refine these principles into essential, consciously chosen values that align with our highest aspirations. Finally, our personal narrative acts as the thread that ties these elements together, reflecting both the beliefs we hold and the values we embody. By actively engaging with and integrating these components into a Must Personal Narrative—a story aligned with who we are meant to be—we can reshape our lives in empowering ways, creating a narrative that supports resilience, authenticity, and ongoing personal development.

Consider how a child who is consistently praised for their intelligence might develop a narrative of "I am smart." Conversely, a child who is frequently criticized might internalize a story of "I am inadequate." These early narratives can set the tone for how we perceive ourselves throughout our lives. Steve Jobs said, "The most powerful person in the world is the storyteller. The storyteller sets the vision, values, and agenda of an entire generation that is to come." I suggest that our storytelling about ourselves sets our self-determined identity.

Research by Dr. Dan P. McAdams, a leading psychologist in narrative identity, emphasizes that our personal stories are not just reflections of our past but also frameworks that shape our future. McAdams's studies show that individuals who craft positive, redemptive narratives about their lives tend to have higher levels of psychological well-being and resilience. McAdams tells us, "We are all storytellers, and the life stories we create, tell, and live contribute to our sense of identity, providing us with a coherent and meaningful way of understanding who we are."

THE INFLUENCE OF LANGUAGE AND SELF-TALK

The language we use, both in our internal dialogue and in our interactions with others, plays a critical role in shaping our narrative. Positive self-talk can reinforce a healthy, empowering story, while negative self-talk can perpetuate self-limiting beliefs.

Consider the difference between saying "I am always failing" and "I am learning from my mistakes." The former cements a narrative of defeat, while the latter fosters a narrative of resilience and growth. Research by Dr. Kristin Neff on self-compassion highlights the importance of kind and supportive self-talk in fostering a positive self-image and reducing negative self-criticism.

> **Journaling Prompt:** Reflect on your self-talk. Write down some of the phrases you frequently use to describe yourself. Are they positive or negative? How do they shape your personal narrative? The companion guided journal and workbook can assist you in this process.

THE POWER OF FOCUS

Where we direct our focus shapes our experiences and reinforces our narrative. Tony Robbins often states, "Where focus goes, energy flows." By focusing on our strengths and accomplishments, we build a narrative of competence and success. Conversely, dwelling on our failures and shortcomings reinforces a narrative of inadequacy.

Journaling Prompt: Think about a recent challenge you faced. Where did you direct your focus? Did you concentrate on the obstacles or on your ability to overcome them? Shifting your focus to your strengths and the lessons learned can help reshape your narrative into one of empowerment.

THE IMPACT OF PHYSIOLOGY

Our physiology—how we carry ourselves physically—affects our internal narrative. Amy Cuddy's research on power poses demonstrates that adopting confident postures can influence our hormone levels and improve our feelings of confidence and power. When we stand tall and adopt open, assertive body language, we reinforce a narrative of strength and capability.

Reflect on your posture and body language throughout the day. Do you carry yourself in a way that communicates confidence and self-assurance? Simple changes in how we hold ourselves can have profound effects on our internal story.

Journaling Prompt: Observe your posture and body language. Do they reflect confidence and strength? What small changes can you make to improve your physical presence?

IDENTITY AND THE ROLES WE ADOPT

Throughout our lives, we adopt various roles or "costumes" that become integral parts of our identity. These roles can include being a student, a parent, a professional, an athlete, or a caregiver, among many others. Each role comes with its own set of expectations and narratives that we internalize, significantly shaping our personal story.

Consider the profound significance of the words "I am." These words are more than just statements of identity; they are declarations that carry the weight of our self-perception and the roles we embody. When we say, "I am a student," "I am a parent," or "I am a professional," we are not just describing what we do, but who we believe ourselves to be. This self-identification influences our behaviors, choices, and how we interact with the world.

You should also consider whether the stories you tell about yourself and the roles you take on might be limiting you. For instance, someone who identifies strongly as a caregiver might develop a narrative centered around selflessness and nurturing. While this role can provide a deep sense of purpose and fulfillment, it can also become limiting if it prevents the individual from exploring other aspects of their identity. They might feel restricted by the expectations of always putting others' needs first, potentially leading to neglect of their own desires and aspirations.

Reflect on the narratives you have adopted over the years. How have they shaped your narrative? Have they empowered you or limited your potential? Do some roles no longer serve you, or have you outgrown them? Embracing a more flexible and multifaceted identity can help you craft a richer, more empowering narrative.

THE POWER OF "I AM"

The statements we make about ourselves, beginning with "I am," are incredibly powerful. They act as affirmations that reinforce our beliefs about who we are. Positive "I am" statements can empower us, while negative ones can limit us. For example, saying "I am capable" or "I am resilient" fosters a sense of strength and determination, whereas saying "I am a failure" or "I am unworthy" can undermine our confidence and potential.

The power of our personal narrative is beautifully illustrated by a story often attributed to a visit by President John F. Kennedy to NASA in 1962. As the president toured the facility, he encountered a janitor carrying a broom. Kennedy paused to shake the man's hand and asked, "What do you do here?" The janitor replied proudly, "I'm helping put a man on the moon." This simple yet profound response shows the transformative power of personal narrative. The janitor didn't define himself by his specific tasks but by the greater purpose he served. His "I am" statement wasn't limited to "I am a janitor," but rather expanded to "I am a crucial part of a historic mission." This story demonstrates how our perception of our role and purpose can elevate our sense of self and contribution. The janitor saw beyond the immediate tasks of cleaning floors and emptying trash bins. He understood that his work, however seemingly small, was an integral part of NASA's monumental goal. By adopting this perspective, the janitor transformed his job into a calling. His narrative wasn't one of menial labor, but of participating in one of humanity's greatest adventures. This shift in perspective likely influenced his work ethic, job satisfaction, and overall sense of fulfillment.

This anecdote serves as a powerful reminder that our personal narratives are not dictated by our job titles or daily tasks, but by how we choose to view our contributions to the world. It challenges us to consider: How can we reframe our roles to align with a greater purpose? What would change if we saw our work, no matter how seemingly insignificant, as part of a larger, more meaningful mission? As we continue to explore the power of personal narrative, let this story inspire you to look beyond the surface of your roles and responsibilities. Consider how you might reframe your own "I am" statements to reflect not just what you do, but the greater purpose you serve.

The concept of personal narrative and the power of "I am" statements are not modern inventions. Ancient luminaries and spiritual traditions have long recognized the profound impact of self-perception and self-declaration on one's life and destiny.

In Hinduism, the Sanskrit phrase *Aham Brahmasmi* translates to "I am Brahman" or "I am the Absolute." This powerful affirmation reflects the belief that one's true self is divine and unlimited. The Upanishads, ancient Sanskrit texts, teach that by realizing and declaring this truth, one can transcend limitations and connect with their highest potential. Similarly, in Buddhism, the concept of *anatta* or "non-self" encourages practitioners to question fixed narratives about the self. By recognizing the fluid nature of identity, Buddhists aim to liberate themselves from limiting self-concepts and achieve enlightenment.

In ancient Egyptian philosophy, the god Ptah was believed to have created the world through thought and speech. This concept extends to human beings, suggesting that our words and thoughts shape our reality. The famous "I am" declarations found in the Egyptian *Book of the Dead*, such as "I am Yesterday, Today, and Tomorrow," reflect the power of self-definition in shaping one's eternal journey.

The ancient Greek aphorism "Know thyself," inscribed at the Temple of Apollo at Delphi, emphasizes the importance of self-awareness in shaping one's life story. Socrates stated, "The unexamined life is not worth living," highlighting the significance of conscious self-reflection in crafting a meaningful personal narrative.

In the Old Testament, God reveals Himself to Moses as "I Am That I Am" (Exodus 3:14 KJV), emphasizing the power of self-declaration. This concept is echoed in the New Testament when Jesus makes several "I am" statements, such as "I am the light of the world" (John 8:12 KJV), demonstrating the power of affirming one's identity and purpose.

These timeless teachings from ancient luminaries offer us a profound wellspring of wisdom to draw upon as we craft our modern self-narratives. They beckon us to recognize the divine spark within, to question the boundaries we've placed on our potential, and to wield our thoughts and words as powerful tools in shaping our reality. As we embark on this journey of self-discovery and transformation, let us embrace the ancient practice of deep self-reflection, peeling back the layers of our being to reveal our truest selves. With each "I am" statement we utter, we have the opportunity to tap into a lineage of self-realization that spans millennia. Let us speak our truth with conviction, affirming our identity and purpose with the same power that has moved mountains and changed the course of history. In doing so, we don't merely engage in a contemporary exercise of self-improvement; we participate in an ageless ritual of awakening, connecting with the boundless potential that has always resided within us. As we align our modern understanding with this ancient wisdom, we open ourselves to a profound sense of empowerment, ready to write the next chapter of our lives with the ink of intention and the quill of limitless possibility.

EXPANDING AND REDEFINING OUR ROLES: REWRITING YOUR NARRATIVE

"You are the author of your own life story. You have the power to create a narrative that reflects your true self."

—UNKNOWN

In my years of legal practice, I have represented thousands of clients who came to me during some of their darkest moments. They are often in turmoil, suffering, and in distress, seeking salvation from their pain. What I frequently encounter are women and men trapped in personal stories that do not serve them and likely never did. These stories, which they ruminate on, are filled with self-limiting beliefs and learned helplessness.

During our personal sessions, I delve into how they currently define themselves and what their present identity is. I ask them to describe themselves, starting with the phrase "I am..." This exercise often reveals extraordinary insights in their moments of open vulnerability. Their tone, pace, and volume reflect the identity and costume they have assumed—whether as a victim or as a self-perceived powerless individual. Their body language mimics the role they are playing, further reinforcing their internal narrative. They unknowingly declare their self-limiting beliefs and embrace the state of learned helplessness, focusing on the guardrails of life rather than where they truly want to go.

After they have poured their souls out to me, I hand them a sheet of paper. I ask them to write their name and then the words "I am..." I encourage them to think of all the negative thoughts they have about themselves, their story, and their personal narrative. Once they have done this, I ask them to place a very large X on the paper, consuming the entire sheet, representing these thoughts, beliefs, and stories. Then I ask them to hand me the sheet of paper. I accept it and tell them they have just given me their old story, painful images, and feelings. I take the paper into another room and place it into the shredder. Their old story no longer exists—it has been given away and destroyed.

When I return, I give them a new sheet of paper. I ask them to write down their name and then the words "I am..." I present this blank canvas and ask them to neatly fold it and start carrying it with them. This blank sheet represents their new canvas, a fresh start, and an opportunity to contemplate who they have always been destined to be. They are free to create a new identity, unshackled from their old story.

As they leave, I ask them to focus on all the blessings in their lives and no longer dwell on the painful experiences of the past, which should hold no power over them. These past experiences are merely memories, chemical interactions, and electrical impulses in their brains that no longer serve them. I encourage them to think about the new, authentic superhero costume that has always been waiting for them. It is there now, ready to be embraced.

This process is reminiscent of an old-school Etch A Sketch, where a few shakes can clear the screen, providing a clean slate to create new and beautiful images. Similarly, each of us holds the power to erase the outdated, harmful narratives and start anew. Your new story, your true "I am," is waiting to be written.

Reflect on your life and the narratives you have been holding on to. Are they serving you or holding you back? Consider this moment as an opportunity to let go of the old and embrace the new. Your blank canvas is in your hands, ready for you to paint the life you desire and deserve. Embrace the new, authentic story of you. As you walk this path, remember the words of C. S. Lewis: "You are never too old to set another goal or to dream a new dream." Your journey is just beginning, and the possibilities are limitless.

Dr. Dan P. McAdams's narrative identity theory provides a comprehensive framework for understanding how we construct our life stories. According to this theory, we create our identities by integrating our experiences into an internalized, evolving story of the self. Research based on this theory has shown that individuals who can construct coherent, positive narratives tend to have better psychological well-being and are more resilient in the face of challenges. This goes beyond individual core beliefs, encompassing how we string these beliefs together into a cohesive life story.

Neuroplasticity plays a crucial role in shaping our core beliefs. This same principle applies to our personal narratives. Research in cognitive psychology has revealed that our autobiographical memories are not fixed recordings but rather reconstructions influenced by our current beliefs and emotions. This malleability of memory explains why our personal narratives can change over time, even when we are recounting past events. As we develop new perspectives or gain new information, we may reinterpret past experiences, altering our narrative in the process.

Each time we reinforce a narrative through thought or action, we strengthen the neural pathways associated with it. Conversely, when we challenge ourselves and replace limiting beliefs or negative narratives with empowering ones, we weaken those old pathways and create new ones that support growth and transformation. This explains why long-held narratives can feel so ingrained and why consistent effort is required to change them. Recent studies have shown that narrative-focused cognitive therapies can lead to measurable changes in brain structure and function, particularly in areas associated with self-perception and emotional regulation.

Understanding the malleability of memory offers you a powerful tool for personal growth. Your memories are not fixed recordings, but reconstructions influenced by your current beliefs and emotions. This flexibility allows you to reframe past experiences in a more positive or constructive light, supporting your journey of self-improvement and helping you build a more empowering narrative.

To harness neuroplasticity effectively, start by practicing intentional reflection. Spend time identifying the recurring thoughts or beliefs that shape your narrative. Write them down and examine their origins. Are they rooted in past experiences, societal expectations, or self-doubt? Next, consciously reframe these beliefs into positive, growth-oriented alternatives. For example, if your current narrative says, "I am not good enough," replace it with "I am capable of learning, growing, and achieving my goals."

Repetition is key to rewiring your brain. Reinforce your new narrative daily through affirmations, visualization, or journaling. Imagine yourself living out this empowering story and taking small actions that align with it. Over time, these practices will strengthen the neural pathways associated with your new narrative, making it feel more natural and authentic.

Recent advancements in social neuroscience have shed light on how our social environments influence our personal narratives. Studies have shown that the brain's default mode network, which is involved in self-referential thinking and autobiographical memory, is highly responsive to social cues and interactions. This research underscores the importance of social context in shaping our narratives, explaining why our stories often reflect the values and expectations of our communities. Surround yourself with supportive environments and people who reflect the values and beliefs you aspire to embody. Positive reinforcement from external sources can amplify your efforts to reshape your personal narrative.

It's crucial to understand that your life story is not set in stone. The concept of narrative identity reveals that you have the power to shape and reshape your personal narrative actively. This empowering realization is at the heart of becoming the person you are meant to be.

As we delve into the transformative power of rewriting our personal narrative, it's essential to understand that this process is intricately linked with the broader journey of embracing our *must*. The combined impact of scientific research on personal growth and narrative psychology reveals that our stories are not set in stone. Rather, we have the agency to actively shape our personal narrative, bringing it into alignment with our deepest aspirations and values.

By examining and reshaping our personal stories, we open ourselves to new possibilities, aligning more closely with our authentic selves and the life we are meant to live.

This journey of narrative transformation is a crucial part of the Must Journey. As you explore and rewrite your personal narrative, you are not just changing your story; you are aligning it with the driving force that propels you toward your true potential. Your *must* is the inner voice that calls you to become the person you were meant to be, and by rewriting your narrative, you are creating a path that honors this call. This process involves recognizing that your experiences, though they may have shaped your current beliefs, do not define your future. By embracing your *must* and rewriting your narrative, you are transforming your life and turning every chapter into a building block toward fulfilling your true purpose.

As you navigate this journey, remember that every aspect of your life—your mindset, core beliefs, values, and actions—plays a role in shaping your narrative. By shifting to a growth mindset and embracing positive core beliefs, you can transform your personal narrative from limitation to empowerment and growth. This transformation is not just about changing your perspective; it's about unlocking the true potential that lies within you and aligning it with your *must*. By doing so, you are not just rewriting your story; you are creating a life that is authentic, meaningful, and filled with purpose.

By understanding these scientific principles underlying personal narrative development and change, we can approach the process of reshaping our stories with greater insight and effectiveness. This knowledge, combined with the techniques we've explored for changing core beliefs, empowers us to make intentional, evidence-based changes to our narratives, leading to more authentic and fulfilling lives.

To fully embrace the power of "I am," it's essential to recognize that we are not confined to a single role or identity. We are dynamic beings capable of growth and change. Changing your personal narrative requires conscious effort and reflection. Next, I present several strategies to help you expand, redefine your roles, and reshape your story.

EXPRESSIVE WRITING

It's worth highlighting the specific benefits of expressive writing in changing personal narratives. James Pennebaker's research on expressive writing demonstrates that writing about our experiences and emotions can lead to improvements in both physical and mental health. When we write about our lives, we externalize our narratives, making them more tangible and easier to examine and reshape. This process can help us gain new perspectives on our experiences and integrate them into a more empowering narrative.

SELF-REFLECTION

Take time to reflect on the various roles you play in your life. Write down your "I am" statements and examine how they make you feel. Are they empowering or limiting? Reflect on your current narrative and identify the sources of these beliefs. Consider how they have shaped your life. Are there roles that feel restrictive or outdated? Challenge the beliefs associated with these roles. Ask yourself if they still serve you or if they are holding you back from exploring new possibilities.

REFRAME

Identify any roles that feel restrictive or outdated. Actively challenge the negative aspects of your narrative. For each limiting belief, find evidence that contradicts it and reframe it into a positive affirmation. For example, change "I am not good enough" to "I am constantly improving and growing." Replace limiting "I am" statements with ones that reflect your potential and aspirations. For example, change "I am just a parent" to "I am a nurturing and creative individual."

SEND ME YOUR OLD STORY—I SHALL ELIMINATE IT FOR YOU

Write down your old "I am" statements and reflect on how they have shaped your life. Feel free to mail or email them to me. They are no longer in your possession. I shall destroy them for you. Then create new "I am" statements that align with your true potential and aspirations. Keep these new statements with you as a reminder of your empowering narrative.

EMBRACE MULTIPLE IDENTITIES AND ADOPT NEW ROLES

Recognize that you can embody multiple roles simultaneously. You can be a parent and a professional, a student and an athlete. Embracing multiple identities allows you to draw from a richer, more diverse set of experiences and strengths. Don't be afraid to explore new roles and identities. If you've always identified as a caregiver, try taking on a role that focuses on self-care and personal growth. If you've seen yourself primarily as a professional, explore creative or recreational activities that bring you joy.

SEEK SUPPORT AND SURROUND YOURSELF WITH POSITIVE INFLUENCES

Engage with a community or support group that encourages you to explore and embrace new roles. Surround yourself with individuals who see and appreciate the multifaceted nature of your identity. Share your journey with trusted friends, mentors, or a therapist. They can provide valuable perspectives and encouragement. Surrounding yourself with positive influences can reinforce your new narrative and provide encouragement along the way.

PRACTICE GRATITUDE AND TAKE ACTION

Cultivate an attitude of gratitude by regularly reflecting on the positive aspects of your life. Gratitude can shift your focus from what is lacking to what is abundant, fostering a more positive narrative. Step out of your comfort zone and take actions that align with your new narrative. Each step you take reinforces your new story and builds confidence in your abilities.

WHAT IS YOUR EXCUSE FOR NOT CHANGING AND IMPROVING YOUR NARRATIVE?

Haben Girma's journey is a powerful testament to the transformative power of personal narrative and determination. Born in California to Eritrean immigrants, Girma was not deafblind from birth but rather experienced progressive loss of hearing and vision due to an unknown condition.

Despite these challenges, she refused to let her disabilities define her story. From an early age, Girma embraced a narrative of possibility rather than limitation. She learned to navigate the world using adaptive technologies and developed a fierce independence.

Girma's pursuit of education was marked by constant innovation. She became the first deafblind student to graduate from Harvard Law School, using a combination of braille and adaptive technologies to excel in her studies. Throughout her time at Harvard, Girma advocated for improved accessibility, not just for herself but for all students with disabilities. In 2013, Girma graduated from Harvard Law, becoming the first deafblind person to do so. This achievement reshaped her narrative, establishing her as a role model and advocate for disability rights.

Today, Haben Girma is an internationally recognized disability rights lawyer, speaker, and author. Her personal narrative continues to evolve as she challenges societal perceptions of disability and advocates for equal opportunities for all.

Girma's story exemplifies how reframing one's personal narrative can lead to extraordinary achievements and societal impact. Her memoir, *Haben: The Deafblind Woman Who Conquered Harvard Law*, provides a detailed account of her journey from her childhood in Oakland, California, to her early professional life as a disability rights lawyer.

Haben Girma's story beautifully illustrates the distinction between core beliefs and personal narrative. Her core beliefs—that disability is not a limitation and that she has the potential to achieve greatness—form the foundation of her worldview. These beliefs are the bedrock upon which she builds her life. Her personal narrative is the dynamic, evolving story she tells about her experiences, challenges, and triumphs. It's how she interprets and presents her journey from a deafblind child to a Harvard Law graduate and internationally recognized advocate. While her core beliefs remain relatively stable, providing a consistent source of strength and motivation, her personal narrative continually expands and evolves as she faces new challenges, achieves new milestones, and redefines what's possible for herself and others with disabilities. This interplay between unwavering core beliefs and an ever-expanding personal narrative is what makes Girma's story so powerful and inspiring.

By embracing your empowering identity, you can craft a richer, more empowering narrative. Remember, the story you tell yourself is not fixed—it can evolve and change as you grow. Each new role you adopt adds depth and dimension to your personal narrative, allowing you to live a more fulfilling and authentic life.

Reflect on your "I am" statements and consider how they shape your identity and potential. Embrace the possibility of change and growth, knowing that you have the power to redefine your story at any time.

Your personal narrative is a powerful force that shapes your reality. By consciously crafting a positive, empowering story, you can unlock your true potential and live a life that reflects your deepest values and aspirations. Celebrate your progress, no matter how small, and trust in your ability to create a life that aligns with your highest potential.

DECLARING YOUR NEW STORY

As we reach the end of this transformative journey through personal narratives, it's time to take a decisive step forward. Your old stories, with their limitations and self-doubt, have been symbolically shredded. They no longer define you or constrain your potential. Now, standing before a blank canvas, you have the opportunity to declare your new story. This is your moment to craft an empowering narrative that aligns with your true self and aspirations. Consider the following as you formulate your new "I am" statements:

What strengths and qualities do you want to embody?

How do you want to contribute to the world?

What goals and dreams will shape your future?

Take a moment to write down your new "I am" declarations. These statements should reflect your highest potential and the person you aspire to become. For example:

"I am resilient and capable of overcoming any challenge."

"I am a source of inspiration and positivity for others."

"I am constantly growing and evolving."

Remember, these new narratives are not fixed. They can and should evolve as you continue to grow and discover more about yourself. Embrace this fluidity and allow your story to unfold authentically.

As you step into this new chapter of your life, carry these empowering statements with you. Let them guide your actions, decisions, and interactions. Your new story is a powerful force for positive change in your life—nurture it, believe in it, and watch as it helps shape a brighter, more fulfilling future.

CHAPTER 7

Must Standards

"The quality of a person's life is in direct proportion to their commitment to excellence, regardless of their chosen field of endeavor."

—Vince Lombardi

From the time I was young, my mother, a teacher, instilled in me the critical importance of education. She believed that education was more than just acquiring knowledge; it was a gateway to opportunity and a reflection of one's character. Her belief shaped the rhythm of my childhood in profound ways. While my peers spent their evenings out playing with friends, I often found myself at home, immersed in textbooks and assignments. I can still picture those nights vividly—the kitchen table piled high with papers, the sound of my mother's voice encouraging me to focus, and the quiet determination I felt as I worked through difficult problems.

Looking back, trade-offs in order to excel in academics were not easy. I sometimes felt isolated from my friends, longing for the carefree moments they seemed to enjoy so effortlessly. Yet even as I struggled with those feelings, I noticed how my mother's standards were shaping me. They instilled in me a sense of discipline and perseverance—a belief that success was not handed out but earned through consistent effort. Her insistence on excellence taught me that hard work and commitment were essential not only for academic achievement but for building a life of integrity and purpose.

From elementary school to high school, through undergraduate studies, my Master of Business Administration degree, and three years of law school, my educational standards and goals steadily evolved. While many of my contemporaries were out socializing and enjoying carefree moments, I often found myself at home, immersed in studying, investing in the gifts of life that were yet to come. Don't get me wrong; I certainly had my fair share of fun and socializing in New Orleans. However, I dedicated a significant portion of my otherwise free time to pursuing academic excellence and personal growth.

These lessons didn't fade as I grew older; they became foundational principles that guided me through every stage of my life. When I pursued higher education, her voice echoed in my mind during late-night study sessions or moments when I doubted myself. When I entered the legal profession, her standards reminded me to approach each case with diligence and care, striving for excellence even when challenges seemed insurmountable. Her influence shaped how I measured success—not by external accolades but by the effort and intention behind my actions.

The educational standards I developed over the years didn't stop after I received my law degree. They expanded into a commitment to personal development and lifelong learning. Decades later, these standards have culminated in the pursuit of my doctorate degree, a milestone that reflects my dedication to acquiring collective knowledge and wisdom. My goal has always been clear: to equip myself with the tools necessary to help others improve their lives in meaningful and impactful ways.

True standards in life are created; otherwise, we measure life without our own ruler and on other people's terms. Without them, we react to life rather than intentionally shaping it. For me, creating these standards meant carrying forward the values my mother instilled in me—prioritizing hard work, valuing education, and striving for excellence in all aspects of life. These standards are not static; they evolve as we grow and adapt, but their foundation remains rooted in intentionality and purpose.

As you reflect on your journey, consider this: What standards have you set for yourself? Are they aligned with your values and aspirations, or are you living by someone else's expectations? By defining and committing to your Must Standards, you can take control of your narrative and shape a life that reflects your true potential. Let this chapter serve as an invitation to explore how intentional standards can elevate your life and empower you to pursue excellence with purpose and authenticity.

Establishing clear, nonnegotiable standards in every area of life is crucial for creating a remarkable life. Must Standards are the core principles and expectations we set for ourselves that align with our deepest values and aspirations. Standards are the invisible boundaries you set for yourself, the nonnegotiable lines that define what you accept, what you strive for, and, ultimately, who you become. They are the silent architects of your destiny, shaping the quality of your actions, the depth of your relationships, and the heights of your achievements. In this chapter, we will explore the profound impact of your standards, how they influence every aspect of your life, and how raising them can propel you toward a life of fulfillment, excellence, and purpose.

Once I determined my Must Standards in each area of my Circle of Life—from relationships to career, from health to personal growth, and so on, I experienced an exponentially positive impact. These standards became the foundation upon which I built a life of purpose and fulfillment. They guided my decisions, shaped my actions, and ultimately transformed me into the person I was meant to be. The journey from a life without defined standards to one built on unwavering principles has been nothing short of revolutionary for my personal growth and success.

As you continue this journey of self-discovery—transforming your core beliefs, rewriting your personal narrative, and aligning with your deepest values and purpose—it becomes clear that your standards are the foundation upon which your future is built. They are the compass that guides you, the engine that drives you, and the lifeblood that fuels your journey toward becoming the person you are destined to be.

REFLECTING ON YOUR STANDARDS

I invite you to reflect on your journey of improved standards. Think back to the various areas of life where you've raised the bar for yourself. How has this impacted the quality of your life? Perhaps you've set higher standards for your education, leading to greater knowledge and opportunities. Maybe you've elevated your expectations in your relationships, resulting in more fulfilling connections. Or possibly you've raised your standards for personal growth, leading to increased self-awareness and life satisfaction. Take a moment to appreciate how these improved standards have shaped your life for the better and consider where you might continue to raise the bar moving forward.

The formation and maintenance of high standards is an intentional and purposeful endeavor with lasting effects—both positive and negative—that permeate every facet of our existence. I invite you to consider how the standards you've set and maintained have shaped your life's trajectory. What lessons have you learned, and how might you apply these insights in the future?

Consider deeply the standards you currently hold. How would you describe them? Are they elevating your existence, or are they holding you back? Be brutally honest with yourself. Perhaps you've recognized areas where you've settled for less—whether out of fear, complacency, or the remnants of an old personal narrative that no longer serves you. It's natural to feel apprehensive about raising your standards, fearing the loss of familiar comforts, relationships, or even your current lifestyle. But here lies the critical question: Are these comforts worth sacrificing the extraordinary life you truly desire? Earl Nightingale, an American radio personality, author, and motivational speaker, stated, "We are all self-made, but only the successful will admit it."

MUST STANDARDS ALIGNMENT WITH MUST MINDSET, MUST CORE BELIEFS, MUST CORE VALUES, MUST PERSONAL NARRATIVE, AND PURPOSE

For your standards to truly empower you and lead you to an exceptional life, they must be in perfect harmony with your Must Mindset, your Must Core Beliefs, your Must Core Values, your Must Personal Narrative, and your purpose (to be discussed in the next chapter). When your standards are aligned with these foundational aspects of your being, they transform into what I call your Must Standards—the unwavering principles that you must live by in every area of your life to ensure you are living authentically, in harmony with your inner being, and fully aligned with your becoming.

Must Standards are the essential, nonnegotiable benchmarks that you set for yourself in every aspect of your life. They are not merely preferences or ideals; they are the standards you absolutely must uphold to live in alignment with your authentic self and to achieve your highest potential. These standards are born out of a deep understanding of who you are, what you value most, and what you believe you can become.

Your Must Standards are directly tied to everything you have learned about yourself in this journey:

1. **Must Mindset:** Your Must Standards should reflect a commitment to continuous growth and improvement. They should push you to challenge yourself, to learn from failures, and to embrace every opportunity for personal and professional development.
2. **Must Core Beliefs:** Your Must Standards are an expression of your deepest beliefs. They must be in harmony with the principles that guide your life, ensuring your actions are always aligned with what you hold to be true.
3. **Must Core Values:** Your Must Standards are built upon the foundation of your core values. These are the values that define who you are at your essence, and your standards must uphold and reflect these values in every area of your life.

4. **Must Personal Narrative:** Your Must Standards are intricately woven into your personal narrative, serving as the framework for the story you tell yourself about who you are and who you aspire to become. They ensure that your narrative reflects resilience, authenticity, and a commitment to living intentionally, empowering you to continually evolve and align your life with your highest potential.
5. **Purpose:** Your Must Standards are the bridge between who you are and the impact you are meant to have in the world. They are directly tied to your sense of purpose, guiding your actions and decisions to ensure they align with the larger meaning you seek in life. By defining and adhering to these standards, you create a clear path toward fulfilling your purpose, whether that involves making a difference in the lives of others, achieving personal excellence, or leaving a lasting legacy. Your Must Standards ensure that every step you take is intentional and purpose-driven, helping you stay focused on what truly matters and empowering you to live a life of significance and authenticity.

By setting Must Standards, you are committing to a life of integrity, excellence, and authenticity. These standards become the guiding principles that shape every decision you make, every action you take, and every interaction you have. They are the standards that you must uphold to ensure your life is not just lived but lived exceptionally.

Your Must Standards are directly tied to everything you have learned about yourself in this journey of self-discovery and personal growth. These standards serve as a practical application of your core beliefs, values, and purpose across all aspects of your life. They ensure you are living in alignment with your authentic self and striving toward your highest potential.

By applying these Must Standards across all life areas, you create a harmonious and purposeful existence. They serve as a practical guide for daily decisions and actions, ensuring that every aspect of your life contributes to your overall purpose and authenticity.

STEPPING UP TO YOUR MUST STANDARDS

As you journey through the process of self-discovery and growth, it's crucial to remember that your Must Standards are nonnegotiable. These are the standards that reflect the very essence of who you are and who you are meant to become. If you live by standards that fall short of your Must Standards, it's time to step up your game. Having standards is not enough, as you may be selling yourself short. Hence, Must Standards ensure that you have defined for yourself your highest level of expectations.

This is your call to action: step up your vision, step up your mindset, and refuse to tolerate anything less than excellence. Do not allow yourself to exist in a space that is misaligned with your true potential. The life you are meant to live demands that you operate from a place of authenticity and purpose, fully aligned with the highest version of yourself.

To live a fulfilling life, you must elevate your standards to match the greatness within you. Anything less is a disservice to your journey and to the person you are destined to be. Embrace this challenge, rise to the occasion, and commit to living every day in full alignment with your Must Standards.

So when we talk about Must Standards, we are not talking about something imposed upon us. We are talking about the standards that naturally arise when we embrace our full potential and commit to living a life without regret. *Must* is our path to exuberant living, a life that leaves no room for hesitation or compromise but instead celebrates the joy of being exactly who we are meant to be.

THE IMPORTANCE OF STANDARDS

Standards are not mere guidelines; they are the embodiment of your self-worth and the essence of what you believe you deserve. High standards challenge you to transcend mediocrity, to reach for the extraordinary in every facet of your life. They drive you toward a life of integrity, purpose, and fulfillment. Low standards can keep you ensnared in a cycle of dissatisfaction, mediocrity, and unrealized potential. When you tolerate low standards, you send a message to yourself and the world that you are willing to accept less than what you are truly worth.

"You don't get what you want; you get what you tolerate" is attributed to Tony Robbins. Similarly, Les Brown states, "You don't get in life what you want; you get in life what you are." This powerfully underscores the critical importance of setting and maintaining high standards. When you refuse to tolerate anything less than excellence, you elevate your life to a level where your aspirations are not just dreams but inevitable realities. You begin to attract opportunities, relationships, and experiences that resonate with your highest vibrations and potential.

Research consistently demonstrates the significant impact of high standards on student achievement and success. Studies have shown that when teachers and schools maintain high expectations for all students, regardless of background or perceived ability, students tend to rise to meet those expectations. This phenomenon, known as the "Pygmalion effect" or "self-fulfilling prophecy," has been documented in numerous educational settings. The importance of setting high standards and expectations extends far beyond education. It impacts success across various domains, including business, finance, relationships, and athletics.

KEY PRINCIPLES FOR EFFECTIVE HIGH STANDARDS

Across domains, several key principles emerge for effectively implementing high standards:

1. Standards should be ambitious yet attainable, providing motivation without causing burnout.
2. Expectations should be clearly communicated and reinforced consistently.
3. High standards should be coupled with appropriate support and resources.

4. Regular assessment and adjustment of standards maintain their relevance and impact.
5. Standards should be tailored to individual/organizational contexts rather than generic.

While the specific applications vary, science consistently shows that thoughtfully implemented high standards drive improved performance and achievement across business, relationships, athletics, and beyond. The key is striking the right balance—setting expectations high enough to inspire growth and excellence without becoming unrealistic or demoralizing.

EXAMINING OUR STANDARDS

To fully grasp the concept of Must Standards, it's essential to break them down into various categories of your Circle of Life.

As we explore the Circle of Life, it's important to recognize that the standards we set for ourselves can vary across different domains. While some standards may apply universally, others may be specific to certain areas of our lives. For instance, the standards you set for your health and well-being might differ significantly from those you establish for your career or relationships. You may have certain nonnegotiables in one area that don't apply in another. This nuance is what makes the Circle of Life such a powerful tool for personal growth. It allows you to tailor your approach to each aspect of your life, ensuring you're aligning with your values and aspirations in a way that feels authentic and meaningful.

Now, take a moment to reflect on the different segments of your Circle of Life. What are the unique standards you hold for each area? How do these standards support your overall well-being and fulfillment? Remember, these should be your Must Standards—the nonnegotiable benchmarks that align with your core values, beliefs, and aspirations. It's essential to establish clear standards for each domain. These standards serve as a guide, helping you align your actions and decisions with your values and aspirations.

Consider writing down your personal standards for each domain—those essential habits and practices that you commit to daily to ensure you're living your best life. By defining these standards, you're not just setting goals; you're creating a blueprint for a life of vitality and purpose. Ask yourself, "Are there areas where I am settling for mediocrity instead of striving for excellence? What changes can I make today to raise my standards and align them with my highest aspirations?" Grab a pen and paper, and let's start crafting your vision for a life of excellence. Here are some standards to reflect upon.

Remember, these standards are personal and may evolve over time. The act of writing them down is a powerful step toward making them a reality.

By setting these standards, you're taking a significant step toward becoming the extraordinary individual you're meant to be. Remember, these standards are not rigid rules, but guiding principles that align with your core values and aspirations. They are the foundation upon which you'll build a life of purpose, fulfillment, and impact.

HEALTH AND VITALITY STANDARDS

"Take care of your body. It's the only place you have to live."
—Jim Rohn, author and motivational speaker

Health and vitality standards may include regular exercise, a balanced diet, and sufficient rest. These standards reflect your commitment to well-being and vitality, ensuring that you maintain the physical and mental energy needed to pursue your purpose. High health standards mean prioritizing your physical and mental well-being, seeking balance, and making conscious choices that promote a healthy lifestyle.

Examples

- **Nutrition:** "I must fuel my body with nutrient-rich whole foods that energize and sustain me."

- **Exercise:** "I must engage in regular physical activity that challenges my body and strengthens my heart."
- **Rest:** "I must prioritize adequate sleep and recovery to maintain my physical and mental well-being."

In sports, setting ambitious yet attainable goals is crucial for reaching peak performance. A comprehensive model of athletic performance emphasizes the importance of establishing high standards across multiple domains, including physiology, biomechanics, psychology, and tactics. Elite athletes consistently demonstrate higher expectations for themselves compared to non-elite peers. However, research also cautions against unrealistic expectations. A study on young elite athletes found that excessively high academic expectations alongside intense athletic demands can negatively impact overall performance. This highlights the need for balance when setting standards.

Arnold Schwarzenegger exemplifies high health standards through his lifelong commitment to physical fitness and overall wellness. During his bodybuilding career, he followed a strict high-protein diet and intense exercise regimen, often training twice daily. Even in his seventies, Schwarzenegger maintains a focus on nutrition, shifting toward a more plant-based diet, and continues to exercise daily, adapting his routine to suit his age and physical condition. His dedication extends beyond physical fitness to overall wellness, emphasizing the importance of mental health, mindfulness, sleep, and regular health checkups.

Schwarzenegger's approach to health is not just about personal achievement but also about inspiring others. He has consistently used his platform to promote fitness and healthy living, encouraging people of all ages to prioritize their health. His commitment to maintaining high health standards has not only contributed to his personal success but has also motivated millions worldwide to focus on their health and fitness. As Schwarzenegger said, "The last three or four reps is what makes the muscle grow. This area of pain divides the champion from someone else who is not a champion."

This philosophy extends beyond just physical fitness to overall health and wellness, emphasizing the importance of pushing oneself to achieve optimal health. I've elevated my own standards for physical health, which has led to improved energy levels, mental clarity, and overall well-being.

Your health standards encompass not only physical fitness but also mental resilience, emotional stability, and spiritual vitality. Take a moment to reflect on what health means to you. What are your nonnegotiables when it comes to your physical and mental health? How do you prioritize self-care and stress management? Perhaps it's exercising regularly, maintaining a balanced diet, or dedicating time to mindfulness practices, such as meditation or journaling.

RELATIONSHIP STANDARDS

"Don't settle for a relationship that won't let you be yourself."
—OPRAH WINFREY, VISIONARY MEDIA MOGUL

Relationship standards govern your interactions with others. They include mutual respect, support, and communication. Standards here could involve open communication, showing appreciation daily, and setting healthy boundaries. These standards embody your values of love, trust, and respect, fostering meaningful connections that support your personal growth and purpose. High relationship standards ensure that you cultivate healthy, meaningful connections with people who uplift and encourage you.

Examples

- **Communication:** "I must communicate with honesty, respect, and empathy in all my interactions."
- **Boundaries:** "I must set and honor healthy boundaries to protect my emotional and mental health."
- **Support:** "I must nurture relationships that are supportive, loving, and reciprocal."

Having high standards for romantic partners is associated with greater long-term relationship satisfaction. While excessively high standards can lead to disappointment, having reasonably high expectations for warmth, attractiveness, and status in a partner predicts more satisfying relationships.

Ronald and Nancy Reagan's fifty-two-year marriage exemplifies high relationship standards through their unwavering mutual respect, support, and communication. Ronald often referred to Nancy as his "secret weapon," valuing her opinions on political matters, while Nancy stood by him through his political career and his battle with Alzheimer's disease. Their relationship was characterized by open communication, including regular love letters and notes, even during their time in the White House.

The Reagans cultivated a partnership that was both personally fulfilling and professionally advantageous. Their deep connection enabled them to navigate the challenges of public life while maintaining a strong personal bond. Nancy's devotion during Ronald's decade-long struggle with Alzheimer's embodied their wedding vows "in sickness and in health," demonstrating their commitment to loyalty and support. Their relationship serves as an inspiring example of how high standards in mutual respect, support, communication, and commitment can create a lasting, meaningful partnership.

Ronald Reagan captured the essence of their relationship when he wrote to Nancy, "I more than love you; I'm not whole without you." This reflects the depth of their connection and the high standards they maintained in their relationship, setting an example of a partnership built on mutual admiration, support, and enduring love.

Take a moment to reflect on your relationships, whether they are romantic or platonic. What standards do you have for the relationships in your life? For example, do you prioritize honesty, empathy, or mutual support? How do you nurture meaningful connections with friends and family?

PROFESSIONAL STANDARDS

"Whatever you are, be a good one."
—William Makepeace Thackeray, English novelist (This quote is often misattributed to Abraham Lincoln.)

Professional standards apply to your work life. They include your work ethic, the quality of your work, and how you interact with colleagues and clients. Maintaining high professional standards involves continuous learning, punctuality, and a commitment to excellence in your field. These standards align with your values of growth and achievement, pushing you toward your professional goals while maintaining integrity in pursuit of your purpose.

Examples

- **Excellence:** "I must consistently produce work that reflects my best effort and dedication to quality."
- **Leadership:** "I must lead by example, inspiring and uplifting those around me with integrity and vision."
- **Growth:** "I must continually seek opportunities for professional development and skill enhancement."

In the business world, setting high standards is strongly correlated with improved performance and financial outcomes. Successful entrepreneurs and business leaders consistently set expectations for themselves and their organizations much higher than is normal. This progressive escalation of expectations over time drives continuous improvement and innovation.

Similarly, research on high-performing companies reveals that maintaining rigorous standards is a key factor in sustained success. Jim Collins's influential *Good to Great* study identified a culture of discipline and high expectations as critical in transforming companies from good to great performers.

Satya Nadella exemplifies high professional standards through his leadership at Microsoft. He demonstrates a strong work ethic and dedication to continuous learning, often emphasizing the importance of a growth mindset. Under his guidance, Microsoft has seen significant transformation, particularly in cloud computing and AI, showcasing his commitment to innovation and quality work. Nadella is known for his empathetic leadership style, fostering a collaborative and inclusive work environment. He consistently pushes for excellence in Microsoft's products and services while also prioritizing ethical considerations in technology development. Nadella's commitment to professional development extends beyond himself; he encourages it throughout the company, promoting a culture of continuous improvement and adaptation. His leadership style and focus on innovation have not only transformed Microsoft's culture but also restored its position as one of the world's most valuable companies.

Nadella explains his approach to professional standards: "Our industry does not respect tradition—it only respects innovation." This statement underscores his commitment to continuous improvement, forward thinking, and excellence in his field, all key aspects of maintaining high professional standards in a rapidly evolving industry.

In my professional journey, I've experienced firsthand the transformative power of setting high standards. When I decided to open my law firm, it was a leap of faith that required me to push beyond my comfort zone and strive for excellence in every aspect of my practice. By setting high standards for myself and my team, I was driven to continually enhance my skills, seek new opportunities for growth, and deliver exceptional value to my clients. This commitment to excellence led not only to greater career satisfaction but also to tangible success. The firm flourished, and I found myself at the forefront of my profession, respected by peers and valued by clients.

This journey taught me that setting high standards is not just about achieving success; it's about creating a culture of continuous improvement and growth. By embracing this mindset, I navigated challenges with confidence, turned obstacles into opportunities, and built a fulfilling and impactful career.

As you reflect on your life, consider how setting high standards in your personal and professional domains can propel you toward greater fulfillment and success. What standards do you hold for your career advancement and skill development? Are there specific courses or certifications you aim to complete each year?

An important component of your career is balancing it with other aspects of your life. How do you ensure your work aligns with your personal values and doesn't encroach on other areas of your life? How do you ensure you have time for fun and relaxation? What activities bring you joy and relaxation? How often do you engage in these activities?

FINANCIAL WELL-BEING

"Financial freedom is available to those who learn about it and work for it."

—Robert Kiyosaki, author of *Rich Dad Poor Dad*

Financial standards involve your approach to managing money. High financial standards mean being responsible for your finances, planning for the future, and making informed decisions that align with your financial goals. These standards reflect your commitment to financial security and abundance, enabling you to live freely and contribute to causes that align with your purpose.

Examples

- **Savings:** "I must prioritize saving a portion of my income to ensure long-term financial security."
- **Investment:** "I must make informed investment decisions that align with my financial goals."
- **Generosity:** "I must give back to my community and support causes that matter to me."

Ray Dalio, founder of Bridgewater Associates, exemplifies exceptional financial standards through his disciplined approach to investment and life management. Despite his immense wealth, Dalio maintains a modest lifestyle, focusing on long-term financial stability rather than lavish spending. His investment strategies are rooted in thorough analysis of economic cycles and long-term trends, emphasizing diversification and risk management. Dalio's commitment to "radical transparency" in both personal and professional dealings underscores his high ethical standards in financial matters. He consistently applies data-driven decision-making processes, which he has codified into a set of principles for both personal finances and company investments.

Dalio's approach to finance demonstrates how high financial standards, when consistently applied, can lead to extraordinary success while maintaining integrity and a commitment to continuous learning. His pledge to give away more than half of his wealth to charitable causes further illustrates his belief in using financial success for the greater good. Dalio's financial wisdom is shown in his declaration, "He who lives by the crystal ball will eat shattered glass," emphasizing the importance of thorough analysis and risk management over reliance on predictions or hunches in financial decision-making. This philosophy underscores Dalio's commitment to informed, disciplined financial management and his high standards for financial stewardship.

As you reflect on your financial standards, consider the following questions: What are your standards for saving, investing, and budgeting? Do you have a specific savings goal or investment strategy? How do you define financial freedom, and what steps are you taking to achieve it?

PERSONAL GROWTH AND LEARNING

"The quality of a leader is reflected in the standards they set for themselves."

—RAY KROC, THE BUSINESSMAN WHO BUILT MCDONALD'S INTO A GLOBAL FRANCHISE

Your standards around personal growth and learning might include daily reflection, regular reading, or pursuing new skills. These standards embody your dedication to self-discovery and authenticity, ensuring you continue to evolve and align with your true self and purpose.

Personal standards are the rules you set for your personal behavior. They include integrity, honesty, and the way you treat yourself and others. High personal standards mean you consistently strive to be the best version of yourself regardless of the circumstances.

Examples

- **Integrity:** "I must live in alignment with my core values, always being honest and true to myself and others."
- **Self-Respect:** "I must treat myself with kindness and hold myself to a standard of self-care that reflects my worth."
- **Accountability:** "I must take full responsibility for my actions and decisions, learning from mistakes and striving for continuous improvement."

Michelle Obama exemplifies high personal standards across various aspects of her life. She prioritizes authenticity, refusing to compromise her identity for political gain while maintaining a strong focus on family and her role as a mother. Education and self-improvement are cornerstones of her standards, evident in her academic achievements and her advocacy for learning. Obama's commitment to health and wellness is reflected in initiatives like Let's Move! and her emphasis on physical and mental well-being. She consistently works to empower others, especially women and girls, through her various initiatives and public speaking engagements. Integrity is a key standard for Obama, as she maintains high ethical standards and emphasizes the importance of honesty and respect in all interactions. Her dedication to community service and giving back is a testament to her standards of social responsibility. Obama also strives to maintain a work-life balance, demonstrating the importance of personal time alongside professional duties. Her resilience in the face of challenges and her consistent pursuit of excellence in her various roles further illustrate her high personal standards. Through these standards, Michelle Obama has shaped her approach to life and public service as well as her role as a leader and role model for many.

"For me, becoming isn't about arriving somewhere or achieving a certain aim. I see it instead as forward motion, a means of evolving, a way to reach continuously toward a better self. The journey doesn't end." Michelle Obama's book *Becoming* reveals her commitment to continuously striving to be the best version of herself regardless of circumstances—a hallmark of high personal standards.

The evolution of my personal standards has been a transformative journey that has profoundly impacted every aspect of my life. As I've raised my standards over the years, I've witnessed a remarkable shift in the quality of my experiences, relationships, and achievements. Where I once settled for mediocrity, I now strive for excellence. This shift has led me to pursue more challenging goals, surround myself with inspiring individuals, and consistently push beyond my comfort zone. The result has been a life filled with greater fulfillment, purpose, and success than I ever thought possible.

Now I invite you to reflect on your own personal standards. What standards do you hold for yourself in terms of personal growth, relationships, career, and overall well-being? Take a moment to write down your current standards and then consider the following: "Are there areas where you're settling for mediocrity instead of striving for excellence? What changes can you make today to raise your standards and align them with your highest aspirations? How do you cultivate a positive mindset and resilience in the face of challenges?"

"Education promotes equality and lifts people out of poverty. It teaches children how to become good citizens. Education is not just for a privileged few, it is for everyone. It is a fundamental human right."
—BAN KI-MOON, FORMER UNITED NATIONS SECRETARY-GENERAL

Educational standards include your commitment to lifelong learning. While education may not be one of the traditional categories in the Circle of Life framework, it plays a foundational role in shaping every other aspect of your life. High educational standards mean continuously seeking knowledge, staying curious, and striving for intellectual growth. These standards are not limited to formal education but extend to personal development, self-reflection, and resilience in the face of challenges.

Examples

- **Curiosity:** "I must maintain a lifelong commitment to learning and expanding my knowledge."
- **Self-Awareness:** "I must regularly reflect on my actions and behaviors to foster personal growth."
- **Resilience:** "I must develop resilience to overcome challenges and persist in the face of adversity."

Leonardo da Vinci exemplifies the highest standards of lifelong learning and intellectual curiosity. Throughout his life, he continuously sought knowledge across a vast array of disciplines, from anatomy and engineering to botany and hydrodynamics. His insatiable curiosity led him to explore and connect seemingly disparate fields, demonstrating an interdisciplinary approach that was far ahead of his time. Da Vinci's commitment to learning was not limited by formal education; he taught himself Latin, higher mathematics, and anatomy through self-directed study and keen observation.

Da Vinci's approach to learning was characterized by his exceptional observational skills and his belief in the importance of applying knowledge practically. He honed his ability to see and understand the world around him, famously stating that *saper vedere* (knowing how to see) was crucial to comprehending the universe. This philosophy guided his scientific studies and artistic works alike, allowing him to make groundbreaking discoveries and create masterpieces that continue to inspire centuries later.

"Learning never exhausts the mind," da Vinci once said, encapsulating his belief in the endless possibilities of knowledge and the joy of continuous learning. This reflects his view that the pursuit of knowledge is not a burden but a source of perpetual enrichment and growth. Da Vinci's life and work demonstrate how a commitment to high educational standards, characterized by lifelong learning, curiosity, and intellectual growth, can lead to extraordinary achievements and a lasting impact on human knowledge and culture.

What are your standards for personal growth? Are there specific books you aim to read or skills you want to develop each year?

SPIRITUALITY, RELIGION, AND INNER PEACE

"The higher the standard of your spiritual life, the higher the quality of your existence."

—Attributed to Paramahansa Yogananda,
Indian spiritual teacher

Spiritual standards pertain to your spiritual beliefs and practices. High spiritual standards involve seeking inner peace, practicing gratitude, and maintaining a connection to something greater than yourself.

Examples

- **Mindfulness:** "I must practice mindfulness and meditation to cultivate inner peace and clarity."
- **Gratitude:** "I must express gratitude daily for the blessings and lessons in my life."
- **Faithfulness:** "I must nurture my faith through prayer, reflection, and consistent spiritual practices to deepen my connection to God or the higher power I believe in."

Amy Carmichael exemplifies high spiritual standards through her unwavering commitment to her faith and her selfless service to others.

As an Irish missionary who spent over fifty years in India, she dedicated her life to rescuing young girls from temple prostitution and providing them with a safe haven. Her spiritual standards were evident in her willingness to leave behind the comforts of home and fully immerse herself in a challenging and often dangerous mission field.

Carmichael's spiritual standards were reflected in her daily practices and her approach to ministry. She maintained a rigorous prayer life and consistently sought God's guidance in her work. Her commitment to spiritual growth was not just personal but extended to those under her care. She established the Dohnavur Fellowship, an orphanage that not only provided physical shelter but also nurtured the spiritual lives of the children. Carmichael's high standards led her to create an environment where love, compassion, and Christian values were paramount.

Throughout her life, Carmichael wrote extensively on Christian spirituality, producing over thirty-five books that continue to inspire readers today. Her writings reflect her deep spiritual insights and her high standards for Christian living. One of her most famous sayings displays her spiritual philosophy: "You can give without loving, but you cannot love without giving." This statement exemplifies Carmichael's belief that true spirituality is expressed through sacrificial love and service to others. Her life and work stand as a testament to the transformative power of maintaining high spiritual standards, demonstrating how such commitment can lead to profound and lasting impacts on the lives of others.

What spiritual practices do you commit to regularly, such as prayer, meditation, or spending time in nature? How do you prioritize your inner peace and calm in a chaotic world?

"Moral authority comes from following universal and timeless principles like honesty, integrity, and treating people with respect."

—STEPHEN COVEY, AUTHOR OF *THE 7 HABITS OF HIGHLY EFFECTIVE PEOPLE*

Ethical standards govern your moral principles and values. While ethics may not be one of the traditional categories in the Circle of Life framework, it serves as a critical foundation for how you interact with the world and navigate your relationships, decisions, and responsibilities. High ethical standards mean making choices that are aligned with your principles, even when it is challenging. These standards act as a moral compass, guiding your behavior in a way that reflects integrity and accountability.

Examples

- **Honesty:** "I must always speak the truth and act with integrity regardless of the circumstances."
- **Fairness:** "I must treat others with respect and fairness, ensuring that my actions are just and equitable."
- **Responsibility:** "I must take ownership of my choices and their impact on others, striving to do what is right."

Harriet Tubman, an American abolitionist and political activist, demonstrated exceptional ethical and moral standards throughout her life, particularly in her work with the Underground Railroad. Born into slavery, Tubman escaped to freedom in 1849 but chose to repeatedly risk her life to help other enslaved people reach freedom.

Tubman's ethical standards were evident in her unwavering commitment to justice and human rights, even in the face of extreme danger. She made approximately thirteen missions to rescue around seventy enslaved people, including family and friends, using the network of activists and safe houses known as the Underground Railroad. Her actions demonstrated a profound belief in the inherent dignity and worth of every human being regardless of the laws of the time.

Tubman's ethical standards extended beyond her rescue missions. She later served as a scout, spy, and nurse for the Union army during the Civil War, continuing to fight for the freedom and rights of others. Even in her later years, she remained committed to social causes, advocating for women's suffrage. Tubman's ethical standards are revealed as she said, "I was the conductor of the Underground Railroad for eight years, and I can say what most conductors can't say—I never ran my train off the track, and I never lost a passenger." This statement reflects her unwavering commitment to her principles and her dedication to the safety and freedom of others, even at great personal risk.

As you reflect on your ethical standards, consider the moral principles that guide your decision-making, particularly in challenging situations. Are there areas where you feel you could strengthen your commitment to honesty or fairness? Think about how your actions reflect accountability for their impact on others. Do they align with the values you hold most dear? In moments of adversity or pressure, how do you ensure your choices remain consistent with your ethical standards? Finally, who inspires you as an example of unwavering ethical commitment? Reflect on how their example can shape and influence the ethical standards you set for yourself.

COMMUNITY AND LEGACY STANDARDS

"The greatness of a community is most accurately measured by the compassionate actions of its members."

—Coretta Scott King, civil rights leader and widow of Dr. Martin Luther King Jr.

Community and legacy standards reflect your involvement in and contribution to your community. High community standards mean actively participating in community service, supporting local initiatives, and striving to make a positive impact.

Examples

- **Service:** "I must contribute to the well-being of others through acts of kindness and service."

- **Impact:** "I must strive to make a positive impact on the world, leaving a legacy of love and compassion."
- **Mentorship:** "I must guide and support others in their journey of growth and development."

Dolores Huerta exemplifies exceptionally high community standards through her lifelong commitment to social justice and community organizing. As a co-founder of the National Farm Workers Association alongside Cesar Chavez, Huerta dedicated over six decades to advocating for workers' rights, civil rights, and women's rights. Her activism began in her local community, where she saw firsthand the struggles of farm workers and their families. This grassroots involvement led her to organize on a larger scale, fighting for better working conditions, fair wages, and dignity for some of society's most marginalized members.

Huerta's community standards extend beyond her professional activism. She has consistently encouraged civic engagement, particularly among Latinx and women voters, understanding that community empowerment starts with political participation. Through the Dolores Huerta Foundation, she continues to train organizers and advocates for policy changes that benefit underserved communities. Her work embodies the idea that true community service involves not just addressing immediate needs but also working to change the systemic issues that create those needs. Huerta's famous rallying cry, "Sí, se puede" (Yes, we can), emphasizes her belief in the power of community action to effect change. As she once said, "Every moment is an organizing opportunity, every person a potential activist, every minute a chance to change the world." This reflects Huerta's unwavering commitment to community involvement and her belief that everyone has the power to make a positive impact in their community.

What are your standards for giving back to your community? Do you volunteer regularly or support specific causes? How do you ensure that your actions align with your values of social responsibility?

> "The greatest threat to our planet is the belief that someone else will save it."
> —Robert Swan, British explorer and environmental activist

Environmental standards involve your responsibility toward the environment. This may be part of your desire to have a legacy. High environmental standards mean making conscious choices to reduce your carbon footprint and promote sustainability.

Examples

- **Sustainability:** "I must adopt sustainable practices in my daily life, such as reducing waste and conserving resources."
- **Awareness:** "I must stay informed about environmental issues and support initiatives that protect our planet."
- **Action:** "I must take actionable steps to reduce my carbon footprint and advocate for environmental preservation."

Yvon Chouinard, founder of Patagonia, an American outdoor clothing and gear company, exemplifies exceptional environmental standards through his unwavering commitment to sustainability in both his personal life and his business practices. Under his leadership, Patagonia has become a trailblazer in sustainable business, using recycled materials, encouraging repair and reuse, donating to environmental causes, promoting transparency, and investing in innovative, sustainable processes. In 2022, Chouinard took his commitment to an unprecedented level by transferring Patagonia's ownership to trust and nonprofit organizations dedicated to combating climate change and protecting undeveloped land.

Chouinard's personal lifestyle mirrors his high environmental standards; he lives modestly and spends much time in nature. His philosophy is displayed as he states, "We're a part of nature. As we destroy nature, we destroy ourselves. It's a selfish thing to want to protect nature."

This statement reflects Chouinard's deep respect for nature and underscores his commitment to environmental stewardship by emphasizing humility and reverence toward the natural world, driving his actions to protect and preserve it.

What standards do you have for your living environment? For example, do you prioritize cleanliness, organization, or sustainability? How do you contribute to your community or environment?

BALANCE: EMBRACING PRESSURE AND UNCERTAINTY IN THE PURSUIT OF EXCELLENCE

While maintaining high standards is essential for an extraordinary life, true balance isn't about avoiding discomfort—it's about thriving within it. The path to greatness inherently involves pressure and uncertainty, which should be embraced rather than shunned.

When harnessed correctly, pressure can be a powerful catalyst for growth. Instead of seeking to eliminate it, learn to leverage it as a driving force. High achievers often perform best under pressure, using it to sharpen focus and elevate performance. Embrace challenging situations as opportunities to test and expand your capabilities.

An exceptional life is rarely predictable. Uncertainty, while uncomfortable, often precedes breakthrough moments. Cultivate a mindset that views the unknown not as a threat but as a realm of possibility. This perspective shift allows you to navigate ambiguity with confidence and creativity. This process of self-discovery and alignment empowers us to overcome limiting beliefs, adopt a growth mindset, and reach our full potential. As we integrate these values into our daily lives, we cultivate a more balanced and fulfilling existence that reflects our true selves and aspirations. Ultimately, by living in accordance with our core values and challenging our limiting beliefs, we pave the way for personal transformation and become the person we are meant to be.

True balance isn't about avoiding difficulties but about developing the resilience to overcome them. Embrace setbacks as integral parts of your journey, not as deviations from it. Each obstacle you overcome strengthens your resolve and contributes to your extraordinary narrative.

Self-care in this context isn't about escape but about strategic rejuvenation. It's a tool to maintain peak performance in high-pressure environments. Prioritize practices that enhance your ability to withstand and thrive under stress rather than those that merely provide temporary relief.

While maintaining high standards, calibrate your expectations to align with the realities of pushing boundaries. Understand that progress often involves setbacks and that perfection is an ideal, not a constant state. This mindset allows for the relentless pursuit of excellence without being derailed by inevitable challenges.

Balancing high standards with realism doesn't mean settling for less or avoiding discomfort. Instead, it's about developing the mental fortitude and strategic approach necessary to sustain extraordinary efforts over time. Embrace the pressures and uncertainties as essential elements of an exceptional life, using them to fuel your growth and achievements.

ANTICIPATING ALIGNMENT WITH YOUR PURPOSE

As you conclude this chapter on high standards, recognize that all the elements of personal development you've explored are interconnected. They are the foundation upon which you build a life of excellence and fulfillment.

You can embrace high standards and become the extraordinary, self-actualized person you're meant to be. The power to set and maintain high standards lies within you. By doing so, you honor your potential and pave the way for a life of purpose, fulfillment, and impact.

CHAPTER 8

Must Purpose

"The mystery of human existence lies not in just staying alive, but in finding something to live for."
—Fyodor Dostoevsky, Russian author of *Crime and Punishment*

I want to start this chapter with a moment of vulnerability—a moment where I let you into a part of my life that I once struggled to understand. For many years, I wandered through life without a clear sense of purpose. I didn't know what my purpose was, and I often found myself standing alone, unsure of what to do, where to go, or whom to turn to. The steps that lead to the discovery of our purpose can be elusive, and it took me decades to truly find mine.

It wasn't until I witnessed my mother's journey that I grasped the profound nature of purpose. After her first husband abandoned her and her second, most beloved husband tragically took his life, I saw her at her most vulnerable.

One night, a few days after my dad killed himself, I went into my mother's bedroom, and she was alone in her closet, on her hands and knees, scrubbing the blood-soaked carpet, trying to clean the mess of our lives. She peered up and saw me. With a look I will never forget, she lifted her broken soul off the floor, looked straight at me, and said, "Honey, I got this. I will never let something like this ever happen to us again." At that moment, I learned the meaning of resilience and determination. My mother's purpose was crystal clear: she would dedicate the rest of her life to her children.

Despite her own suffering, she resolved that she *must* protect and take care of her children. Nothing else mattered.

She could have easily been consumed by despair, but instead she found a strength within herself I had never seen before. Through her suffering, she discovered her purpose—to be a source of love and support for those around her, to rebuild a life that had been shattered, and to give her children the foundation they needed to thrive.

Watching my mother navigate these unimaginable hardships, I realized that purpose often emerges from our deepest pain. It took me years—decades, even—to piece together the lessons life had been trying to teach me. My purpose became clear as I gathered knowledge, experience, and wisdom from luminaries through books, seminars, one-on-one interviews, and countless hours of contemplation. I came to understand that my purpose is to help those who, like my mother, have faced tragedies, obstacles, and suffering and who desire to find fulfillment, happiness, and self-realization in life.

My purpose in life evolved from witnessing my mother's unwavering dedication to her children. After the tragic loss of my stepfather, she faced unimaginable challenges, yet her commitment to providing the best possible life for my sister and me never wavered. Her intentional dedication and discipline in doing whatever it took to give us opportunities became the foundation of my life's purpose.

My mother's resilience in the face of adversity, her tireless efforts to ensure our education and well-being, and her ability to find strength in the darkest of times left an indelible mark on my soul. As I grew older, I realized the greatest way to honor her sacrifice was to extend that same level of dedication and care to others in need.

This realization led me to a life dedicated to helping others overcome their challenges and reach their full potential. Whether through my legal practice, motivational speaking, or personal mentoring, I strive to embody the same intentional dedication and discipline my mother exemplified. My purpose has become clear: to be a beacon of hope and a catalyst for positive change in the lives of others, just as my mother was for me.

Now I invite you to reflect on your life experiences. What events, relationships, or challenges have shaped your sense of purpose? Perhaps it was a mentor who believed in you when no one else did or a personal struggle that revealed your inner strength. Maybe it was a moment of clarity during a difficult time or a gradual realization over years of introspection.

A Must Purpose is a concept that aligns closely with the core themes of personal transformation and self-actualization presented in this book. It represents the essential, nonnegotiable reason for one's existence and actions, deeply rooted in an individual's core values, beliefs, and aspirations. A Must Purpose goes beyond a simple life goal or ambition. It embodies an unwavering commitment. It's not just something you want to do, but something you feel compelled to pursue with urgency and dedication. This purpose reflects your deepest beliefs and the principles you hold most dear, aligning with your core values. It represents the truest expression of who you are and who you are meant to become, embodying personal authenticity.

A Must Purpose has transformative power, with the potential to positively impact not just your life, but the lives of others and the world around you. It is fueled by intrinsic motivation, driving you forward even in the face of challenges, powered by internal passion rather than external rewards. Your Must Purpose serves as a guiding light for decision-making, personal growth, and life direction. It's the culmination of understanding your core beliefs, values, and personal narrative, integrated into a compelling reason for being that propels you toward becoming the person you are meant to be.

For those who feel they haven't yet found their purpose, I want to assure you it will come. The journey to discovering your purpose is one of the most exhilarating and rewarding endeavors you can undertake. It requires an earnest desire to find your purpose and a willingness to explore yourself more deeply than ever before. This exploration might involve examining your passions, values, and the experiences that have shaped you.

Remember, finding your purpose is not a destination but a journey. It may evolve and change as you grow and gain new experiences. The key is to remain open, curious, and reflective. Engage in activities that bring you joy and fulfillment, pay attention to what energizes you, and notice where you naturally want to contribute.

Your purpose is the catalyst for the meaning of your existence. It's what gets you out of bed in the morning with excitement and determination. When you align your actions with your purpose, you'll find a sense of fulfillment that permeates every aspect of your life.

So whether you're clear on your purpose or still searching, embrace the journey. Be patient with yourself but also be proactive in your exploration. Your purpose is waiting to be discovered, and when you find it, it will illuminate your path forward, giving depth and meaning to your life's work.

Last night, as I reflected on this chapter, it was as though God once again whispered in my ear and reminded me, "Stephen, your true purpose is singular at any given moment. Your purpose is to lovingly help the person who is reading or hearing these words right now. Your purpose is them."

UNDERSTANDING OUR PURPOSE

Purpose is not merely a goal to achieve; it is the very essence of who we are. It is the force that compels us to move forward, even when the path is uncertain. Purpose is the heartbeat of our existence, manifesting in our choices, relationships, and contributions to the world.

I honor and value the diverse beliefs and spiritual paths that individuals follow. As someone who embraces the Christian faith, I believe it is not our desires that solely drive our purpose, but something deeper—something that aligns with what God has intended for us.

Our purpose, in this view, is to uncover God's plan for our lives. This perspective doesn't negate the importance of our own dreams and aspirations but frames them within the context of a higher calling. Whether you are religious or spiritual or not, the concept remains consistent: our purpose should be aligned with our true authentic self, our mindset, beliefs, values, and standards—all of which are innately ours, unique to us alone, and, in my personal view, God-given. So, my friend, my purpose is *you*.

Consider the lives of individuals who have discovered and embraced their purpose through this lens. Jimmy Carter's life is a testament to the power of purpose, service, and unwavering faith. My encounter with this remarkable man left an indelible mark on my life, shaping my understanding of what it means to live with purpose and dedication to others.

I first met President Carter when I was a young man, full of idealism but unsure of my path. His warm handshake and genuine smile immediately put me at ease. As we spoke, I was struck by his humility and the depth of his commitment to serving others. This brief interaction planted a seed in my mind about the potential for one person to make a significant difference in the world.

Carter's postpresidency years were nothing short of extraordinary, solidifying his place as one of the most giving former presidents in US history. After leaving the White House in 1982, he and his wife, Rosalynn, founded the Carter Center, dedicated to advancing human rights and alleviating suffering worldwide.

Their work has spanned continents, tackling issues from disease eradication to conflict resolution. One of Carter's most visible and hands-on commitments has been his involvement with Habitat for Humanity. Beginning in 1984, the Carters worked alongside volunteers building and renovating homes for those in need.

This annual Carter Work Project has not only provided shelter for thousands but has also inspired countless others to volunteer and give back to their communities. Carter's faith was a cornerstone of his life and service. As a devout Christian, he taught Sunday School for decades, even into his nineties. His faith informed his commitment to peace and justice, driving him to work tirelessly for the betterment of others.

Rosalynn Carter was an equal partner in these endeavors, working alongside her husband in their humanitarian efforts. Their partnership, spanning over seven decades, is a testament to the power of shared purpose and mutual support in achieving lasting impact. Decades after our first meeting, I had the incredible fortune to once again shake President Carter's hand. This time, I expressed how profoundly he had influenced my life. His example inspired me to seek my own purpose and to dedicate myself to serving others. The warmth in his eyes and the firmness in his handshake remained unchanged, a living embodiment of a life well lived in service to others.

Jimmy Carter's story reminds us that our purpose can extend far beyond our formal roles or titles. His life after the presidency arguably had an even greater impact than his time in office, showing that when we align our actions with our deepest values and commit to serving others, we can create a legacy of positive change.

But is purpose always this singular and clear? For many, it may not be. Purpose can be multifaceted, evolving as we grow and as our understanding of ourselves deepens. For instance, Oprah Winfrey's purpose evolved from being a media mogul to being a global advocate for personal empowerment. Reflecting on her journey, she stated, "The key to realizing a dream is to focus not on success but on significance—and then even the small steps and little victories along your path will take on greater meaning."

Another example of a remarkable person with a purpose-driven life is a fellow New Orleanian, Steve Gleason. Steve Gleason's journey is a powerful testament to finding purpose through adversity. A former NFL player for the New Orleans Saints, Gleason became a symbol of resilience and hope for the city when he blocked a punt in the team's first home game after Hurricane Katrina. His life took an unexpected turn in 2011 when he was diagnosed with amyotrophic lateral sclerosis (ALS), a terminal neuromuscular disease. Rather than succumbing to despair, Gleason chose to face his diagnosis head-on, transforming his suffering into a catalyst for change and inspiration. He and his wife, Michel, founded Team Gleason, an organization dedicated to raising awareness about ALS and improving the lives of those affected by the disease.

Gleason's unwavering determination led him to accomplish remarkable feats despite his physical limitations, summiting Machu Picchu and fathering two children. Gleason's advocacy efforts resulted in the passage of the Steve Gleason Act by Congress, ensuring access to vital communication devices for ALS patients. His journey has been captured in documentaries and his memoir, *A Life Impossible: Living with ALS: Finding Peace and Wisdom Within a Fragile Existence*, which he wrote entirely using eye-tracking technology. Through his struggles, Gleason discovered a profound purpose: to inspire others to find strength in adversity and live meaningful lives regardless of their circumstances. His story reminds us that even in our darkest moments, we have the capacity to create positive changes and touch the lives of others. In 2024, Gleason received the Arthur Ashe Courage Award.

Gleason's legacy extends far beyond his football career. He has become a beacon of hope, showing that life's challenges can be transformed into opportunities for growth, wisdom, and extraordinary impact. His journey embodies the idea that true strength lies not in the absence of suffering but in how we choose to respond to it.

Now let's pause and reflect together. Have you ever felt uncertain about your own purpose? Have you stood at a crossroads, unsure of which path to take? If so, know that you are not alone. Each of us has moments of doubt, but it is through these moments that we uncover the purpose that lies within us, a purpose that may very well be part of a divine plan for our lives.

THE FLUID NATURE OF PURPOSE

One of the profound truths about purpose is its fluidity. As we navigate life, accumulating experiences and wisdom, our purpose can—and often does—change. This change reflects our growth and transformation. As we evolve, so too does our understanding of what brings us fulfillment.

In our youth, our purpose might be tied to exploration, learning, and self-discovery. As we mature, it might shift toward building relationships, contributing to our communities, or nurturing the next generation. In later stages of life, our purpose may become more introspective, focused on leaving a legacy or finding peace within ourselves. This evolution of purpose is not inconsistency; it is a natural reflection of our ever-changing lives and, in my view, a deeper understanding of God's unfolding plan for us.

Ancient philosophers and thinkers have long pondered the nature of purpose. Socrates famously declared, "The unexamined life is not worth living," suggesting that a life devoid of purpose, reflection, and self-examination is a life unfulfilled. To Socrates, purpose was intrinsically linked to the pursuit of wisdom and virtue. Similarly, Aristotle believed purpose was connected to the concept of *eudaemonia*, often translated as "flourishing" or "the good life." He argued that living in accordance with one's virtues and striving for excellence in all things leads to a life of true happiness and fulfillment.

In Eastern philosophy, Confucius taught that purpose was found in living a life of moral integrity and fulfilling one's duties within the social order. He emphasized the importance of harmony, both within oneself and within society, as a path to discovering one's true purpose. The teachings of Zoroaster, an ancient Persian prophet, highlight the struggle between good and evil as central to human purpose, urging individuals to choose righteousness and contribute to the triumph of good in the world.

Reflecting on these ancient teachings, consider how they resonate with your experiences. Have you found that living in accordance with your values and striving for excellence brings you closer to a sense of purpose? Do you feel a connection between your purpose and the greater good, as these philosophers suggest? And if you share my Christian perspective, how does this alignment with your values and virtues help you uncover the purpose God has for you?

DISCOVERING AND EVALUATING YOUR AUTHENTIC PURPOSE

But how do we know if we have found the right purpose? How can we be sure the path we are on is the one we are meant to follow? The answer lies in the alignment between our purpose and our authentic self, which, in my belief, is intricately connected to God's purpose for us.

Your authentic self is the truest expression of who you are, free from societal expectations and fears. It is the embodiment of your growth mindset, core beliefs, core values, and standards—the elements that define your essence and guide your actions. When your purpose aligns with your authentic self, you experience a profound sense of harmony and fulfillment. You feel energized and motivated, knowing you are living in accordance with your true nature and, potentially, God's plan for your life.

Modern-day luminaries offer additional perspectives on the discovery and alignment of purpose. Simon Sinek, in his widely acclaimed book *Start with Why: How Great Leaders Inspire Everyone to Take Action*, emphasizes the importance of identifying the underlying reason behind our actions—the "why" that drives us. He argues that true fulfillment comes from understanding and living by this "why." According to Sinek, "People don't buy what you do; they buy why you do it. And what you do simply proves what you believe." This idea encourages us to align our purpose with our deepest beliefs, ensuring our actions are a true reflection of who we are.

Similarly, Eckhart Tolle, in *A New Earth: Awakening to Your Life's Purpose*, speaks of purpose in both an outer and an inner sense. He suggests that our outer purpose—our actions and achievements—should always be in service of our inner purpose, which is to awaken to our true self and live in alignment with it. Tolle writes, "You are here to enable the divine purpose of the universe to unfold. That is how important you are!" His perspective reinforces the idea that purpose is not just about what we do but about who we are and how we connect with the greater flow of life. For those who hold a belief in God, this divine purpose is deeply connected to the idea that we are here to fulfill a specific role God has set for us, a role that aligns with the gifts and talents He has bestowed upon us.

Reflect on your life. Have you ever achieved a significant milestone only to feel a lingering sense of dissatisfaction? This may be a sign that your actions, while successful by external standards, were not fully aligned with your deeper purpose. Understanding this misalignment can be the first step in rediscovering or redefining your true purpose.

ADJUSTING AND REFINING YOUR PURPOSE

Sometimes, despite our best efforts, we may find that our defined purpose no longer feels right. Perhaps it was shaped by external pressures, or maybe we have outgrown it as we've evolved. If your purpose no longer aligns with your authentic self—or with what you feel is God's purpose for your life—it's essential to recognize this and take steps to adjust or refine it.

My mother's story is a poignant testament to how life's tragic circumstances can shape our Must Purpose in profound and unexpected ways. When she lost my father, her world shattered in an instant. Suddenly, she became a single parent, responsible for raising three young children alone. In that moment of overwhelming grief and uncertainty, her purpose crystallized with stark clarity: to live for her children to ensure our well-being and future.

This purpose wasn't something she chose in a moment of calm reflection. It was thrust upon her by the cruel hand of fate. Yet in embracing this purpose with unwavering commitment, she discovered a wellspring of strength she never knew she possessed. Her dedication to us became her North Star, guiding every decision, every sacrifice, and every moment of perseverance through the darkest of times.

As I reflect on her journey, I'm struck by how this externally imposed purpose became intrinsically tied to her deepest values and her authentic self. Her love for us, her resilience, her selflessness—these were not new traits born of tragedy, but core aspects of her being that found their fullest expression through her newfound purpose.

In living for us, she wasn't just fulfilling a duty; she was manifesting the truest version of herself.

My mother's story reminds me that sometimes our Must Purpose finds us in our moments of greatest vulnerability. It may not always arise from joyous self-discovery, but from the crucible of life's harshest challenges. Yet when we embrace that purpose with all our heart, it can become a transformative force, not just for ourselves, but for those whose lives we touch. Her unwavering commitment to her purpose didn't just shape her life—it shaped ours, instilling in us values of love, resilience, and selflessness that continue to guide us to this day.

Steve Jobs, in his famous Stanford commencement speech, said, "Your work is going to fill a large part of your life, and the only way to be truly satisfied is to do what you believe is great work. And the only way to do great work is to love what you do. If you haven't found it yet, keep looking. Don't settle." Jobs's words remind us that purpose is not static. It is something we must continuously seek and refine until it resonates deeply with who we are.

If you question your purpose, start by revisiting your core beliefs and values. What has changed in your life? What new insights have you gained? How have your experiences shaped your understanding of what truly matters? These reflections can guide you in tweaking or even completely redefining your purpose.

For those who, like me, believe their purpose is aligned with God's plan, this process might involve prayer, meditation, or seeking counsel from trusted spiritual advisors. It's about being open to the possibility that God's purpose for you might be evolving, that He might be guiding you toward a new direction that better suits who you've become.

Take a moment now to think about your life. Have there been times when you felt disconnected from your purpose? What led you to that point, and how did you respond? Were there any external pressures or internal conflicts that caused you to question your path? Understanding these moments is crucial to rediscovering and realigning your purpose.

Remember, your purpose doesn't have to be grand or world-changing in the traditional sense. As Mother Teresa once said, "Not all of us can do great things. But we can do small things with great love." Your purpose may be as simple as being a source of kindness in a harsh world or as complex as leading a movement for social change. What matters is that it resonates deeply with who you are, aligns with your authentic self, and, if you share my faith, is in harmony with God's will for your life.

LIVING IN ALIGNMENT WITH YOUR PURPOSE

Living in alignment with your purpose requires more than just understanding it; it demands commitment, discipline, and integrity. You must be willing to make difficult choices, let go of what no longer serves you, and embrace the unknown with an open heart. Your Must Core Beliefs, Values, and Standards will be your compass, ensuring you stay true to yourself even in the face of challenges.

Your purpose is dynamic, evolving as you do. As you navigate life's twists and turns, your purpose may shift, expand, or deepen. This evolution is a testament to your resilience and commitment to living a life of meaning and fulfillment.

Consider Jane Goodall's journey, which exemplifies the transformative power of living with purpose. Born in London in 1934, Jane developed a deep love for animals and nature at an early age. Despite limited opportunities for women in science at the time, her passion for understanding the natural world drove her to pursue her dreams. Without formal scientific training, she traveled to Tanzania in 1960 to study chimpanzees under the mentorship of renowned anthropologist Louis Leakey.

What began as a simple desire to observe chimpanzees in their natural habitat soon evolved into a groundbreaking scientific career. Jane's observations revolutionized our understanding of primates and challenged long-held beliefs about what separates humans from other animals. Her discovery that chimpanzees use tools—a behavior previously thought to be uniquely human—reshaped the field of anthropology and deepened humanity's connection to the natural world.

As Jane's work progressed, so did her sense of purpose. Witnessing the destruction of chimpanzee habitats and the suffering caused by deforestation and poaching, she realized her mission extended far beyond research. She became an advocate for conservation and environmental protection, dedicating her life to preserving the planet for future generations. Through the Jane Goodall Institute, she has worked tirelessly to promote sustainable practices, protect endangered species, and inspire people around the world to take action.

Jane's story reminds us that purpose is not static. It grows as we grow and adapts as we encounter new challenges and opportunities. Her journey from a curious young woman with a passion for animals to one of the world's most influential environmentalists demonstrates how aligning our actions with our values can create profound change.

Jane once said, "What you do makes a difference, and you have to decide what kind of difference you want to make." Her life challenges us to reflect on our own purpose: How can we use our passions and talents to contribute meaningfully? What steps can we take today to align our lives with what truly matters? By embracing our purpose with courage and determination, we can leave a lasting impact on both the people around us and the world we share.

For those of us who view our purpose as part of a divine plan, living in alignment with that purpose also means trusting in God's timing and direction. It means having faith that the challenges we face are shaping us for the roles we are meant to play and that even when we feel lost, we are being guided toward a greater good.

Reflect on your own life. How are you living in alignment with your purpose? Are there areas where you might need to adjust? Are there choices you've made that feel out of sync with your true self—or with what you believe God's purpose is for you? These reflections can help you course-correct and ensure that your actions are in harmony with your purpose.

THE PROFOUND IMPACT OF PURPOSE

Purpose is essential for every human being. It imbues our lives with meaning and connects us to something greater than ourselves. Without it, we may achieve success, accumulate wealth, and gain recognition, yet still feel an underlying emptiness—a void that no external accomplishment can fill.

The significance of a well-aligned purpose cannot be overstated. It is the cornerstone of a fulfilling life, the source of our deepest joy and satisfaction. When you live in alignment with your purpose, you experience a sense of wholeness and connection to something greater than yourself. You find meaning in your work, relationships, and daily experiences. You become more resilient, compassionate, and capable of navigating life's challenges.

Your purpose has a ripple effect on those around you. When you live with purpose, you inspire others to do the same. You become a beacon of light, guiding others toward their path of fulfillment. Your purpose, therefore, is not just a personal journey; it is a gift you share with the world, enriching the lives of others and leaving a lasting legacy.

Living without purpose can lead to a sense of aimlessness, where life feels unanchored and devoid of direction. Purpose, on the other hand, gives us a reason to persevere, even when the path is difficult and the destination is unclear. It provides a framework through which we view our experiences and a foundation upon which we build our identity.

Think about someone in your life who has inspired you with their sense of purpose. What qualities do they embody? How have they influenced your journey? Reflecting on these influences can help you recognize the impact that living with purpose can have, not just on your own life, but on the lives of those you touch, creating a ripple effect that strengthens your community and leaves a lasting legacy for future generations. The search for purpose is one of the most profound and rewarding journeys you can undertake. It requires courage, self-reflection, and a deep commitment to living authentically. As you explore your purpose, be open to change, willing to grow, and ready to embrace the challenges and opportunities that life presents.

DEFINING YOUR PURPOSE

The journey to discovering your purpose often begins with a quiet moment of reflection—a pause in the hustle of life where you allow yourself to look back and reconnect with the experiences that have shaped you. It's in these moments of stillness when you may begin to uncover the subtle yet powerful clues that have been guiding you all along.

As you reflect, think back to the times when you felt most alive, fully engaged, and deeply fulfilled. These moments aren't just random occurrences; they are signposts, gently pointing you toward your true calling. What were you doing during these times? Were you immersed in an activity that made time feel irrelevant, where you were so deeply involved that the world around you seemed to fade away? These experiences often align with your purpose because they resonate with the core of who you are.

Yet our purpose does not only reveal itself in moments of joy and fulfillment. Often the most profound insights into our purpose come through the crucible of suffering and strife. Life's hardships, though painful, have a way of stripping away the superficial, forcing us to confront the deepest parts of ourselves. It is in these moments of trial that we are often called to reflect on what truly matters and to reexamine the paths we have chosen.

Consider the challenges you've faced and the lessons you've learned. Life's hardships are not just obstacles; they are powerful teachers. The resilience you've built, the wisdom you've gained—these are the raw materials from which your purpose is often crafted. What have these challenges taught you? How have they shaped your perspective, your values, and your sense of what truly matters? In many cases, our purpose is intricately tied to the difficulties we've overcome, and our mindset plays a crucial role in how we interpret these experiences.

In the midst of suffering, we may question the very fabric of our lives. Why is this happening to me? What am I supposed to learn from this? These are not easy questions, and the answers are rarely immediate. But it is through this process of questioning, of wrestling with our pain, when we often uncover the deeper purpose of our lives. The very struggles that once seemed insurmountable can become the foundation upon which we build a life of meaning and purpose. Reflect on your moments of suffering. What did those experiences teach you about yourself? Did they reveal a strength you didn't know you had, a compassion that had been buried, or a resolve to change something in your life or the world around you? These are the moments that, while deeply painful, can illuminate your path with a clarity that is often obscured in times of comfort.

As you continue to explore, think about your core beliefs—those deeply held convictions about yourself, others, and the world around you. What do you believe about your own worth and capabilities? How do you view the people you encounter, and what is your perspective on the broader world? These beliefs are foundational, shaping how you interpret your experiences and interact with the world. They also provide vital clues to your purpose. If you believe in your capacity to grow, contribute, and find meaning, you are already aligning yourself with a purpose that resonates with these beliefs.

Your personal story and narrative—how you view the journey you've taken thus far—hold further insights into your purpose. What themes emerge when you recount your life's story? Are there recurring challenges you've faced or particular passions that have consistently driven you? Your narrative is not just a recounting of events; it's a reflection of how you see yourself and your role in the world. In these reflections, you can find hints of your purpose—whether it's in overcoming adversity, helping others, or pursuing a passion that has been a constant thread throughout your life.

Another layer of reflection involves looking outward at the people you admire. Who are they, and what is it about them that draws you in? The qualities and actions you respect in others often mirror the values that are important to you. These traits can serve as a compass, guiding you toward the kind of life you want to lead and the purpose that will bring you the most fulfillment.

Passion is another powerful indicator of purpose. It goes beyond mere moments of deep engagement, representing a sustained and intense emotional connection to an activity or pursuit. Unlike fleeting periods of absorption, passion persists over time, driving individuals to return to their chosen endeavor repeatedly, even in the face of challenges. This enduring enthusiasm is primarily fueled by intrinsic motivation, with passionate individuals pursuing their interests for inherent satisfaction rather than external rewards.

Passion often becomes intertwined with one's identity and self-expression, involving a long-term vision and willingness to make significant sacrifices. Its transformative power can influence major life decisions, career paths, and personal growth in profound ways. By exploring both moments of deep engagement and areas of passion, individuals can gain a more comprehensive understanding of what truly resonates with them, providing valuable insights for identifying and articulating their purpose.

What issues or causes stir something deep within you? What compels you to act, to speak out, to engage? These passions are not just fleeting interests; they are connected to the deeper currents of your purpose. When you identify what ignites your passion, you are uncovering a significant clue to your life's calling.

As we turn to your values, consider what you hold most dear in the various areas of your life, including your relationships, work, health, spirituality, and so on. What are your Must Core Values in these areas? They reveal what you stand for and what you strive to embody in your daily life. By understanding your core values, you see the contours of your purpose taking shape. These values serve as the compass points that guide you toward a life that feels authentic and meaningful.

Your standards—those benchmarks you set for yourself in how you live and engage with the world—are equally revealing. What does it mean to live up to your own standards? What would it look like to embody these standards fully? When you reflect on your standards, you are not just considering how you want to be perceived but how you wish to show up in the world, day after day. Living according to your standards brings you closer to realizing your purpose because it means you are acting in alignment with your true self.

All these elements—your mindset, beliefs, narrative, values, and standards and the lessons learned through passion and suffering—are interconnected. They are not separate paths but guideposts that lead you toward the discovery of your purpose. The entire journey we've taken together in this book has been about uncovering these building blocks, understanding them, and seeing how they align to form a clear picture of who you are and what you are meant to do.

Take your time with these reflections. Write down your thoughts and feelings as they emerge. This isn't about rushing to find a definitive answer but rather about allowing the threads of your life to reveal themselves, showing you the patterns and themes that have been quietly weaving together your sense of purpose. As you reflect on these aspects of your life, from a high standpoint, you begin to see your purpose not as something external or elusive but as something deeply personal and innate. Your purpose is not outside of you, waiting to be found. It is within you, ready to flourish as you reveal and embrace the person you are meant to be. It is the natural extension of all that you are—your experiences; your growth; your beliefs, values, and standards; and, yes, your moments of passion and suffering.

In the end, the discovery of your purpose is a journey of coming home to yourself. It is about recognizing that everything you need to understand and live your purpose is already within you. It is a process of unveiling, of allowing the layers of your authentic self to emerge and guide you toward a life of meaning and fulfillment. So, as you reflect on your answers to the questions we've explored, know that you are not just finding your purpose; you are revealing it, piece by piece, as you align with the person you were always meant to be. Through joy and through pain, your purpose is there, waiting to be fully realized.

CRAFTING YOUR DECLARATION OF PURPOSE

Crafting your purpose statement is not just an exercise in self-reflection; it is an act of profound significance, much like the drafting of America's Declaration of Independence. As an attorney with decades of experience, I deeply appreciate the power of the written word. In my profession, words are not just tools of communication; they are instruments of change, foundations of justice, and guardians of rights. The importance of writing with *precision and intention* cannot be overstated, for the words we choose have the power to shape lives, define legacies, and carve the path forward.

In the same way that the framers of the Declaration of Independence carefully chose their words to articulate a vision of freedom and self-determination, you are now crafting your own declaration—a Declaration of Purpose. This is more than just a statement; it is a contract with yourself, a binding agreement to live a life that is driven by meaning, integrity, and authenticity.

Think of your purpose statement as your personal Declaration of Independence. It is a clear and concise expression of who you are, what you stand for, and the impact you wish to have on the world. Just as the founders of this nation asserted, "We hold these truths to be self-evident," you too are identifying the self-evident truths that define your life. These are the core beliefs and values you know to be true, the guiding principles you hold above all else. When the framers of the Declaration of Independence signed their names to that historic document, they were not just affirming a set of beliefs; they were committing themselves to a cause greater than themselves, fully aware of the sacrifices and challenges that lay ahead. Similarly, when you write and sign your purpose statement, you are making a commitment to live in alignment with the values, passions, and goals that define your true self.

Writing, signing, and dating your purpose statement is a powerful ritual. It transforms an abstract idea into a tangible commitment. It is a promise you make to yourself to live according to the principles you have defined, to pursue the path that leads to your highest potential, and to embrace the challenges that will undoubtedly arise along the way. By putting your purpose in writing, you give it weight and substance, turning it into a guiding force in your life.

Your purpose statement is a living document. It is not static; it is meant to evolve as you grow, learn, and deepen your understanding of yourself and your place in the world. Revisit it often, refine it as needed, and let it guide your actions and decisions. This process of continuous reflection and revision ensures that your purpose statement remains relevant and true to who you are becoming.

Life is about more than significance; it is about meaning—true, authentic meaning that comes from living a purpose-driven life. Significance, while important, is often tied to external achievements and recognition. Meaning, however, is a higher-level concept, one that is rooted in self-actualization and the fulfillment of your unique potential. It embodies contribution and service to others but also transcends these acts by connecting them to your deeper sense of self and purpose.

By crafting your purpose statement, you engage in a process of self-actualization. You define what it means to live a life of meaning, not just for others, but for yourself. This statement becomes your North Star, guiding you toward a life that is not only successful but also deeply fulfilling.

And like any contract, this Declaration of Purpose is something you must uphold with integrity. Sign it, date it, and keep it close. Revisit it daily, if you must, and allow it to remind you of the commitment you have made to yourself. This is your contract with your existence, a precious statement of who you are and what you are here to do. It is a testament to your resolve to live a life of purpose, driven not by external accolades but by the inner conviction that you are living in alignment with your true self.

As you mold this statement, remember that you are not just writing words on a page; you are sculpting a declaration that reflects the essence of your existence and becoming. It is your unique contribution to the world, a statement of meaning that will guide you through life's challenges and triumphs. This is your unique Declaration of Purpose—crafted with intention, signed with commitment, and lived with passion.

Now, as we reach this pivotal moment in our journey together, I invite you to take the next step—one that is as significant as it is symbolic. Below, you will find a few blank lines, a space reserved for you to write and sign your life's purpose. This is your moment to put into words the truths you hold to be self-evident, the guiding principles that will shape the path ahead.

Believe it or not, you already know your purpose. It has been within you, quietly guiding your decisions and your passions, perhaps even before you consciously realized it. Now is the time to bring it to the surface, to give it form and substance. Tell yourself it is time to acknowledge what has been within you all along. It is time to write it down and celebrate its birth on paper.

Here is your Declaration of Purpose—a true new beginning toward becoming the person you have always been meant to be. Take a deep breath, and as you write, let the words flow from the deepest part of your soul. This is your contract with yourself, your commitment to live a life of meaning and authenticity.

Date:

My Declaration of Purpose:

Signature: _____

By writing and signing this declaration, you are not just acknowledging your purpose; you are embracing it, committing to it, and taking a decisive step toward living it each and every day. This is your new beginning, and it is a moment worth celebrating. Your purpose is now written, seen, and affirmed—a guiding light that will lead you forward on the journey.

Now you are not merely following a path; you are forging it, driven by the clarity of your purpose and the commitment to your authentic self.

LIVING YOUR PURPOSE: A COMMITMENT TO YOUR AUTHENTIC SELF

As I conclude this chapter, let me remind you once more of what I shared at the beginning. My purpose, as I've come to understand it, is singular in this moment: it is to help you, the reader, who is walking alongside me on this journey. I am here to share the knowledge, experience, and wisdom I've gathered so that you, too, can find and live your purpose, despite any tragedies, pain, obstacles, perceived failures, and suffering you may face.

Your purpose is waiting to be discovered or, perhaps, rediscovered. It is already within you, waiting to be aligned with your authentic self—and, if you share my faith, with God's plan for you. So take that step, embrace the journey, and live the purpose that is uniquely yours. The world needs it, and so do you.

So let's move forward with purpose and passion. With your Declaration of Purpose as your guide, it's time to define and embrace your *musts*—those essential actions that will ensure you are not just living but truly becoming the person you are meant to be. This is where the journey deepens, where the theory becomes practice, and where your purpose is lived, day by day, action by action.

PART TWO

Implementation

Implementation builds on the foundation of self-discovery established in Exploration by focusing on translating your *musts*—your core beliefs, values, and purpose—into actionable steps. This section is about bridging the gap between intention and reality, equipping you with the tools and strategies to align your daily actions with your authentic self. Implementation is where clarity meets commitment, and the lessons learned in Part 1 are put into practice to create meaningful change in your life.

Through this process, you will learn how to cultivate Must Habits with your Must Mindset and live fully in the Must Zone. These concepts provide a structured framework for building resilience, prioritizing what matters most, and eliminating distractions that pull you away from your purpose. Implementation is not about perfection but about consistent progress—taking deliberate steps each day to create a life that reflects your deepest values. By the end of this section, you will have the practical tools to turn your aspirations into reality and move closer to becoming the person you are meant to be.

CHAPTER 9

Must Actions

"The key to One More Try is to be intentional. You must have the strength and the focus to take steps that will drive you closer to where you want to be in life."

—Ed Mylett, bestselling author of *The Power of One More: The Ultimate Guide to Happiness and Success*

As I reflect on my journey, I recall a pivotal moment when I felt deeply unhappy with my life. The weight of past family tragedies and personal setbacks had led me into a dark place of depression and a diminished personal narrative. I was trapped in a cycle of pain and stagnation, feeling as though I was merely existing rather than truly living. This realization was both painful and liberating, as it compelled me with every fiber of my soul to seek a way out of this darkness.

    I knew I had to take deliberate and focused actions—what I now refer to as Must Actions—to transform my life. These actions were not just about personal growth; they were about survival and rebirth. I became determined to learn everything I could from the luminaries of personal development and self-improvement. I immersed myself in ancient wisdom and contemporary insights from leaders in the self-help field. I read voraciously, attended seminars, and sought opportunities to meet those who were helping others achieve profound transformation.

These Must Actions were not optional; they were essential to my transformation. By engaging with the wisdom of individuals such as Tony Robbins, Les Brown, Jack Canfield, and Brian Tracy, I began to view the world in a new light. I learned to reframe my past experiences, transforming them from burdens into catalysts for growth. I started to view my challenges as opportunities rather than obstacles, and my mindset shifted from one of limitation to one of empowerment.

As John C. Maxwell eloquently puts it, "An unintentional life accepts everything and does nothing. An intentional life embraces only the things that will add to the mission of significance." This is precisely what my Must Actions were about—being intentional and focused on creating a better life.

By committing to these Must Actions, I broke free from the cycle of suffering and created a new narrative for myself. I saw myself not as a victim of circumstance but as a survivor with a unique story to tell. My journey taught me that Must Actions are not just tasks; they are the deliberate efforts that drive us toward our true potential. They are the nonnegotiable steps we must take to align our lives with our deepest aspirations, our Must Values, and our Must Standards.

Must Actions are the deliberate and focused efforts that drive you forward, even when challenges arise. By consistently applying Must Actions to your daily tasks, you create a strong foundation for achieving your goals.

THE CUMULATIVE POWER OF *MUSTS*: SMALL STEPS, BIG CHANGES

As we delve into the concept of *musts*, it's essential to understand that this term encompasses a comprehensive framework for personal growth and transformation. Your *musts* are not just isolated actions or beliefs. They represent a holistic integration and alignment of your Must Mindset, Must Core Beliefs, Must Values, Must Personal Narrative, Must Standards, and Must Purpose. These elements work together to guide your decisions, shape your mindset, and drive your actions toward a life of authenticity and fulfillment. By embracing your *musts*, you are committing yourself to a journey where every aspect of your life aligns with your deepest aspirations and values. This alignment is what propels you toward becoming the person you were meant to be, ensuring that every step you take moves you closer to your true potential.

In this context, Must Actions are the tangible steps you take to honor your Must Core Beliefs, Values, and Purpose. They are the deliberate efforts that drive you forward, even when challenges arise, and are essential for creating a life that reflects your highest standards and aspirations. By consistently applying these Must Actions, you build momentum that eventually becomes unstoppable, leading to profound changes both in your external circumstances and within yourself.

In the journey of embracing your *musts*, it's essential to understand that progress may not always be immediate or obvious. There will be times when the daily efforts you invest in aligning with your purpose and values may seem insignificant, as if they make little to no difference. It's easy to become discouraged, feeling as though you're taking three steps backward for every step forward. However, the true power of embracing your *musts* lies not in the immediate results but in the cumulative effect of consistent, intentional action over time.

When you engage in Must Actions—those essential, nonnegotiable behaviors that align with your purpose—you are not just making decisions; you are engaging in a process that literally rewires your brain. These actions are driven by your Must Core Beliefs and Must Mindset, which serve as the foundation for your transformation.

Consider the story of Howard Schultz, the former CEO of Starbucks. Before Starbucks became the global coffee powerhouse it is today, Schultz faced numerous challenges that could have easily derailed his vision. Schultz grew up in a poor neighborhood in Brooklyn, where he witnessed the hardships of his working-class family.

This background instilled in him a drive to succeed, but also a deep empathy for others. When Schultz first joined Starbucks, it was a small company with a handful of stores selling only coffee beans and equipment. Schultz had a vision to transform it into a café-style chain where people could gather, relax, and enjoy a cup of coffee.

However, his vision was initially met with resistance. The original Starbucks owners were not interested in expanding into the café business. Schultz could have accepted this as a setback, but instead, he remained committed to his *must*—the core belief that Starbucks could be more than just a coffee retailer. After a trip to Italy, where the vibrant coffee culture inspired him, Schultz took the leap to start his own chain of coffee shops, which eventually led him to acquire Starbucks.

Schultz's journey was anything but smooth. He faced financial struggles, skepticism from investors, and intense competition. Progress was often slow, and there were many moments when it seemed like his vision might never come to fruition. But Schultz remained steadfast, driven by the *must* that had become his guiding force. He once said, "Dream more than others think practical. Expect more than others think possible. Care more than others think wise." This reflects his understanding that while setbacks and challenges are inevitable, staying true to your *musts* can lead to the fulfillment of what truly matters.

The long-term benefits of consistently applying your Must Actions can be profound, even if the day-to-day progress feels minimal. Think of it as building a mosaic: each tiny piece of glass or tile might seem insignificant on its own, but when viewed as a whole, these small pieces come together to create a stunning, intricate work of art. Schultz's dedication to his vision was like placing each small tile in a mosaic, gradually constructing the Starbucks experience that millions of people enjoy today.

It's also crucial to recognize that setbacks are a natural part of this journey. Just as Schultz faced numerous obstacles—financial, strategic, and personal—you may encounter challenges that make you question your path. These challenges are not indicators of failure; rather, they are opportunities to strengthen your resolve and refine your approach. The key is to maintain your commitment to your *musts*, even when progress is slow or setbacks arise.

This is where the power of consistency becomes evident. By continuing to take small steps, by applying your Must Actions with determination and patience, you build momentum that eventually becomes unstoppable. What may have started as a seemingly insignificant effort can lead to profound changes, both in your external circumstances and within yourself.

As you apply this to your life, remember that every great achievement is the result of many small, consistent actions. Your Must Actions may not yield immediate results, and there will be days when it feels as though you're moving backward. But if you stay the course, if you continue to honor your *musts* despite the setbacks, you will look back one day and see that each small step was a crucial part of a much larger journey.

In essence, your Must Actions are the catalysts for a profound transformation, not just in your behavior but in the very fabric of your brain. They are the instruments through which you craft a life that is in harmony with your deepest values and aspirations. Embrace them with the knowledge that every step you take is not only moving you closer to your goals but also forging the neural foundation upon which your extraordinary life is built.

NEUROPLASTICITY AND COGNITIVE REFRAMING

When you consistently choose your Must Actions, you're doing far more than changing habits—you're actively reshaping the architecture of your mind. Each intentional action, aligned with your deepest values, sends a powerful signal to your brain: this is who I am becoming. Over time, these repeated choices lay down new neural pathways, forming the foundation for lasting transformation and an inspired life.

This process is possible because of neuroplasticity, the brain's remarkable ability to rewire itself in response to new experiences and intentional practice. On my journey from suffering and anger to joy and forgiveness, I learned firsthand that change is not only possible but inevitable when you commit to new patterns of thought and behavior. I'll explore the science and practical steps of this process in more detail later, but for now, know this: every Must Action you take is not just moving you forward—it is actively training your brain to support the person you are meant to become.

The beauty of neuroplasticity is that it empowers you to take control of your own evolution. You are not bound by the limitations of your past. Instead, you have the power to shape your future, one *must* at a time. Each small, deliberate action contributes to the construction of a brain that is aligned with the person you aspire to become—a person who lives with intention, purpose, and a deep sense of fulfillment. Transformation becomes a force that constantly reshapes your life, much like a river reshapes the land it flows through. By embracing this force, you align it with your soul's evolution, and it beats in harmony with your growth.

Your transformation starts with a clear vision of the person you want to be—a vision of a brighter future and a more vibrant life. Give yourself permission to dream big and imagine the best version of yourself. This vision will serve as your guiding light on your transformation journey.

Cognitive reframing is a psychological technique rooted in cognitive behavioral therapy (CBT) that involves changing the way we perceive and interpret events in our lives. By consciously shifting our perspective, we can transform challenges into opportunities for growth.

Research has shown that cognitive reframing can significantly impact mental health. Studies indicate that individuals who practice reframing techniques experience lower levels of anxiety and depression as well as increased resilience in the face of adversity. For instance, research in cognitive behavioral therapy has consistently found that cognitive reframing techniques help individuals manage stress and negative emotions effectively. This evidence highlights the effectiveness of reframing as a tool for transforming suffering into opportunities for growth.

From a neuroscience perspective, cognitive reframing taps into the brain's neuroplasticity—its ability to reorganize and form new neural pathways. When we consciously choose to reframe negative thoughts, we are essentially rewiring our brains to adopt more adaptive thought patterns. Over time, this practice can strengthen neural connections associated with positive thinking and resilience, making it easier to maintain a growth-oriented mindset.

In your personal development journey, applying cognitive reframing can help you shift your perspective on challenges and setbacks. For example, consider a situation where you faced a job rejection. Initially, you may have felt discouraged and defeated, thinking, "I am not good enough." However, by reframing this thought to "This is an opportunity to learn and grow," you can view the rejection as a gateway toward future success. This shift in mindset allows you to focus on self-improvement rather than dwelling on perceived failures.

William James, influential American philosopher, psychologist, and educator, said, "The greatest weapon against stress is our ability to choose one thought over another." This emphasizes that we have the power to influence our mental state through our thoughts. By consciously choosing to reframe negative thoughts, we can combat stress and foster a more positive outlook on life.

To illustrate the application of cognitive reframing, consider the story of Zara, who struggled with feelings of inadequacy after receiving critical feedback on her work. Initially, she interpreted the feedback as a reflection of her abilities, leading her to doubt herself and withdraw from new opportunities. However, after learning about cognitive reframing techniques, Zara viewed the feedback as constructive rather than punitive. She told herself, "This feedback is valuable information that can help me improve." By adopting this new perspective, Zara not only regained her confidence but also actively sought additional feedback and mentorship, ultimately enhancing her skills and career prospects.

Cognitive reframing is a powerful tool you can use to challenge negative thought patterns and promote personal growth. By recognizing that your thoughts shape your perceptions and emotions, you can take proactive steps to cultivate a more positive mindset. As you incorporate reframing techniques into your daily life, remember that you have the ability to choose how you respond to challenges. This practice not only helps transform suffering into opportunities for growth but also empowers you to navigate life's complexities with resilience and clarity.

OUR *MUSTS* PROVIDE A PATH FOR PRODUCTIVITY ALIGNED WITH OUR PURPOSE

Embracing your *musts* is not just about necessity; it's about prioritization and alignment with your deepest aspirations. By establishing your *musts*, you are making a deliberate choice to focus on what truly matters in your life—the actions, behaviors, and core beliefs critical to fulfilling your purpose and passions. When you declare something as a *must*, you place it at the top of your priorities, ensuring it receives your full attention and energy. This process involves recognizing that your musts encompass not just specific actions but also the core values and standards that guide them. By prioritizing your *musts*, you align every aspect of your life with your true purpose, acknowledging that not everything can be a *must*. Other tasks or actions must be placed in a lesser realm of importance, either delegated to others or eliminated altogether, allowing you to maintain focus on what truly drives you toward becoming the person you were meant to be.

Consider this: when we use the word *must*, we invoke a sense of urgency and importance. We are telling ourselves this is not just something we want to do or think we should do. It is something we absolutely have to do if we want to honor our purpose and live authentically. This shift in language from *should* to *must* transforms our mindset. It moves us from a place of passive intention to one of active commitment. It is the difference between hoping for change and making it happen.

A personal example from my life illustrates the power of prioritizing *musts* in the face of overwhelming obstacles. After my father abandoned us and my stepfather committed suicide, my mother faced seemingly insurmountable challenges. Yet she made the courageous decision to focus on what she *must* do to persevere and provide for her family. She did not have the luxury of getting lost in the *coulds* or *shoulds* of her situation. Instead, she chose to prioritize her actions, focusing on the essential tasks that would keep our family afloat. Through sheer determination and the prioritization of her *musts*, she navigated the darkest moments of her life, ensuring we had a future, even when the present seemed unbearable.

Her Must Purpose became clear: to ensure our well-being and create a stable future for us. From this purpose, her Must Actions were derived. She prioritized securing stable employment, managing our household finances, and maintaining a strong support network. She worked tirelessly to provide for us, often sacrificing her own needs to ensure we had everything we required to thrive. Her commitment to these essential tasks—her Must Actions—allowed her to create a sense of stability and hope, even in the midst of chaos.

These actions were not just about survival; they were about creating a better life for us. She became determined to give us the opportunities she never had, to educate us, and to instill in us the values of resilience and hard work. Her Must Actions were guided by her core beliefs in the importance of family, education, and personal growth.

In essence, my mother's Must Purpose and Must Actions were intertwined. Her purpose drove her actions, and her actions fulfilled her purpose. This alignment is what allowed her to transform her challenges into opportunities for growth and to create a life of meaning and fulfillment for herself and our family.

My mother's story is not unique in its lessons of perseverance and prioritization. Consider the extraordinary example of United States Supreme Court Justice Ruth Bader Ginsburg. Ruth Bader Ginsburg's story is a powerful testament to perseverance and prioritization, showcasing how she dedicated her life to the pursuit of justice and equality. Born in 1933, in Brooklyn, New York, Ginsburg faced significant challenges from an early age, including gender discrimination in a male-dominated society. Despite these obstacles, she excelled academically, earning a place at Harvard Law School, where she was one of only nine women in a class of over five hundred. Ginsburg's commitment to her education and her belief in the importance of gender equality fueled her determination to succeed. After transferring to Columbia Law School, she graduated at the top of her class but struggled to find employment due to her gender. Rather than succumbing to despair, Ginsburg persevered, taking on various roles that allowed her to advocate for women's rights and civil liberties.

Ruth Bader Ginsburg's remarkable journey to becoming a US Supreme Court Justice is a testament to the transformative power of Must Actions. Ginsburg's Must Purpose was clear: to fight for gender equality and justice. Her Must Actions were the deliberate and focused efforts she made to align with this purpose. Her Must Actions included co-founding the Women's Rights Project of the ACLU and strategically litigating landmark cases like *Reed v. Reed*, which challenged discriminatory laws. These actions were not just tasks; they were the nonnegotiable steps she took to fulfill her purpose. By consistently applying these Must Actions, Ginsburg transformed her challenges into opportunities, ultimately becoming a cultural icon and a symbol of resilience. Her legacy inspires us to prioritize our own Must Actions, aligning them with our deepest values and aspirations to achieve extraordinary success.

Ginsburg's tireless efforts culminated in her appointment to the Supreme Court in 1993, where she continued to champion gender equality and civil rights. Known for her fierce advocacy and unwavering commitment to justice, she became a cultural icon and a symbol of resilience for many.

Throughout her life, Ginsburg prioritized her mission to create a more equitable society, demonstrating that one's purpose can evolve through dedication and hard work. Her legacy will inspire future generations to pursue their passions relentlessly and fight for what they believe is right regardless of the obstacles they may face. Ruth Bader Ginsburg's extraordinary feats are a testament to the power of perseverance and prioritization in fulfilling one's purpose.

By establishing and executing our *musts*, we are not just taking action—we are making a profound statement about what we value and what we are willing to fight for. We are saying that in the face of fear, uncertainty, and adversity, we will not waver in our commitment to our purpose. We will prioritize what matters most, delegating or eliminating anything that does not serve our higher goals, and in doing so, we will move closer to fulfilling our potential.

TRANSITIONING TO THE MUST ZONE

As we transition from establishing our *musts* to exploring the revolutionary concept of the Must Zone, we're about to embark on a paradigm shift that will fundamentally change how you approach personal growth and achievement. The next chapter will challenge the conventional wisdom of merely "stepping out of your comfort zone" and introduce you to a more powerful, purpose-driven state of being.

The Must Zone represents a radical departure from the traditional comfort zone model. It's not about occasional forays into discomfort but about creating a new normal where your actions are consistently aligned with your deepest values and highest aspirations. This shift in perspective will redefine how you approach challenges, growth, and the pursuit of your goals.

Prepare yourself for a transformative journey that will reshape your understanding of personal development. The Must Zone isn't just a place you visit; it's a state of being where your purpose and actions are in perfect harmony. As we delve into this concept, you'll discover how to transcend the limitations of the comfort zone paradigm and embrace a life of continuous growth, fulfillment, and extraordinary achievement.

CHAPTER 10

The Must Zone

"Life begins at the end of your comfort zone."
—Neale Donald Walsch, author of *Conversations with God*

For years, I had been contemplating the ideas and principles that would form the foundation of this book, constantly thinking about how to inspire others to break free from self-imposed limitations. Then, one night, I awoke from a dream with startling clarity. The words Must Zone were clear in my mind, and with them came a profound realization: the concept of "stepping out of the comfort zone" was, in itself, a limiting belief.

The Must Zone is not about merely stepping out of something comfortable—it's about embracing a state of being where there is no desire or need to retreat to comfort. It is a shift away from the limiting belief that growth requires us to escape our own comfort, and instead, it embraces the idea that we thrive beyond the boundaries of comfort, in a space where the challenges and opportunities of true living vitalize us.

I recall a moment when I realized that my comfort zone was holding me back. Despite achieving success in my career, I couldn't shake the feeling that something was missing—a sense of significance and meaning that went beyond external accomplishments. This realization sparked a profound quest for self-discovery, as I sought to understand what truly drove me and what I was meant to achieve in life.

My journey into the Must Zone began with two simple yet profound questions: What are my nonnegotiables? What are the essential actions and beliefs that align with my deepest values and aspirations? As I explored these questions, I felt drawn to the concept of Must Actions and Must Core Beliefs. These were not just tasks or beliefs; they were the foundation upon which I would build a life of purpose and fulfillment.

The Must Zone became a state of being where I no longer felt the need to retreat to comfort. Instead, I learned to thrive in the midst of challenges and pressures, embracing them as opportunities for growth. This zone is not about escaping the pressures of life; it's about becoming accustomed to them, using them as fuel for continuous improvement and transformation. It's a place where the desire to achieve and grow becomes an unquenchable fire, driving every action and decision.

As I stepped into the Must Zone, I began to see challenges as opportunities rather than obstacles. I viewed setbacks as stepping stones toward growth, and my mindset shifted from fear to empowerment. The Must Zone became a dynamic, purpose-driven state where my actions were fueled by a deep commitment to my core values, highest goals, and authentic self, transcending the limitations of the traditional comfort zone.

Living in the Must Zone meant fully integrating my purpose into daily life, ensuring that every action, habit, and decision moved me closer to fulfilling my potential and living an extraordinary life of fulfillment, resilience, and unwavering intentionality. This journey taught me that the Must Zone is not just a place you visit; it's a state of being you can cultivate and maintain, leading to an authentic and meaningful life filled with purpose.

The Must Zone is a dynamic, purpose-driven state where your actions are fueled by a deep commitment to your core values, highest goals, and authentic self, transcending the limitations of the traditional comfort zone. In this zone, you operate at the optimal level of arousal, where the right amount of constructive pressure enhances performance and drives continuous growth. The Must Zone is not about making radical changes overnight but about cultivating sustainable habits that align with your Must Standards—nonnegotiable benchmarks that guide every aspect of your life. Here, challenges are embraced as opportunities, discipline transforms initial pressure into a structured routine, and incremental progress leads to profound long-term transformation. Living in the Must Zone means fully integrating your purpose into daily life, ensuring every action, habit, and decision moves you closer to fulfilling your potential and living a meaningful life of fulfillment, resilience, and unwavering intentionality.

THE ORIGINS OF THE COMFORT ZONE

The concept of the comfort zone has become a fixture in our everyday language. It often describes the psychological space where we feel secure, in control, and unchallenged. The origins of this concept can be traced back to early psychological research on arousal and performance.

One of the most relevant theories is the Yerkes-Dodson law, developed by psychologists Robert M. Yerkes and John Dillingham Dodson in 1908. This law describes the relationship between arousal and performance, suggesting that performance increases with physiological or mental arousal, but only up to a certain point, after which performance decreases.

The Yerkes-Dodson law is crucial to understanding the Must Zone because it highlights the importance of finding an optimal level of arousal for peak performance. In the Must Zone, you operate at this optimal level, where the right amount of constructive pressure enhances your performance and drives continuous growth. This zone is not just about stepping out of your comfort zone; it's about embracing a state of being where challenges and opportunities vitalize you and you are fully engaged in pursuing your goals.

The concept of the comfort zone, often associated with the Yerkes-

Dodson law, is a psychological state where a person operates in an environment that feels safe, predictable, and free from stress or anxiety. However, in this zone, our abilities are neither stretched nor tested, and as a result, our growth is often stunted. The comfort zone is where one feels safe and in control yet where growth does not occur. The Must Zone transcends this limitation by embracing challenges as opportunities for growth rather than threats to comfort.

In the Must Zone, you don't just tolerate challenges; you seek them as catalysts for transformation. This mindset aligns with the Yerkes-Dodson law's principle that optimal performance requires the right level of arousal. By consistently applying your Must Actions and maintaining this optimal level of arousal, you create a dynamic, purpose-driven state where every action moves you closer to fulfilling your potential and living an extraordinary life of fulfillment, resilience, and unwavering intentionality.

THE SCIENCE BEHIND THE COMFORT ZONE

The comfort zone is not just a convenient metaphor; it is grounded in the very biology of our brains. Understanding the neuroscience behind the comfort zone reveals why we are naturally inclined to remain within its confines and what it takes to break free.

THE BRAIN'S ROLE IN COMFORT SEEKING

At its core, the comfort zone is a product of the brain's inherent desire to minimize risk and conserve energy. The human brain is designed for efficiency. It constantly seeks to automate tasks, forming habits and routines that require less cognitive effort. This efficiency is managed primarily by the brain's basal ganglia, structures responsible for habit formation. The basal ganglia help us execute well-rehearsed behaviors with minimal conscious thought, which is why driving a familiar route or performing routine tasks feels effortless.

This drive for efficiency also explains why the brain prefers the comfort zone. When we are within this zone, our brain does not have to expend much energy processing new information or handling uncertainty. The prefrontal cortex, the part of the brain responsible for decision-making, planning, and problem-solving, is less engaged when we stick to familiar routines. This allows the brain to conserve energy, which is why the comfort zone feels so safe and unchallenging.

However, the trade-off for this energy conservation is stagnation. Dr. Mihaly Csikszentmihalyi, a pioneering Hungarian psychologist known for his work on "flow," emphasized that the comfort zone is a place where creativity and peak performance often wither. In his research, Csikszentmihalyi found that individuals enter a state of flow—where they perform at their best—when they are challenged just beyond their current capabilities. This state of flow exists outside the comfort zone, in what he describes as the "sweet spot" between boredom and anxiety. He notes, "Flow is being completely involved in an activity for its own sake. The ego falls away. Time flies. Every action, movement, and thought follows inevitably from the previous one, like playing jazz."

THE FEAR RESPONSE AND THE COMFORT ZONE

When we consider stepping outside our comfort zone, our brain's amygdala—the region responsible for processing fear and emotional responses—becomes activated. This triggers the fight-or-flight response, releasing stress hormones like cortisol and adrenaline. As a group of University of West Alabama researchers explain, "A threat stimulus, such as the sight of a predator, triggers a fear response in the amygdala, which activates areas involved in preparation for motor functions involved in fight or flight. It also triggers the release of stress hormones and the sympathetic nervous system." While this response was crucial for our ancestors' survival in the wild, it can now act as a barrier to personal growth.

However, modern neuroscience also shows that our brains are incredibly plastic, meaning that while the brain may initially resist leaving the comfort zone, repeated exposure to new challenges can rewire it to become more comfortable with discomfort. As Kelly Blackmon emphasizes, "When we step out of our comfort zones, we're actually helping to increase our brain's neuroplasticity. Neuroplasticity refers to the brain's ability to change and adapt in response to new experiences and challenges." The more we push ourselves out of our comfort zone, the more our brain adapts, gradually reducing the fear response and making it easier to embrace new experiences.

This is echoed in the work of Carol Dweck. Her research on fixed and growth mindsets highlights the importance of challenging ourselves beyond our comfort zones to foster a mindset of continuous improvement. Dweck states, "This growth mindset is based on the belief that your basic qualities are things you can cultivate through your efforts, your strategies, and help from others. Although people may differ in every which way—in their initial talents and aptitudes, interests, or temperaments—everyone can change and grow through application and experience."

Consider the story of Sara Blakely, the founder of Spanx, who started her business with $5,000 in savings and a relentless belief in her product. Blakely had no background in business or fashion, and the odds were stacked against her. Yet she pushed beyond the comfort zone of a secure job selling fax machines and ventured into the risky world of entrepreneurship. Her journey was filled with rejection and obstacles, but her determination to succeed was unwavering. "Failure is not the outcome—failure is not trying. Don't be afraid to fail," Blakely said. Her courage to leave the comfort zone and pursue her vision led Spanx to become a billion-dollar company, and she became one of the youngest self-made female billionaires in the world.

CHALLENGING THE COMFORT ZONE CONCEPT: A SHIFT IN PERSPECTIVE

While the comfort zone metaphor has been widely accepted as a model for growth, it can be limiting. It implies a binary state of either being comfortable or uncomfortable, without fully capturing the dynamic nature of personal development and the intensity of commitment required to fulfill your life's purpose. The comfort zone is often seen as a place of rest and safety, but it lacks the proactive energy needed to drive meaningful change.

In fact, the very idea that we must "step out of the comfort zone" to grow can itself be a self-limiting belief. This perspective suggests that we must escape from a place of comfort to reach new heights, as if comfort is a refuge we need to abandon rather than an obstacle to be conquered. This mindset creates an unnecessary tension between comfort and growth, implying that we are somehow betraying our natural instincts for safety and security by seeking progress.

The Must Zone redefines this dynamic by embracing the fact that we live outside the comfort zone as a natural state of being. In the Must Zone, there is no need or desire to retreat to the comfort zone because our existence is vitalized by the challenges, opportunities, and experiences that lie beyond it. The comfort zone becomes a "kiddie pool" of refuge we no longer need as we grow in all aspects of our being. Instead of feeling like we must escape the comfort zone, we recognize that we have outgrown it, much like a child outgrows a small pool and craves the excitement of swimming in the vast ocean.

In the Must Zone, we are driven not by the fear of discomfort but by the exhilarating thrill of living a life explored. We thrive in the wilderness of existence, where every challenge is an opportunity to test our limits, every obstacle a chance to prove our resilience, and every fear a call to courage. This is where we truly come alive, where we are not merely surviving but thriving.

The Must Zone often comes with a provocative feeling of pressure, which is essential for growth and change. This pressure is not to be feared; instead, it should be embraced as a sign that you are pushing beyond your comfort zone and challenging yourself to achieve greatness.

The pressure you feel in the Must Zone can initially serve as a powerful motivator. It propels you to take action, make decisions, and move forward. This initial motivation is crucial for breaking free from inertia and starting your journey toward fulfilling your purpose.

Much like the spark that ignites a flame, this pressure kick-starts your momentum, pushing you to step into the unknown with courage.

Over time, the pressure transforms into a disciplined approach to life. You begin to appreciate the structure and routine that come with high standards and committed actions. This discipline helps you stay focused and consistent, ensuring that you continue to make progress even when the initial motivation wanes. Consider an athlete training for a major competition. The initial pressure to perform well drives them to train hard, but it is the disciplined routine of daily practice and commitment to excellence that sustains their progress. Similarly, in your journey, the pressure you feel in the Must Zone will evolve into a disciplined approach that supports long-term success.

ALIGNING THE MUST ZONE WITH THE YERKES-DODSON LAW

As we delve into the concept of the Must Zone, it's essential to understand how it aligns with the Yerkes-Dodson law. Remember, this law suggests there is an optimal level of arousal that enhances our performance, beyond which further increases in stress or pressure can lead to decreased performance. The Must Zone is a state of being where you operate at this optimal level of arousal, where the right amount of constructive pressure enhances your performance and drives continuous growth. By aligning with the Yerkes-Dodson law, the Must Zone ensures that you are neither understimulated nor overwhelmed, but rather, you are fully engaged and motivated to tackle challenges. This alignment is crucial because it allows you to harness the power of your Must Actions and Must Core Beliefs effectively, propelling you toward your goals with clarity and purpose. By understanding how the Yerkes-Dodson law supports the Must Zone, you can better navigate the delicate balance between challenge and comfort, ensuring that every step you take moves you closer to fulfilling your potential and living a wonderful life of fulfillment, resilience, and unwavering intentionality. This exercise is useful because it provides a scientific foundation for why the Must Zone is effective, helping you maintain motivation and performance over time.

THE MUST ZONE AS THE OPTIMAL AROUSAL POINT

The Must Zone can be interpreted as the state where an individual operates at the optimal point of the Yerkes-Dodson curve. In this zone, a person is not merely stepping out of their comfort zone to experience random discomfort but is purposefully engaging with challenges that align with their deepest values and goals. These challenges provide just the right amount of stress or arousal to push the individual toward growth without tipping into anxiety or burnout.

In the Must Zone, the pressure you feel is constructive—it keeps you engaged, focused, and driven. This aligns perfectly with the Yerkes-Dodson law's idea that moderate arousal can improve performance. The key difference is that in the Must Zone, this optimal arousal is not incidental but intentional, created by the commitment to purpose-driven actions.

SUSTAINABLE HIGH PERFORMANCE

Yerkes and Dodson's theory suggests that too much stress can lead to diminished performance, which ties into the importance of sustainability in the Must Zone. The Must Zone encourages individuals to consistently engage with challenges that push them toward their potential, but it also recognizes the importance of balance. By focusing on incremental growth and habit building, the Must Zone helps maintain the optimal arousal level over time, preventing the burnout that Yerkes and Dodson warned against.

This sustainable approach to high performance ensures that individuals do not merely peak temporarily but continue to grow and perform at high levels throughout their journey. The Must Zone, therefore, is a practical and evolved application of the Yerkes-Dodson law, where the focus is on creating conditions for sustained optimal performance.

TRANSFORMING PRESSURE INTO DISCIPLINE

Yerkes and Dodson highlighted that too much arousal could be counterproductive. The Must Zone addresses this by emphasizing the transformation of initial pressure into disciplined actions. As individuals settle into the Must Zone, the pressure that might initially feel overwhelming becomes a source of structure and routine, helping them maintain their performance levels without succumbing to stress.

By fostering a disciplined approach, the Must Zone allows individuals to stay within that optimal arousal state, where the challenges are sufficient to stimulate growth but are managed in a way that avoids excessive stress. This is how the Must Zone can be seen as a practical application of Yerkes and Dodson's theory, tailored to personal development and long-term growth.

INCREMENTAL GROWTH AND THE AROUSAL CONTINUUM

The Yerkes-Dodson law also implies that different tasks require different levels of arousal for optimal performance. Simple tasks might benefit from higher arousal, while complex tasks require lower arousal. The Must Zone incorporates this understanding by promoting incremental growth—small, manageable steps that build toward larger goals.

This incremental approach ensures that the level of challenge, and thus the arousal, is appropriate for the task at hand, allowing the individual to stay within the optimal performance zone. Over time, as the individual grows and their capacity increases, they can handle more complex tasks and higher levels of arousal, continually pushing the boundaries of the Must Zone.

The Must Zone is consistent with the Yerkes-Dodson law as it encourages individuals to operate at an optimal level of arousal by engaging with purpose-driven challenges. It transforms pressure into disciplined action, promotes incremental growth, and sustains high performance without tipping into burnout. By understanding and applying these principles, individuals can navigate the Must Zone effectively, maximizing their potential while staying aligned with their deepest values and purpose.

THE MUST ZONE AND PEAK PERFORMANCE

The Must Zone is not just a theoretical construct; it is a living reality for some of the most successful and impactful individuals in the world. Let's explore how contemporary peak performers embody the Must Zone.

Tyler Perry, the acclaimed playwright and entrepreneur, is another individual who exemplifies the Must Zone. Perry's journey to success was anything but easy; he faced years of struggle, homelessness, and rejection. However, Perry's unwavering belief in his purpose and his commitment to his vision drove him to keep creating despite the obstacles. "Focus on one thing, make it your priority, and stick with it no matter what," Perry said, illustrating his determination to succeed against all odds. Perry's Must Zone was fueled by his passion for storytelling and his desire to inspire and uplift others, particularly within the African American community. His story is a powerful example of how living in the Must Zone requires not just talent, but an unshakable commitment to your purpose, even when the path is difficult.

Also consider the story of Serena Williams, one of the greatest athletes of all time. Williams's journey to the top of the tennis world was not without its challenges—she faced racism, sexism, and countless obstacles along the way. Yet her unwavering commitment to excellence and her refusal to accept anything less than the best propelled her to greatness. "I really think a champion is defined not by their wins but by how they can recover when they fall," Williams has said, emphasizing resilience and determination. Her mindset is what is required to live in the Must Zone. For Williams, tennis is more than a game; it is a platform to challenge herself and inspire others to pursue their dreams with the same relentless drive.

Then there's David Goggins, a retired Navy SEAL, ultra-endurance athlete, author of *New York Times* bestselling books, and motivational speaker whose life is a living example of what it means to operate within the Must Zone. Goggins transformed himself from an overweight, struggling young man into one of the most resilient and mentally tough individuals on the planet. His motto, "You are in danger of living a life so comfortable and soft, that you will die without ever realizing your true potential," shows the essence of breaking free from the comfort zone. Goggins doesn't just step out of the comfort zone; he lives far beyond its borders, constantly pushing his limits in grueling endurance challenges that test his physical and mental capacity. Goggins lives in alignment with his own Must Zone, a place where there is no option but to give everything, every day, regardless of the pain or discomfort. His story reminds us the Must Zone is not just a state of mind, but a lifestyle where we demand the best of ourselves in every situation.

THE MUST ZONE: A PLACE WHERE GROWTH AND FLOW CONVERGE

The Must Zone is where your growth mindset can truly flourish. It is within this space that you begin to see challenges as opportunities, where you no longer shy away from obstacles but rather embrace them as the catalyst to your growth and transformation. A growth mindset, as Dweck's research emphasizes, thrives on the belief that abilities and intelligence can be developed through effort, learning, and persistence. The Must Zone nurtures this mindset by pushing you to continuously evolve, to learn from each experience, and to seek the discomfort that comes with true growth.

The Must Zone is where you are most likely to experience flow—the state of optimal engagement where time seems to stand still and you are fully immersed in what you are doing. Csikszentmihalyi describes flow as the experience of being completely involved in an activity for its own sake. It is the sweet spot where your skills are perfectly matched to the challenge at hand, creating a sense of energized focus and deep satisfaction.

In the Must Zone, your actions are not optional; they are essential. This zone represents a shift from merely wanting to achieve something to needing to achieve it. When you merely want something, it's optional. You might pursue it if the conditions are right or if it's convenient. But when you need to achieve something—when it's a *must*—it becomes a priority, and you are driven to act regardless of obstacles or difficulties.

This shift from comfort to *must* is essential for truly living out your purpose. It requires a radical change in mindset and behavior. It's about moving from a passive state of wishing and hoping to an active state of doing and achieving. In the Must Zone, you are not waiting for opportunities to come to you; you are creating them.

As you navigate through the Must Zone, it's essential to recognize that this space is not just a temporary state of mind but a lifestyle that permeates every aspect of your existence. The Must Zone is where your growth mindset can truly flourish. It's a place where you are continuously learning, evolving, and pushing your limits. This is where your flow is engaged, where you lose yourself in the pursuit of your goals, and where time seems to stand still as you immerse yourself fully in your purpose.

As you become more comfortable living in the Must Zone, the discomfort associated with growth and change begins to fade. What once felt daunting now feels exhilarating. The Must Zone becomes your new normal—a place where you constantly evolve, thrive, and move closer to your true potential.

In this space, there is no retreating to the comfort zone, because it no longer serves you. The comfort zone becomes a relic of the past, a place you've outgrown. You no longer seek refuge in it because you've discovered something far more fulfilling—the wild, exhilarating wilderness of the Must Zone, where you are fully alive, fully engaged, and fully committed to living out your purpose.

INTEGRATING THE MUST ZONE WITH YOUR PURPOSE

Integrating your purpose with the principles of the Must Zone is a transformative process that aligns your deepest motivations with your most essential actions, creating a life of intentionality and fulfillment. This powerful integration begins with clarifying your purpose, ensuring it reflects your core values and long-term vision. Once your purpose is clearly articulated, you can identify the critical activities that directly contribute to fulfilling it within your Must Zone.

Creating purpose-driven goals is the next crucial step. By setting specific, measurable objectives that align with both your purpose and Must Zone activities, you create a roadmap for meaningful action. Establishing daily practices and routines that consistently reinforce your purpose through Must Zone actions helps embed this alignment into your everyday life.

Fostering a purpose-driven mindset is essential for successful integration. Regular reflection on how your Must Zone activities are advancing your purpose keeps you focused and motivated. Using your purpose as a guiding principle when prioritizing tasks and making choices within your Must Zone ensures that your actions remain aligned with your broader vision. Embracing challenges as opportunities for growth and purpose fulfillment transforms obstacles into pathways toward your goals.

The synergy between purpose and the Must Zone significantly enhances motivation and performance. Tapping into the power of purpose fuels intrinsic motivation for Must Zone tasks, driving you forward even when faced with difficulties. Aligning your skills and challenges within the Must Zone can help you achieve a state of flow, enhancing both productivity and satisfaction. Continuous improvement through regular assessment and refinement of the alignment between your purpose and Must Zone activities ensures ongoing growth and impact.

By thoughtfully integrating your purpose with the principles of the Must Zone, you create a powerful catalyst for personal transformation. This integration drives meaningful action, enhances personal fulfillment, and maximizes your potential for impact in areas that truly matter to you. It's a journey of continuous growth and alignment, leading to a life of greater intention, satisfaction, and purpose-driven achievement.

ALIGN YOUR ACTIONS WITH YOUR PURPOSE

Ensure that your Must Actions are directly aligned with your purpose. Every step you take should move you closer to realizing your goals and fulfilling your mission. For instance, if your purpose is to improve the lives of others through healthcare, your Must Actions might include furthering your education, gaining practical experience, and advocating for better healthcare policies. When your actions are in sync with your purpose, they become more than tasks—they become the exemplification of your mission.

EMBODY YOUR PURPOSE IN EVERYDAY LIFE

Live out your purpose in your daily interactions and decisions. Let it guide your behavior and shape your identity. The Must Zone is not a separate part of your life; it is integrated into everything you do. Reflect on how your purpose influences your relationships, career choices, and personal habits. Make adjustments to ensure you are consistently living in alignment with your purpose. This integration transforms ordinary moments into opportunities for purpose-driven action.

INSPIRE OTHERS TO JOIN YOU IN THE MUST ZONE

Share your journey with others and encourage them to embrace the Must Zone in their own lives. Your commitment and success can serve as a powerful example and inspire others to pursue their purpose with the same dedication. Engage with communities and networks that support purposeful living. Surround yourself with individuals who are also committed to living in the Must Zone and who can provide support and encouragement along the way. Collective growth amplifies the impact of the Must Zone, turning individual achievements into a ripple effect that transforms communities.

LIVING IN THE MUST ZONE

Living in the Must Zone is not always easy, but it is always rewarding. It's a journey that requires courage, resilience, and a deep commitment to your purpose. But the rewards are immeasurable. As you continue to embrace the Must Zone, remember that this is where true growth happens. This is where you discover who you really are and what you are truly capable of achieving.

So step boldly into the Must Zone, knowing that this is where you belong. This is where you will find the fulfillment, purpose, and success you've been searching for. This is where your dreams become reality, and where your potential is fully realized. This is your journey, and it starts here, in the Must Zone.

As you step into the Must Zone, recognize that this is not just a place of obligation—it's the gateway to your greatest achievements. It is where your growth mindset finds fertile ground, where your capacity for flow is unleashed, and where you move from mere existence to purposeful living. The Must Zone challenges you to rise to the occasion, to live with intention, and to embrace the discomfort that comes with growth. This is where your life truly begins, where you shed the limitations of the comfort zone and step boldly into the extraordinary life you were meant to live.

Embracing the Must Zone represents a profound shift in how you approach your life and purpose. It moves you from a state of passive wishing to active doing, from comfort to commitment, and from mediocrity to excellence. By identifying and committing to your Must Actions and by applying productivity principles to maximize efficiency, you align your life with your highest goals and create a path to success.

The Must Zone is more than a concept; it's a way of life. It requires you to continuously challenge yourself, embrace the pressures that come with growth, and remain committed to your purpose. As you move forward, remember that living in the Must Zone is a journey of constant evolution. You will encounter obstacles and setbacks, but each challenge is an opportunity to reinforce your commitment and refine your actions.

CHAPTER 11

Goal Setting

"The great danger for most of us lies not in setting our aim too high and falling short; but in setting our aim too low, and achieving our mark."
—Michelangelo

As a young man, I was in the audience when Zig Ziglar, with the warmth of his charming southern drawl, captivated us with this story.

In a quaint village nestled among rolling hills, there lived an archer of great renown. Wherever he went, he amazed the locals with his seemingly supernatural ability to hit the bullseye every single time. People would gather from far away and witness his incredible feats of marksmanship.

The archer would stride confidently into the village square, bow in hand, and a quiver of arrows slung across his back. With a flourish, he'd pull an arrow, draw his bow, and let it fly. Thwack! The arrow would embed itself in a nearby tree, barn, or fence post. From a distance, the crowd would hold its breath in anticipation. Then, with a mischievous twinkle in his eye, the archer would saunter over to where his arrow had landed. He'd pull out a small cloth from his pocket and carefully wipe the area around the arrow, claiming he was cleaning off any debris that might have affected his shot. The villagers would nod in appreciation of his attention to detail.

This went on for years, with the archer's reputation growing with each perfect shot. People marveled at his consistency and skill, never questioning how he managed to hit the bullseye every time, regardless of the target.

One day, a wise old woman in the village decided to follow the archer after one of his performances. As she watched from afar, she saw him pull out a small pot of paint and a brush from his pocket. With great ceremony, he carefully painted a perfect brilliantly red bullseye circle around the arrow he had just shot.

The old woman couldn't help but chuckle at the clever deception and the villagers' willingness to believe in this "magical" accuracy. She realized that the archer had been creating his own false success all along, adjusting his targets to match his results rather than truly improving his skill.

Zig Ziglar used the archer's story to illustrate a profound point about how many of us approach goal setting in our lives. He observed that, unfortunately, most of us treat our goals much like the deceptive archer in the tale. We often believe we have clear objectives in mind, but in reality, we're simply painting targets around wherever our arrows of effort happen to land. Different versions of this story have been told throughout the millennia. In fact, one version dates to the *Huainanzi*, a Chinese philosophical text from the second century BCE. This ageless wisdom still applies today.

This approach to life and goal setting is haphazard at best. We convince ourselves we're living with intention and purpose when, in fact, we're merely justifying our random actions after the fact. By doing so, we fail to take control of our destiny or aim for specific, meaningful targets in life.

Ziglar emphasized that true success requires a different approach. Instead of retroactively defining our goals based on our actions, we need to develop the necessary skills in goal setting. This involves carefully contemplating our true desired destinations before we take action. By clearly defining our targets first, we can then align our efforts and develop Must Skills needed to hit those marks consistently. Must Skills are the critical abilities and knowledge you must acquire to hit your targets and fulfill your purpose consistently. They are not just desirable skills; they are the foundational elements that ensure your success and growth. By identifying and mastering these Must Skills, you create a strong foundation for achieving your aspirations and living a life of purpose and fulfillment. Your Must Skills are the critical abilities and knowledge you must acquire to consistently hit your targets and fulfill your purpose. These skills are not just about achieving success; they are about aligning your actions with your core values and purpose, ensuring that every step you take moves you closer to your true potential. By integrating your *musts* into your goal-setting process, you transform your goals from mere aspirations into essential components of your life's journey, propelling you toward a future that is authentic, meaningful, and filled with purpose. This approach to goal setting is not just about achieving success; it's about living a life that reflects your deepest aspirations and values, where every action and decision aligns with your Must Purpose.

Ziglar urges us to be more deliberate and proactive in shaping our lives. By mastering the art of goal setting, we can take control of our destiny and ensure that our efforts are directed toward achieving the specific outcomes we truly desire rather than simply rationalizing whatever results we happen to achieve. Ziglar asks us this profound question: "How can we hit a target that we don't have?"

Goals are the beacons that guide our actions, infusing our lives with direction and purpose. They are the bridge between our present state and the future we aspire to create. In this chapter, we will explore the profound impact of goal setting on our lives, drawing from the wisdom of historical studies, contemporary thought leaders, and scientific research. We will also reflect on how to integrate these principles into every aspect of our lives, as reflected in the Circle of Life.

Despite compelling evidence that proper goal-setting strategies can significantly enhance one's life across all areas, surprisingly few people take advantage of this powerful tool. This paradox stems from various factors, including lack of awareness, fear of failure, comfort with the status quo, perceived complexity, and lack of self-belief.

This chapter will help you overcome these obstacles and join the elite group of goal setters who consistently achieve *must* aspirations. By addressing common barriers and providing practical strategies, we'll equip you with the knowledge and tools to harness the full potential of goal setting. You'll learn how to transform goal setting from a potentially daunting task into a natural, empowering practice that not only gives you a competitive advantage in life but also aligns your actions with your deepest purpose. Through this process, you'll discover how to use goal setting as a compass for personal growth and professional success and, ultimately, to become the person you are meant to be.

EFFECTIVE GOAL SETTING

To take your goals to the next level, remember that effective goal setting cannot exist in isolation. It must be deeply rooted in the foundational aspects of who you are and who you aspire to become. This requires the integration of your Must Mindset, Must Core Beliefs, Must Personal Narrative, Must Values, Must Standards, and Must Purpose into the goal-setting process. This holistic approach ensures that your goals are not just arbitrary targets but are deeply connected to who you are and what you aspire to become.

Understanding the theoretical foundations of goal setting is the cornerstone of personal development, but the true power of these concepts lies in their application. Theory provides the "why"—the rationale behind setting goals, the science that supports their efficacy, and the principles that guide their creation. However, it is through practice that these theoretical ideas are transformed into tangible results. To achieve this transformation, it's essential to bridge the gap between knowledge and your Must Actions, ensuring that your goals are not just lofty ideas but actionable steps that lead to real change. You only change your life through actions.

SET GOALS THAT REFLECT THESE MUST VALUES

For each value, set a corresponding goal that exemplifies how you will live by that value on a daily basis. For example, if excellence is one of your Must Values, a related goal might be to continuously improve your professional skills through ongoing education or training, or by seeking mentorship. If compassion is a Must Value, you might set a goal to volunteer regularly or to make daily efforts to be more empathetic and supportive in your interactions with others. When you write down your own associated goals, provide much more specificity.

These goals should be specific and actionable, providing clear steps you can take to embody your values. By doing so, you ensure that your goals are not just tasks to complete but are reflections of who you are and who you aspire to be.

REVIEW AND REFLECT

After setting these goals, take a moment to step back and reflect on how they align with your overall life purpose. Ask yourself, "Are these goals helping me become the person I want to be? Do they resonate with my sense of purpose and direction?" If you find any misalignment, adjust your goals accordingly to ensure that they truly reflect your Must Values.

This reflection is crucial because it allows you to assess whether your actions are in harmony with your beliefs, values, and purpose. It ensures that your goals are not just externally imposed tasks but deeply personal commitments that resonate with your authentic self.

By regularly practicing this exercise, you ensure that your goals are not just theoretical but are integrated into the very fabric of your daily life, guiding your actions and decisions. Apply your goals in each area of your Circle of Life. This practice helps to anchor your goals in your identity, making them a natural extension of who you are. Over time, this alignment between theory and practice creates a powerful synergy that drives you toward continuous growth and fulfillment.

The process of aligning your goals with your Must Values is not a one-time task; it is an ongoing journey. As you evolve, your values may deepen, and your goals may need to be adjusted to reflect this growth. Regularly revisiting and refining your goals in light of your *musts* ensures that you remain on a path that is not only successful but also deeply satisfying.

THE SCIENCE OF GOAL SETTING

The concept of goal setting is not a modern invention; its roots stretch deep into history. The ancients understood the power of clear intentions and the disciplined pursuit of objectives. Aristotle spoke of telos, the ultimate purpose or aim that everyone strives to achieve. This early understanding laid the groundwork for what we now recognize as the importance of setting clear, purposeful goals. Greek Stoic philosopher Epictetus proclaimed, "First say to yourself what you would be; and then do what you have to do."

Fast-forward to the twentieth century, when the power of goal setting was scientifically validated. In my research of goal setting, virtually every book I read spoke of the famous Yale and Harvard goal-setting studies. Let me tell you about these studies on goal setting. In 1953, Yale University conducted a goal-setting study, finding that *only 3 percent* of the student participants had written goals. A follow-up decades later found that the 3 percent who had written goals were more successful in both wealth and life satisfaction. In 1979, researchers at Harvard Business School conducted a study that revealed a startling finding: *only 3 percent* of graduates had written goals and plans for their future. Twenty years later, those 3 percent were earning ten times more than the other 97 percent combined. This study, often referenced in discussions on goal setting, underscores the profound impact of having clear, written goals on long-term success.

Here's the problem with these two widely cited goal-setting studies. Besides claims in mainstream personal development books, there is absolutely no evidence these studies ever occurred. Yale University has expressly stated it has no record of this study, and Harvard Business School claims to have no record of this study attributed to its institution; these studies are merely urban myths.

In contrast, Dr. Gail Matthews, a psychology professor at Dominican University of California, conducted a legitimate study that sheds real light on the power of goal setting. Dr. Matthews's research found that individuals who wrote down their goals and shared them with others were 42 percent more likely to achieve them than those who merely kept their goals in mind. Matthews demonstrated that the act of writing goals brings clarity and focus, while accountability—through regular progress updates to a friend or partner—fuels sustained commitment. Her findings provide scientific backing to the long-held belief that written goals are a critical tool for success, proving that intentionality and accountability, not folklore, drive meaningful achievements.

Furthermore, Edwin A. Locke and Gary P. Latham, in their book *New Developments in Goal Setting and Task Performance*, discuss other validated studies on goal setting from which several key findings emerged that strongly suggest great advantages for those who apply goal setting in their life. Specific, challenging goals lead to better performance than vague or easy objectives. A clear relationship exists between goal difficulty and task performance, provided that the individual is committed, capable, and does not face conflicting priorities. Goals appear to have an energizing effect, with more ambitious targets inspiring greater effort.

The practical significance of goal setting has been demonstrated in diverse settings, including workplaces, sports, and healthcare. This broad applicability underscores the value of structured goal-setting practices in enhancing motivation and performance across various areas of life.

An essential component of successful goal setting is the role of feedback and commitment. Regular feedback keeps individuals on track and allows them to adjust their strategies, while commitment ensures sustained effort over time. The researchers also underline the importance of writing goals down, as this solidifies intent and bridges the gap between abstract aspirations and concrete actions. Locke and Latham's work provides a scientific foundation for the power of goal setting, illustrating its potential to enhance performance across various areas of life.

A 2016 study by Benjamin Harkin and his colleagues offers fascinating insights into the power of tracking our progress toward goals. This comprehensive meta-analysis involved a thorough examination of 138 studies, encompassing nearly twenty thousand participants. The researchers aimed to understand how monitoring progress impacts goal achievement. Their findings were profound: simply paying attention to how we're doing can significantly boost our chances of success. Imagine you're on a road trip—checking your map regularly makes you more likely to reach your destination. That's essentially what this study discovered about goal achievement.

The researchers found that when people monitored their progress, they were much more likely to achieve their goals. This effect was particularly pronounced when the outcomes were reported or made public and when the information was physically recorded. For instance, writing down progress or sharing it with others appeared to be especially powerful in promoting goal achievement. It's akin to the difference between silently thinking about your diet and actually keeping a food journal or joining a weight loss group. The study suggests that the act of monitoring itself—not just setting goals—plays a crucial role in helping us succeed.

This meta-analysis was a significant contribution to the field of goal-setting research, providing robust evidence that tracking progress is a key factor in achieving success. By synthesizing data from numerous studies, Harkin and his team were able to draw broad conclusions about the effectiveness of progress monitoring across various contexts. Their work underscores the importance of making progress tangible—either through social accountability or physical documentation—to reinforce commitment and motivate individuals to push harder toward their goals. Whether you're trying to save money, learn a new skill, or make a lifestyle change, regularly checking in on your progress could be the key to turning your aspirations into reality.

A 2020 study published in the *European Journal of Social Psychology* highlights the effectiveness of intentions in goal achievement. This research demonstrates that creating specific, detailed plans for pursuing goals significantly increases success rates. Declaring and writing down these intentions makes it more likely for individuals to take desired actions when opportunities arise. The study found that participants who formed these concrete plans were markedly more successful in achieving their goals.

While most of the research I've discussed up to this point has focused on just one aspect of the goal-setting process, a 2023 study by Dr. John Bird and his colleagues at the University of Stirling, published in the journal *Personality and Social Psychology Bulletin*, offers a more holistic perspective. This groundbreaking research reveals that setting goals is far more than simply writing down what you want to achieve. Instead, the study identified goal setting as a dynamic, multifaceted process that involves not only clarifying your ambitions but also regularly monitoring your progress, adjusting your strategies as you go, and reflecting on setbacks and successes along the way.

Bird and his team demonstrated that people who actively engage in this ongoing process—by tracking their progress, revisiting and refining their goals, and learning from their experiences—are significantly more likely to achieve meaningful outcomes than those who simply set a goal and leave it at that. Their findings highlight that effective goal pursuit requires flexibility, self-reflection, and a willingness to adapt, making the journey toward your ambitions just as important as the destination itself.

Here's where it gets exciting: the study emphasizes that one size does not fit all when it comes to goal setting. It's not about following a rigid formula but about crafting a personalized roadmap to success. This means your journey to achieving your goals can be as unique as you are!

Whether you're an athlete aiming for Olympic gold, a student targeting straight A's, or an entrepreneur building the next big thing, this research offers a fresh, powerful approach to turning your dreams into reality. It's not just about setting goals anymore—it's about embarking on a thrilling journey of self-discovery and achievement.

These findings offer robust scientific support for the use of goal-setting techniques across various areas of our lives. Whether in professional and business endeavors, academic pursuits, or personal development, setting clear and ambitious goals is a must to enhance performance and drive success significantly. This research underscores the value of incorporating structured goal-setting practices to achieve desired outcomes in diverse areas of your life.

But what is it about goal setting that makes it so effective? Psychologically, goals provide a sense of purpose and direction, which enhances motivation and focus. They serve as a roadmap, helping us navigate the complexities of life with a clear sense of where we are headed. Neuroscientific research further supports this, showing that goal setting activates the brain's reward system, releasing dopamine, a neurotransmitter associated with pleasure and motivation, whenever we make progress toward our goals.

BEST PRACTICES IN GOAL SETTING

What follows is a practical overview of the most effective goal-setting strategies, drawn not only from the latest scientific research but also from the proven methods of leading productivity experts, coaches, and high achievers. These best practices combine evidence-based insights with real-world wisdom, offering you a tool kit to set, pursue, and achieve your most important goals with clarity and confidence.

WRITTEN GOALS

Even though the 3 percent study has been shown to be an urban myth, the research supports the main point: writing down your goals makes you more likely to achieve them.

Brian Tracy, one of the foremost authorities on personal development, is not just an expert in the field; he is also a personal friend and mentor of mine. Tracy is a strong advocate for *writing down your goals*. He argues that the act of writing crystallizes your thoughts and strengthens your commitment. Written goals serve as a constant reminder of what you are working toward and make it easier to track your progress.

When I spoke to Tracy about this book, I asked him what he thought was the most important concept in goal setting that he could share with you that would have the most impact on your life. His answer was definitive: "You must write down your most important goals in all areas of your life, every single day." He insisted this daily practice of writing and rewriting your goals keeps them in alignment with your conscious and subconscious mind, ensuring they remain at the forefront of your focus. While numerous experts agree with this practice, others suggest a slightly less demanding regime of reviewing your goals every day.

Tracy's advice is based on his decades of experience and observation. He has found that individuals who engage in this daily practice not only stay more focused but also significantly increase their chances of achieving their goals. If your goals change over time, as they naturally might, Tracy advises that you update your list immediately and continue the practice without interruption. This relentless focus on your goals, he says, is what keeps you aligned with your true purpose and drives you toward success.

THE IMPORTANCE OF CLARITY

Tracy stresses that clarity is the starting point of all success. He advises that goals must be specific, measurable, and time-bound. A vague goal, like "I want to be successful," is far less effective than a specific goal, such as "I will increase my annual income by 20 percent within the next year by securing five new clients each quarter." This level of specificity helps focus your efforts and provides a clear target to aim for.

The concept of SMART goals, a cornerstone of effective goal setting, has its roots in the management philosophy of Peter Drucker, who introduced the general idea of management by objectives in the 1950s. Drucker emphasizes the importance of specified focus, as the saying, "What gets measured gets managed" is attributed to him. The specific SMART acronym was first articulated by George T. Doran in a 1981 issue of *Management Review*. Doran proposed that goals should be Specific, Measurable, Assignable, Realistic, and Time-Related (SMART). This framework provides a clear structure for setting objectives that are well defined and achievable.

Over time, the acronym has evolved, with some variations replacing "Assignable" with "Achievable" or "Attainable" and occasionally adding "Relevant" to create SMARTER goals. The SMART criteria quickly gained traction in the business world and beyond, becoming a widely adopted tool for personal and professional development. Its enduring popularity stems from its simplicity and effectiveness in transforming vague aspirations into concrete, actionable plans. By applying the SMART criteria to goals, individuals and organizations can create a roadmap for success, ensuring that objectives are not only clear and measurable but also aligned with broader aims and realistically attainable within a specified time frame.

Michael Hyatt expands on these principles by emphasizing the importance of purposeful and intentional goal setting. In his book *Your Best Year Ever*, Hyatt advocates for setting SMARTER goals—Specific, Measurable, Actionable, Risky, Time-keyed, Exciting, and Relevant. Hyatt's approach to goal setting goes beyond merely achieving success; it's about living a life that aligns with your deepest values and aspirations. He argues that goals should not only be clear and specific but should also resonate with your passions and purpose.

Hyatt believes goals should stretch you beyond your comfort

zone; hence the inclusion of "Risky" in his SMARTER framework. He explains that taking risks is essential for growth and achievement, as it pushes you to develop new skills, overcome fears, and discover strengths you didn't know you had. "You don't grow by staying in your comfort zone."

Hyatt emphasizes the need for goals to be exciting. He suggests that goals should ignite a sense of enthusiasm and anticipation, motivating you to take consistent action toward their achievement. This excitement, Hyatt argues, is what keeps you engaged and persistent, even in the face of obstacles.

VISUALIZATION: MAKING GOALS COME ALIVE

While setting clear and specific goals is essential, the practice of visualization can significantly enhance one's ability to achieve those goals. Tracy teaches that visualization is a powerful tool for achievement. By regularly visualizing your goals as already accomplished, you program your subconscious mind to work toward making them a reality. Visualization is the process of creating a vivid mental image of what one wants to achieve, engaging all one's senses to make the experience as real as possible.

WHY VISUALIZATION WORKS

Visualization works by engaging your subconscious mind, which does not distinguish between real and imagined experiences. When you vividly imagine yourself achieving your goals, your subconscious mind treats these imagined experiences as reality. This mental rehearsal strengthens the neural pathways associated with the actions and behaviors needed to achieve your goals, making it easier to perform these actions in real life.

Visualization is more than a mental exercise—it's a scientifically supported practice that can reshape your brain and enhance your ability to achieve your goals. At its core, visualization works by engaging the brain's neural pathways, like the way physical practice does. Through neuroplasticity, the brain's ability to reorganize itself by forming new neural connections throughout life, when you visualize performing a task, your brain sends signals through the same pathways that would be activated if you were physically performing the task. This mental rehearsal effectively strengthens these pathways, making the task easier and more natural to execute in real life.

Neuroscientific studies have shown that visualization can have a tangible impact on physical performance. For example, research involving athletes who mentally rehearsed their sports performances found that they experienced improvements in actual performance that were comparable to those achieved through physical practice. This occurs because the brain does not distinguish between real and imagined actions; it treats vivid mental imagery as though the events are actually happening. This is why athletes, musicians, and even surgeons often use visualization to refine their skills and improve their performance.

To maximize the effectiveness of visualization, it's crucial to imagine your goals in the present tense, as if they are already happening. Engage all five or six senses—sight, sound, smell, touch, taste, and even the emotion associated with achieving your goal. For instance, if your goal is to deliver a powerful keynote speech, visualize yourself standing on the stage. Feel the texture of the microphone in your hand, hear the applause of the audience, see the expressions of engagement on their faces, and sense the confidence and satisfaction that comes with delivering your message effectively.

The more detailed and sensory-rich your visualization, the more real it becomes to your subconscious mind. This practice not only reinforces your commitment to your goals but also prepares your mind and body to take the necessary actions to achieve them. Visualization helps transform your goals from abstract concepts into tangible realities your subconscious mind can work toward.

Many successful leaders and high achievers have recognized the power of visualization. One such leader is Oprah Winfrey, who has often spoken about the importance of visualization in her life. Oprah believes that visualization, combined with hard work, is a key ingredient for success. She has said, "Create the highest, grandest vision possible for your life, because you become what you believe." Visualization is not just about seeing your goals but about believing in their realization.

Tony Robbins teaches that visualization helps to condition your mind and body to perform in a certain way. He often says, "Whatever you hold in your mind on a consistent basis is exactly what you will experience in your life." Robbins encourages people to use visualization to program their subconscious mind to focus on their goals, which helps to turn those goals into reality.

In the realm of sports, Michael Phelps, the most decorated Olympian of all time, with twenty-eight Olympic medals, is another powerful advocate of visualization. Phelps has shared that he visualized every single race before it happened, down to the smallest details. He would mentally rehearse the swim, seeing himself in the pool, feeling the water, and even imagining how he would respond if something went wrong. Phelps tells us, "I've always been able to think through my swims, but I started getting much more detailed. I would visualize my races from start to finish, thinking about every stroke, every turn, and even my celebration at the end." This mental preparation was a key factor in his ability to perform under pressure and achieve extraordinary success.

VISUALIZATION'S IMPACT ON BEHAVIOR AND SUCCESS

Beyond improving physical skills, visualization also plays a crucial role in shaping behavior. When you regularly visualize achieving your goals, you are essentially training your brain to recognize and prioritize opportunities that align with those goals. Visualization activates the brain's reticular activating system (RAS), a network of neurons that filters information and determines what you pay attention to. By focusing on your goals through visualization, you prime your brain to notice and seize opportunities that can help you achieve those goals.

Visualization and the RAS form a powerful synergy in goal achievement. By consistently visualizing our desired outcomes, we activate the RAS, priming it to notice relevant opportunities, resources, and information in our environment. This process heightens our awareness, aligns our subconscious mind with our objectives, boosts motivation, enhances focus, and stimulates creative problem-solving. The RAS, attuned to our visualized goals, acts as a filter, directing our attention to our *musts*, what truly matters, while screening out distractions. This creates a self-reinforcing cycle where our mind continuously works toward our aspirations, even subconsciously. Through this dynamic interplay between visualization and the RAS, we transform abstract dreams into tangible objectives, propelling us toward success with increased efficiency and purpose.

Visualization has been shown to reduce anxiety and increase confidence. When you mentally rehearse a successful outcome, you build a sense of familiarity with the process, which reduces the fear of the unknown and increases your confidence in your ability to achieve it. This is particularly important when facing high-pressure situations, such as public speaking, important meetings, or competitive sports.

HOW TO VISUALIZE EFFECTIVELY

Visualization is a powerful tool that taps into the brain's ability to shape reality through the vivid rehearsal of desired outcomes. When used with intention and consistency, visualization can significantly enhance your ability to achieve your goals, embedding your aspirations deep within your subconscious mind and guiding your actions toward their realization. To fully harness the power of visualization, it's essential to approach it with a structured and deliberate methodology. Here's how you can bring your visions to life in the most effective way.

Set a Clear Vision

The foundation of effective visualization is clarity. Begin by clearly defining what you want to achieve. The more specific and detailed your vision, the more potent your visualization will be. Ambiguity dilutes the power of visualization, as the brain needs a clear and concise image to focus on. For example, if your goal is to achieve financial independence, don't just visualize wealth in general terms. Instead, imagine the specific amount of money you wish to earn, the investments you will make, the financial decisions you will take, and the lifestyle you will lead. The clearer your vision, the stronger the impact on your subconscious mind and the more likely you are to recognize and act upon opportunities that align with this vision.

Engage All Senses

To deepen the impact of your visualization, don't just see your goal—experience it. Engage all your senses to make the visualization as vivid and real as possible. Imagine what your goal looks like in detail, what sounds you hear as you achieve it, what sensations you feel, and even what it smells and tastes like. For example, if you are visualizing achieving a long-distance run, imagine the crisp morning air filling your lungs, the steady rhythm of your feet striking the pavement, the scent of fresh-cut grass and blooming flowers, the taste of cool water as you hydrate, and the exhilarating wave of accomplishment as you cross the finish line. This multisensory approach makes the visualization more immersive, thereby reinforcing the belief in its eventual realization. Author and motivational speaker Simon Sinek reminds us, "The clearer your vision, the easier it is to create it."

Visualize in the Present Tense

One of the most effective techniques in visualization is to picture your goal as if it has already been achieved. Visualizing in the present tense tricks your brain into thinking the event is happening now, which can significantly boost your confidence and motivation. For instance, if you are working toward becoming a successful entrepreneur, visualize yourself running a thriving business, interacting with satisfied clients, and celebrating business milestones. This technique convinces your brain that success is not a distant possibility but a present reality, thereby aligning your thoughts and actions with the achievement of your goals.

Repetition Is Key

Consistency is the cornerstone of effective visualization. The more frequently you visualize your goals, the more ingrained these images become in your subconscious mind. Set aside dedicated time each day to practice visualization, making it a *must* nonnegotiable part of your routine. Over time, these repeated mental images become powerful motivators that guide your behavior and decision-making processes. Just as physical practice hones a skill, regular visualization conditions your mind to focus relentlessly on your goals, making them an integral part of your everyday consciousness.

Pair Visualization with Affirmation

To further reinforce the effectiveness of your visualization, pair it with positive affirmations—statements that reflect your belief in your ability to achieve your goals. Affirmations serve as powerful reminders of your capabilities and commitment, helping to override any negative thoughts or doubts that might arise. For example, if you're visualizing a successful business presentation, you might affirm, "I am a confident and persuasive speaker." This combination of visualization and affirmation creates a synergistic effect, embedding your goals deeper into your subconscious and fortifying your resolve to achieve them.

Carli Lloyd, former US women's soccer midfielder, exemplifies the power of visualization and affirmations in achieving athletic greatness. Her remarkable performance in the 2015 FIFA Women's World

Cup final, when she scored a hat trick in just sixteen minutes, was a direct result of her mental preparation. Lloyd's dedication to these techniques is evident in her statement, "I've basically visualized so many different things on the field, making these big plays, scoring goals...I've envisioned playing in a World Cup final and visualized scoring four goals." This powerful combination of mental imagery and positive self-talk, coupled with her rigorous physical training, enabled Lloyd to turn her visualizations and affirmations into reality on soccer's biggest stage, demonstrating the profound impact these mental techniques can have on athletic performance.

Incorporating a Vision Board

One of the most effective tools for enhancing your visualization practice is a vision board. A vision board is a physical or digital collage of images, words, and phrases that represent your goals and aspirations. Creating a vision board allows you to bring your goals to life in a tangible way, making them more concrete and compelling.

To create a vision board, gather images and words that resonate with your goals in various areas of your Circle of Life, such as health, career, relationships, finances, spirituality, and contribution. Arrange these images on a board or a digital platform in a way that feels inspiring to you. Place your vision board in a location where you will see it daily, such as your office, bedroom, or even as the wallpaper on your computer or phone.

Steve Harvey, the renowned comedian, television host, and motivational speaker, is a passionate advocate for the power of vision boards. His journey from homelessness to becoming a household name is a testament to the effectiveness of this visualization technique. Harvey's unwavering belief in vision boards stems from his personal experiences and the transformative impact they've had on his life. "Everything I've ever gotten in life, I've written," Harvey emphasizes, highlighting the crucial link between putting your dreams on paper and manifesting them in reality. This practice aligns with the biblical principle he often quotes, "Write the vision and make it plain" (Habakkuk 2:2 KJV). By consistently writing down his goals and aspirations, Harvey has turned seemingly impossible dreams into tangible achievements.

Harvey's enthusiasm for vision boards encourages others when he offers a glimpse into the magnitude of his ambitions and the limitless potential he sees for his future. As you grow and succeed, your goals and visions should evolve to match your new circumstances and aspirations. Perhaps most inspiring is Harvey's unwavering confidence in the process. He demonstrates the kind of unshakable belief that is crucial for turning visions into reality. This mindset, coupled with the tangible reminder of his goals that a vision board provides, creates a powerful formula for success.

In my life, a few years ago, over the course of a week, I embarked on creating a vision board, carefully selecting and cutting out images from magazines and online sources that resonated with my aspirations. I pasted these onto a board purchased from a local drugstore, assembling a visual representation of my dreams. The board featured the beautiful home I imagined, the precise car I aspired to own, a photo symbolizing the relationship I wanted to maintain and enhance with my fiancée, and various other aspects of my life, both material and nonmaterial. I placed this vision board in my office, where I saw it every day for just over a year. Astonishingly, a little more than a year after creating this collage of dreams, I was amazed to discover how many of these items had materialized in my life. I was able to continue to work very hard, purchase our dream home, acquire the exact car I had envisioned, and enjoy the ongoing extraordinary relationship with the love of my life. Many other visualized elements had also become reality. This experience has solidified my belief in the remarkable power of vision boards, visualization, and affirmations in shaping one's life. I will never doubt their wondrous value.

In fact, one of the main focal points on my present vision board is the cover of my book *Must: Becoming the Person You Are Meant to Be*. Adjacent to the book cover image is a carefully crafted representation of the *New York Times* Best Seller list, prominently featuring my book's title. Complementing these aspirational images is a photograph capturing my ongoing journey as a keynote speaker, personal coach, and counselor to numerous beautiful souls seeking guidance on their individual paths to enlightenment. This vision board serves as a daily reminder of my goals and the impact I hope to make. The juxtaposition of these elements—the book, the bestseller status, and my role as a guide—creates a powerful visual narrative of my present and future aspirations. It's a testament to the dreams I hold dear and the lives I hope to touch through my work.

Interestingly, you, my friend, are indirectly present on this vision board. Your journey, along with those of countless others I aim to reach, is represented in the imagery of my speaking engagements and coaching sessions. This visual representation fuels my determination to transform these aspirations into reality.

Regularly spending time with your vision board—studying the images, reflecting on your goals, and visualizing yourself achieving them—can reinforce your commitment and keep your goals at the forefront of your mind. This practice not only enhances your motivation but also increases the likelihood of taking actions that align with your goals.

THE POWER OF AFFIRMATIONS: FROM SATIRE TO SCIENCE

Affirmations have become a well-known tool in the world of self-improvement, often associated with the practice of repeating positive statements to oneself to foster a sense of confidence and purpose. However, they are not without their critics and have even been the subject of satire. One of the most famous examples comes from the iconic *Saturday Night Live* skit featuring Stuart Smalley, a character played by Al Franken. In this skit, Stuart, a self-help guru with a penchant for over-the-top positivity, looks in the mirror and recites his now-famous affirmation: "I'm good enough, I'm smart enough, and doggone it, people like me!" The skit humorously exaggerates the practice of affirmations, portraying Stuart as somewhat out of touch with reality yet clinging to his positive mantras in the face of life's challenges.

While the skit is undeniably funny and highlights some of the potential absurdities in self-help culture, it also raises a valid question: Do affirmations actually work? Are they merely feel-good statements, or can they truly play a role in helping us achieve our goals?

THE SCIENCE BEHIND AFFIRMATIONS

When used correctly, affirmations are more than just positive thinking—they are tools that can rewire the brain to reinforce certain beliefs and behaviors. The practice of using affirmations is rooted in cognitive behavioral therapy (CBT), a well-established psychological approach that helps individuals change unhelpful patterns of thought and behavior. The basic premise of affirmations is that by regularly repeating positive statements, we can influence our subconscious mind, which in turn shapes our actions and decisions.

Through neuroplasticity, when you repeatedly focus on a specific thought, such as an affirmation, you strengthen the neural pathways associated with that thought. Over time, this can lead to changes in your mindset and behavior. For example, if you frequently affirm, "I am confident and capable," you may start to internalize this belief, leading yourself to take actions that align with greater confidence and capability.

Research in psychology supports the effectiveness of affirmations, particularly when they are used to combat negative self-talk or to reinforce positive behavioral changes. Studies have shown that affirmations can reduce stress, increase resilience, and improve performance in various tasks. For instance, a study published in the journal *Social Cognitive and Affective Neuroscience* found that affirmations activate the brain's reward centers, much like other positive experiences, suggesting that they can indeed influence our emotional state and motivation.

However, for affirmations to be effective, they need to be realistic and believable. The brain is less likely to accept an affirmation that feels blatantly untrue, such as "I am a millionaire" when you are struggling financially. Instead, affirmations should be grounded in reality, focusing on qualities or behaviors you can genuinely develop or improve. For example, rather than affirming "I am rich," a more effective affirmation might be "I am taking steps every day to improve my financial situation and wealth."

HOW TO USE AFFIRMATIONS EFFECTIVELY

To maximize the impact of affirmations in your goal-setting process, it's important to use them thoughtfully and consistently. Here are some guidelines for creating and using affirmations effectively:

1. **Be Specific and Positive:** Your affirmations should be specific and positive. Instead of saying, "I won't fail," say, "I am capable of succeeding in this task." This shifts the focus from avoiding failure to achieving success.
2. **Align with Your Values and Goals:** Your affirmations should resonate with your core values and be aligned with your long-term goals. This ensures they are meaningful and motivating. For example, if one of your Must Core Values is personal growth, an affirmation might be "I am continuously learning and improving every day."
3. **Use the Present Tense:** Phrase your affirmations as if the desired outcome is already happening. This helps train your brain to believe in the reality of affirmation, thereby influencing your actions. For example, say, "I am confident in my abilities" rather than "I will become confident."
4. **Repetition Is Crucial:** Like visualization, affirmations require consistency. Repeating your affirmations daily, ideally at the same time each day, helps reinforce the message to your subconscious mind. Over time, these repeated statements can lead to real shifts in your mindset and behavior.

5. **Pair with Visualization:** For even greater impact, combine affirmations with visualization. As you say your affirmation, close your eyes and visualize yourself embodying the statement. If your affirmation is "I am a successful leader," imagine yourself in a leadership role, confidently guiding your team and achieving your goals.

PERSISTENT ACTION: REPEAT, REVISE, REFINE

Tracy asserts that the key to achieving any goal is a consistent daily action. He encourages setting aside time each day to work on your most important goals, no matter how small the step. This persistent effort, compounded over time, leads to significant results. Tracy reminds us that obstacles and setbacks are inevitable, but persistence is what separates those who achieve their goals from those who do not.

It's essential to recognize that setting goals is only the first step in achieving success. The real challenge lies in creating a plan to achieve those goals and maintaining the momentum needed to see them through to completion. This is where persistent action comes into play—a crucial process that involves not only setting goals but also consistently revisiting and refining them as progress is made. By embracing this mindset, you ensure that your goals remain aligned with your evolving aspirations and that every step you take moves you closer to realizing your vision.

In this final part of our goal-setting journey, we will delve into the strategies that make persistent action effective. This includes reverse engineering your goals to break them down into manageable steps, setting micro goals that provide immediate motivation and feedback, and establishing stretch goals that challenge you to grow beyond your current limits. By integrating these techniques into your goal-achieving process, you create a dynamic framework that adapts to your growth and ensures that every effort you make is purposeful and impactful. This approach transforms goal setting from a static exercise into a living, breathing process that propels you toward your highest potential.

REVERSE ENGINEERING YOUR GOALS

Setting ambitious goals is the first step, but achieving them requires a clear, actionable plan. This is where reverse engineering comes into play—taking your end goal and breaking it down into the smallest, most manageable increments. This process transforms daunting objectives into bite-sized tasks that are within your perceived reach, making the journey toward your goal not only achievable but also sustainable.

Begin with the end in mind. Visualize your goal as if it's already accomplished. Then work backward from that point, identifying the key milestones that need to be reached along the way. Break these milestones down further into smaller tasks and continue this process until you have a clear list of specific actions that you can start taking immediately.

For example, if your goal is to launch a successful online business within a year, you might start by visualizing your fully operational business. Then reverse engineer the steps needed to get there: developing a business plan, building a website, creating a marketing strategy, sourcing products, and so on. Each of these steps can be broken down further into daily or weekly tasks, such as researching competitors, writing content, or designing product packaging.

By breaking your goal into small, actionable steps, you make the process less overwhelming and more manageable. These bite-sized chunks are easier to tackle on a daily basis, allowing you to maintain momentum and stay motivated. As you complete each small task, you gain confidence and build the necessary skills to take on the next challenge.

To effectively reverse engineer the goal of losing twenty pounds of unwanted weight within twelve months, you can break down the journey into manageable steps, making the goal feel more achievable. First, start by defining the end goal clearly: losing twenty pounds in a year translates to approximately 1.67 pounds per month or about 0.4 pounds per week. This realistic target helps to alleviate the pressure of an overwhelming goal.

Next, identify specific activities that contribute to this weight loss. For instance, one could aim to exercise for at least 150 minutes per week, which can be chunked into manageable sessions, such as thirty minutes of brisk walking five times a week. Additionally, incorporating strength training exercises twice a week can further support weight loss and muscle maintenance.

In terms of dietary changes, set smaller, actionable goals, such as reducing daily caloric intake by 500 calories or increasing vegetable intake to at least five servings per day. Meal planning and preparation can also be broken down into weekly tasks, such as dedicating Sundays to plan and prep healthy meals for the week ahead. This example of reverse engineering and breaking down tasks into bite-sized chunks can be applied in all areas of your life.

Tracking progress is essential for maintaining motivation and accountability. Consider using a journal or an app to log daily food intake and exercise, allowing for regular reflection on achievements and adjustments as needed.

By chunking down these activities into specific, actionable steps and setting regular check-ins, such as monthly weigh-ins or progress photos, this approach not only makes the example goal of losing twenty pounds feel more attainable but also instills a sense of accomplishment and celebration along the way. Ultimately, this structured method empowers individuals to take control of their goals and turn them into future outcomes.

To ensure these small steps lead to your desired outcome, it's crucial to apply your Must Actions—those nonnegotiable tasks that align with your Must Values and Standards. Must Actions are the deliberate and focused efforts that drive you forward, even when challenges arise. By consistently applying Must Actions to your daily tasks, you create a strong foundation for achieving your goals.

For instance, if one of your Must Values is excellence, your Must Actions might include dedicating time each day to refine your skills, seeking feedback from mentors, and continuously improving your work. These actions, applied consistently to the tasks you've reverse engineered, ensure that every step you take is purposeful and aligned with your highest standards.

THE USE OF MICRO GOALS

While reverse engineering provides a roadmap to success, micro goals serve as the stepping stones along the way. Micro goals are small, manageable steps that lead you toward your larger objectives. They provide a clear path forward, making the seemingly overwhelming journey to achieving your goals more accessible.

For example, if your goal is to write a book, the process can seem daunting. However, by setting a micro goal of writing 500 words a day, the task becomes more manageable. Each day's accomplishment builds momentum, and over time, these small daily efforts culminate in the completion of your book. Micro goals also offer frequent opportunities to experience success, which reinforces your motivation and keeps you moving forward.

The beauty of micro goals lies in their ability to create a sense of progress and achievement on a regular basis. Each micro goal you accomplish serves as a building block toward your larger goals, providing a sense of forward motion and satisfaction that keeps you engaged in the process.

THE POWER OF STRETCH GOALS

While micro goals help manage daily progress, stretch goals push you beyond your current capabilities, challenging you to reach new heights. Stretch goals are ambitious targets that force you to be in your Must Zone and think creatively about how to achieve them. They are designed to stretch your abilities, requiring you to develop new skills, adopt innovative strategies, and take calculated risks.

For instance, a business leader might set a stretch goal to double the company's revenue in a year. This goal is intentionally challenging and requires the leader and their team to think beyond the usual strategies, explore new markets, and innovate in ways they haven't before. While achieving a stretch goal may seem daunting, even if you don't fully achieve it, the effort required to pursue it often leads to substantial growth and progress.

Stretch goals are powerful because they encourage you to break through perceived limitations. They challenge you to think bigger, act bolder, and embrace the possibility of achieving what once seemed impossible. By setting and pursuing stretch goals, you create opportunities for significant personal and professional growth. Billionaire Richard Branson reminds us, "If your dreams don't scare you, they are too small."

NAVIGATING THE OBSTACLES: COMMON PITFALLS IN GOAL SETTING

Goal setting is an invaluable tool for achieving personal and professional growth, offering a clear roadmap toward success. However, the journey from setting a goal to achieving it is rarely straightforward. It is filled with challenges and potential pitfalls that can derail even the most well-intentioned plans. Recognizing and addressing these pitfalls is essential for maintaining momentum and ensuring that your goals remain achievable and relevant. Let's explore some of the most common obstacles and how to navigate them effectively.

VAGUE GOALS: THE TRAP OF AMBIGUITY

One of the most prevalent mistakes in goal setting is setting goals that are too vague. While well-meaning goals like "be healthier" or "be successful" may be appropriate, they lack the specificity needed to turn aspirations into reality. When goals are not clearly defined, they become difficult to measure, and without measurable progress, it's easy to lose motivation and direction.

To avoid this pitfall, it's crucial to set goals that meet the SMART or SMARTER goal-setting criteria. For example, instead of setting a goal to "be healthier," you might aim to "exercise for thirty minutes, five days a week" or "reduce sugar intake by 50 percent over the next three months." These goals provide clear targets to aim for, making it easier to track your progress and stay focused on the steps needed to achieve them.

Specificity not only clarifies what success looks like but also helps you identify the actions required to reach your goal. It breaks down an abstract desire into concrete steps, making the journey more manageable and less overwhelming.

LACK OF FLEXIBILITY: THE RIGIDITY DILEMMA

While determination and commitment to your goals are important, so is the ability to adapt when circumstances change. Life is inherently unpredictable, and unforeseen events—whether they are personal challenges, shifts in priorities, or external factors—can render your original goals less relevant or even unattainable. Rigidly adhering to a goal without considering these changes can lead to frustration, burnout, and a sense of failure.

Flexibility in goal setting is not about abandoning your objectives but rather about being willing to modify them as necessary. Regularly reviewing your goals allows you to assess their relevance in light of your current circumstances. If a goal needs to be adjusted, refined, or even replaced, embracing this change can keep you on track toward your broader life purpose.

Consider flexibility a strength, not a weakness. It's about being resilient and responsive, ensuring that your goals evolve alongside you. This adaptability not only helps you stay aligned with your values and purpose but also keeps your journey dynamic and responsive to life's changes.

OVEREMPHASIS ON OUTCOMES

A common trap in goal setting is focusing too much on the result at the expense of the process. While it's natural to be motivated by the outcome—whether it's achieving a promotion, reaching a financial milestone, or completing a project—this singular focus can lead to frustration, particularly if progress is slower than expected or if setbacks occur.

The danger of an outcome-centric approach is that it can make you blind to the importance of the journey itself. When the emphasis is solely on the destination, the daily actions and habits that lead to that outcome can feel like burdens rather than opportunities for growth.

To counter this, shift your focus from purely the result to the process—the small, consistent steps you take every day that bring you closer to your goal. Celebrate the small wins along the way, as these are the building blocks of long-term success. Embracing the process helps maintain motivation, even when the goal seems distant, and it fosters a growth mindset where learning from setbacks becomes part of the journey.

BRAINSTORMING AND DOWNLOADING YOUR WILDEST DREAMS

Now that we've explored the importance and benefits of goal setting, it's time to dive into the creative process of brainstorming and downloading your wildest dreams onto paper. This exercise is about giving yourself permission to dream big and explore all the possibilities that life has to offer.

Begin by setting aside time in a quiet, uninterrupted space. Take out a blank piece of paper or open a new document on your computer and start writing about everything you've ever wanted to achieve, experience, or become in all aspects of your life. Don't limit yourself by thinking about what's realistic or achievable—this is a space for pure imagination and aspiration.

Consider all areas of your life—career, relationships, health, personal growth, spirituality, travel, hobbies, and more. What things have you always wanted to do but never had the chance to do? What are the experiences that would bring you joy and fulfillment? What legacy do you want to leave behind?

Once you've written down all your ideas, begin the process of categorizing and prioritizing them. Group similar dreams together and look for patterns or themes that emerge. This helps to organize your thoughts and identify the goals that resonate most deeply with you.

Next, prioritize these dreams based on their alignment with your core beliefs, values, standards, and purpose(s). Which of these aspirations align with who you are and the life you want to live? Which goals will bring you the most fulfillment and help you achieve your long-term vision?

This process of brainstorming, categorizing, and prioritizing transforms your wildest dreams into a structured list of Must Goals that are meaningful, inspiring, and aligned with your authentic self.

REFLECTION AND PERSONAL INTEGRATION

I invite you to reflect on how you can harness the power of goal setting in every area of your life. Are your goals clear, intentional, and aligned with your Must Core Values and Purpose? Have you taken the time to visualize your success and mentally prepare for the challenges you may face? Have you given yourself permission to dream big and set goals that inspire and excite you?

Remember, goal setting is not just about achieving success in one area of life. It's about creating a balanced, fulfilling life that reflects your true potential. By setting goals in your career, relationships, mental health, personal growth, and beyond, you are taking control of your future and shaping it according to your highest aspirations. Become one of the 3 percent of the world that have purpose-driven written goals, which have been scientifically proven to dramatically enhance your chances of success in life.

In the words of my friend Brian Tracy, "Your ability to set goals is the master skill of success." Let this chapter be a catalyst for you to harness that ability, shaping the life you are meant to live. Embrace the power of goal setting, visualization, affirmations, and persistent action with the dedication and discipline they deserve and watch as your life transforms in ways you never thought possible.

CHAPTER 12

Time Management and Productivity

"Time management is about life management."
—Robin Sharma, author of *The Monk Who Sold His Ferrari* and *The 5 AM Club*

For years, I prided myself on being a "go with the flow" attorney, thriving on the adrenaline of living in the moment. My approach to law was akin to a jazz improvisation—spontaneous and creative, with each case unfolding like a unique melody. I believed that structure and rigid scheduling were for the mathematically inclined, not for a creative legal mind like mine. This approach allowed me to focus on what truly mattered: the nuances of each case, the emotional depth of my clients' stories, and the thrill of finding innovative solutions.

However, as my law practice grew and responsibilities multiplied, I found myself overwhelmed and struggling to maintain a work-life balance. The once-manageable chaos began to feel like a maelstrom, pulling me under with each new case and client. I realized that without proper time management, I was losing sight of my *must* priorities—

the very things that defined my purpose and drove my success. It was as if I were trying to navigate a dense forest without a compass, unsure which path led to my true north.

Initially, I was reluctant to explore time management techniques and productivity systems. They seemed constraining and unnatural, like trying to fit a wild bird into a cage. However, as I began to implement these strategies, I noticed a remarkable transformation. My days became more structured, my work more focused, and I had more free time than ever before. By prioritizing tasks, eliminating time wasters, and creating efficient systems, I gained control over my schedule. This newfound control allowed me to dedicate more energy to high-value activities and meaningful personal pursuits—my true *musts*.

The shift in perspective was profound. It led to an improved quality of life, reduced stress, and greater success in my thriving law firm. I was no longer just a "go with the flow" attorney; I was a master navigator, charting my course through the complexities of law and life with clarity and purpose. My journey taught me that embracing structure wasn't about losing creativity; it was about harnessing it to achieve more than I ever thought possible. As I looked back on the transformation, I realized that sometimes the most powerful tool for success is not spontaneity, but strategy.

I discovered that effective time management isn't about rigid control, but about harnessing time to work in your favor. It's about ensuring we allocate our precious time to what truly matters—our *musts*. Time management and productivity tools became my compass, guiding me toward what was truly important in my life and career.

Our purpose-driven Must Goals provide us with direction and clarify our priorities. Now it is time to shift our focus to the execution of the Must Actions necessary to achieve these meaningful goals. To bring these actions to life, we must master the effective use and allocation of our time. This requires us to cultivate strong time management skills and establish the productivity habits essential for implementation. By aligning our time with our purpose, we can create the momentum needed to turn our aspirations into reality.

Mastering time management and productivity is crucial in the quest for self-improvement. I'm excited to help you unlock the potential of effective time management, guiding you to identify your *musts* and create a system that allows you to focus on what truly matters. Remember, the goal is to ensure your productivity aligns with your most important priorities.

Effective time management and enhanced productivity allow us to make the most of our time, achieve our goals, and maintain a healthy work-life balance. By learning to prioritize tasks, eliminate distractions, and leverage productivity techniques, you can transform your life and reach your full potential.

THE IMPORTANCE OF TIME MANAGEMENT

Time is our most valuable resource, and how we use it determines the *quality* and success of our lives. Effective time management allows us to make the most of our time, achieve our goals, and maintain a healthy work-life balance. Benjamin Franklin wisely said, "Lost time is never found again." This emphasizes the need to be intentional with our time, ensuring each moment is spent in pursuit of our goals and purpose.

Imagine for a moment that time is like a river. It flows continuously, and you cannot stop it. You can only decide how to navigate its currents. Are you drifting aimlessly, or are you steering your life toward meaningful destinations? Effective time management and productivity skills are the tools that allow you to take control of your journey, ensuring that you spend your days achieving what truly matters to you.

To truly harness the power of time management, you must engage with your time intentionally. This means making conscious decisions about how you spend your hours and minutes and aligning your daily actions with your long-term goals and values. Ask yourself, "Are my daily activities bringing me closer to my purpose, or are they merely filling time?"

Consider the difference between a day spent reacting to urgent demands and a day spent proactively working toward your goals. The former leaves you feeling exhausted and unfulfilled, while the latter brings a sense of accomplishment and progress. By being intentional with your time, you can ensure that each day contributes to your overall purpose and well-being.

Tim Ferriss, the *New York Times* bestselling author of *The 4-Hour Workweek*, has revolutionized the way many people think about time management, productivity, and personal freedom. His approach challenges traditional notions of work and lifestyle, emphasizing efficiency and effectiveness over mere busyness. Ferriss introduces the DEAL framework to achieve what he calls "lifestyle design." This framework aligns closely with the *must* principles, as it encourages individuals to take decisive action in shaping their lives. The acronym DEAL begins with Defining one's ideal lifestyle and goals, a crucial step that resonates with the *must* concept of identifying what truly matters. The Elimination phase urges people to remove unnecessary tasks and distractions, much like the *must* focus on prioritizing essential actions. Automation involves implementing systems to handle routine tasks, freeing up time and energy for *must* priorities. Finally, the Liberation stage empowers individuals to break free from traditional work constraints, embodying the Must Mindset of pursuing what's truly important without compromise.

Through this systematic approach, Ferriss challenges readers to reimagine their relationship with work and personal time, offering a roadmap to create a life that aligns more closely with their deepest aspirations and values. His methodology has inspired countless individuals to pursue alternative career paths, embrace entrepreneurship, and prioritize experiences over conventional measures of success, all of which resonate strongly with the transformative power of the *must* principles.

Tim Ferriss advocates for a transformative approach to work and life centered on maximizing efficiency and personal fulfillment. At the core of his philosophy is the concept of "selective ignorance," which encourages individuals to curate their information intake, focusing solely on what's relevant and actionable. This principle aligns with his broader vision of streamlining life to create more time for meaningful pursuits.

Ferriss's practical applications are designed to revolutionize daily routines and work habits.

WHAT TIME DO YOU GET UP?

Rising early in the morning, before most people are awake, offers numerous advantages that can significantly enhance your daily life. This quiet time allows for increased productivity, as you can tackle important tasks without distractions. It provides an opportunity for self-care activities like exercise, meditation, or enjoying a leisurely breakfast, which can improve both physical and mental well-being. Early risers often report reduced stress levels and improved mood throughout the day.

Additionally, waking up early can help regulate your body's natural circadian rhythm, leading to better sleep quality at night. The extra time in the morning also allows for a more relaxed start to the day, reducing the rush and anxiety often associated with hectic mornings. Whether you use this time for personal growth, planning your day, or simply enjoying tranquility, the benefits of early rising can have a profound impact on your overall quality of life. I remember my grandmother often quoting Benjamin Franklin, who also said, "Early to bed and early to rise makes a man healthy, wealthy, and wise."

The science behind early rising paints a compelling picture of its potential benefits for success and well-being. It appears that Benjamin Franklin was correct. Harvard biologist Dr. Christoph Randler's research reveals that early birds tend to be more proactive, a trait strongly linked to better academic performance, enhanced career prospects, and superior problem-solving abilities. This proactive mindset can be a catalyst for increased productivity and success across various life domains. The early morning hours offer a unique window of opportunity for focused work and creative endeavors, free from the usual distractions that populate our busy days. Dr. Randler proclaims in the *Harvard Business Review* that "when it comes to business success, morning people hold the important cards. My earlier research showed that they tend to get better grades in school, which get them into better colleges, which then lead to better job opportunities. Morning people also anticipate problems and try to minimize them. They're proactive...A number of studies have linked this trait [of getting up early], proactivity, with better job performance, greater career success, and higher wages."

Beyond productivity, early rising may also contribute to improved mental health and overall well-being. A comprehensive genomic study suggests that individuals genetically predisposed to early rising may experience greater well-being and a reduced risk of certain mental health conditions. This finding is complemented by research from the University of Westminster, which found that early risers tend to have higher cortisol levels upon waking, potentially contributing to increased alertness and energy to tackle the day ahead. These scientific insights underscore the potential of early rising as a powerful tool for personal and professional growth, offering a compelling reason to consider embracing the early morning hours as a pathway to achieving our *musts* in life, enhanced productivity, creativity, and overall life satisfaction.

New York Times bestselling author Hal Elrod of *The Miracle Morning: The Not-So-Obvious Secret Guaranteed to Transform Your Life (Before 8AM)* introduced me to the splendor and advantages of getting up early. I was not a "morning person." In fact, I was the furthest thing from it. That was until I was introduced to Hal Elrod's Miracle Morning concept.

Elrod's journey to discovering the Miracle Morning concept is a testament to human resilience and the power of personal transformation. At the age of twenty, Hal's life took a devastating turn when he was hit head-on by a drunk driver at over seventy miles per hour. The accident left him clinically dead for six minutes, broke eleven bones, and caused permanent brain damage. Doctors told him he would never walk again.

Despite this grim prognosis, Elrod defied the odds and not only learned to walk but went on to run an ultramarathon and become a hall-of-fame business achiever. However, Hal's challenges were far from over. At age thirty-seven, he faced another life-threatening situation when his heart, lungs, and kidneys began failing and he was diagnosed with a rare, aggressive form of cancer. Given only a 20 percent chance of survival, Elrod once again overcame seemingly insurmountable odds. It was during these periods of extreme adversity that Elrod developed and refined the concepts that would become *The Miracle Morning*. Desperate to turn his life around, he realized he needed to commit to a daily personal development ritual to become the person he needed to be. This realization led to the birth of the Miracle Morning routine, which has since transformed millions of lives worldwide.

Elrod's Miracle Morning concept centers on the transformative power of a structured morning routine to enhance personal development and overall life success. At its core, *The Miracle Morning* is built around six key practices, known by the acronym SAVERS: Silence (meditation or prayer), Affirmations, Visualization, Exercise, Reading, and Scribing (journaling). Elrod advocates dedicating the first hour of each day to these activities, believing that this intentional start sets the tone for a more productive, fulfilling day.

The essence of the Miracle Morning lies in its ability to create a daily space for self-improvement and reflection regardless of one's circumstances. Elrod found that by consistently practicing these morning rituals, individuals can cultivate a growth mindset, increase their motivation, and make significant progress toward their goals. The Miracle Morning is not just about early rising; it's about making a committed investment in oneself each day, fostering personal growth, and creating a positive ripple effect that extends into all areas of life.

Elrod is not the only expert to advocate for a structured morning routine. Tim Ferriss also emphasizes the importance of a structured morning routine, incorporating practices like meditation and goal setting to set a positive tone for the day.

The Miracle Morning concept resonates profoundly with the *must* principles explored in this book, offering a sacred window of opportunity at the dawn of each day. In these precious moments, as the world awakens, we can align our hearts and minds with our deepest aspirations and most cherished values. By embracing this intentional practice, we set the stage for a day infused with purpose and meaning. As we greet the morning light, we illuminate the path to our true potential, focusing our energy on what truly matters. This daily ritual becomes a powerful catalyst for transformation, enabling us to sculpt our lives with intention and grace, one sunrise at a time. In the quiet of these early hours, we nurture the seeds of our *musts*, allowing them to blossom into the beautiful reality we are destined to create.

THE BENEFITS OF STRUCTURED PRODUCTIVITY

As we explore the transformative power of starting our day with intention, we see how these early morning rituals can set the stage for a day of purpose and productivity. However, the true magic happens when we integrate these practices into a broader framework of structured productivity and work-life balance. By prioritizing our time and focusing on high-value activities, we can create a life that is not just efficient but also deeply fulfilling.

As we transition into the realm of work-life balance, we find that structured productivity becomes the foundation upon which we build a harmonious and successful existence. This journey from morning mindfulness to a life of purposeful action is a testament to the idea that our daily habits are the building blocks of our long-term success and happiness. By embracing structured productivity, we ensure that every moment counts, leading to a more balanced and satisfying life that aligns with our core values and aspirations. Structured productivity brings greater control and clarity into your life. When you have a clear plan for how to spend your time, you eliminate the chaos and stress that comes with disorganization. Structured productivity means you are intentional about your actions, which leads to more effective and efficient use of your time.

With structured productivity, you gain clarity, knowing what needs to be done and when, allowing you to focus on the task at hand without being overwhelmed by a never-ending to-do list. You gain control by planning and organizing your time, reducing the feeling of being at the mercy of external demands. Structured productivity ensures that you are working on high-priority tasks, maximizing your output, and achieving more in less time. Additionally, proper time management helps you allocate time for work, rest, and personal activities, leading to a more balanced and fulfilling life.

PRIORITIZING TASKS: THE EISENHOWER MATRIX

Dwight D. Eisenhower, the thirty-fourth President of the United States and a five-star general during World War II, laid the foundation for what would become known as the Eisenhower Matrix. In a 1954 speech, Eisenhower referenced a concept that would later inspire this decision-making tool. He quoted a former, unnamed university president, saying, "I have two kinds of problems, the urgent and the important. The urgent are not important, and the important are never urgent." This insight into task prioritization reflected Eisenhower's approach to managing his numerous responsibilities as a military leader and president.

While Eisenhower did not create the matrix in its current form, his philosophy on distinguishing between urgent and important tasks became the cornerstone of this time-management principle. It was later developed into the four-quadrant matrix by productivity experts, most notably popularized by Stephen Covey in his book *The 7 Habits of Highly Effective People*, where it gained widespread recognition and was later referenced as the Eisenhower Matrix.

The Eisenhower Matrix categorizes tasks based on urgency and importance:

1. **Important and Urgent:** Tasks that must be done immediately
2. **Important but Not Urgent:** Tasks that are important for your goals but do not require immediate action

3. **Not Important but Urgent:** Tasks that require immediate attention but are not crucial to your goals
4. **Not Important and Not Urgent:** Tasks that can be delegated or eliminated

Using this matrix helps focus energy on what truly matters, ensuring time is spent on high-impact activities while delegating or discarding distractions. Applying this principle reveals that our *musts*—the actions essential to our success—fall into the "Important and Urgent" category. By prioritizing these *musts*, we align our time with what drives us toward our goals, avoiding the trap of urgent but trivial tasks.

This framework is more than theoretical—it has profound practical implications. By consistently categorizing tasks, you can enhance productivity in areas that count most, delegate nonessential work, and free up mental space for meaningful pursuits. In doing so, you empower yourself to focus on what truly matters, propelling you toward a life of purpose and fulfillment.

THE 80/20 RULE: MAXIMIZING EFFICIENCY

Joseph M. Juran was a Romanian-born American engineer and management consultant who became one of the most influential figures in quality management. Born in 1904, Juran had a career that spanned over seven decades, during which he made significant contributions to the field of quality control and management theory.

Juran's background in electrical engineering and statistics led him to work at Western Electric's Hawthorne Works, where he was exposed to early quality control techniques. His experiences there, combined with his later work during World War II, shaped his understanding of quality management and its importance in organizational success.

One of Juran's most significant contributions to quality management was his application of the Pareto principle, also known as the 80/20 rule. This principle, originally observed by Italian economist

Vilfredo Pareto in 1896, states that roughly 80 percent of effects come from 20 percent of causes. Pareto initially noted this distribution in land ownership in Italy, where 80 percent of the land was owned by 20 percent of the population. Juran adapted this concept to quality issues, coining the phrase "the vital few and the trivial many." He recognized that this principle could be applied to various aspects of life and business, not just economics. Richard Koch, author of *The 80/20 Principle*, further elaborated on this concept, explaining that "a minority of causes, inputs, or effort usually led to a majority of the results, outputs, or rewards." Juran's insight into applying this principle to quality management revolutionized the field, helping organizations focus their efforts on the most critical issues that would yield the greatest improvements in quality.

The 80/20 rule emphasizes that 80 percent of your results come from 20 percent of your efforts. This principle helps you work smarter, not harder, by prioritizing high-impact activities. Identify the tasks and activities that generate the most significant results and focus your energy on them. This principle is not a strict mathematical law but more of a rule of thumb that highlights the frequent imbalance between inputs and output in life. The Pareto principle is a very useful tool for prioritization and analysis.

For instance, if you're an entrepreneur, you might find that a small portion of your clients generate most of your revenue. Focus on nurturing these key relationships and streamlining processes that serve them. Apply this rule to all areas of your life, ensuring that your efforts are directed toward activities that yield the highest returns.

Applying the 80/20 principle to personal growth means identifying the few key activities, skills, or areas of focus that bring the greatest joy, fulfillment, and progress toward our goals. By homing in on the passions and talents that resonate most deeply with us, we can channel our energy into what truly matters rather than spreading ourselves thin across less impactful pursuits. This alignment not only accelerates growth but also fosters a sense of purpose and clarity.

In the context of following one's passions, the Pareto principle aligns seamlessly with the *must* principles discussed in this book. It encourages us to prioritize our *musts*—those nonnegotiable aspects of life that define who we are and what we are meant to achieve. By focusing on the core 20 percent of activities that align with our unique talents and deepest aspirations, we create a life centered around intentionality and purpose. This approach allows us to eliminate distractions and time wasters, ensuring our efforts are directed toward meaningful growth and self-actualization. In essence, the Pareto principle empowers us to live a life where our passions and talents are not just pursued but fully realized in alignment with our *musts*.

Consider this: what are the few critical tasks that contribute most to your success and happiness? Focus on these high-leverage activities and let go of the rest. This shift in focus will allow you to achieve more with less effort, enhancing your productivity and overall satisfaction.

TIME BLOCKING AND DEEP WORK

Time blocking is a time management technique where you divide your day into blocks of time, each dedicated to specific tasks or activities. This method helps you stay focused and avoid multitasking, which can reduce productivity. The origins of time blocking can be traced back to ancient practices of structured daily routines, but it was popularized in the modern era by productivity experts like Cal Newport, author of *Deep Work*. Newport values the importance of focused, uninterrupted time for achieving high-quality work.

Newport's *Deep Work* concept emphasizes intense focus on demanding tasks without distractions, enabling efficient mastery of complex information. This increasingly rare skill in our hyperconnected world involves distinguishing deep from shallow work, creating distraction-free environments, and embracing boredom to enhance concentration. Implementation involves scheduling focused time, establishing rituals, and tracking progress. Newport states, "The ability to perform deep work is becoming increasingly rare at exactly the same time it is becoming increasingly valuable in our economy.

As a consequence, the few who cultivate this skill, and then make it the core of their working life, will thrive."

To implement time blocking, start by identifying your priorities. List the tasks and activities you need to accomplish. Allocate specific time blocks for each task, ensuring you have dedicated time to focused work. Schedule breaks to rest and recharge, maintaining productivity throughout the day. Stick to your schedule as closely as possible, making adjustments as needed.

Time blocking transforms your daily routine into a well-orchestrated symphony, where each hour is purposefully dedicated to your most important activities. By structuring your day with time blocks, you can maintain a rhythm that keeps you productive and focused on what truly matters.

In personal development, time blocking can be used to ensure you are dedicating time to activities that foster growth and self-improvement. Time blocking aligns powerfully with the *must* principles across all areas of our Circle of Life. By deliberately allocating specific time slots to our most important priorities, we ensure that our *musts* receive the focused attention they deserve. This intentional scheduling approach forces us to confront and prioritize what truly matters in each life domain—career, relationships, health, or personal growth. When we time block for our *musts*, we're making a concrete commitment to our core values and goals, transforming abstract aspirations into tangible actions. This method not only boosts productivity but also cultivates a sense of purpose and fulfillment as we consistently dedicate time to what's most meaningful. Time blocking for our *musts* across various life areas helps maintain balance, ensuring that no crucial aspect of our lives is neglected. By visually mapping out our commitments, we can easily identify any imbalances and adjust accordingly, aligning our daily actions with our holistic life vision. Time blocking and our *must* principles empower us to live with greater intention, making consistent progress toward becoming the person we are meant to be in all facets of life.

PARKINSON'S LAW

Parkinson's law, articulated in 1955 by C. Northcote Parkinson, a British naval historian, author, and academic, asserts that "work expands to fill the time available for its completion." This principle holds profound implications for productivity, time management, and personal development, aligning closely with the Must Mindset of intentional growth and purposeful action. At its core, Parkinson's law illuminates our tendency to utilize all allocated time for a task regardless of its actual complexity or importance. For instance, given a week to complete a report that could be finished in a day, we often find ways to stretch the work to fill the entire week. This expansion of work can manifest through overthinking, perfectionism, or simply working at a slower pace.

Understanding and applying Parkinson's law can be transformative for productivity and time management. By recognizing this tendency, we can set tighter deadlines, break larger projects into smaller time-bound tasks, prioritize effectively, and minimize distractions. Allocating less time for tasks can increase focus and efficiency, while breaking projects into smaller components helps maintain momentum and prevents work from expanding unnecessarily. This approach aligns with the *must* principle of taking decisive action and maintaining unwavering commitment to our goals. For personal development, Parkinson's law challenges us to be more intentional with our time, encouraging self-awareness about how we work and pushing us to develop better time management skills. By setting self-imposed deadlines and holding ourselves accountable, we can boost our productivity and create more time for other important aspects of our lives. This self-discipline and intentional growth mirror the Must Mindset's emphasis on continuous improvement and purposeful living. However, it's crucial to strike a balance. While Parkinson's law can drive efficiency, applying it too rigidly might lead to stress or compromised quality. The goal is to use this principle as a tool for optimizing our time and efforts, not as a means to create undue pressure. By understanding and strategically applying Parkinson's law, we can enhance our productivity, refine our time management skills, and foster personal growth, ultimately leading to a more balanced and fulfilling life—a key aspiration of the *must* philosophy.

THE POMODORO TECHNIQUE: BOOSTING FOCUS

The Pomodoro Technique, developed by Francesco Cirillo in the late 1980s, is a popular time management method that enhances focus and productivity. It involves working in short, focused bursts (usually twenty-five minutes) followed by a short break (five minutes). After completing four pomodoros, take a longer break (fifteen to thirty minutes). This technique helps maintain high levels of concentration and prevents burnout.

Cirillo named the technique after the tomato-shaped kitchen timer he used as a university student. The core idea is to work with time rather than against it, leveraging short bursts of productivity to accomplish tasks more efficiently. By breaking your work into manageable intervals, you can maintain your focus and make steady progress without feeling overwhelmed.

Imagine tackling a challenging project. By breaking it down into manageable chunks with the Pomodoro Technique, you can maintain your focus and make steady progress without feeling overwhelmed. This method is particularly effective for tasks that require deep concentration and mental stamina. As Cirillo said, "If you try to improve your productivity and spend less time working, you'll find that the time you do spend working is more productive."

MANAGING DISTRACTIONS: STAYING FOCUSED

In today's digital age, distractions are abundant. To stay productive, it's essential to manage and minimize these distractions. Create a distraction-free workspace, free from the clutter and chaos that can pull your focus away from your tasks. Use technology wisely, leveraging apps and tools to block distracting websites and notifications. Set boundaries, communicating your work hours and limits to family, friends, and colleagues to minimize interruptions. Practice mindfulness techniques such as meditation to improve focus and concentration.

By creating an environment that supports your focus, you can reduce distractions and maintain productivity. Remember, each moment of distraction is a moment lost. Protect your time as you would any valuable resource, ensuring that it is spent wisely and intentionally. As Tim Ferriss says, "Focus on being productive instead of busy."

DELEGATING AND OUTSOURCING: MAXIMIZING EFFICIENCY

Recognize that you can't do everything yourself. Delegating tasks to others or outsourcing certain activities can free up your time for more critical tasks. Determine which tasks can be handled by others and choose individuals with the skills and capabilities to complete these tasks. Provide clear instructions and expectations, then trust and empower your team to take ownership of the tasks.

SWIFT DECISIONS FOLLOWED BY SWIFT INITIAL ACTIONS

The greatest tool in time management, decision-making, and overcoming procrastination is the ability to make swift decisions. The art of swift decision-making emerges as a transformative force, capable of reshaping our destinies and propelling us toward greatness. This invaluable skill, when honed and embraced, becomes the catalyst for seizing life's fleeting opportunities, conquering formidable challenges, and maintaining an unwavering momentum toward our most cherished aspirations.

The wisdom of quick decision-making is not merely anecdotal; it is grounded in scientific research. Studies reveal that our initial instincts often guide us toward the optimal path, while prolonged deliberation can lead us astray, causing us to miss golden opportunities. The act of deciding swiftly aligns us with our innate wisdom, tapping into the wellspring of intuition that often holds the key to our success.

We must recognize that *indecision is, in itself, a choice and a decision*—one that often bears a heavy toll on our mental well-being and quality of life. By embracing decisive action, even in the face of uncertainty, we liberate ourselves from the shackles of anxiety and stress that indecision imposes upon us.

The science of action is intrinsically linked to our brain's natural inclination toward comfort and familiarity. Yet it is in the realm of the unfamiliar—in the bold act of swift decision-making—that we find the power to transcend our limitations and propel ourselves toward positive transformation.

This powerful skill can significantly impact on our personal and professional lives, as it allows us to seize opportunities, overcome challenges, and maintain momentum toward our goals. Research has shown that making quick decisions can lead to better outcomes and increased productivity. A study by Florida State University found that when decision-makers come to a conclusion quickly, their choices are more influenced by their initial thoughts. Our instincts often guide us toward the right path, and overthinking can lead to unnecessary delays and missed opportunities. Indecision can lead to increased mental burden, anxiety, and stress.

A global study by Oracle titled "The Decision Dilemma" provides insight into the real-world impacts of decision-making challenges. The study, which surveyed over fourteen thousand employees and business leaders across seventeen countries, revealed a startling statistic: 85 percent of respondents reported that the inability to make decisions negatively impacts their quality of life. This indecision leads to increased mental burden, anxiety, and stress.

The Oracle study also uncovered that 74 percent of people say the number of decisions they make daily has increased tenfold over the last three years. Simultaneously, 78 percent report being bombarded with more information from more sources than ever before. This data deluge is making decision-making increasingly complex, with 86 percent of respondents stating that the volume of data is complicating decisions in both their personal and professional lives.

The McKinsey study on decision-making in organizations, conducted in 2019, is a comprehensive analysis of how companies make and execute critical decisions. This research, which involved over twelve hundred managers across various industries and regions, aimed to understand the factors that contribute to effective decision-making processes in businesses. The study found that organizations with fast and efficient decision-making processes were twice as likely to report financial returns of at least 20 percent from their recent decisions compared to slower decision-makers. It also revealed that companies making decisions quickly were twice as likely to make high-quality decisions compared to slow decision-makers. Additionally, the study emphasized that good decision-making practices tend to yield decisions that are both high quality and fast, challenging the notion that there must be a trade-off between speed and quality.

These studies collectively highlight the importance of developing effective decision-making skills in our information- and data-rich world. While quick decisions in business or in our personal lives can sometimes lead to biased outcomes, the alternative—chronic indecision—can be equally, if not more, detrimental to our well-being and success. The key lies in striking a balance: leveraging our instincts and quick thinking when appropriate, while also knowing when to gather more information for complex, high-stakes decisions.

This highlights the importance of taking action, even when faced with uncertainty. The science behind taking action is rooted in our brain's tendency to avoid change or discomfort. By making swift decisions, we can interrupt this instinctive hesitation and propel ourselves toward positive change as we do so while in our Must Zone.

Mel Robbins stands as a beacon of inspiration in the realm of personal development and motivation. A *New York Times* bestselling author, renowned speaker, and influential podcaster, Robbins has touched the lives of millions with her practical, no-nonsense approach to self-improvement. Her dynamic presence and relatable style have made her one of the most sought-after voices in the field, captivating audiences worldwide with her transformative insights.

At the heart of Robbins's philosophy lies her groundbreaking concept: the 5 Second Rule. This simple yet powerful technique has revolutionized the way people approach change and personal growth. The rule states that if you have an instinct to act on a goal, you must physically move within five seconds, or your brain will kill it.

This deceptively straightforward approach has proven to be a game changer for countless individuals struggling with procrastination, self-doubt, and inaction. By counting backward from five to one and then immediately taking action, people have found themselves breaking through mental barriers and accomplishing tasks they previously thought impossible.

The beauty of the 5 Second Rule lies in its simplicity and universal applicability. Whether we need to get out of bed for our Miracle Morning, make that important phone call, or take the first step toward a long-held dream, Robbins's technique provides a practical tool for overcoming hesitation and embracing action. It's a method that bypasses the brain's tendency to overthink and instead propels individuals into motion. This underscores the critical nature of acting swiftly on our instincts and goals.

Making swift decisions and acting on them is *not* just about efficiency—it's about embracing a life of purpose and intention. By utilizing tools like the 5 Second Rule and adopting a Must Mindset, we can overcome procrastination, reduce decision fatigue, and unlock our full potential. Remember, every moment of hesitation is a missed opportunity for growth and success.

MASTER TIME AND PRODUCTIVITY: TAKE CHARGE OF YOUR LIFE

Mastering time management and productivity is essential for achieving your goals and living a fulfilling life. By prioritizing tasks, focusing on high-impact activities, and leveraging effective techniques, you can make the most of your time and energy. Remember, time is a finite resource; use it wisely and intentionally to create the life you desire.

As you continue your journey of self-improvement, embrace the power of habits, goal setting, and effective time management. These elements work together to propel you toward your highest potential, helping you achieve your dreams and live a life of purpose and fulfillment.

Ultimately, the goal of effective time and productivity management is not just to do more but to do what matters most. It's about creating space in your life for growth, relationships, and the pursuit of your passions. By mastering your time and productivity, you master your life. As we move forward, let's commit to becoming organized based on what matters most, making swift, purposeful decisions that align with our purpose and values, and transforming our lives one decision at a time. We will do this next with examining our habits.

CHAPTER 13

Must Habits

"We are what we repeatedly do. Excellence, then, is not an act, but a habit."

—Will Durant, historian, philosopher, and author of *The Story of Philosophy*

As I reflect on my journey, I realize that the concept of Must Habits has been a guiding force in my life since childhood. Growing up, I faced challenges that many would find daunting. My biological father left when I was just six years old, and my stepfather's tragic passing a few years later left my family shattered. In that moment, I felt an overwhelming sense of responsibility. I was the only son, and I believed it was my duty to become the "man of the house" to be strong for my family.

This sense of responsibility became the foundation upon which I built my habits. I knew that doing well in school was crucial, not just for my own future but for the stability and hope it could bring to my family. So I dedicated myself to creating habits that would ensure my success. I established a strict routine, waking up early each morning to study before school and spending hours each evening reviewing my notes and completing homework.

As I grew older, these habits became more refined. I began to see that success wasn't just about grades; it was about personal growth and development. I immersed myself in books on personal development, attended seminars, and sought out mentors who could guide me on my journey. My educational pursuits became a testament to the power of Must Habits. I pursued a law degree, followed by a master's in business, and even began a doctorate program, driven by the belief that knowledge and education were the keys to unlocking my true potential.

The Must Habits I developed during those formative years—discipline, resilience, and a relentless pursuit of excellence—have stayed with me to this day. They have been the foundation upon which I've built my career as an attorney and my personal life. These habits have taught me that success is not just about achieving goals; it's about the person you become in the process. By embracing Must Habits, I've been able to transform my life from one of adversity to one of purpose and fulfillment.

This journey has shown me that our habits are not just actions we perform; they are the building blocks of our character. They define who we are and what we stand for. By cultivating Must Habits, we can overcome obstacles, achieve greatness, and live a life that is true to who we are meant to be. My story is a testament to the transformative power of embracing these habits, and I hope it inspires others to do the same.

Confucius, the renowned Chinese philosopher, emphasized the power of habit in shaping character and achieving personal growth. He believed that virtue and excellence are not innate qualities, but rather the result of consistent practice and habit formation over a lifetime.

In the Confucian classic text *Liji* (Book of Rites), there is a famous passage that illustrates this perspective: "The Master said, 'At fifteen, I set my heart upon learning. At thirty, I had planted my feet firm upon the ground. At forty, I no longer suffered from perplexities. At fifty, I knew what were the biddings of Heaven. At sixty, I heard them with docile ear. At seventy, I could follow the dictates of my own heart; for what I desired no longer overstepped the boundaries of right.'"

This passage demonstrates Confucius's belief that developing good habits is a gradual process requiring dedication and perseverance. He taught that by cultivating proper conduct (*li*) through daily practice, one could internalize virtuous behavior and achieve harmony with the natural order. This concept of *li* went beyond mere etiquette, representing an internalized code of civility that defined proper human conduct. Habits have significant application far beyond learning how to conduct oneself in life. We can apply habit formation to all aspects of our being.

In a very real sense, we are the embodiment of our habits. Our repeated behaviors shape not only our daily lives but also our physical brains and bodies. Through neuroplasticity, our habits create and strengthen neural pathways, literally rewiring our brains. Each time we perform a habitual action, we reinforce these pathways, making the behavior more automatic and ingrained. Our habits also influence our physical health, from the foods we habitually consume to our exercise routines (or lack thereof). Even our posture and the way we carry ourselves are reflections of habitual patterns. In this way, our habits are not just things we do; they become integral parts of who we are, manifesting in our thoughts, actions, and physical being.

Habits are the invisible architecture of our lives. They shape our days, influence our decisions, and ultimately determine our destiny. While goals give us direction, habits are the steady footsteps that carry us toward those goals. They are the silent, consistent actions that, when compounded over time, can lead to extraordinary outcomes or devastating results.

When your goals are anchored in your purpose, your habits become more than just daily routines—they become the deliberate actions that propel you toward living out your purpose. This alignment between habits and purpose ensures that every step you take is not just productive but meaningful. Purpose-driven goal setting requires you to identify your Must Actions—the nonnegotiable steps you must take to achieve your goals and live in alignment with your deepest values. These Must Actions are the habits that form the foundation of your daily life, guiding you consistently toward your most authentic self.

THE POWER OF NEUROPLASTICITY

The field of neuroscience offers profound insights into why embracing your *musts* with unwavering commitment is not just a matter of discipline but a transformative process that reshapes who you are at the very core of your being. Neuroplasticity refers to the brain's extraordinary ability to reorganize itself, to form new neural connections, and to adapt in response to our experiences, behaviors, and thoughts. Contrary to the long-held belief that our brains are fixed and unchangeable after a certain age, science has revealed that our brains are, in fact, dynamic and ever-changing. They are malleable, like clay, constantly being sculpted by the actions we take, the habits we form, and the thoughts we cultivate.

In his groundbreaking work *The Brain That Changes Itself*, Dr. Norman Doidge explains how our thoughts and experiences physically alter our brain structure. Your brain has the ability to reorganize itself by forming new connections throughout your life. It's like having a superpower that allows you to rewire your own brain! This means that no matter how deeply ingrained a thought or behavior or pattern might be, there's always potential for change.

Each time you take a step toward fulfilling your purpose, you are strengthening the neural pathways that support that behavior. Imagine these pathways as trails in a forest: the more you walk a particular trail, the clearer and more defined it becomes. Similarly, the more you engage in your *musts*, the more robust and efficient these neural connections become, making the behavior easier and more natural over time.

This scientific insight underscores the transformative power of consistent, intentional action. Your *musts* are not merely habits to be formed; they are the very building blocks of a new, empowered identity. With each *must* you fulfill, you are shaping the structure of your brain in ways that align with your highest goals and values. Over time, these actions lead to the creation of a brain that is finely tuned to your purpose, a brain that instinctively supports the behaviors and decisions that propel you toward your true potential.

But the power of neuroplasticity extends even further. Not only does it help you establish new, positive habits, but it also allows you to break free from old, limiting patterns. Just as you can create new pathways, you can also weaken and eventually eliminate the neural connections that support behaviors and beliefs that no longer serve you. By consistently choosing your *musts* over old habits of procrastination, self-doubt, or fear, you are actively rewiring your brain to favor growth, resilience, and purposeful living.

THE SCIENCE OF HOW HABITS ARE FORMED

Understanding how habits are formed is crucial to mastering them. Habits are created through a process that involves repetition, reinforcement, and neurological patterns that make behaviors automatic over time. Here, we shall briefly describe habits in scientific terms and then reframe this science in terms of how we can apply this knowledge to improve our lives.

William James, the pioneering American psychologist and philosopher of the late nineteenth century, laid the foundation for our modern understanding of habits through his groundbreaking research and insights, which continue to influence contemporary neuroscience and psychology.

James described habits as new pathways of discharge formed in the brain, through which certain incoming currents tend to escape. This concept aligns with our present understanding of neural plasticity and the formation of new neural connections in the basal ganglia during habit formation. James observed that habits simplify movements, make them accurate, and diminish fatigue. Our brain is made up of billions of neurons (brain cells) that communicate with each other through electrical and chemical signals. These neurons form networks, and the strength and structure of these networks determine our thoughts, behaviors, and beliefs.

James noted that habits "diminish the conscious attention with which our acts are performed." This observation is consistent with modern neuroscience's understanding of how habit formation shifts activity from the prefrontal cortex to the basal ganglia, reducing cognitive load—the amount of mental effort and working memory resources required to process information and complete a task.

James introduced the concept of plasticity in relation to habit formation, describing it as "the possession of a structure weak enough to yield to an influence, but strong enough not to yield all at once." This concept is fundamental to our current understanding of neuroplasticity and its role in habit formation within the basal ganglia. Modern neuroscience has confirmed James's insights, identifying the basal ganglia as crucial for habit formation. The basal ganglia are involved in learning relationships between sensory information and motor responses based on trial-by-trial feedback. This aligns with James's emphasis on repetition and practice in habit formation.

In essence, William James's work and our current understanding of habits offer valuable insights for anyone looking to improve themselves or take control of their life. Habits are essentially brain shortcuts created to save energy. As behaviors become habitual, they require less mental effort, freeing up your mind for other tasks. The key to forming habits is repetition; the more you repeat a behavior, the stronger the neural pathways become, making the habit easier to perform and harder to break. Consistency is crucial, as James emphasized never allowing exceptions when forming a new habit. Each time you perform the desired behavior, you're reinforcing it.

James advised starting strong by making new habits as robust as possible from the beginning, which means committing fully and creating a supportive environment consistent with our new concept of Must Actions. It's important to remember that habits can be changed due to the brain's plasticity. Even though habits become automatic, they're not permanent and can be modified with conscious effort. Small changes can lead to significant long-term results, as habits are formed through repetition. James recommended seizing opportunities and acting on resolutions immediately to overcome inertia and start building the habit. Patience is crucial in this process, as habit formation is gradual and it takes time for behaviors to become truly automatic.

The habit loop, popularized by Charles Duhigg in his book *The Power of Habit*, is at the core of habit formation. It consists of three components: the cue, the routine, and the reward.

1. **Cue:** The cue is the trigger that initiates the habit. It can be anything from a specific time of day to an emotional state or an environmental context. For example, feeling stressed (the cue) might trigger the habit of eating comfort food (the routine).
2. **Routine:** The routine is the behavior that follows the cue. It's the action you take in response to the trigger. In the example above, the routine would be eating comfort food.
3. **Reward:** The reward is the benefit you get from the routine, which reinforces the habit. The reward can be physical, emotional, or psychological. In the case of eating comfort food, the reward might be a temporary relief from stress.

Over time, this loop becomes ingrained in the brain, making the behavior more automatic. The more often the loop is repeated, the stronger the habit becomes, as the brain begins to associate the cue directly with the reward, bypassing the need for conscious decision-making.

For decades it was widely proclaimed that a habit could be formed in twenty-one days. The old notion of a fixed twenty-one-day period for habit formation, which originated from anecdotal observations by plastic surgeon Maxwell Maltz in the 1960s, has been debunked and replaced by a more nuanced understanding of habit formation as a gradual process that varies widely based on the individual and the specific behavior being adopted.

A seminal study conducted by Phillippa Lally and her colleagues at University College London, published in the *European Journal of Social Psychology*, has provided significant insights into the true nature of habit formation. This research found that, on average, it takes about sixty-six days for a new behavior to become automatic. However, the study also revealed a striking range in the time required for habit formation, spanning from as few as 18 days to as many as 254 days, depending on various factors, such as the complexity of the behavior and individual differences.

The complexity of the habit being formed plays a crucial role in determining the time required for it to become automatic. For instance, simpler habits like drinking a glass of water with lunch may form more quickly, while more complex behaviors, such as regular exercise routines, take considerably longer. A 2015 study focused specifically on exercise habits found that new gym-goers needed to maintain a routine of at least four workouts per week for six weeks before the behavior began to feel habitual.

These findings highlight the importance of setting realistic expectations when attempting to form new habits. This research underscores the need for patience and persistence in habit formation, especially for more complex behaviors, and suggests that individuals should be prepared for a potentially lengthy process when working to incorporate new habits into their daily lives. Understanding these findings can help you approach habit formation and change more effectively, giving you greater control over your behaviors and, ultimately, your life.

DISCOVERING AND RECOGNIZING YOUR HABITS

Before we can change or cultivate new habits, we must first recognize the ones we already have. Many of our habits operate on autopilot, embedded so deeply into our daily routines that we might not even notice them. These unconscious habits, whether good or bad, influence our behavior and outcomes in significant ways.

Recognizing your habits requires a level of self-awareness that comes from introspection. This process involves taking a step back and observing your daily routines and behaviors with a critical eye. What do you do when you first wake up? How do you spend your free time? What actions do you take when you're stressed or tired? These are the moments when your habits reveal themselves. Introspection allows you to bring these habits to the forefront of your consciousness, where they can be examined and evaluated.

One effective way to discover your habits is to keep a daily journal where you record your actions and behaviors throughout the day. By documenting what you do, when you do it, and how it makes you feel, you can identify patterns that may have gone unnoticed. For instance, you might discover that you have a habit of reaching for your phone every time you feel bored or that you snack mindlessly while watching TV in the evening. These habits, once recognized, can then be addressed and modified if they do not serve your best interests.

In addition to introspection, observation is a powerful tool for recognizing habits. Sometimes it's easier to see patterns in others before we see them in ourselves. Observing the habits of those around you—whether they are family, friends, or colleagues—can provide valuable insights into your behavior. You might notice that a colleague who consistently arrives early to meetings is more organized and less stressed, prompting you to reflect on your time-management habits.

Observation can also involve seeking feedback from others. Sometimes those closest to us can see habits we are blind to. Asking a trusted friend or mentor for their observations about your habits can be an eye-opening experience. They might point out habits—both positive and negative—you hadn't fully recognized.

As you observe and introspect, you may also discover your unique or quirkier habits—those amusing or odd little behaviors you never really thought about. Perhaps you always put on your left shoe before your right, or you hum the same tune every time you brush your teeth. Maybe you check the refrigerator multiple times a night, even though you know there's nothing new inside. These quirky habits can be endearing and often harmless, but they also provide insight into how our brains create patterns of behavior, sometimes for no other reason than comfort or familiarity.

Consider the example of Albert Einstein, who had some famously quirky habits. He often wore the same outfit every day because he didn't want to waste mental energy on deciding what to wear. This habit was not only practical but also a reflection of his focus on conserving his cognitive resources for more important tasks. Einstein also had a habit of playing the violin whenever he was stuck on a complex problem, using the music to stimulate his mind and foster creativity.

Or think of Thomas Edison, who had the habit of taking catnaps throughout the day. Rather than sleeping for long periods at night, Edison would rest for a few minutes at a time, sometimes holding a steel ball that would drop and wake him when he dozed off. This quirky sleep habit, known as polyphasic sleep, was Edison's way of maximizing his productivity and staying alert.

Then there's the famous example of Agatha Christie, who had the habit of eating apples in the bath while dreaming up her murder mysteries. This quirky habit became part of her creative process, allowing her to relax and think more freely.

Recognizing these funny, quirky habits can be a lighthearted way to start the process of habit discovery. They remind us that habits aren't just about discipline and self-improvement. They're also about the unique ways we navigate our daily lives. Embracing these quirks can add a touch of humor to the journey of personal development, making it easier to address more challenging habits with a positive attitude.

OUR GOOD HABITS AS BLESSINGS

Good habits are not just beneficial to us; they are blessings that extend beyond ourselves and positively impact others. When we cultivate habits of kindness, generosity, and integrity, we contribute to a ripple effect that touches the lives of those around us, often in ways we may never fully realize.

Consider the habit of being consistently kind and considerate to others. A simple habit of offering a smile or a kind word can brighten someone's day and create a positive atmosphere. Over time, these small acts of kindness can build stronger relationships, foster a sense of community, and inspire others to adopt similar behaviors. The blessing of kindness extends far beyond the immediate moment, influencing the emotional and social well-being of those we encounter.

Similarly, habits of generosity—whether it's giving your time, resources, or support to others—can create a culture of giving that benefits entire communities. When you consistently practice generosity, you not only help those in need, but you also set an example that encourages others to do the same. The blessing of generosity is that it creates a cycle of giving and receiving that enriches the lives of everyone involved.

Good habits also bless us by reinforcing our sense of integrity and self-respect. When we consistently act in alignment with our values, we build a strong foundation of trust and reliability. Others come to see us as dependable and trustworthy, which strengthens our personal and professional relationships. The blessing of integrity is that it fosters a deep sense of inner peace and confidence, as we know that we are living in a way that allows us to be true to ourselves.

Consider the example of Jane, a schoolteacher who developed the habit of daily gratitude journaling. Jane began this practice to cope with stress and improve her mental well-being. Every evening, she would take a few minutes to write down three things she was grateful for that day, no matter how small. Over time, this simple habit transformed her outlook on life. Jane found that by focusing on the positive aspects of her day, she became more resilient, happier, and more present in her relationships. Her habit of gratitude journaling not only improved her mental health but also strengthened her connections with family and friends, as she became more appreciative and supportive in her interactions with others.

IDENTIFYING AND CONCENTRATING ON YOUR MUST HABITS

It's crucial to identify and concentrate on the habits that are most aligned with our Must Core Beliefs, Must Values, Must Standards, and Must Purpose. These habits, which we call Must Habits, deserve special attention, focus, and care because they are directly aligned with our core self and our true, authentic identity.

These Must Habits are the daily expressions of your most cherished values and beliefs. By giving them special attention, you ensure that your actions are consistently aligned with your identity and purpose. This alignment brings a sense of coherence and fulfillment to your life, as you are not just going through the motions but living in a way that truly reflects who you are.

Concentrating on Must Habits helps to reinforce your identity as someone who is committed to living according to their highest standards. This focus builds confidence and self-respect, as you know your actions are in harmony with your beliefs. It also makes it easier to resist temptations or distractions that might lead you away from your path, as your commitment to your Must Habits acts as a guiding star.

Stephen Covey's *The 7 Habits of Highly Effective People* is a seminal work in the field of personal development, and its themes align closely with the concept of Must Habits. Covey's seven habits are principles-based, meaning they are rooted in universal truths that guide effective behavior. These habits help individuals live in harmony with their values and achieve their full potential—goals that resonate deeply with the idea of Must Habits.

Covey's first three habits—Be Proactive, Begin with the End in Mind, and Put First Things First—focus on personal mastery and the alignment of actions with one's values and goals. These habits emphasize the importance of taking responsibility for one's life, having a clear vision of what you want to achieve, and prioritizing tasks that align with your purpose. These are the very essence of Must Habits, which are also centered around living intentionally and in alignment with your core self.

The next three habits—Think Win-Win; Seek First to Understand,

Then to Be Understood; and Synergize—deal with interpersonal effectiveness and the importance of relationships. Covey's emphasis on collaboration, empathy, and mutual benefit aligns with the idea that Must Habits are not only about personal success but also about contributing to the well-being of others. Good habits like kindness, integrity, and generosity are Must Habits that extend beyond the self and create positive impacts in relationships and communities.

The seventh habit, Sharpen the Saw, emphasizes the importance of self-renewal and continuous growth. This habit reflects the ongoing process of evaluating and refining Must Habits to ensure they remain aligned with your evolving goals and values. Covey's holistic approach to habit development and his focus on aligning habits with principles provides a robust framework that complements and enhances the concept of Must Habits.

While Stephen Covey's *The 7 Habits of Highly Effective People* offers valuable insights into personal development, the concept of Must Habits goes beyond prescriptive lists or universal principles. Must Habits are deeply personal and unique to each individual, reflecting their core values, aspirations, and life circumstances.

Must Habits are not just about routine actions like brushing your teeth; they are transformative practices that actively shape your life's trajectory. These habits are the deliberate, consistent behaviors that align with your purpose and propel you toward your most meaningful goals. They are the daily choices that, over time, sculpt your character and determine your life's direction.

For instance, a Must Habit for an aspiring writer might be dedicating an hour each morning to writing regardless of inspiration or mood. For someone prioritizing physical health, it could be preparing nutritious meals at home instead of relying on convenience foods. A person focused on personal growth might make it a habit to read or listen to educational content during their daily commute.

The power of Must Habits lies in their personalization. What's essential for one person may be inconsequential for another. The key is to identify the habits that resonate with your unique values and aspirations and then commit to them with unwavering consistency. These habits become the building blocks of your ideal life, shaping your skills, mindset, and, ultimately, your destiny.

THE IMPACT OF BAD HABITS

While good habits can lead to success, bad habits can be equally powerful in their ability to derail our progress. Bad habits are behaviors that are detrimental to our goals and well-being, yet we often find them difficult to break because they are ingrained in our routines.

Consider the habit of procrastination. Many people struggle with this bad habit, which can significantly impact productivity and stress levels. Procrastination often starts as a small habit—putting off tasks that seem daunting or unpleasant—but can quickly spiral into a pattern of avoidance that hinders personal and professional growth. Breaking the habit of procrastination requires not only recognizing the underlying triggers, such as fear or perfectionism, but also developing strategies to address them, such as breaking tasks into smaller steps or setting specific deadlines.

The destructive power of bad habits is also evident in the case of unhealthy eating patterns. For instance, someone who has developed a habit of turning to junk food for comfort may become trapped in a cycle of poor nutrition, weight gain, and declining health. This bad habit not only affects physical well-being but can also lead to emotional and psychological distress. Breaking free from such a habit requires a conscious effort to replace unhealthy foods with nutritious alternatives and to develop new coping mechanisms for stress, such as exercise or mindfulness practices.

CREATING MUST HABITS IN OUR LIFE

In our journey to become the person we were meant to be, embracing Must Habits is a crucial step toward unlocking our true potential. These habits are not just routines; they are the foundational elements that align our daily actions with our core values, purpose, and aspirations. By cultivating Must Habits, we ensure that every moment counts, leading to a life of purpose, resilience, and profound fulfillment.

Creating Must Habits begins with understanding the transformative power of intention and commitment. It's about recognizing that our habits are not just actions we perform but the building blocks of our character. They define who we are and what we stand for. By integrating mindfulness practices, structured productivity, and a growth mindset into our daily routines, we can transform our lives from one of mere existence to one of purposeful living.

Here are some strategies you can use as you develop your Must Habits.

REPLACING BAD HABITS WITH GOOD ONES

Breaking bad habits is challenging, but it is possible with the right approach. Wolfram Schultz, a renowned neuroscientist at the University of Cambridge, has conducted research on dopamine, a crucial neurotransmitter in the brain, which has provided invaluable insights into how our brains process rewards and form habits. Schultz's key contribution to the science of habits lies in his discovery of how dopamine neurons act as a reward prediction system in the brain. He found that these neurons respond strongly to unexpected rewards and reward-predicting stimuli. This finding has profound implications for how we form, maintain, and break habits.

One of the most effective strategies is to replace a bad habit with a good one. This involves identifying the cue that triggers the bad habit and substituting a new, positive routine in its place while ensuring that the reward remains satisfying.

For example, if you have a habit of reaching for your phone first thing in the morning to scroll through social media, the cue might be the moment you wake up. Instead of this routine, you could replace it with a healthier one, such as spending the first few minutes of your day stretching, meditating, or reading something inspirational. The reward—feeling more energized and focused—remains the same, but the new habit is aligned with your goals of starting the day with intention and calm.

James Clear suggests the use of implementation intentions to help replace bad habits. An implementation intention is a plan that specifies when and where you will perform a new habit. For example, if you want to replace the habit of snacking on unhealthy foods in the afternoon, you might create an implementation intention like this: "When I feel hungry at 3:00 p.m., I will eat a piece of fruit instead of a candy bar." By clearly defining the cue and the desired action, you make it easier to follow through with the new habit.

To really tap into the dopamine high, home in on the rewards of the good habits and the negative consequences of the bad ones.

To form positive habits:

- **Make the new behavior as rewarding as possible.** For instance, if you're trying to establish a reading habit, choose books you truly enjoy and create a cozy reading nook.
- **Introduce unexpected rewards.** Surprise yourself with small treats when you stick to your new habit. This could be as simple as a favorite snack after a week of consistent behavior.
- **Celebrate small wins.** Each time you successfully perform your new habit, take a moment to acknowledge your progress. This positive reinforcement can boost dopamine release, strengthening the habit.

To break unwanted habits:

- **Disrupt the expected reward.** If you're trying to reduce social media use, for example, try to break the association between scrolling and relaxation. Find alternative ways to unwind, like short walks or deep breathing exercises.
- **Associate the habit with negative outcomes.** Remind yourself of the long-term consequences of the bad habit. For excessive

social media use, this could mean reflecting on lost productivity or missed real-life interactions.
- **Replace the habit with a more positive one.** When you feel the urge to engage in the unwanted habit, consciously choose a different, more beneficial action.

Understanding Schultz's work can help you approach habit change with greater patience and more effective strategies. Remember, you're working with your brain's fundamental reward system. This means that forming or breaking habits takes time, and setbacks are a normal part of the process. By consistently applying these dopamine-informed strategies, you can effectively reshape your habits and, ultimately, your life.

CHUNKING

Ann Graybiel, a brilliant scientist at MIT, has revolutionized our understanding of habits and how our brains create them. Her groundbreaking research has shed light on a fascinating part of our brain called the basal ganglia, which plays a crucial role in forming habits. This area doesn't just control our movements; it's also deeply involved in how we learn, what motivates us, and how we make decisions.

One of Graybiel's most exciting ideas is what she calls "chunking." Imagine you're learning a new skill, like playing a song on the piano. At first, you have to think about each note separately. But as you practice, your brain starts to group these individual notes into larger chunks. Eventually, you can play the whole song without thinking about each note. That's chunking in action.

Graybiel found that when we're forming a habit, our brain activity shifts from the thinking part of our brain to this habit-forming area. It's like our brain is going on autopilot. This is why habits can feel so automatic and why they can be hard to break.

Understanding how our brains form habits isn't just interesting science—it's incredibly useful for personal growth. By knowing how our brains create and maintain habits, we can better understand how to build positive habits and break negative ones. Graybiel's work gives us a roadmap for personal change, showing us that with the right approach, we can rewire our brains and transform our lives.

When you're trying to form a new good habit, consistency is key. By repeating the desired behavior regularly, you're helping your brain to "chunk" it into an automatic routine. For instance, if you want to start a daily meditation practice, consistently meditating at the same time each day helps your brain chunk the individual steps (sitting down, setting a timer, focusing on breath) into one automatic meditation routine.

On the flip side, when trying to break a bad habit, you're essentially working to disrupt this chunking process. The shift in brain activity Graybiel observed—from the thinking part of the brain to the habit-forming area—explains why habits can feel so automatic and hard to change. But here's the good news: knowing this process gives you the power to intervene. You can consciously engage your thinking brain to override automatic behaviors, creating new neural pathways for better habits. For example, if you want to break a habit of late-night snacking, you might need to consciously redirect yourself to a different activity when the urge strikes, gradually forming a new, healthier chunk.

HABIT STACKING: BUILDING MOMENTUM

One of the most powerful techniques for building new habits is habit stacking, a concept popularized by James Clear. Habit stacking involves linking a new habit to an existing one and creating a chain of behaviors that build on each other. This technique makes it easier to integrate new behaviors into your routine and ensures that you consistently work toward your goals.

For instance, if you already brew coffee every morning, you could add a new habit, such as practicing a five-minute gratitude meditation while waiting for your coffee to brew. By connecting the new habit to an established routine, you make it easier to incorporate the new behavior into your daily life.

Habit stacking is effective because it leverages the momentum of your existing habits. Each time you complete the first habit, you're reminded to perform the second, and so on. This creates a cascading effect, where each habit reinforces the next, leading to a powerful routine that supports your goals.

THE POWER OF ROUTINES

Wendy Wood is a prominent behavioral scientist and Provost Professor Emerita at the University of Southern California. Her extensive research on the psychology of habits has significantly advanced our understanding of how habits are formed, maintained, and changed in everyday life. Wood's research reveals that habits play a much larger role in our daily lives than most people realize. She found that about 43 percent of what people do every day is repeated in the same context, usually while thinking about something else. This automatic behavior is the essence of habits. Wood's work challenges common misconceptions about habit formation and change, particularly the idea that strong willpower is the key to creating new habits. Instead, she emphasizes the importance of context and repetition in habit formation.

Wood's research offers valuable insights. She suggests that creating new habits requires repeating behaviors in consistent contexts and receiving immediate rewards. Breaking bad habits, according to Wood's research, is often about changing your environment or routine to avoid the triggers that spark the unwanted behavior. For example, if you habitually snack while watching TV, you might break this habit by not keeping snacks in the house or by choosing a different activity instead of watching TV. The key is to identify and alter the situations or cues that usually lead to the bad habit, making it easier to avoid falling into the familiar pattern. Understanding these principles can help individuals approach habit change more effectively, recognizing that it's not just about willpower but about strategically shaping our environment and routines to support desired behaviors.

Routines are a natural extension of habits, forming the structured sequences of actions that define our daily lives. While habits are individual behaviors triggered by specific cues, routines are the larger patterns of activity that incorporate multiple habits into a cohesive whole. The power of routines lies in their ability to create stability, reduce decision fatigue, and enhance productivity.

Routines act as anchors in our day, providing a sense of structure and predictability. When your morning routine includes habits like waking up at the same time, exercising, eating a healthy breakfast, and planning your day, you set a positive tone that influences your mindset and productivity throughout the day. Similarly, an evening routine that involves winding down with relaxation techniques, reflection, and setting intentions for the next day can improve sleep quality and prepare you for a successful tomorrow.

Consistency in routines is what makes them so powerful. When you consistently follow a routine, it becomes ingrained in your daily life, reducing the mental energy required to perform tasks and making it easier to maintain good habits over time. This consistency also reinforces positive behaviors, helping you build momentum and achieve your goals more effectively.

The beauty of routines is that they can be customized to fit your individual needs and goals. Whether your routine is focused on physical health, mental well-being, productivity, or creativity, the key is to design routines that support your priorities. For example, if your goal is to improve your physical fitness, your routine might include morning exercise, healthy meals, and regular hydration. If your focus is on mental clarity, your routine could incorporate mindfulness practices, journaling, and time spent in nature.

THE POWER OF MUST HABITS IN ACHIEVING AUTHENTICITY AND AN EXTRAORDINARY LIFE

Imagine a life where your daily habits are perfectly aligned with your purpose-driven goals, where each small action contributes to the larger vision of who you are becoming. This is the essence of living in the Must Zone. It's a dynamic state where you are constantly challenging yourself, learning, and expanding your capabilities. Your habits, in this context, are the tools that carve out your path to success, not just in achieving goals but in realizing your fullest potential.

Must Habits are powerful because they are the actions that bring your inner values and beliefs to life. When practiced consistently, they lead to a life that is not just successful but deeply fulfilling and authentic. When you concentrate on your Must Habits, you are not just working toward external goals—you are aligning your daily actions with your deepest self, ensuring that you live in harmony with your true identity.

This focus on Must Habits also enhances your ability to achieve your long-term goals, as these habits are directly tied to your purpose. When your habits are aligned with your purpose, you create a strong foundation for achieving your highest aspirations. This alignment ensures that every action you take is meaningful and contributes to the realization of your true potential.

The journey of personal development is one of continuous evolution, where habits play a central role in shaping who you are and what you achieve. By cultivating habits that are aligned with your identity, narrative, beliefs, values, standards, and purpose, you set the stage for a life that is not only successful but deeply fulfilling. As you continue to refine and focus on your Must Habits, you'll live more authentically and achieve truly meaningful goals.

CHAPTER 14

Tenacity and Perseverance

"Never give in. Never, never, never, never—in nothing, great or small, large or petty—never give in, except to convictions of honour and good sense. Never yield to force. Never yield to the apparently overwhelming might of the enemy."

—British Prime Minister Winston Churchill

My mother's life is a testament to tenacity and perseverance. After my stepfather's tragic suicide, she became a young widow with two small children to raise. Despite her own grief and struggles, she never wavered in her commitment to provide for us and ensure we had the best possible future. She worked tirelessly as a public school teacher, often tutoring children at our kitchen table late into the night to make ends meet. Her unwavering determination to see us go through school, get a good education, and become successful and happy adults was a constant source of inspiration.

The depth of my mother's tenacity was truly remarkable. She faced countless worried days and sleepless nights, grappling with the overwhelming challenge of providing for our every need. The financial burden of ensuring we had an excellent education weighed heavily on her shoulders. Yet she never let her anxiety show, always presenting a strong and optimistic front to us. Her ultimate goal was to ensure we could depend on ourselves for life's advancements as adults. This meant sacrificing her own comforts and desires, often going without so we could have the opportunities she believed we deserved. Her resilience in the face of such daunting odds was nothing short of heroic.

This spirit of tenacity and perseverance is a legacy I carry into my own life.

After I started deliberately exploring my beliefs and values, I left the law firm I was working for to start my own independent journey as a lawyer. I hung up my lawyer shingle and started representing people from all walks of life and in all types of cases. I wasn't making much money, but I loved what I was doing—helping people in need.

One day, I passed by an old boarded-up steak and egg restaurant that had sat vacant for years. No one wanted to buy it, as they saw the building as it once was and not as it could be. I saw a blank slate, a new canvas on which to create my future. I had little money, but I located the elderly owner of the property and told him my story. He graciously allowed me to owner-finance the property for a few years.

When I first entered the building, it literally had the orange booths and decor that had been popular for that restaurant in the 1970s. The restaurant had a long steel grill that traveled the length of the back wall and a long booth where people would sit on round, orange stools. I sold everything and gutted the place.

As I built the first building I ever owned, I had to sleep in the back room of the office for a year and a half as I couldn't afford to also get an apartment. All my income went to paying for ongoing debts, the building, construction, and advertising. I bought the biggest Yellow Pages ad, which I could not even afford. I had faith in myself and believed it would pay off. After all, I was my mother's child, and she had greater tenacity and resilience than anyone I had ever known.

When you have gone through great adversity in your life, it actually gives you a sense of freedom that you can get through anything, including the financial struggles that lie ahead, I had already endured so much more suffering in my life. With God's grace, and with the determination forged from my past, over the years I saw my law firm grow to numerous offices around the Greater New Orleans area. My law firm now stands as a well-known, established law practice where people know they are welcome and will receive the "Excellence in Action" that our core values promise.

This journey was not easy. But the tenacity and perseverance I learned from my mother, combined with my own determination to help others and stay true to my values, carried me through. It's a testament to the power of innate and learned resilience and the importance of never giving up on your dreams, no matter how difficult the path may seem.

Life is a journey marked by peaks and valleys, moments of triumph, and times of trial. As we navigate this journey, we are often faced with challenges that test our resolve, obstacles that seem insurmountable, and setbacks that threaten to derail us from our path. In these moments, it is not merely our talent or intelligence that determines our success, but our tenacity and perseverance—our ability to keep going despite the difficulties we encounter.

Take a moment to reflect on your life journey and the tremendous challenges you've already faced. Think about those pivotal moments when you stood at the crossroads of adversity and perseverance. What sense of courage did you muster from deep within? Where in the recesses of your being did you find that positive, motivating self-talk that urged you forward?

Remember the actions you took to push through, over, under, and around the walls that tried to impede your progress. What prior experiences of pain and suffering did you recall that were even worse than what you imagined might occur in the future? How did these memories comfort you, reminding you that you had already endured more, assuring you that you could survive the impending struggles?

Consider the outcomes you desired. Were they greater than the work and hardship you would encounter along the way? Think about the times when failure knocked you down once, or more. Remember the ancient Japanese proverb to "fall seven times, stand up eight." Was the potential for failure insufficient to thwart the momentum of your desire to accomplish your goals? Recall that moment when the last of many so-called failures was finally followed by success.

These experiences are the crucible in which our *musts* are forged. They are the foundation of our perseverance, tenacity, and determination. As we reflect on the transformative power of embracing our *musts*, we find ourselves at a pivotal moment where the principles of mindset, core beliefs, and core values converge to guide us toward creating lasting habits.

In previous chapters, we explored how our mindset shapes our potential for growth and how identifying and aligning with our core values provides clarity and purpose. We learned that mindset is the lens through which we view challenges, while core beliefs act as the silent architects of our self-perception. Together, these elements influence everything from our daily decisions to the pursuit of our long-term goals.

But this chapter asks us to go deeper. It challenges us to examine how the trials and tribulations of our past have shaped who we are today. The moments of pain and struggle—the heartbreaks, failures, and setbacks—are not just obstacles; they are the forge in which our character is tempered. These experiences have given us resilience, taught us lessons, and revealed strengths we may not have known we possessed.

This chapter builds upon the foundation laid earlier by showing how perseverance and tenacity are born from those very hardships. It connects the dots between mindset, beliefs, values, personal narrative, standards, and purpose, illustrating how they come together to fuel our determination to overcome adversity. Here we will explore how embracing our *musts* with unwavering commitment enables us to transform suffering into purpose, setbacks into stepping stones, and challenges into opportunities for growth.

As you read on, consider this: What moments in your life have tested you? How have they shaped your beliefs about yourself and your capacity to persevere? This chapter is an invitation to honor those experiences, not as sources of regret or pain but as the defining moments that have prepared you for greatness. Together, we will uncover how perseverance and tenacity are not just traits but choices—choices that align with your *musts* and propel you toward becoming the person you were meant to be.

TENACITY AND PERSEVERANCE: THE PILLARS OF THE MUST ZONE

The journey into the Must Zone is not merely about optimizing daily life; it is about constructing a robust foundation for long-term resilience and purpose. As we embrace our *musts*—our nonnegotiable habits, mindset, and values—we simultaneously develop the mental and emotional tools necessary to face life's challenges head-on. These *musts* are not just routines; they are the crucible in which tenacity and perseverance are forged, empowering us to transform adversity into growth and setbacks into stepping stones toward greatness.

Tenacity and perseverance are essential qualities that elevate our Must Habits into a force capable of overcoming life's greatest challenges. While Must Habits provide the structure for our daily routines, tenacity and perseverance infuse these routines with the resilience and determination needed to thrive in the face of adversity. Tenacity is not merely about persistence. It is about strategic persistence—adapting and improving our approach with every setback, ensuring we grow stronger and more effective. Perseverance is the unwavering commitment to stay the course, even when obstacles seem insurmountable. Together, these virtues transform our Must Habits into tools for achieving greatness.

Our Must Habits, combined with a Must Mindset, serve as the foundation for cultivating tenacity and perseverance. By integrating practices such as mindfulness, structured productivity, and a growth mindset into our lives, we create a framework that supports resilience. Mindfulness helps us maintain focus and emotional balance during difficult times, structured productivity ensures we prioritize tasks effectively to avoid distractions, and a growth mindset fosters the belief that failure is an opportunity for learning and improvement. These habits allow us to approach challenges with clarity and purpose, ensuring that setbacks become stepping stones rather than roadblocks.

Adversity plays a critical role in strengthening tenacity. The moments of pain, struggle, and loss shape our character and teach us invaluable lessons about resilience. These experiences—whether heartbreaks, failures, or setbacks—are not obstacles but crucibles in which our character is tempered. They remind us that setbacks are opportunities to innovate, adapt, and grow stronger. By embracing these challenges with unwavering determination, we honor our journey and prepare ourselves for future triumphs.

Living in the Must Zone offers immediate benefits, like increased productivity, clarity of purpose, and alignment with core values. However, its true power lies in cultivating qualities essential for overcoming adversity. The discipline required to maintain Must Habits strengthens your ability to persevere through difficult times, creating a ripple effect that touches every aspect of your life. This chapter builds upon previous lessons by showing how perseverance and tenacity are born from hardships while connecting mindset, beliefs, values, personal narrative, standards, and purpose into one cohesive framework for resilience.

Consistent application of Must Zone principles leads to a compounding effect on resilience. Each day lived in alignment with your *musts* not only improves immediate well-being but also incrementally builds the strength needed to face larger life challenges. This cumulative growth in resilience is like compound interest for your personal development—small but consistent efforts yield exponential results over time.

By embracing tenacity and perseverance as essential qualities that build upon Must Habits, we ensure that every moment counts toward becoming our best selves. These virtues empower us to face life's challenges head-on while transforming suffering into purpose, setbacks into stepping stones, and challenges into opportunities for growth. As Winston Churchill said, "Success is not final; failure is not fatal: it is the courage to continue that counts." Let this courage guide you as you craft a life of purpose, resilience, and fulfillment within the Must Zone—a space where your habits align with your deepest values and fuel your journey toward greatness.

Research shows that individuals with a clear purpose are better equipped to handle stress and recover from setbacks. By defining your purpose through the Must Zone framework, you're not just improving your daily life; you're preparing yourself for future challenges. This sense of purpose acts as an anchor during turbulent times, providing stability and direction when you need it most.

Must Habits transform our choices into nonnegotiable commitments, propelling us forward despite the odds. As you reflect on these moments, recognize how they've shaped your resilience and fueled your growth mindset. These are the experiences that have prepared you for the journey ahead, equipping you with the strength to face whatever challenges may come.

At its core, tenacity is the determination to keep pursuing a goal, no matter how difficult or elusive it may be. It is the relentless drive that pushes us to continue striving for success, even when the odds are stacked against us. Perseverance, on the other hand, is the steadfastness to endure through trials and tribulations. It is the quality that enables us to weather the storms of life with grace and resilience, holding on to our vision even when the going gets tough.

These two qualities are inextricably linked. Tenacity fuels our perseverance, giving us the energy to keep pushing forward. Perseverance sustains our tenacity, allowing us to maintain our efforts over the long haul. Together, they form the backbone of any successful endeavor.

Tenacity and perseverance are not mere buzzwords; they are the bedrock of any significant achievement. These qualities are what separate those who achieve their goals from those who give up along the way. They are the quiet, steady forces that propel us forward, even when the road is long and the journey is hard.

THE WRIGHT BROTHERS: THE POWER OF TENACITY AND *MUST*

As we explore the profound commitment implementing our *musts* requires, it's impossible not to draw inspiration from the story of the Wright brothers, Wilbur and Orville. Their journey from obscurity to achieving one of the most significant technological feats of the twentieth century—the first powered, controlled flight—serves as a powerful example of what it means to embrace your *musts* with unwavering determination.

The Wright brothers were not formally trained engineers or scientists; they were self-taught inventors driven by a passion for solving the mystery of flight. Their path was anything but smooth. The world at the time was skeptical, and many experts in the field doubted that powered flight was even possible. Yet the Wright brothers were not deterred. They possessed a relentless *must*—the unshakable belief of achieving human flight. This belief, goal, and purpose were not just a desire or dream; they were convictions so strong that they guided their every action.

The brothers' journey was marked by numerous challenges, including technical failures, harsh environmental conditions, and even a serious injury that nearly ended Wilbur's life. Yet their unwavering commitment to their *must*—the deep purpose driving their efforts—propelled them forward. They spent years meticulously studying aerodynamics, testing countless models, and enduring repeated failures, each time returning to the drawing board with greater resolve.

One of the most striking examples of their perseverance was their methodical approach to overcoming technical obstacles. When they needed a lightweight engine for powered flight but could not find one suitable, the brothers designed and built it themselves. Their first powered flight attempt stalled after three seconds and resulted in a crash that damaged the aircraft. Undeterred, they repaired the plane and tried again three days later, achieving a historic twelve-second flight that laid the foundation for modern aviation. This iterative process of failure and improvement highlighted their ability to adapt and innovate under pressure.

The Wright brothers also faced skepticism from experts and competitors with greater resources. Despite lacking formal education in aeronautics and financial backing, they relied on systematic experimentation to refine their designs. For instance, they conducted over two hundred wind tunnel tests to perfect airfoil shapes and developed a groundbreaking three-axis control system that made controlled flight possible. Their persistence in addressing challenges like stability and lift efficiency set them apart from others in the field.

Even after achieving a powered flight in 1903, the brothers continued to improve their designs, demonstrating that tenacity is not just about reaching a milestone but about striving for excellence beyond it. Their ability to transform setbacks into stepping stones was rooted in their Must Mindset, which combined resilience, strategic problem-solving, and an unyielding belief in their purpose. By living in alignment with their Must Zone, they not only achieved success but inspired generations to pursue ambitious goals despite adversity.

Orville Wright once remarked, "If we worked on the assumption that what is accepted as true really is true, then there would be little hope for advance." This resonates deeply with the essence of the Wright brothers' journey and the lesson it offers to us. The Wright brothers understood that achieving something extraordinary often requires questioning the status quo and pursuing your *musts* with a tenacity that defies conventional wisdom. They knew their success would not come from accepting limitations, but from challenging them and pushing beyond what was considered possible.

The Wright brothers' story is a testament to the idea that when we commit to our *musts*, we are not just making a choice; we are engaging in a process of continual learning, adaptation, and growth. Their success was not a sudden, singular event. It was the culmination of years of persistent effort, of small, incremental steps taken with purpose and resolve. Each experiment, each failure, and each discovery brought them closer to their goal because they remained steadfast in their commitment to their *must*.

The Wright brothers exemplify the power of embracing your *musts* with total dedication. They remind us that the path to fulfilling our purpose is rarely straightforward. It is in the daily, deliberate actions we take, no matter how challenging or uncertain, that our success is forged. Just as the Wright brothers' *must* led them to reshape the boundaries of what was possible, your *musts* have the power to redefine your life, push you beyond perceived limitations, and lead you toward extraordinary achievements.

THE SCIENCE OF TENACITY AND PERSEVERANCE

The qualities of tenacity and perseverance are not just inspirational; they are grounded in rigorous scientific research. Studies in psychology and neuroscience have demonstrated that these traits can be developed and strengthened over time, akin to muscle growth. Understanding the underlying mechanisms can empower us to cultivate these qualities more effectively in our lives.

Recent neuroimaging research has begun to uncover the neural mechanisms underlying perseverance and goal-directed behavior. A 2019 study identified the anterior mid-cingulate cortex (aMCC) as a central hub for integrating information across multiple brain systems—such as attention, memory, emotion, and motor planning—to assess the costs and benefits of sustained effort. The researchers proposed that this region plays a critical role in "tenacity," enabling individuals to persist in challenging situations by dynamically evaluating whether continued effort is worthwhile.

The power of intentional repetitive thoughts and actions in developing perseverance is supported by neuroscience. The brain's ability to reorganize itself by forming new neural connections throughout life is enhanced when we consistently engage in persevering behaviors and thoughts; we strengthen the neural pathways associated with these traits.

Positive emotions also play a crucial role in building perseverance. According to the broaden-and-build theory, developed by psychologist Barbara Fredrickson, positive emotions expand our awareness and encourage novel, varied, and exploratory thoughts and actions. Over time, this broadened mindset helps build lasting personal resources, such as perseverance.

Fredrickson's research suggests that by cultivating positive emotions, such as joy, gratitude, and hope, we can enhance our perseverance and build a buffer against the effects of stress. Positive emotions not only make us feel good in the moment, but they also help us recover more quickly from adversity and build the psychological resources needed to face future challenges. Fredrickson eloquently cautions, "Just as water lilies retract when sunlight fades, so do our minds when positivity fades." We must maintain our positive emotions to provide fuel for our tenacity and perseverance.

These scientific insights provide a solid foundation for our practical applications of developing tenacity and perseverance. By engaging in intentional repetitive thoughts and actions that reinforce perseverant behavior, we can strengthen the neural pathways associated with these traits. This process involves setting and pursuing challenging goals, which push us beyond our comfort zones and require sustained effort as we stay in our Must Zone. As we work toward these goals, practicing positive self-talk during difficult tasks becomes crucial, helping us maintain motivation and overcome obstacles. Regularly engaging in activities that demand sustained effort further reinforces our capacity for perseverance, whether through physical exercise, learning a new skill, or tackling complex projects. Cultivating a growth mindset through education and self-reflection is equally important, as it allows us to view challenges as opportunities for growth rather than insurmountable barriers. By consistently applying these strategies, we can harness the power of neuroplasticity to enhance our capacity for perseverance and tenacity. This intentional approach to developing these traits not only strengthens our ability to overcome obstacles but also leads to greater personal and professional success, as we become more resilient and determined in pursuing our goals.

GRIT AND LONG-TERM SUCCESS

Angela Duckworth is a prominent psychologist and professor at the University of Pennsylvania who has gained widespread recognition for her research on grit. As a former management consultant and seventh-grade math teacher, Duckworth became intrigued by the disparity between student potential and actual achievement. This curiosity led her to pursue a PhD in psychology and develop her theory of grit.

Duckworth defines grit as "passion and perseverance for very long-term goals." It's a combination of sustained interest (passion) and persistent effort (perseverance) toward challenging objectives. Grit goes beyond mere resilience or tenacity; it encompasses the ability to maintain focus and dedication over extended periods, often years or even decades.

Gritty individuals not only overcome obstacles but also stay committed to their objectives despite temptations to change course or give up. Duckworth's research suggests that grit is a better predictor of success in various fields than factors like IQ or talent alone. Her studies have shown grit's significance in contexts ranging from West Point military cadets to National Spelling Bee contestants.

Duckworth tells us, "Grit is living life like it's a marathon, not a sprint." This metaphor effectively conveys the long-term nature of grit, emphasizing that success often requires sustained effort over time rather than short bursts of intensity. It challenges the notion of overnight success and highlights the importance of perseverance in achieving significant goals.

CONJURING OUR OWN TENACITY, PERSEVERANCE, AND GRIT

Where do we find the tenacity, perseverance, and grit to keep going when the road becomes unbearably tough? These traits are not gifts bestowed upon a select few; they are qualities that reside within each of us, waiting to be called upon in times of need. But how do we access them? How do we summon the strength to persevere when everything inside us screams to give up?

Our Must Mindset empowers us to see failure not as a reflection of our inherent abilities but as a stepping stone to success. It allows us to persist in the face of adversity, knowing that each setback is simply part of the journey. By cultivating a Must Mindset that compels us, we tap into an inexhaustible well of tenacity and grit, enabling us to keep moving forward, no matter how daunting the challenge.

Another wellspring of tenacity and perseverance is our sense of our purpose derived from our *must* foundations of who we are. When we are deeply connected to our purpose—when we know our "why"—we are far more likely to persevere through difficulties. Purpose gives us a reason to keep going, even when the path is hard. It fuels our determination and keeps us focused on the bigger picture.

Simon Sinek reminds us that our purpose is our motivating engine of progress. Those who understand their "why" are better equipped to inspire action in themselves and others. "Working hard for something we don't care about is called stress; working hard for something we love is called passion," Sinek explains. When we align our goals with our purpose, we transform our efforts from a burden into a mission. This sense of purpose becomes the fuel that drives our tenacity, helping us to stay the course even when the going gets tough.

The way we approach goals can also help us build tenacity. One helpful strategy begins with setting clear long-term goals that are personally meaningful and breaking them down into smaller, achievable milestones. This strategy, known as "goal laddering," has been shown to increase motivation and persistence by up to 30 percent in longitudinal studies. Additionally, engaging in deliberate, focused practice in areas targeted for improvement is crucial.

Research indicates that individuals who dedicate at least ten thousand hours to mastering a skill demonstrate significantly higher levels of grit and expertise in their chosen field. While it may seem circular, the development of tenacity through persistent practice is a self-reinforcing process. The act of dedicating oneself to deliberate, focused practice not only builds skill but also strengthens the mental fortitude required for long-term commitment. As individuals invest time and effort into their chosen pursuits, they develop not just expertise but also resilience, perseverance, and a growth mindset. This process creates a positive feedback loop: the more one practices, the more tenacious they become, which in turn fuels their ability to engage in further practice.

It's important to note that the ten-thousand-hour rule is not a rigid benchmark but rather a representation of the substantial time investment required for mastery. The key takeaway is that consistent, purposeful effort over time not only develops skill but also cultivates the very qualities of grit and determination that enable continued growth and achievement.

Tenacity, perseverance, and grit are often strengthened by the support of others. Surrounding ourselves with a community of like-minded individuals who share our goals and values can provide the encouragement and accountability we need to keep pushing forward. Whether it's a mentor who offers guidance, a friend who lends a listening ear, or a group of peers who share our struggles, the power of community cannot be underestimated.

Research has shown that social support is a critical factor in resilience and perseverance. When we feel supported by others, we are more likely to persevere through challenges and less likely to give up when things get tough. This support helps us to maintain our motivation and stay focused on our goals, even in the face of adversity.

For example, Angela Duckworth and her colleagues conducted a comprehensive study that shed light on the significant role of social support in fostering grit among adolescents. Their research, which involved a large sample of students from diverse backgrounds, revealed a strong correlation between perceived support from teachers and peers and higher levels of grit and perseverance in academic pursuits. Specifically, students who reported feeling valued, encouraged, and supported by their educators and classmates demonstrated a 20 percent increase in grit scores compared to those who felt less supported.

Embracing challenges as opportunities for growth rather than threats is another key component in developing grit. This mindset shift, rooted in Carol Dweck's growth mindset theory, has been associated with an increase in academic performance and resilience in the face of setbacks.

Regularly reflecting on progress and celebrating small victories along the way has been linked to increased motivation and perseverance. Research indicates that individuals who engage in weekly self-reflection and acknowledge their incremental progress have an enhanced likelihood to achieve their long-term goals.

By implementing these evidence-based strategies and maintaining a growth mindset, individuals can develop the tenacity, perseverance, and grit to overcome obstacles and achieve their long-term aspirations. It's important to remember that these qualities are not innate or fixed traits, but rather skills that can be cultivated and strengthened over time through consistent effort, practice, and a supportive environment.

THE BALANCE BETWEEN SURRENDER AND PERSEVERANCE

Does surrender mean failure? When is it wise to surrender one path of pursuit and choose another one? The word "surrender" often conjures images of white flags and defeat, but true surrender can be an act of immense strength and wisdom.

The idea that surrender equals failure is a common misconception. In reality, there are times when surrender is the wisest course of action, a recognition that some battles are not meant to be fought. However, perseverance at all costs can also lead to burnout, diverting us from our true path.

Wisdom lies in knowing when to hold on and when to let go. It's about asking the tough questions: Is this pursuit enhancing my life or draining my spirit? Am I holding on out of fear or genuine aspiration? True courage comes from being honest with ourselves, confronting our fears, and living authentically.

Steve Jobs, the co-founder of Apple, exemplified this wisdom. Known for his relentless drive and vision, Jobs also understood the importance of knowing when to pivot. After being ousted from Apple, the company he co-founded, Jobs could have persisted in trying to regain his position. Instead, he chose to surrender that fight and focus on new ventures, including the creation of Pixar, which revolutionized the animation industry. His decision to let go of one battle allowed him to win another, ultimately leading to his triumphant return to Apple and the creation of iconic products like the iPhone.

Navigating the balance between surrender and perseverance requires courage—the courage to be vulnerable, to admit when we don't have all the answers, and to take the leap of faith that is required, whether in surrender or perseverance. The true measure of knowing if you are on the right path, and whether you should surrender or persevere, is whether your current path is in direct alignment with your Must Core Beliefs, Must Values, Must Standards, and thoroughly examined purpose.

THE UNBREAKABLE HUMAN SPIRIT

Your life is rich not just with sunny meadows but also with deep valleys. Your hardest times often reveal the core of who you are, and it's from that core that you draw the strength to rise. As you traverse life's difficulties, each challenge is a stepping stone on your path to becoming the magnificent being you were always meant to be. Richard Bach, American author of *Jonathan Livingston Seagull*, proclaims, "You are never given a dream without also being given the power to make it true."

Please allow me to bring us back to a moment of poignant significance in my life that merits repeating as it so vividly applies to our discussion of tenacity, perseverance, and grit. In the dark aftermath of my stepfather's suicide, I stumbled upon a scene that would forever etch itself into my memory. There in the shadowy confines of her bedroom closet, my mother knelt, her hands raw from scouring the blood-stained carpet—a futile attempt to cleanse away the chaos that had engulfed our existence. As I stood frozen, her gaze met mine. With a look that spoke volumes of anguish and determination, she rose from the floor, her spirit battered but unbroken. In a voice tinged with both sorrow and steel, she said, "Honey, I got this. I will never let something like this ever happen to us again." She found her tenacity and grit to persevere.

I pray you never have to experience such profound suffering or face a tragedy that shatters the very foundations of your world. But if you are confronted with overwhelming darkness, remember this: within you lies an untapped wellspring of strength, a reservoir of tenacity that you can rise from and that must carry you through the storm. If you have already encountered devastating tragedy in your life, then you know you can handle whatever will happen in the future. For in the end, it is not the absence of suffering that defines us, but how we choose to respond to it. Let your response be one of courage, of compassion, and of unwavering resolve. In doing so, you not only honor your own journey but also inspire others to find their inner strength in times of need.

PART THREE

Integration: Transcendence, Transformation, and the Fullness of Life

As you arrive at Part 3 of this journey, you stand at a threshold—the place where all the insights, habits, and beliefs you've cultivated are ready to be integrated into the fabric of your daily life. This is the stage of becoming, not simply learning or doing, but embodying the person you are meant to be.

Part 3 is about integration: weaving together the lessons of suffering and struggle with the blessings of gratitude, love, and grace. Here you will discover that true transformation is not just about overcoming hardship but about allowing every experience—joyful and painful alike—to shape you into a more authentic, compassionate, and resilient self.

In these chapters, we explore how suffering, when met with courage and perspective, can become the catalyst for purpose and growth. But this section is equally about recognizing and receiving the blessings that life offers: the quiet moments of gratitude, the grace that emerges from forgiveness, and the profound power of love, both for others and for yourself.

Transcendence is the theme running through these pages. It is the process of rising above old patterns and limitations, transforming wounds into wisdom, and choosing to see every challenge as an opportunity for deeper meaning. Integration means living from your *must*—not as an abstract ideal but as a daily practice that brings harmony to your relationships, your work, your spirituality, and your legacy.

As you read, I invite you to reflect on how far you've come. Notice the ways you have already begun to change—not just in thought but also in action and intention. Embrace the blessings that surround you and let love—both given and received—become the foundation of your transformation.

This is the journey of wholeness. In integrating all that you are—the struggles and the strengths, the losses and the loves—you unlock the possibility of a life marked by purpose, peace, and profound fulfillment. Welcome to the final phase of becoming: the art of living your *must* in every moment.

CHAPTER 15

Suffering: The Darkness Before the Light

"To live is to suffer, to survive is to find some meaning in the suffering."
—Friedrich Nietzsche, German philosopher

In reflecting on my own experiences with suffering, I realize now how deeply personal and isolated they felt at the time. There was a pervasive sense that my pain was uniquely targeted at me, as if the universe had singled me out for hardship. This myopic view of suffering clouded my ability to recognize the struggles of those around me. I vividly recall moments when the weight of my challenges felt crushingly heavy and impossibly unfair. The loss of my stepfather, the physical limitations I faced, the bullying during my youth, and the feelings of abandonment all seemed to converge into a narrative that I was somehow marked for misfortune. In those dark times, it was difficult to see beyond my pain.

Tunnel vision of suffering is a common human tendency. When

we're in pain, our focus naturally narrows to our immediate experience. It's as if we're wearing blinders that prevent us from seeing the broader landscape of human struggle. This self-centered perspective isn't born of selfishness but rather a natural response to intense emotional pain.

Looking back, I now understand that my suffering, while deeply personal, was not unique in its intensity or unfairness. It was part of the shared human experience of collective human struggle. The classmate who always seemed cheerful might have been grappling with family issues at home. The neighbor who appeared to have it all together could have been fighting an internal war with depression. This realization doesn't diminish the validity of our pain, but it places it in a broader, more compassionate context.

Now when I encounter personal challenges, I remind myself that I'm not alone in my struggles. This shift in perspective doesn't make the pain disappear, but it makes it more bearable. It allows me to extend the same compassion to myself that I would offer to others facing similar difficulties.

In sharing our stories of suffering, we create bridges of understanding, empathy, and compassion. We realize that while our specific circumstances may differ, the core experience of pain and resilience is something we all share. This shared vulnerability can be a powerful force for connection and healing.

I invite you to embark on a profoundly difficult journey of introspection. Find a quiet sanctuary, free from disturbance, where you can delve into the depths of your soul. Close your eyes, and with each breath, allow your life's struggles, pain, and suffering to vividly and palpably unfold before you. Let the memories of loss, loneliness, and heartache rise to the surface, not to torment you, but to be acknowledged with compassion and courage. The sights, sounds, and feelings associated with your losses may flood back, making those past events seem present once again. This intense recollection serves to bring your experiences of loss into sharp focus, making them tangible and immediate in your consciousness.

In this sacred space of reflection, summon the dark, ethereal traces of your past—the pain of the loss of loved ones who have departed, the moments of crushing rejection, the bitter taste of failure, and the searing pain of both body and spirit. As you breathe life into these vivid memories, feel the weight of ongoing battles that still press upon your heart.

These acts of remembrance and inventory are not meant to reopen old wounds but to illuminate the path of your personal evolution. By bringing these dark chapters to light, we prepare to face them with unwavering resolve. In the conversation that follows, we will not simply recount our suffering but seek to understand its profound purpose in shaping who we are and who we are destined to become.

This moment of reflection is an act of alchemy, transforming the heavy stones of our pain into the gold of self-discovery. It is through this courageous confrontation that we see our struggles not as mere obstacles but as the stepping stones that lead us to our true selves. Take all the time you need in this sacred space of remembrance. When you are ready, open your eyes and carry with you the awareness of your journey. For it is in understanding and transcending our suffering that we unlock the door to profound growth and unshakable resilience. I deeply honor you for your courage to search deep within yourself, as this experience shall ultimately lead to a renewed perspective that shall free our spirit and our worldview. In this chapter, we grab the dragon of suffering by the tail and do not let go until we better understand it and how to deal with it in our lives.

While previous chapters have focused on identifying and pursuing your *must*, this chapter delves deeper, exploring how to maintain alignment with your purpose even in the face of adversity. Suffering is not a detour from your *must* path; it is an inevitable and necessary part of it. By understanding this, we can approach our challenges not as obstacles to be avoided but as opportunities for growth and deeper self-discovery.

FILLING YOUR SUFFERING BASKET

Imagine a metaphorical Suffering Basket that has been woven from the threads of your experiences. Into this basket, gently place each recollection of suffering, both past and present:

- The sharp pangs of *grief* for loved ones lost
- The dull ache of *regrets* and missed opportunities
- The heavy weight of *depression* that once clouded your days
- The burning flames of *anger* that may have consumed you
- The isolating chill of *loneliness* you've endured
- The gnawing discomfort of *guilt* that has lingered
- The deep wounds inflicted by *prejudice* or *hatred*

As you fill this basket, notice the texture of each memory, the weight it carries, and the emotions it stirs within you. Now let us examine the contents of this basket under our microscope of introspection. We must examine our suffering to know it and to release its power over us. Our Suffering Basket is heavy, full of items we wish did not exist, but that presently linger with us and within us.

As we inspect the contents of our basket, we are stricken with the same questions the ancient luminaries confronted. We grapple, trying to understand the enigma of human suffering, seeking to unravel its purpose and place in our lives. Should we view our personal suffering as divine retribution? Is it an inherent aspect of the human condition? Is it a catalyst toward wisdom? Is it an inescapable companion to desire and impermanence? Or is it a means for the opportunity of cultivating virtue and inner strength? It's time to look into your Suffering Basket. We must confront our suffering.

The goal of confronting your Suffering Basket is to transform pain into a catalyst for personal growth and self-actualization. By inspecting the contents of the basket, we unravel the ways suffering shapes our beliefs, values, and resilience. This process is not about dwelling on pain or viewing it as punishment; rather, it is about understanding suffering as an inevitable part of the human experience that, when embraced, can refine our purpose and strengthen our inner resolve.

Through this exercise, we learn to use suffering as both a tool and a teacher, allowing it to reveal hidden strengths, deepen our wisdom, and align us more closely with our authentic selves. At the same time, we let go of the emotional weight that suffering carries by reframing it as an opportunity for growth rather than a source of despair. This duality—using suffering while releasing its burden—helps us evolve into the self-actualized person we were meant to be, fully aligned with our *musts* and capable of transcending life's challenges.

EMBRACING THE UNIVERSALITY OF SUFFERING

As we peer into our Suffering Basket, we find it brimming with an assortment of painful experiences, each unique in its shape and intensity. Some are sharp, cutting into our very being; others burn with the heat of unresolved anger or shame. Some press against us with the weight of guilt or regret, while others refuse to leave us alone, haunting our thoughts with persistent sorrow. These items fill our minds with darkness and an initial sense of hopelessness, compelling us to cry out into the void for release and salvation from the torment they bring.

Yet in a moment of clarity, we lift our gaze from our anguish and notice we are not alone in our suffering. All around us, others carry their own baskets, filled with similar yet distinct elements of pain. We see grief etched on faces, regret weighing down shoulders, depression casting shadows over eyes, anger clenched in fists, loneliness creating invisible barriers, and the wounds of hatred leaving visible scars. In this shared experience of human suffering, we discover a profound truth: the universality of pain. Our individual Suffering Baskets may vary in content and weight, but they are a common thread that binds us all, reminding us of our shared humanity and the collective resilience we possess in facing life's challenges.

In the depths of our pain, it's easy to think our suffering is unique and no one else could possibly understand the profound depths of our despair. Yet as we look around at other baskets of suffering, we see similar ornaments of our own pain. Thich Nhat Hanh, a Vietnamese Zen master, peace activist, and spiritual leader, reminds us, "The illusion of unique suffering is the greatest barrier to empathy, for in pain, we are all the same." This belief that our pain is unique can make our burden feel even heavier, isolating us further from the comfort and support we need. Yet this belief is misleading.

Brené Brown captures this truth with clarity: "We often think our pain is special, but in truth, it is the most common thread of human experience." By recognizing that our suffering is not unique, we dismantle the barriers to empathy and connection. This understanding opens the door to a deeper sense of solidarity with others, reminding us that in our pain, we are not isolated but united with the broader human experience.

Only by walking through the darkness can we fully appreciate and embrace the light on the other side. Recognizing the universality of suffering can be a powerful step toward healing. It allows us to feel less alone in our struggles and more connected to the human experience as a whole. As Viktor Frankl discovered in the concentration camps, finding meaning in suffering can transform our relationship with pain.

Suffering is not the end; it is a passage—a critical and essential part of the human experience that shapes us, strengthens us, and ultimately deepens our understanding of ourselves and the world around us. No matter how overwhelming the pain may seem, there is a beautiful life waiting to be embraced beyond these difficult experiences.

Suffering is an inescapable part of the human condition. It tests our resilience, strength, and character in ways few other experiences can. Whether your suffering takes the form of physical pain, emotional turmoil, psychological struggles, or spiritual crises, each type shapes us in profound ways. Throughout this chapter, we will delve into your Suffering Basket and reveal these various facets of suffering, and I will offer perspectives, empathy, support, and inspiration to help you navigate your personal journey.

As we explore these dark valleys, remember that suffering always simultaneously coexists with blessings, grace, and abundance. These moments of hardship can enrich our lives in unexpected ways, revealing the depth of our resilience and the beauty of the human spirit. Together, we will uncover how, even in the midst of pain, there is light to be found—guiding us toward healing, growth, and a deeper connection to the world around us. Remember that each step through the darkness brings us closer to the light.

THE POWER OF ACKNOWLEDGING SUFFERING

As we peer into our Suffering Basket, it is impossible to deny that it is full of an array of experiences. *We must acknowledge all of our suffering.* Acknowledging suffering is a powerful and essential step in navigating through it with grace and resilience. It is not merely about admitting the presence of pain but about validating your experience and emotions, giving them the recognition they deserve.

Franciscan friar, Catholic priest, and author Richard Rohr beautifully articulates this notion: "To acknowledge suffering is to give it a name, and in naming it, we begin the process of liberation."

When we name our suffering, we confront it head-on rather than evading or denying its existence. This act of acknowledgment is the first step toward healing and transformation. By recognizing our pain, we create space for introspection, which allows us to delve into the roots of our suffering and understand its impact on our lives.

Archbishop Emeritus Desmond Tutu offered profound wisdom and insisted that "suffering that is not acknowledged festers in the dark, but suffering brought into the light begins to heal." By bringing our suffering into the light, we begin the process of healing. This light of acknowledgment doesn't just illuminate our pain; it also reveals the pathways to recovery, resilience, and growth.

Acknowledgment opens the door to compassion—both for us and for others who suffer. Author and therapist Tara Brach emphasizes this further: "The truth is suffering is an essential part of life. If we acknowledge it, it can lead us to deeper understanding and compassion." Embracing this truth empowers us to seek the support we need, develop effective coping strategies, and find meaning in our struggles. Through acknowledgment, we transform our suffering from a source of hidden anguish into a catalyst for personal growth and resilience. It is in this courageous act of facing our pain that we reclaim our power and move toward a place of healing and renewal.

Acknowledging suffering illuminates the ways it has influenced our beliefs, strengthened our resilience, and clarified our purpose. This act of naming and confronting pain allows us to transcend the straightforward lessons of habits and actions by engaging with the emotional and spiritual dimensions of growth. It transforms us by revealing hidden strengths and teaching us compassion for ourselves and others.

It integrates what we've learned by showing how suffering is not separate from the Must Zone but an essential part of it—a force that challenges us to live in alignment with our values even in the face of adversity. Through acknowledgment, we reclaim our power to use suffering as a tool for refinement and renewal, propelling ourselves toward self-actualization.

THE INVENTORY OF OUR COLLECTIVE SUFFERING

At the beginning of this chapter, you took the courageous step of collecting in your mind those times when suffering riveted your being. It is time to take inventory of all the elements of suffering contained in our Suffering Basket, full of types of suffering that we shall pull out and reveal one by one. We have never thoroughly organized our life's moments of suffering in this way before. Now we must do so. Once we address each experience, we will have reframed our experiences into lighter and less personal objects that, once freed from their burden of oppressing us, can simply lie in a drawer, void of their power to cause us to succumb to the false self-limiting belief that we are a victim.

As we begin our inventory of what is contained in our Suffering Basket, we are reminded that our wounds are here so we can be receptive to healing with our efforts and with God's grace. English novelist Charles Dickens offers, "Suffering has been stronger than all other teaching, and has taught me to understand what your heart used to be. I have been bent and broken, but—I hope—into a better shape."

In the midst of suffering, it's crucial to turn inward and listen to that quiet, inner voice—the one that knows the way to healing, even when everything else feels chaotic. Thich Nhat Hanh said, "The most important thing we can do in times of emotional distress is to listen to the voice within us, the one that whispers softly but carries the wisdom of healing." This inner wisdom guides us through the darkness, helping us process our pain and beginning the journey toward recovery.

DESPAIR: THE LOSS OF HOPE

We pull out the experiences of despair and loss of hope from our Suffering Basket. Despair is the profound and crushing feeling that all hope is lost. It often emerges from prolonged suffering or traumatic events that leave us feeling utterly helpless. This overwhelming sense of despair can make the future seem bleak, as if the light at the end of the tunnel has permanently dimmed. Yet even in the darkest of times, glimmers of hope can sustain us, offering a path out of the darkness.

In my life's story, that summer night over fifty years ago, my loving stepfather, Rodney Rue, placed a gun in his mouth. At that moment, I am confident he was experiencing deep despair and an absolute loss of hope in his life. For what reasons, no one will ever know. As an eleven-year-old boy at the time, I was not there and did not have the opportunity to talk with him and tell him what he should realize that would loosen the grip of this despair and hopelessness. What words could have miraculously changed the trajectory of the devastation that was seconds away from being?

To those battling despair and hopelessness, know that your life is precious beyond measure. You are loved more deeply than you can imagine, and your presence in this world is a blessing to those around you. The darkness you feel now is not permanent—it will pass, revealing the light of new possibilities. Your story is not over; it is still being written, and the world needs your unique voice and experiences. Remember, seeking help is not a weakness but an act of immense courage. Reach out, speak your truth, and allow others to support you through this storm. Your life has purpose, your pain has meaning, and your future holds hope. Hold on, for you are stronger than you know, and the world is better with you in it.

If you are in deep despair and hopelessness, I urge you to reach out and talk to someone right now. You do not have to face this alone. There are people who care about you and want to help. Remember, the National Suicide Prevention Lifeline is available 24/7 at 1-800-273-TALK (1-800-273-8255), providing confidential support and resources for anyone in crisis. Please know you are loved, and your life has a purpose. Your presence in this world matters, not just to those who care for you but also to those who may one day benefit from your journey of healing. Your struggles can become a source of strength for others. By sharing your story, you can inspire hope and resilience in those around you. You are not alone in this fight; we love you. Please take this step today. Reach out, share your feelings, and let the light of connection guide you through the darkness.

Any despair and hopelessness that may come into our lives may temporarily cast shadows over our joy and cloud our vision of the future. Yet it is crucial to remember that these feelings, no matter how overwhelming they may seem in the moment, are temporary. They don't last unless you allow them to stay. They are mere temporary visitors. When we find ourselves in the grip of despair, it can feel as though we are trapped in an endless tunnel with no light in sight. The weight of our emotions presses down upon us, and we may struggle to imagine a time when we will feel differently. However, this perception is an illusion—a trick of the mind that convinces us of the permanence of our pain. Persian poet Rumi reminds us that "this too shall pass."

The intensity of our despair is directly linked to the meaning we attach to our circumstances. By shifting our perspective, even slightly, we can begin to see the blessings that surround us, even in our darkest moments. Consider the story of Anne Frank, a young girl who endured the horrors of the Holocaust while hiding from the Nazis. Despite the unimaginable suffering she witnessed and experienced, Frank maintained a remarkable sense of hope and faith in humanity. She once wrote, "I don't think of all the misery, but of the beauty that still remains."

This shift doesn't negate our pain, but it allows us to see beyond it, to recognize that our current state is not the entirety of our existence.

The evidence of the temporary nature of despair and hopelessness is evident in our own lives. Think back to times when you felt consumed by sadness, despair, or hopelessness. Perhaps it was the end of a relationship, the loss of a job, or a personal failure that seemed insurmountable at the time. Yet here you are, reading these words, having survived those moments that once felt unbearable. Our lives are a testament to the transient nature of despair. Time and again, we have emerged from the shadows, often sooner than we expected, to find joy and purpose once more. This pattern is not coincidental—it is the natural rhythm of human resilience.

The key to moving through despair lies in our willingness to let it pass. This doesn't mean denying our feelings or forcing ourselves to "be happy." Rather, it means acknowledging our pain without clinging to it, allowing it to move through us like a passing storm. By loosening our grip on despair, we create space for hope to enter. We allow ourselves to be open to the possibilities that exist beyond our current circumstances.

So if I had been given the opportunity to be in that closet fifty years ago and talk to my stepfather, Rodney, while he was in his moment of deepest despair, what I have told you here is what I would have told him then. If that had happened, the night would have passed without tragic events, the sun would have risen as it did, and my stepfather would have shared a lifetime of wonderful experiences that life has for us. Let's behold the beauty of this wonderous life, full of the fruits of our enduring hope.

DEPRESSION: THE PERSISTENT SHADOW

The next item that we pull from our Suffering Basket is any experience with depression that we have encountered. If you look around at other people, you will see that many of them are pulling their experiences with depression out of their baskets. Depression is a pervasive and often debilitating form of suffering that can cast a long shadow over one's life. It's characterized by persistent feelings of sadness, hopelessness, and a loss of interest in activities once enjoyed. This mental and emotional weight can be difficult to lift, making it seem as though there is no escape from the darkness.

Jeffrey Eugenides captures the essence of depression with a poignant metaphor: "Depression is like a bruise that never goes away. A bruise in your mind. You just got to be careful not to touch it where it hurts. It's always there, though." This image of a persistent, tender bruise illustrates how depression lingers, affecting thoughts, actions, and the ability to find joy in things that once brought happiness.

Depression is more than just feeling sad or going through a rough patch. It's a persistent mental health condition that affects how you think, feel, and handle daily activities. Common symptoms include a persistent sad, anxious, or "empty" mood; loss of interest in hobbies and activities; fatigue and decreased energy; difficulty concentrating or making decisions; changes in sleep patterns or appetite; and in severe cases, thoughts of death or suicide.

Consider the story of a young woman who, after the sudden loss of her mother, found herself slipping into deep depression. The once vibrant and outgoing person she had been seemed to disappear, replaced by a hollow version of herself who struggled to get out of bed each day. Her world had turned gray, and things that once brought joy now felt meaningless. However, in the midst of her darkness, she reached out to a therapist. Through therapy, she began to unravel her grief and understand her depression. She learned to find small moments of light—whether it was a kind word from a friend, a walk in the park, or the simple act of caring for herself. Slowly, she rebuilt her life, piece by piece, and while the bruise of depression didn't completely vanish, she learned how to live with it.

Winston Churchill famously referred to his depression as his "black dog." Despite this persistent shadow, he led Britain through its darkest hours with resilience and determination. He once said, "If you're going through hell, keep going." These words remind us that even when the path is shrouded in darkness, the only way forward is to keep moving. Depression can make it feel as though you are trapped in a never-ending tunnel, but by taking one step at a time, you can find your way out.

It's crucial to seek professional help if you're experiencing symptoms of depression. Mental health professionals can provide accurate diagnoses, tailored treatment plans, psychotherapy (such as cognitive behavioral therapy or interpersonal therapy), medication management if necessary, and coping strategies for managing symptoms. Remember, seeking help is a sign of strength, not weakness.

There are also nonmedical interventions that can complement treatment and help manage depression. Regular exercise can boost mood and reduce stress. Mindfulness and meditation practices can help you stay present and manage negative thoughts. Establishing healthy sleep habits and maintaining a balanced diet can support overall mental health. Importantly, maintaining social connections and avoiding isolation is crucial in combating depression.

One powerful strategy for managing depression is to shift your focus outward. Volunteering or helping others can provide a sense of purpose and connection. Engaging in meaningful activities that align with your values, setting achievable goals, and practicing gratitude can all contribute to improving your mental state.

It's important to recognize that while you may experience depression, it does not define you. You are not a "depressed person," but rather a person who has encountered depression. This distinction is crucial as it acknowledges the temporary nature of your condition, separates your identity from your current experience, and opens the possibility for change and growth.

As you work through depression, focus on becoming the person you are meant to be. Identify your values and strengths, set meaningful goals aligned with your purpose, cultivate self-compassion and self-care practices, embrace personal growth opportunities, and surround yourself with supportive people who encourage your growth.

As you navigate depression, the Must Framework can serve as a powerful guide to help you move forward with purpose and resilience.

By identifying your *musts*—the core values, beliefs, and habits that define your authentic self—you create a foundation for growth even in the midst of struggle. Depression often clouds clarity and purpose, but reconnecting with your *musts* can provide a beacon of light, reminding you of what truly matters and anchoring you to your inner strength. The Must Habits you've cultivated—such as mindfulness, structured productivity, and self-compassion—are invaluable tools for managing the emotional weight of depression. Mindfulness helps you stay present and grounded. Structured productivity allows you to take small, meaningful steps toward your goals, and self-compassion fosters kindness toward yourself during difficult times. Fighting depression and pursuing self-growth are deeply intertwined. By aligning your actions with your *musts*, you not only work toward healing but also evolve into the person you were meant to be. This journey is not about perfection but about progress—using the lessons from earlier chapters to reclaim your power and move closer to living fully in the Must Zone.

Remember, overcoming depression is a journey, not a destination. There may be setbacks along the way, but with persistence, support, and the right tools, you can move toward a more fulfilling life. You are more than your experiences with depression. You are a complex, valuable individual with the capacity for growth, resilience, and joy.

Depression may seem like a persistent shadow, but with the right support, treatment, and a focus on the small joys of life, it is possible to find your way back to the light. As you navigate through depression and work toward healing, it's crucial to remember that this experience is part of your larger journey of self-discovery and personal development. While depression can feel all-consuming, it doesn't define you or negate the progress you're making. Even in the midst of managing your symptoms and seeking treatment, continue to engage with the insights and exercises in this book. Your efforts to understand yourself better, to grow, and to become the person you are meant to be are still valid and important.

Depression may slow your pace, but it doesn't have to halt your journey entirely. In fact, the work you're doing to manage depression can often complement and deepen your overall personal growth. The coping strategies you develop, the self-awareness you gain, and the resilience you build all contribute to your broader journey of self-improvement. Remember, healing from depression and pursuing personal growth are not mutually exclusive. They can happen simultaneously, each informing and enriching the other. Stay committed to your path of self-discovery, knowing that every step forward, no matter how small, is a victory both in managing depression and in becoming your best self.

ANGER: THE FIRE WITHIN

As you reach into your Suffering Basket, you pull out the next element of your emotional experiences: anger. This fiery emotion is fierce and hard to handle, often igniting feelings of injustice and betrayal. Anger can feel like a raging inferno, consuming everything in its path and leaving destruction in its wake. It's an intense force that can either empower you or overwhelm you, depending on how you choose to manage it.

In my life, the deepest well of long-term anger that had festered within me for decades stemmed from my profound resentment toward my biological father, Robert. He abandoned us when I was just a child, leaving a gaping hole in my heart. The pain of his absence haunted me and transformed my anger into a simmering rage that colored my perceptions of love and trust. Each time I reflected on his choice to walk away, I felt the weight of rejection and loss, emotions that had, at one time, shaped my beliefs about myself and others. This unresolved anger was not just a fleeting feeling. It was a relentless shadow that reminded me of the love I was denied and the family bonds that were severed. The scars of his abandonment had altered my view of relationships, instilling a fear of loss and a deep-seated belief that I was unworthy of love.

Anger rises from deep within, ignited by feelings of injustice, betrayal, stress, frustration, or unmet needs. When left unchecked, anger can spiral into destructive behaviors that harm not only us but also those we care about. Confucius wisely cautioned, "When anger rises, think of the consequences." This simple yet profound reminder encourages us to pause and reflect before we act, allowing us to redirect our anger toward constructive ends instead of letting it lead us down a path of regret.

The Buddha poignantly articulated the dangers of clinging to anger when he said, "Holding on to anger is like drinking poison and expecting the other person to die." This powerful analogy underscores how anger festers within us, becoming toxic—not just for those around us but primarily for us. It corrodes our peace of mind and clouds our judgment, leaving us trapped in a cycle of negativity. Yet when we take the time to understand and channel our anger effectively, it can transform into a powerful force for change.

Anger often has deep roots that can be traced back to various sources. Trauma plays a significant role; experiences of abuse or neglect can leave emotional scars that manifest as anger later in life. Emotional dysregulation—where one struggles to manage one's emotions effectively—can also lead to explosive outbursts or prolonged periods of simmering rage. Altered brain development, particularly in childhood due to adverse experiences, may hinder one's ability to process emotions healthily.

Internalized pain and helplessness can further fuel anger. When we feel powerless in our circumstances, anger may become the only way we feel we can assert control. Learned behavior from family or societal influences can shape how we express anger. If we grow up witnessing others react with rage to stressors, we may adopt similar responses.

At its core, anger is a natural emotional response to perceived threats or injustices. It can manifest in various forms, ranging from mild irritation to explosive rage. When we feel wronged or powerless, anger serves as a protective mechanism—a way for us to assert ourselves and reclaim control over our circumstances. However, unchecked anger can lead to destructive outcomes that strain relationships and impair decision-making.

A research study from the National Epidemiologic Survey on Alcohol and Related Conditions found that approximately 7.8 percent of the US population experiences excessively inappropriate or poorly controlled anger, indicating a significant public health concern. Frequent feelings of anger can lead to chronic stress, affecting both mental and physical health, resulting in issues such as anxiety, depression, and even cardiovascular problems. It can strain relationships with family, friends, and colleagues, creating a cycle of conflict and resentment that undermines trust and connection.

Engaging in exercises to express anger can initially feel enjoyable and liberating, providing a temporary release of pent-up emotions before leading to potentially devastating consequences. Unchecked anger can lead to severe personal acts of violence with devastating consequences. It manifests in road rage incidents that escalate into aggressive confrontations or shootings, as well as tragic school shootings driven by feelings of alienation.

In domestic settings, uncontrolled anger often results in physical and emotional abuse, while workplace conflicts can lead to violent outbursts. Additionally, interpersonal disputes fueled by rage can culminate in homicides, and individuals may turn their aggression inward, resulting in self-harm or suicide attempts. Anger can also contribute to substance abuse and child abuse, where caregivers lash out at vulnerable individuals. In extreme cases, collective anger may motivate acts of terrorism against innocent civilians. These examples underscore the critical need for effective anger management strategies to prevent such destructive outcomes.

Anger can profoundly impact your personal life in numerous and less dramatic ways that can alter your core beliefs about yourself, others, and the world around you. Unresolved anger can distort your perceptions, leading to a more cynical view of others and fostering feelings of isolation. It may cause you to react impulsively or lash out verbally, which can damage important relationships and create a sense of regret. Over time, these experiences can shape negative beliefs about your self-worth and the intentions of those around you, making it difficult to engage positively with others. Ultimately, recognizing and managing anger is essential not only for emotional well-being but also for nurturing healthy relationships and maintaining a balanced perspective on life.

Consider the story of David, a man who was unfairly dismissed from his job. The sense of injustice burned within him like an unquenchable fire, threatening to consume his spirit. Initially, he lashed out at those around him; his frustration spilled over into his personal life, damaging relationships with friends and family who cared for him. He would snap at loved ones over trivial matters, feeling as though he was losing control over everything that mattered. But as time passed, David realized this anger would ultimately destroy him if he left it unchecked. He searched for ways to channel his anger constructively.

David decided to volunteer at a local advocacy group dedicated to workers' rights, using his experiences not only as a means of healing but also as a way to help others facing similar injustices. Through this work, he found renewed purpose in advocating for those who had been wronged in their workplaces. His anger transformed into a force for positive change—turning pain into empowerment.

Now reflect on your own experiences with anger. Have there been moments when it felt overwhelming? Perhaps you've experienced the sting of injustice or betrayal that ignited an intense fire within you. Reflect on how you harnessed this powerful emotion. Did you allow it to push you toward actions you later regretted? Or did you find a way to channel it into something constructive?

Effectively managing and curbing the anger that may linger in your life requires conscious effort and reflection. When you feel that familiar heat rising within you, pause and take a deep breath. Reflect on what triggered your anger and ask yourself whether your response will lead to constructive outcomes. Often, anger stems from unmet needs or feelings of injustice. Identifying what you need in that moment—whether it's respect, understanding, or support—can guide you toward communicating those needs assertively rather than aggressively.

Channeling your energy into positive action is another powerful strategy. Use your anger as fuel for physical activities like exercise or sports that allow you to release pent-up energy healthily. Practicing mindfulness techniques can help you stay present and manage negative thoughts associated with anger. Meditation or deep-breathing exercises create space between your feelings and reactions. Engaging in creative outlets provides another avenue for processing emotions—

writing, art, or music can serve as therapeutic relief while allowing you to express complex feelings constructively.

Don't hesitate to reach out for support when managing your emotions feels overwhelming. Talking with friends or mental health professionals can provide valuable perspectives and coping strategies that help you navigate through difficult times. Instead of dwelling on what made you angry, focus on finding solutions that address the root causes of your feelings.

Cultivating empathy is also essential in transforming anger into understanding. Try to see things from the perspective of others involved in the situation that triggered your anger. This practice can soften hostility and open pathways for constructive dialogue.

By transforming anger from a destructive force into a motivating one, you can turn this powerful emotion into a tool for personal growth and societal change. Remember that while anger is an inevitable part of life's emotional landscape, it does not have to dictate your actions or define who you are as a person.

Embracing the fire within requires understanding its origins and potential consequences while also recognizing its capacity for positive transformation. By reflecting on your experiences with anger and employing strategies to manage it constructively, you can harness this powerful emotion as a catalyst for meaningful change—not only in your own life but also in the lives of those around you.

As Maya Angelou beautifully stated, "You may not control all the events that happen to you, but you can control your attitude toward them." By choosing how we respond to our emotions—particularly anger—we reclaim our power and pave the way toward healing and growth. Let this fire within become a guiding light rather than an all-consuming blaze. Let it illuminate your path forward as you navigate the complexities of life with resilience and purpose.

My biological father passed away shortly after his eightieth birthday, leaving behind a legacy of unresolved pain and unfulfilled potential. Despite my heartfelt attempts to reach out and mend our fractured relationship, he never sought to reconnect. For decades, I kept the flames of rage and anger kindled within me, believing these emotions somehow honored my hurt. Yet, in truth, they only served to imprison me in a cycle of suffering.

On the day of his funeral, as I watched his ashes drift away with the wind, a profound revelation washed over me: "I cannot be angry at ashes." In that moment, I felt an unexpected relief. It dawned on me that all those years of anger had not harmed him; they had only harmed me. This realization was a breakthrough, illuminating the futility of holding on to such destructive feelings.

With further reflection and the support of my personal faith, I discovered the power of forgiveness. This act was not just for him; it was a precious gift to myself and to those around me. By choosing to forgive, I lightened my burdens and released the weight of resentment that had weighed heavily on my heart. In essence, I took that ornament of suffering out of my Suffering Basket, allowing space for healing and renewal in my life. Embracing forgiveness has opened new pathways for love and connection, freeing me from the shackles of the past and inviting peace into my present.

Forgiveness plays an essential role in this journey as it is not merely about absolving others but liberating ourselves from the chains of resentment that bind us. Consider how releasing your anger through forgiveness can change your life. Imagine carrying around heavy stones representing every hurt you've endured. Each stone weighs down your spirit and clouds your joy. These currently reside in your Suffering Basket. Now picture yourself slowly setting down each stone, one by one, through acts of forgiveness—first forgiving others who have hurt you and then forgiving yourself for holding on to these burdens for so long.

GRIEF: THE DEEP SORROW OF LOSS

Grief has been a constant companion in my life since the day my biological father left. It deepened when my stepfather took his own life, and it lingered as I witnessed my mother struggle through years of depression. I know this feeling all too well. If you have experienced loss, you understand that haunting ache that never truly leaves you.

Grief lingers like a heavy veil over your existence, casting shadows on moments of joy and peace. It doesn't adhere to anyone else's timeline; it has its own rhythm and pace. Well-meaning friends may tell you that you will be fine or you should feel better soon, but they don't grasp the profound depth of your sorrow. Healing is not a linear path, and there's no set schedule for when the weight of grief will lift.

It raises itself in its own time, often when you least expect it, and sometimes it feels as if it will never fully go away. Yet in this struggle, I've learned to honor my grief as a part of my journey—a testament to the love I once had and the connections that shaped me. It reminds me of the fragility of life and the importance of allowing ourselves to feel deeply, even when it hurts. In embracing this process, I've found moments of clarity and strength, learning that it's okay to grieve at my own pace, without judgment or expectation from others.

Grief is the profound sorrow that accompanies loss, especially the death of a loved one. It is an emotion that touches the deepest parts of our being, a reminder of how intertwined our lives are with those we love. The depth of grief is a testament to the depth of our love and connection. Queen Elizabeth II knew that "grief is the price we pay for love." The queen's words capture the essence of grief—it is the cost of love, the inevitable consequence of forming deep bonds with others. The more we love, the more we grieve when that love is severed by loss.

Consider the story of Arthur, who, after the passing of his lifelong partner, found himself engulfed in grief. The pain of waking up alone, the silence of an empty home, and the constant reminders of the life they had shared were overwhelming. He felt as though he had lost a part of himself, and the future seemed bleak and uncertain. But amid the sorrow, he found solace in the memories they had created together. He would sit in their favorite park, reminiscing about their shared moments of joy, and slowly these memories became a source of comfort rather than pain. He kept a journal, writing down these memories, which helped him feel connected to his partner even after their passing. Through this process, he found a way to honor his grief while also cherishing the love that had brought it about.

C. S. Lewis, in his book *A Grief Observed*, offers a raw and honest reflection on his own experience of grief after losing his wife. He tells us, "No one ever told me that grief felt so like fear." Lewis's comparison of grief to fear highlights the anxiety and uncertainty that often accompany loss. Grief is not just sadness—it is a complex mix of emotions, including fear, confusion, and even anger. The world can feel unpredictable and unsafe when someone we love is no longer there, and navigating this new reality can be incredibly daunting.

Reflect on your own experiences with grief. Have you ever lost someone close to you and felt the profound emptiness that follows? Perhaps it was a parent, a partner, or a dear friend. The pain of their absence can feel unbearable, as though a piece of your heart has been torn away. But within that grief, there is also a deep well of love and memories that can offer comfort and a sense of continuity.

Grief is not something to be "overcome" or "moved past"; it is something to be lived with, a process that evolves over time. It's important to honor your feelings and the memories of those you have lost while finding a path forward that allows you to live fully in the present. Megan Devine, author of *It's OK That You're Not OK*, challenges prior concepts about grief. She states, "Grief is not a problem to be solved; it's an experience to be carried."

In 1969, Elisabeth Kübler-Ross introduced to us the concept that there are five stages of grief, which are denial, anger, bargaining, depression, and acceptance. These stages were initially developed to describe the emotional responses of terminally ill patients facing their own mortality. She tell us, "The reality is that you will grieve forever. You will not 'get over' the loss of a loved one; you will learn to live with it. You will heal and you will rebuild yourself around the loss you have suffered. You will be whole again, but you will never be the same. Nor should you be the same nor would you want to."

Later in her life, Kübler-Ross clarified that these stages were not meant to be a rigid, linear progression that everyone experiences. In her book *On Grief and Grieving*, coauthored with David Kessler and published posthumously in 2005, she emphasized that the stages are "not stops on some linear timeline in grief" and that "not everyone goes through all of them or goes in a prescribed order."

Contemporary grief research supports this view, recognizing that grief is a highly individual experience that doesn't follow a predictable pattern. Some people may not experience all stages, while others might experience them in a different order or even simultaneously. Kübler-Ross's model is now seen as a flexible framework for understanding various emotional responses to loss rather than a strict sequence of events.

Understanding that grief is a natural and necessary response to loss can help you navigate this painful journey with compassion for yourself. Grief may change you, but it also offers an opportunity for growth, for deepening your understanding of love, life, and the connections that define us.

Near where I write this book is a bookshelf that holds my late stepfather's coffee mug, which he obtained in the navy. His pipe sits in it. Periodically, I smell remnants of the cherry tobacco that he last placed in that pipe; it has the scent of what he smelled like when he smoked it while he was alive. I look at his picture, cherishing that smell and the memories of our love for each other. The bittersweetness of it is profoundly comforting.

Grief, while deeply painful, is also a reflection of the love that binds us to others. By embracing your grief, honoring your memories, and allowing yourself the time and space to heal, you can navigate this journey with a sense of compassion and hope, knowing your loved one's legacy lives on in the love you continue to carry.

LONELINESS: THE FEELING OF ISOLATION

The next item of our life experiences that we pull from the Suffering Basket is loneliness. Loneliness is a profound feeling of being alone, isolated from others, and disconnected from the world around us. It can be one of the most painful human experiences, cutting deep into our sense of belonging and self-worth. Mother Teresa said, "Loneliness and the feeling of being unwanted is the most terrible poverty." Mother Teresa's words remind us that loneliness, like physical poverty, can leave us feeling empty and deprived. This state of being can lead to despair if not addressed, but it also carries within it the potential for extraordinary self-discovery and growth.

Loneliness is a profound and haunting emptiness that echoes through the chambers of the heart, a silent ache that yearns for connection in a world that feels increasingly distant. It's the weight of isolation pressing down on your chest, making each breath a reminder of the void where companionship should reside. Loneliness is the cold touch of solitude when you long for the warmth of a human embrace, the deafening silence in a room full of people, and the invisible barrier that seems to separate you from the world around you. It's a complex mix of emotions—fear and a deep-seated longing for understanding and acceptance.

In a startling recognition of this pervasive issue, in 2023 the surgeon general of the United States, Dr. Vivek Murthy, declared that the country is in the midst of a "loneliness epidemic." As we retreat into the digital cocoons of our smartphones and social media, we're sacrificing genuine face-to-face connections for the illusion of connectivity. Dr. Julianne Holt-Lunstad and colleagues in 2015 examined data from over 3.4 million participants in global research, which had findings consistent with the surgeon general's findings. The statistics presented by the surgeon general are alarming: the health risks associated with loneliness are equivalent to smoking up to fifteen cigarettes a day, and approximately half of US adults report experiencing measurable levels of loneliness.

This social disconnection increases the risk of premature death by nearly 30 percent while also elevating the likelihood of stroke, heart disease, depression, anxiety, and dementia. The impact is particularly severe among young people aged fifteen to twenty-four, who reported a staggering 70 percent drop in time spent with friends over the past two decades. Dr. Murthy emphasizes the gravity of the situation, stating, "Our epidemic of loneliness and isolation has been an underappreciated public health crisis that has harmed individual and societal health. Our relationships are a source of healing and well-being hiding in plain sight—one that can help us live healthier, more fulfilled and more productive lives."

Scientific research supports the notion that self-acceptance and comfort with solitude are crucial first steps in addressing loneliness. A study published in the *Journal of Personality and Social Psychology* found that loneliness predicts increases in depressive symptoms over one-year intervals, suggesting a reciprocal relationship between loneliness and depression. The study also found that individuals who developed a strong sense of self-compassion and self-acceptance reported lower levels of loneliness and higher overall well-being. The research found that loneliness was characterized by greater negative affect and more negative interactions. Lonely individuals were found to not only communicate negativity to others but also elicit it from others and transmit it through social networks. This creates a cycle of negative interactions and effects for the lonely person, while also spreading negativity to others they interact with.

Applying this knowledge to our personal lives and our personal bouts with loneliness, we should develop a comfortable and thriving relationship with ourselves. This is one of the most significant goals of this book—to introduce you to your true authentic self. When we are sitting in solitude, alone, that does not equate to being lonely unless we accept that narrative.

Quintessential American writer and humorist Mark Twain said, "The worst loneliness is not to be comfortable with yourself." Twain speaks to this deeper layer of loneliness—the loneliness that comes from not being at peace with oneself. This kind of loneliness can persist even in the presence of others, as it stems from an internal disconnect rather than an external one.

Before we seek remedies for loneliness through social interactions with others, let us first turn inward and nurture our own hearts. It is essential to cultivate a deep sense of self-love, compassion, and forgiveness within ourselves. We must become our own greatest cheerleader, our steadfast coach, and our most trusted mentor and friend. By embracing this inner support, we can build a foundation of self-acceptance that allows us to connect more authentically with the world around us.

By identifying your *musts*—the values, beliefs, and purpose that define your authentic self—you create a foundation for cultivating self-love and compassion. Living in alignment with your *musts* means honoring who you truly are, even in moments of loneliness or struggle. The Must Habits you've developed—such as mindfulness, self-compassion practices, and structured reflection—become essential tools for nurturing your heart and building inner resilience.

When you embrace your *musts*, you strengthen your ability to be your own greatest cheerleader and mentor, creating a wellspring of self-acceptance that empowers you to connect with others authentically. This inner alignment not only remedies loneliness but also deepens your capacity to live fully in the Must Zone, where your actions and relationships reflect the truest version of yourself.

Our inner dialogue, or self-talk, is a fascinating aspect of human psychology that plays a crucial role in our cognitive development, self-regulation, and emotional well-being. This internal voice, which develops from childhood social interactions, isn't simply us talking to ourselves. Our relationship with ourselves and our experience of loneliness are deeply influenced by our self-talk, according to current scientific understanding. This internal dialogue, which can involve multiple perspectives or a single voice, shapes our well-being. When we engage in positive self-talk, we can boost our self-esteem, motivation, and resilience, potentially reducing feelings of loneliness by fostering a sense of self-companionship.

Conversely, negative self-talk can exacerbate feelings of isolation and undermine our confidence in social situations. By becoming aware of and actively shaping our self-talk, we can improve our relationship with ourselves, develop greater self-compassion, and build a stronger foundation for connecting with others, ultimately addressing the root causes of loneliness from within.

In *The Untethered Soul*, author Michael A. Singer offers profound insights into how our inner voice influences our relationship with ourselves and our experience of loneliness. He emphasizes the importance of separating our awareness from our thoughts and emotions, which can often amplify feelings of isolation. By observing our thoughts rather than identifying with them, we can gain a new perspective on loneliness. As Singer notes, "Loneliness is just like a thorn…it will run your entire life." This practice of self-observation allows us to create distance from negative self-talk, helping us recognize that we are not defined by our inner critic. Singer powerfully declares, "You are not the voice of your mind; you are the one who hears it." By applying these teachings, we can learn to navigate our inner dialogue more effectively, reducing feelings of loneliness and fostering a more compassionate relationship with ourselves.

In my own life, I spent many years grappling with loneliness, often unconsciously pushing away relationships due to a deep-seated fear of abandonment and a pervasive sense of unworthiness. It was a painful cycle that kept me isolated, longing for connection but unable to reach out. Through years of steadfast and incremental personal development, I gradually learned to become comfortable in my own skin and to accept and love myself. This journey of self-discovery was transformative; only when I embraced my own worthiness was I truly ready to welcome the love, affection, and companionship that life has to offer. Today I feel blessed to be in a loving relationship with the partner of my dreams and to have formed deep friendships with incredible people from around the world. These connections blossomed only after I became a true friend to myself, opening my heart to the richness of relationships that I once feared.

William Butler Yeats proclaimed, "There are no strangers here; only friends you haven't yet met." Will Rogers made a very similar statement. These sentiments emphasize the idea that every unfamiliar person we encounter has the potential to become a friend, highlighting the connections that can be formed through openness and shared experiences.

In our moments of loneliness, it's easy to become self-centered in our evaluation of our feelings, believing we are the only ones who deeply experience this ache. We often overlook the reality that, from a bird's-eye view of any neighborhood, we might see ourselves isolated in our homes yet fail to recognize the lonely individuals living right next door, each trapped in their own self-centered perception of solitude. The truth is that many people are waiting for someone to reach out and invite them into a connection.

The greatest solution to loneliness lies in our willingness to act proactively and extend the offer of friendship. By being the one to initiate a conversation or suggest an outing, we can break the cycle of isolation. When we take that first step and become the inviter, we not only open ourselves up to new friendships but also create opportunities for others to join us, transforming our loneliness into shared experiences and meaningful connections.

Consider the story of Olivia, who, after moving to a new city for work, found herself feeling deeply isolated. The excitement of starting a new job was overshadowed by the loneliness of not knowing anyone in this unfamiliar place. Her evenings were spent alone in her apartment, the silence echoing the absence of companionship. At first, the loneliness felt overwhelming, like a weight she couldn't shake. But as time passed, she used this solitude to her advantage. She began exploring the city on her own, finding comfort in its parks and libraries, visiting different coffeehouses, and slowly starting to build new connections—first with work colleagues, then with neighbors, and eventually with a local hiking group. Through this process, she not only found new friends but also discovered a deeper sense of independence and resilience. Her loneliness faded away.

Reflect on your experiences with loneliness. Have there been times when you felt disconnected from those around you, as if you were navigating life alone? Perhaps it was after a significant life change, such as a move, a breakup, or the loss of a loved one. How did you cope with those feelings, and what steps did you take to reconnect with others or to find strength in your solitude?

Addressing loneliness can feel overwhelming, but there are practical and accessible solutions that anyone can embrace. One effective way to combat loneliness is by using a simple technique inspired by cognitive behavioral therapy (CBT). This approach helps us see how our thoughts, feelings, and actions are connected. When we notice negative thoughts that make us feel lonely, we can work on changing them to more positive ones. For example, instead of thinking, "No one wants to be my friend," we can remind ourselves, "I can reach out and make new friends." This shift in thinking can help us feel better and respond more positively in social situations. By focusing on what we can do right now to improve our mood, we can take practical steps toward feeling less lonely and more connected.

Developing strong social skills is also essential for building connections. This can be as simple as practicing active listening or starting small conversations with those around us. Engaging in community activities or joining clubs based on our interests can provide opportunities to meet new people and practice these skills in a supportive environment.

We need to be intentional to develop relationships with positive, authentic people who have good intentions and who do not foster negative beliefs in you. The late American comedian and actor Robin Williams struggled with depression and feelings of loneliness. He said, "I used to think the worst thing in life was to end up all alone. It's not. The worst thing in life is to end up with people that make you feel all alone."

Let's gather the strength and self-love to demand high standards of those we choose to relate to. Surrounding ourselves with people who bring joy and encouragement into our lives is essential. We should seek those who not only express their support through positive words but also demonstrate their connection through meaningful actions that uplift and inspire us.

Another wonderful solution is to consider getting a pet. Pets offer companionship and unconditional love, significantly reducing feelings of loneliness. Studies show that pet ownership can increase happiness levels and provide emotional support, making it easier to connect with others.

Finding purpose-driven activities—whether through hobbies, volunteering, or joining support groups—can also enrich our lives and help us feel more connected. Support groups provide a sense of community where we can share experiences and find encouragement from others who understand what we're going through. Even the simple act of turning to someone nearby and saying, "Hello, please tell me about yourself," can spark meaningful conversations and connections.

By taking these proactive steps, we not only combat loneliness but also open ourselves up to the joy of companionship and shared experiences.

GUILT: THE BURDEN OF RESPONSIBILITY

Now the Suffering Basket displays the next type of suffering for us to confront in our lives—our feelings of guilt. Guilt is a complex and weighty emotion, often rooted in feelings of responsibility or remorse for something we perceive as an offense or wrongdoing. It can weigh heavily on the heart, influencing our thoughts and actions as we grapple with the consequences of our past decisions and actions.

Recent research on guilt published in the *Psychological Bulletin*, titled "When Guilt Works: A Comprehensive Meta-Analysis of Guilt Appeals," has provided valuable insights into how individuals experience and cope with this complex emotion. This comprehensive study reveals that guilt can motivate positive behavior change when individuals feel responsible for their actions. The feeling of guilt can influence attitudes and behaviors. Factors such as personal responsibility and the nature of the relationship between the perceiver and the victim were found to moderate these effects, suggesting that context matters greatly in how guilt is experienced and acted upon.

Carrying the burden of guilt can weigh heavily on our hearts and minds, but it also presents an opportunity for profound personal development and growth. The first step in resolving negative feelings associated with guilt is to acknowledge the emotion without judgment. Recognizing that guilt is a natural response to our actions allows us to confront it honestly. Once we have acknowledged our feelings, seeking forgiveness—whether from ourselves or those we may have wronged—becomes essential. This act of reaching out can foster healing and restore relationships, allowing us to move forward with a lighter heart. Atonement is another vital component. Taking proactive steps to make amends demonstrates our commitment to change and accountability. Engaging in acts of kindness or service can transform guilt into a catalyst for positive action, ultimately leading us to a deeper understanding of ourselves and a more compassionate connection with others. By embracing these steps, we can turn the weight of guilt into a powerful force for personal growth and renewal.

John C. Maxwell, *New York Times* bestselling author and leadership expert suggests that "the burden of guilt is heavy, but the weight of unfulfilled responsibility is heavier still." Maxwell's insight highlights the idea that while guilt is a heavy burden to carry, the regret of not fulfilling our responsibilities or living up to our values can be even more crushing. This realization can motivate us to address our guilt head-on, seeking ways to atone for our mistakes and realign our actions with our deepest values.

Understanding that guilt often arises from a misalignment between our actions and our values ties directly to the Must Framework. Your *musts*—the core values and beliefs that define your authentic self—serve as a compass for living a life of integrity and purpose. When guilt emerges, it signals that you may have strayed from these guiding principles, offering an opportunity for reflection and realignment. By reconnecting with your *musts*, you can identify where the misalignment occurred, take meaningful steps to make amends, and commit to actions that honor your values moving forward. This process not only alleviates guilt but also strengthens your ability to live fully in the Must Zone, where your choices consistently reflect the person you are meant to be. Acknowledging where you've gone wrong and taking steps to correct your course can be deeply liberating. It's a way of transforming guilt from a paralyzing burden into a catalyst for positive change.

SHAME: THE PAIN OF HUMILIATION

Shame is one of the most painful and isolating emotions we can experience. It's the deep feeling of humiliation or distress that arises when we perceive ourselves as having fallen short, made a mistake, or been exposed in a way that makes us feel unworthy. Unlike guilt, which focuses on our actions, shame is a more pervasive feeling that attacks our sense of self-worth.

June Tangney and Ronda Dearing are prominent psychologists known for their extensive research on the emotions of shame and guilt. Their research on shame provides profound insights into how this complex emotion affects our lives and relationships. In their book, *Shame and Guilt*, they emphasize that shame is a self-focused emotion that often leads to feelings of worthlessness and isolation, while guilt is more adaptive, focusing on specific behaviors and motivating reparative actions.

Their findings indicate that individuals prone to shame are more likely to experience psychological difficulties, such as low self-esteem and depression, which can impair empathy and lead to interpersonal challenges. They argue that while guilt can encourage positive change and strengthen relationships, shame tends to push individuals away from others, exacerbating feelings of loneliness.

To effectively deal with shame, Tangney and Dearing suggest acknowledging the emotion without judgment, understanding its triggers, and seeking support from trusted friends or professionals. Engaging in open conversations about our feelings can help dismantle the isolating effects of shame. By fostering self-compassion and focusing on personal growth rather than self-criticism, individuals can transform their relationship with shame into an opportunity for healing and connection. Ultimately, their research underscores the importance of distinguishing between these two emotions, as addressing shame constructively can lead to healthier relationships and a more fulfilling life.

Brené Brown, whose research on shame and vulnerability has shed light on this difficult emotion, explains that shame is universal—

everyone experiences it, but it doesn't have to control us. Brown offers, "Shame is the most powerful, master emotion. It's the fear that we're not good enough." This captures the essence of shame—it is the fear that at our core, we are not worthy of love, respect, or belonging. This fear can be paralyzing, leading us to hide our true selves, to retreat into isolation, and to avoid situations where we might be judged or rejected.

Brown's Shame Resilience Theory has garnered significant attention and acceptance among both academics and personal development practitioners. Her research and findings, which span over two decades, offer a compassionate and constructive approach to navigating the difficult emotions of shame. She emphasizes that recognizing our experiences of shame is the first step toward healing. By understanding what triggers these feelings, we can address them rather than allowing them to fester in silence. Brown also encourages us to reach out to others for support, reminding us that vulnerability is not a weakness but a pathway to deeper connections. She states, "Shame resilience is not all or nothing; it exists on a continuum between fear and disconnection on one end and empathy and connection on the other." This insight highlights that while shame can isolate us, empathy can bridge the gap and foster authentic relationships.

To effectively deal with shame, Brown advocates for practicing self-compassion and engaging in open conversations about our feelings. When we share our experiences with trusted friends or family members, we create a safe space where empathy can flourish. This connection not only helps diminish the power of shame but also reinforces the understanding that we are not alone in our struggles. By embracing vulnerability and seeking supportive relationships, we can transform shame into an opportunity for growth, ultimately leading to stronger connections with ourselves and others. In this way, we learn that acknowledging our shame can open the door to healing and deeper human connection.

Reflect on your experiences with shame. Have there been moments when you felt deeply humiliated or unworthy, when the fear of not being good enough held you back? Perhaps it was after a mistake that you couldn't forgive yourself for or an experience where you felt exposed in a way that left you feeling small. How did this shame affect your behavior, and how did you begin to overcome it?

Understanding that shame often arises from a fear of disconnection or rejection can empower us to embrace our true selves and cultivate genuine connections with others. When we confront our shame and acknowledge it without allowing it to define who we are, we unlock the potential for deeper, more authentic relationships. This process is not just about healing ourselves; it's about creating a safe space for others to share their vulnerabilities as well.

Overcoming shame can lead to profound personal empowerment and foster a sense of shared humanity that transcends the superficial perfection that shame often demands. By embracing our vulnerabilities, we not only mend our wounds but also invite others to do the same, building connections that are far more meaningful and fulfilling. In this journey toward self-love and self-compassion, we rise above the dark feelings of shame that have tried to negatively shape our personal narratives. Instead, we redefine ourselves through our beliefs and experiences, which allows us to live fully and authentically, free from the burdens of shame. This transformative process enriches our lives and also enhances the lives of those around us, creating a ripple effect of empathy and connection in a world that so desperately needs it.

COPING WITH HATRED AND PREJUDICE

Dealing with hatred and prejudice is one of the most profound challenges we face as human beings, striking at the very core of our shared humanity. Prejudice manifests in many forms—racial prejudice that unjustly targets people of color, gender discrimination that undermines the rights and dignity of women and non-binary individuals, and homophobia and transphobia that marginalize those who dare to love differently. We cannot ignore the historical horrors of xenophobia, which has led to the persecution of immigrants and refugees, or classism, which perpetuates cycles of poverty and inequality. Religious prejudice has also fueled violence and division throughout history, as seen in the brutal acts against those who practice faiths deemed "other," from the Inquisition to modern-day attacks on places of worship.

As individuals, we are often confronted with these harsh realities, not just in isolation but within our families, friendships, and the broader society. Conversations around the dinner table can reveal deeply ingrained biases that challenge our values and beliefs. Friends may unknowingly perpetuate stereotypes or engage in discriminatory jokes that reinforce harmful narratives. In workplaces and schools, we witness the impact of systemic prejudice that can marginalize colleagues or classmates based on their identity.

English essayist and philosopher William Hazlitt wrote, "Prejudice is the child of ignorance." Hazlitt's words, from his essay titled "On Prejudice," highlight the root of prejudice, which is ignorance. Prejudice often stems from a lack of understanding or exposure to different perspectives, and its consequences can be deeply damaging to those on the receiving end.

Riveting examples of hatred and prejudice remind us that hatred is not just an abstract concept; it is a living reality that affects countless lives every day. To confront these injustices is to acknowledge the pain they inflict, not only on individuals but on society as a whole. Understanding that these biases often stem from fear and ignorance compels us to rise above them, embracing empathy as our guiding principle. By fostering genuine connections with those who are different from us, we can dismantle the barriers that prejudice erects.

Being the target of hatred and prejudice is a deeply isolating and painful experience that cuts to the core of one's identity. It feels like walking through a world where the very essence of who you are is met with disdain or indifference, where your worth is diminished by the biases of others. Each derogatory comment or dismissive glance feels like a sharp knife, slicing through the fabric of self-esteem, leaving behind scars that are often invisible but profoundly felt. In those moments, you may grapple with a whirlwind of emotions—anger at the injustice, sadness for the connections that could have been, and an overwhelming sense of loneliness. It's as if you are standing on the outside looking in, yearning for acceptance and understanding while being met with walls built from fear and ignorance. The weight of prejudice can feel suffocating, casting a shadow over your spirit and making it difficult to breathe freely or express your true self.

You may question your place in the world, wondering if you will ever be seen for who you truly are rather than through the distorted lens of someone else's prejudice. The internal struggle can be exhausting. You might feel compelled to hide parts of yourself to fit in or to protect yourself from further hurt. Yet amid this darkness there is a flicker of resilience—a desire to rise above the hatred and reclaim your narrative.

When you encounter empathy and kindness from others, it feels like a lifeline thrown into turbulent waters. Those moments remind you that connection is possible and that love can transcend the barriers erected by prejudice. It is this hope for understanding and acceptance that fuels your journey toward healing, pushing you to advocate not only for yourself but for others who share similar struggles. In embracing vulnerability, you learn that while hatred may seek to define you, it cannot extinguish your light or diminish your worth. You are more than the labels assigned to you. You are full of strength, compassion, and an unyielding spirit that refuses to be silenced.

In this journey toward healing, we must actively seek to create spaces where every voice is heard and valued. It is through these connections that we can transform our outrage into action, ensuring we never forget the lessons of history while striving for a future defined by compassion, equality, and respect for all. Together we can forge a world where understanding triumphs over hatred, allowing us to reclaim our shared humanity in the face of adversity.

Audre Lorde, a poet and civil rights activist, understood the importance of recognizing and celebrating differences to combat prejudice. She believed, "It is not our differences that divide us. It is our inability to recognize, accept, and celebrate those differences." Lorde's insight emphasizes that the true challenge lies not in our diversity but in our failure to embrace it. Acknowledging and celebrating differences can pave the way for a more inclusive and empathetic society.

Reflect on your experiences with hatred or prejudice. Have you felt marginalized or judged because of your identity, beliefs, or background? Perhaps it was an offhand remark that cut deeper than expected or a more systematic exclusion that made you feel invisible. How did these experiences shape your sense of self and influence your interactions with others? Now take this reflection a step further and ask yourself, "Have there been moments when you harbored prejudice or judgment toward others? Perhaps it was based on assumptions, stereotypes, or unconscious biases. How might these attitudes have affected your relationships, your decisions, or even your sense of integrity? Confronting both the prejudice we've faced and the prejudice we may hold is essential for personal growth and self-awareness. By examining these patterns honestly, we foster greater empathy and understanding for ourselves and others while taking meaningful steps toward living in alignment with our values and creating a more inclusive and compassionate world. Acknowledging the impact of hatred and prejudice on emotional well-being is essential. These experiences can lead to feelings of anger, frustration, and helplessness, which, if left unaddressed, can fester and cause lasting harm. It is important to validate these emotions, recognizing that they are natural responses to the pain of being treated unjustly.

Dr. Martin Luther King Jr. said, "Darkness cannot drive out darkness; only light can do that. Hate cannot drive out hate; only love can do that." Dr. King's words remind us of the power of love and compassion in overcoming hatred. Understanding, empathy, and positive action are the ways to begin healing from prejudice's wounds.

Dr. King also understood the potential of anger to drive meaningful action. He channeled his anger at the injustices of racial discrimination into peaceful activism, changing the course of history with his leadership in the Civil Rights Movement. King believed deeply in the power of love to overcome hate. King's approach to anger teaches us that while anger can ignite the desire for change, it is love and constructive action that truly transform the world. By channeling anger into peaceful and purposeful efforts, we can create lasting positive change rather than perpetuating cycles of harm.

The lessons on hatred and prejudice serve as crucial touchstones in our personal development journey, reminding us that growth begins with self-awareness and empathy. As we confront our own biases and challenge the prejudices that surround us, we cultivate a deeper understanding of ourselves and others. This journey compels us to embrace vulnerability, fostering connections that transcend differences and promote healing. By applying these lessons, we not only enrich our own lives but also contribute to a more compassionate world, transforming our personal growth into a collective movement toward justice and equality for all.

Coping with hatred and prejudice is not merely a personal struggle; it is a collective battle that demands our unwavering commitment to empathy, understanding, and action. We must confront the harsh realities of a world where prejudice manifests in many forms.

Let us stand together, not just as individuals fighting our own battles but as a united force against hatred in all its forms. By acknowledging our vulnerabilities and embracing our differences, we can transform our outrage into action and create spaces where every voice is heard and valued. In doing so, we reclaim our narrative—not as victims of prejudice but as champions of understanding and advocates for equality. Together we can forge a world where empathy triumphs over hatred, allowing us to rise above the darkness and illuminate the path toward a more inclusive and compassionate society. In this fight for justice and dignity, let us be relentless in our pursuit of a future where love prevails over fear and every individual is celebrated for their unique contributions to humanity.

PHYSICAL PAIN: THE BODY'S CRY FOR HELP

"The human spirit can endure a sick body, but who can bear a crushed spirit?"

—Proverbs 18:14 (New International Version [NIV])

Physical pain is often the most immediate and tangible form of suffering. Whether it stems from an injury, illness, or condition, physical pain can wear down not just the body but also the spirit. It is a constant reminder of our vulnerability, and yet it also presents an opportunity for profound resilience and growth.

Physical suffering is often the body's cry for help—a signal that something needs attention, whether it's rest, medical care, or a change in lifestyle. By listening to your body's signals, you can develop greater self-awareness and self-care practices that address the pain and promote overall well-being.

Physical pain can leave scars—both visible and invisible—but these scars are a testament to your strength and perseverance. "Out of suffering have emerged the strongest souls; the most massive characters are seared with scars," said Kahlil Gibran, Lebanese American writer, poet, artist, and philosopher. They are a reminder that you have endured, that you have faced the trials of your body and emerged on the other side, perhaps not unscathed, but certainly stronger and more resilient.

My grandmother, Memaw, battled cancer and painful rheumatoid arthritis. Every morning it was a struggle for her to move, the pain gnawing in her joints, but she chose not to be defined by her condition. Through physical therapy, mindful movement, and the support of a community of fellow sufferers, she learned to manage her pain. More importantly, she found ways to live a full life despite it—pursuing her passions, maintaining her relationships, and finding joy in small everyday moments.

Her story, like yours, shows that physical pain, while deeply challenging, does not have to define your existence. Instead, it can serve as a powerful catalyst for growth, for finding strength you never knew you had, and for developing a deeper appreciation of the moments of grace and healing that come, sometimes unexpectedly, in the midst of suffering.

Consider the story of Helen Keller, a woman who faced immense physical challenges. An illness caused her deafblindness at nineteen months old. She also suffered from chronic pain in her eyes, which eventually led to the removal of both eyes to improve her health and lessen her suffering. Keller could have easily succumbed to her body's limitations. Yet she found a way to communicate, learn, and eventually inspire millions around the world. She said, "Although the world is full of suffering, it is also full of the overcoming of it."

Keller's journey reminds us that even in the face of physical pain, there is hope and healing. Your journey through physical pain, whether it resulted from a significant injury, a chronic illness, or the lingering effects of surgery, can be a testament to the resilience of the human spirit. Perhaps you've experienced moments where the pain seemed overwhelming, yet you found strength in the care and support of loved ones, in the small victories of your healing process, or even in the simple act of getting through another day.

As you continue your journey, remember that each step you take, each moment of pain endured is part of a larger narrative—one of resilience, survival, and the indomitable human spirit. And as you navigate this path, know that you are not alone. Your story of overcoming physical pain is shared by many, and it can inspire others, just as Helen Keller and countless others have inspired you.

ADDRESSING OTHER ELEMENTS OF SUFFERING

We must acknowledge the additional types of suffering that may reside in our Suffering Basket, each deserving of our attention and compassion.

Existential suffering often involves grappling with deep questions about the meaning and purpose of life. This struggle can lead to feelings of emptiness and disconnection, as we seek to find our place in the world. For instance, a successful individual may feel unfulfilled despite their achievements, prompting a journey of self-discovery. Embracing this suffering can lead to profound personal transformation as we align our actions with our Must Values and uncover what truly matters in life.

Social suffering arises from adverse social conditions like poverty, discrimination, and isolation. These external forces can create significant distress, highlighting the impact of societal issues on our personal well-being. Reflecting on experiences of discrimination or social exclusion can deepen our empathy and inspire us to advocate for change. By transforming our pain into action—much like individuals who rise from their struggles to mentor others—we can create pathways for healing, not just for ourselves but for our communities.

Moral or ethical suffering stems from the inner conflict between our actions and our moral beliefs. This type of suffering forces us to confront our integrity and the principles by which we live. Moments of moral dilemma can lead to intense feelings of guilt and shame, but they also present opportunities for growth. By choosing to act in accordance with our Must Values, even when faced with difficult choices, we can find peace and alignment within ourselves.

Spiritual suffering arises from a sense of disconnection from one's beliefs or a higher power, often leading to a crisis of faith. This profound struggle can shake the foundations of our understanding and purpose. Yet it is often in these moments of despair when we find seeds of spiritual growth. By reaching out through prayer, meditation, or community support, we can rebuild our faith into something deeper and more resilient.

Cognitive suffering is characterized by confusion and negative thought patterns that cloud our minds. It can feel like an overwhelming fog, making it difficult to see a way forward. However, this inner battle presents an opportunity for transformation. Through mindfulness practices and self-reflection, we can challenge negative thoughts and cultivate resilience, turning cognitive suffering into a source of creativity and clarity more fully in line with our Must Core Beliefs, Values, Standards, and Purpose.

ONE LAST TASK REGARDING YOUR SUFFERING BASKET

By acknowledging these diverse forms of suffering in our lives, we empower ourselves to confront them with compassion and courage. Each type offers valuable lessons that can guide us toward deeper self-understanding and connection with ourselves and others. As we navigate this journey together, let us embrace the opportunity for growth that comes from facing our suffering head-on, transforming pain into purpose and isolation into community.

In this self-exploration, you have bravely unearthed the various forms of suffering that have shaped your life. You have meticulously examined the emotional burdens you carried, the emotional and psychological suffering of despair, depression, anger, grief, helplessness, loneliness, guilt, shame, being the focus of hatred and prejudice, physical pain, and other forms of suffering, including existential suffering, social suffering, moral dilemmas, spiritual crises, and cognitive struggles. Each type of suffering has influenced your thoughts and actions, often leaving you feeling trapped in a cycle of pain and limitation. But now, as you stand at the threshold of transformation, it is time to reclaim your power and redefine your narratives.

Imagine your Suffering Basket, once filled to the brim with memories of loss, regret, anger, and despair. As you have reflected on these experiences, you have begun to see them not as chains binding you but as stepping stones on your path to growth that no longer control or inhibit you. You have confronted the sharp pangs of grief for loved ones lost, the heavy weight of guilt from past actions, and the isolating chill of loneliness that has sometimes left you feeling invisible. Each item in that basket represents a chapter in your story—one that has shaped who you once perceived yourself to be but now does not define your present life or your future.

Now envision yourself standing before your Suffering Basket, full of all the items you have thoroughly examined and addressed as you never had before. Fill the basket with all the elements of suffering that no longer serve you. If you need more time to cling to elements of grief or similar feelings, that's fine. We can deal with the remnants of that suffering later. For now, place into the basket those items of suffering from which you know it's time to become untethered.

The Suffering Basket is now outside of you, outside of your mind, heart, and soul, and you are gazing at it outside of your being. It is on the table before you. Acknowledge the pain it once held; recognize how it no longer serves the person you have become. What do you want to do with it? Do you want to pour its contents back into you? Or do you want to rid yourself of those past burdens forever?

I want you to do something for me now that will change your life. Envision yourself picking up that Suffering Basket, once heavy and once burdensome on you; it's much lighter now. Walk and carry your personal Suffering Basket outside. Walk over to the garbage can. Drop the Suffering Basket into the garbage can. Close the lid, then place the garbage can on the edge of your street for sanitation to pick up and empty its contents. It is now something that simply needs to be disposed of. Walk away from the garbage can. Do not look back. Walk inside your home and feel the new sense of uplifting freedom.

By placing your Suffering Basket in the garbage can outside and away from your mind, heart, and soul, you now understand that this act is one of profound liberation. You are choosing to step into a new chapter of your life, one where you are no longer weighed down by unexamined pain. You are reclaiming control over your narrative.

The Suffering Basket metaphor provides a valuable framework for visualizing and processing our pain; it is essential to recognize that it exists alongside various therapeutic avenues that can further assist you in navigating your suffering. This metaphor encourages introspection and personal reflection, yet it does not negate the importance of seeking professional help through counseling, therapy, or support groups. These avenues can offer critical insights and coping strategies that address the complex nature of suffering, allowing individuals to unpack their experiences more thoroughly. By using your Suffering Basket as a tool for self-exploration, you can better understand your past emotional burdens while also being open to external support systems that facilitate healing and growth.

In this newfound space within yourself, make room for healing and growth. Fill it with compassion for yourself and others, with love that transcends past hurts, and with a commitment to live authentically aligned with your core values and beliefs. Embrace the lightness that comes from letting go; it is an invitation to explore new possibilities and connections.

You possess the power to rewrite your story. The suffering you have experienced does not diminish your worth; rather, it enriches your understanding of life's complexities. As you move forward, remember that each step taken in self-compassion brings you closer to a life filled with purpose and joy.

Reflect on how far you've come: from being held captive by your suffering to standing empowered in your truth. You have faced the darkness and emerged stronger on the other side. Embrace this transformation. Let it guide you toward deeper connections with yourself and those around you.

Carry this knowledge with you that pain is inevitable in life, but suffering is optional. You have the strength to choose how you respond to life's challenges, turning them into opportunities for resilience and renewal.

As you have now walked away from the disposed Suffering Basket, let it be a symbol of release—a testament to your courage in facing what once felt heavy, permanent, and insurmountable. The future is bright. It awaits your embrace with open arms. Step into it boldly, knowing you are not defined by your past but empowered by your purified vision for yourself.

Please remember my personal message to you: as you have faced and rid yourself of the darkness, you now will create your own light.

CHAPTER 16

Transforming Suffering into Purpose

As we embark on our journey through the Must Zone, we inevitably encounter moments of darkness, challenge, and suffering. These experiences, while often painful, are not detours from our path but integral parts of it. In this chapter, we will explore how suffering, when approached with intention and awareness, can become a powerful catalyst for growth, resilience, and, ultimately, the fulfillment of our deepest purpose.

The Must Zone is not a place of constant comfort and ease. It is a realm where we confront our deepest truths, face our fears, and push beyond our perceived limitations. Suffering, in this context, becomes a crucible for transformation. It challenges us to reassess our values, priorities, and purpose, often revealing aspects of ourselves we never knew existed. As we navigate these difficult experiences, we are compelled to grow, adapt, and evolve, aligning more closely with our authentic selves and our true *must*.

Developing resilience through adversity is not just a coping mechanism; it is a vital Must Skill. The ability to transform suffering into purpose is essential for anyone seeking to live authentically in their Must Zone. This resilience allows us to maintain our course even when faced with setbacks, to find meaning in our struggles, and to emerge stronger and more aligned with our purpose. By cultivating this skill, we prepare ourselves not just for current challenges but for the inevitable obstacles that lie ahead on our Must Journey.

Søren Kierkegaard, the Danish philosopher, posited that confronting necessary suffering is integral to finding meaning in life and becoming one's authentic self. This profound insight aligns perfectly with our *must* philosophy. By facing our suffering head-on, we strip away pretenses and societal expectations, revealing our true selves. This process of confronting pain and emerging renewed is a powerful path to authenticity, allowing us to live more fully in our Must Zone.

PRACTICAL APPLICATIONS: TRANSFORMING PAIN INTO PURPOSE

To help you navigate this transformative process, we will explore practical exercises designed to help you apply these insights to your own Must Journey. These reflective practices will guide you in identifying how past challenges have shaped your values and purpose and how current struggles can be reframed as stepping stones toward your most authentic self.

As we delve into this chapter, remember that the ability to transform suffering into purpose is not just for those currently in pain. It is a universal skill that empowers us to live more fully in our Must Zone regardless of our current circumstances. By embracing this perspective, we open ourselves to a deeper, more resilient, and ultimately more fulfilling journey of becoming who we are truly meant to be.

Frame adversity not as an obstacle but as an opportunity to deepen your commitment to the Must Zone. Challenges serve as powerful reminders of why you've chosen your *musts*, reinforcing their importance and motivating you to stay true to them even in difficult times. By viewing setbacks through this lens, you transform struggles into stepping stones for personal growth.

The journey to the Must Zone and the development of resilience are not separate goals but two aspects of the same transformative process. As you embrace the Must Zone philosophy, you're not just optimizing your daily life—you're building a foundation of resilience that will serve you well in all of life's adventures. Remember, every challenge you face is an opportunity to reinforce your *musts* and emerge stronger, more focused, and more aligned with your true self.

REWIRING AND SUFFERING

The thirteenth-century Persian poet and Islamic scholar Rumi stated, "The wound is the place where the Light enters you." This profound insight from Rumi illuminates the transformative power of suffering.

The path from suffering to growth is not always linear or easy, but it is rich with opportunities for self-discovery, resilience, and profound change. As we delve into the strategies and insights for transforming suffering, remember that this process is deeply personal and often requires patience, courage, and compassion for yourself. Whether you're grappling with existential questions, social injustices, moral dilemmas, spiritual crises, or cognitive struggles, the journey of transformation begins with a single step: the decision to seek meaning and growth in the midst of your pain.

Post-traumatic growth (PTG) is a profound psychological transformation that can occur in the aftermath of significant adversity or trauma. It refers to positive changes in an individual's life outlook, relationships, and sense of self that emerge as a result of struggling with highly challenging life circumstances.

PTG is a fascinating phenomenon that highlights the human capacity for resilience and positive change in the face of adversity. Research in the field of positive psychology has revealed that a significant proportion of individuals who experience trauma or severe life challenges report positive personal growth as a result. According to studies conducted by researchers such as Richard Tedeschi and Lawrence Calhoun, pioneers in the field of PTG, approximately 50–60 percent of trauma survivors report experiencing some form of positive change or growth following their traumatic experiences. This growth manifests itself in various domains of an individual's life, often leading to profound and lasting transformations.

The areas of growth commonly associated with PTG are multifaceted and interconnected. Survivors often report a deepened appreciation for life, finding joy and meaning in everyday experiences they may have previously taken for granted. Relationships with others tend to improve, with many individuals experiencing increased empathy, compassion, and a stronger sense of connection to their loved ones and community. PTG can also open up new possibilities in life, as individuals reassess their priorities and discover new paths or opportunities they haven't considered before. Personal strength is another area of growth, with survivors often developing a greater sense of self-reliance and confidence in their ability to overcome future challenges. Many individuals also report spiritual or existential growth, experiencing a deeper connection to their beliefs or developing a more profound understanding of life's meaning and purpose.

It's important to note that PTG doesn't negate the pain and suffering experienced during trauma. Rather, it coexists with the distress, showcasing the remarkable human ability to find light even in the darkest of circumstances. As research in this field continues to evolve, it offers hope and insight into the transformative potential of life's most challenging experiences.

The great news is that your suffering is not in vain. This research on post-traumatic growth reveals a remarkable opportunity for profound personal transformation. If you have experienced varied levels of suffering or trauma in your life, you have the potential to find a silver lining and experience significant positive changes. These changes can manifest across multiple domains: deeper and more meaningful relationships, increased personal strength and resilience, a renewed appreciation for life's simple joys, discovery of new possibilities and paths, and potential spiritual or existential growth.

Rather than trauma being a potential source of self-limiting beliefs and learned helplessness, you can use it as a catalyst for remarkable personal development. The statistics of those facing trauma and significant suffering reporting meaningful positive changes is encouraging. This suggests your pain can become a powerful pathway to resilience, wisdom, and unexpected personal evolution. Your suffering does not have to be an endpoint. Instead, it can be a transformative beginning with a chance to rebuild, reimagine, and rediscover yourself in ways you might never have anticipated. As you reflect on your experiences, consider how they might guide you toward a deeper understanding of yourself and your purpose in life. I have no doubt your life's experiences have drawn you to this book and your desire for extraordinary personal growth.

Further good news is that the neuroscience of PTG offers fascinating insights into the brain's remarkable capacity for adaptation and resilience. Building on the foundation of neuroplasticity discussed earlier, research has shown that PTG is associated with specific neurobiological changes. Brain imaging studies have revealed increased activity and connectivity in regions associated with emotional regulation, such as the prefrontal cortex and anterior cingulate cortex. This enhanced neural connectivity may underlie the improved emotional processing and resilience observed in individuals experiencing PTG. Additionally, studies have found changes in the amygdala's response to stress-related stimuli, suggesting a recalibration of the fear response system. These neurobiological changes not only support the psychological aspects of PTG but also demonstrate how adversity can literally reshape our brains, creating new neural pathways that support growth and adaptation.

The neuroscience behind post-traumatic growth offers hope and empowerment for your personal journey through suffering. Your brain's inherent plasticity means you have the potential to recover from trauma and emerge stronger and more resilient. As you navigate challenging experiences, your brain actively forms new neural connections, particularly in areas responsible for emotional regulation and stress response. This biological process can translate into tangible improvements in your daily life, such as enhanced emotional control, increased resilience to future stressors, and a more balanced perspective on life's challenges. By engaging in activities that promote PTG, such as mindfulness practices or therapy, you're not just coping—you're actively reshaping your brain's architecture. This neurobiological transformation can lead to profound personal growth, enabling you to find new meaning and purpose in the aftermath of adversity.

PTG is not something that happens overnight. It is a gradual process that unfolds as individuals work through their experiences and seek meaning in their suffering. This journey often requires time, patience, and self-reflection. Initially, the emotional and psychological impacts of trauma can feel overwhelming, making it difficult to see any potential for growth. However, as you process your feelings and confront the challenges you've faced, you may notice subtle shifts in your perspective. These shifts can lead to a deeper understanding of yourself and your values, ultimately fostering resilience and personal development.

The time factor in PTG emphasizes that healing and growth are not linear; they may involve setbacks and moments of doubt. Yet with each step taken toward understanding your pain, you open the door to new insights and opportunities for transformation. Remember that finding meaning in suffering is a personal endeavor that unfolds at your own pace. Embracing this process can lead to profound changes in how you view yourself and the world around you, allowing you to emerge from your experiences with a renewed sense of purpose and strength.

RELIGIOUS AND SPIRITUAL PERSPECTIVES ON SUFFERING AND PERSONAL GROWTH

While scientific research offers valuable insights into how we can grow through suffering, it is not the only way we can understand this journey. Across cultures and throughout history, religious and spiritual traditions have also sought to make sense of suffering, offering their own wisdom about how adversity can lead to personal and spiritual transformation. Despite the diversity of religious teachings, many spiritual traditions share common views on suffering. They often emphasize growth, learning, community, support, faith, and resilience as key aspects of navigating the challenges of life. These shared perspectives offer valuable insights into how suffering can be transformed into a source of strength and spiritual development.

Suffering is frequently seen as a catalyst for personal growth and learning across various religious traditions. Enduring suffering is believed to lead to the development of virtues, such as patience, compassion, and wisdom, as well as a deeper understanding of life's complexities.

In Christianity, suffering is viewed as a path to spiritual maturity and moral development. The Bible often references trials and tribulations as opportunities to strengthen faith. As James 1:2–4 states, "Consider it pure joy, my brothers and sisters, whenever you face trials of many kinds, because you know that the testing of your faith produces perseverance. Let perseverance finish its work so that you may be mature and complete, not lacking anything." This passage highlights how challenges are seen as essential to achieving spiritual completeness.

Christianity also places a strong emphasis on community support. The early Christian church was known for its communal living and mutual aid. Galatians 6:2 advises, "Carry each other's burdens, and in this way, you will fulfill the law of Christ." This directive underscores the importance of helping one another through difficult times, reinforcing the idea that we are stronger together.

In Christianity, faith in God's love and wisdom provides comfort during times of suffering. Romans 8:28 reassures believers, "And we know that in all things God works for the good of those who love him, who have been called according to his purpose." This belief that suffering has a divine purpose encourages resilience and trust in God's plan, helping believers endure hardships with hope.

Additionally, Christianity teaches acceptance through faith in God's will. Jesus's prayer in the Garden of Gethsemane, "Not my will, but yours be done" (Luke 22:42 KJV), exemplifies the surrender to divine will. Believers are encouraged to trust in God's plan and accept their suffering as part of their spiritual journey, finding solace in the belief that it serves a higher purpose.

In Judaism, suffering is often viewed as a catalyst for personal growth and spiritual development. The tradition emphasizes that through suffering, individuals can gain deeper insights into their lives and their relationship with God. One key aspect of this understanding is the concept of *tikkun olam*, which means "repairing the world." This idea suggests personal suffering can lead to a greater awareness of the suffering of others, motivating individuals to engage in acts of kindness and social justice.

A relevant verse from the Hebrew Bible reflects this perspective and is found in the book of Psalms: "The Lord is close to the brokenhearted and saves those who are crushed in spirit" (Psalm 34:18KJV). This verse underscores the belief that suffering is not a sign of abandonment but rather an opportunity for divine connection and healing. It suggests that in moments of pain, individuals can find solace and strength, ultimately leading to personal transformation.

In Judaism, the sense of community (*kehilla*) is paramount. The collective responsibility to care for one another is deeply embedded in Jewish law and tradition. The Talmud states, "All Israel is responsible for one another" (Shevuot 39a), highlighting the importance of mutual support. This principle fosters a supportive environment where individuals are encouraged to share their burdens and receive help from their community.

Similarly, in Buddhism, suffering (*dukkha*) is recognized as an inherent part of life and a fundamental aspect of the Four Noble Truths. The Buddha taught that understanding and overcoming suffering is crucial for achieving enlightenment. Through the practice of mindfulness and meditation, individuals learn to observe their suffering without attachment, leading to wisdom and liberation. This approach encourages a deep internal journey where suffering becomes a teacher, guiding practitioners toward a state of enlightenment.

In Buddhism, the Sangha, or community of monks and practitioners, provides a supportive environment where individuals can share their experiences and grow together. The Sangha offers guidance, encouragement, and companionship, helping individuals stay on the path of dharma and overcome suffering. This communal aspect is vital for sustaining one's practice and finding strength in collective wisdom.

Buddhism, while not centered on a deity, teaches faith in the Buddha's teachings and the path to enlightenment. This faith in dharma helps practitioners remain steadfast in their practice, knowing that understanding and liberation from suffering are possible. Resilience in Buddhism is cultivated through the trust that the path will lead to the cessation of suffering.

In Buddhism, the practice of mindfulness and nonattachment is fundamental. The Buddha taught that attachment to desires and outcomes is the root cause of suffering. By practicing detachment and mindfulness, individuals learn to accept the impermanent nature of life and find peace amidst suffering. This approach allows practitioners to experience life with a calm and balanced mind, reducing the impact of suffering.

In Islam, suffering is often viewed as a test from Allah, intended to purify believers and strengthen their faith. The Quran emphasizes this perspective, stating, "Do you think that you will enter Paradise without Allah testing those of you who fought hard and remained steadfast?" (Quran 3:142). This viewpoint encourages Muslims to see hardships as opportunities to demonstrate patience (*sabr*) and trust in God's plan, ultimately fostering spiritual growth and resilience.

Islam encourages the *ummah*, or global community of Muslims, to support one another. Acts of charity (*zakat*) and community service are fundamental aspects of Islamic practice, ensuring those who suffer are not left to face their challenges alone. The Prophet Muhammad said, "The believers, in their mutual love, mercy, and compassion, are like one body; when any limb aches, the whole body reacts with sleeplessness and fever" (Sahih Bukhari), illustrating the interconnectedness of the Muslim community in supporting one another through hardships.

Islam teaches that reliance on Allah (*tawakkul*) is crucial in overcoming suffering. Believers are encouraged to maintain their faith and trust that God will provide relief and guidance. The Quran states, "And whosoever fears Allah and keeps his duty to Him, He will make a way for him to get out (from every difficulty)" (Quran 65:2). This trust in divine wisdom fosters resilience, allowing Muslims to navigate suffering with patience and hope.

Islam also emphasizes acceptance through the concept of *sabr* (patience) and reliance on Allah's wisdom. Believers are taught to accept their circumstances with patience and trust that God knows best. The Quran states, "Indeed, Allah is with the patient" (Quran 2:153), highlighting the importance of patience and trust in navigating suffering.

Hinduism perceives suffering as a means to achieve higher states of consciousness and spiritual evolution. The concept of karma plays a significant role, where suffering is seen as a result of past actions and enduring it with grace can lead to spiritual growth. The Bhagavad Gita teaches that one should perform their duty without attachment to results, viewing both pleasure and pain as transient. This mindset is displayed in the verse "Be steadfast in yoga, O Arjuna. Perform your duty and abandon all attachment to success or failure. Such evenness of mind is called yoga" (Bhagavad Gita 2:48).

In Hinduism, the concept of surrender to the divine will (*prapatti*) is a source of strength. Believers trust that their suffering is part of a larger cosmic order and that the divine will ultimately guide them to liberation. The Bhagavad Gita emphasizes devotion and surrender to Krishna as a path to overcoming life's challenges, encouraging resilience through faith.

MORE STRATEGIES FOR COPING WITH AND OVERCOMING SUFFERING

In your transformation of suffering into purpose, employing effective strategies for coping with and overcoming challenges is essential. After you explore the release of the elements of suffering from your Suffering Basket, you can explore these various other techniques that can empower you to navigate your experiences and foster resilience. Together, these strategies form a comprehensive approach to not only cope with suffering but to harness it as a catalyst for personal growth and transformation.

MINDFULNESS

Mindfulness is the practice of being fully present and engaged in the moment, allowing us to observe our thoughts, feelings, and sensations without judgment. Rooted in ancient contemplative traditions and popularized in the West by figures like Jon Kabat-Zinn, mindfulness has become a cornerstone of personal development. This practice fosters a deeper understanding of ourselves and our experiences, paving the way for personal growth. By focusing on the present, we can break free from the cycle of rumination and anxiety that often accompanies suffering. Zinn tells us, "Mindfulness is not just a technique; it's a way of being." This perspective highlights that mindfulness extends beyond mere practices like meditation; it involves adopting an attitude of openness and curiosity toward our experiences.

Research has shown that mindfulness enhances emotional regulation, reduces stress, and promotes overall well-being. Neuroscience research studies indicate consistent mindfulness practice can lead to structural changes in the brain, particularly in areas associated with attention, emotion regulation, and self-awareness.

Consider Kyle, who has recently faced a significant loss. Initially overwhelmed by grief, he decides to practice mindfulness by setting aside time each day to apply mindfulness and meditation. During these sessions, he focuses on his breath and allows himself to feel his emotions without trying to push them away. As he continues this practice, he notices subtle shifts in his perspective. Instead of feeling consumed by sadness, he experiences moments of peace and even gratitude for the memories shared with his loved one. This newfound awareness helps him navigate his grief more effectively, fostering resilience and a deeper connection to his emotions.

The benefits of mindfulness extend far beyond stress reduction; it serves as a powerful tool for personal growth and healing. By cultivating present-moment awareness, we can learn to navigate our suffering with grace and insight. Mindfulness not only enhances our emotional well-being but also empowers us to embrace life's challenges as opportunities for transformation. As we become more attuned to our inner experiences, we open ourselves up to profound insights and a greater sense of purpose in our lives.

MEDITATION

Meditation is a practice that involves focusing the mind and eliminating distractions to achieve a state of mental clarity, emotional stability, and heightened awareness. Its origins can be traced back thousands of years, with roots in ancient spiritual traditions, particularly within Hinduism and Buddhism. Initially developed as a means to deepen spiritual understanding and connect with the divine, meditation has evolved into a widely recognized tool for personal development and mental well-being. Today it is practiced globally, transcending cultural and religious boundaries, and is supported by a growing body of scientific research that highlights its numerous benefits.

The application of meditation in transforming suffering is profound. By engaging in regular meditation practice, individuals can cultivate mindfulness. Meditation allows people to observe their suffering rather than become overwhelmed by it. For instance, consider someone who experiences anxiety due to a traumatic event. Through meditation, they learn to focus on their breath and acknowledge their anxious thoughts without becoming entangled in them. Over time, this practice can lead to reduced anxiety levels, improved emotional regulation, and a greater sense of peace. Academy Award–winning actor Jared Leto professes the importance of his meditations on peeling back the layers of external distractions and societal expectations, saying, "Meditation is a way to connect with your true self, to find out who you really are beneath all the noise."

Research has shown that meditation can induce changes in brain structure and function. Studies using neuroimaging techniques have found that regular meditation can increase the thickness of the prefrontal cortex, an area associated with higher-order thinking and emotional regulation. Additionally, meditation has been linked to decreased activity in the amygdala, which plays a key role in the stress response. These changes suggest that meditation not only helps individuals cope with their suffering but also fosters resilience and personal growth.

DEVELOPING EMOTIONAL INTELLIGENCE

Emotional intelligence (EI) is a vital skill that enables you to recognize, understand, and manage your emotions while also empathizing with the emotions of others. The concept of emotional intelligence was popularized by psychologist Daniel Goleman, who emphasized its importance in personal and professional success. Goleman's work built on earlier theories by psychologists Peter Salovey and John D. Mayer, who initially defined emotional intelligence as the ability to monitor one's own and others' feelings and emotions. Their research highlighted how emotional intelligence could significantly impact interpersonal relationships, decision-making, and overall well-being.

Goleman published his bestselling book *Emotional Intelligence* in 1995. In this work, Goleman expanded on the concept of emotional intelligence, arguing it is just as important as traditional intelligence (IQ) for success in life. He identified five key components of emotional intelligence: self-awareness, self-regulation, motivation, empathy, and social skills. Goleman's emphasis was on how these emotional competencies can enhance personal and professional relationships, making his work highly influential in both educational and corporate settings.

Understanding and developing emotional intelligence can lead to profound personal growth. When you cultivate EI, you enhance your ability to navigate complex social situations, communicate effectively, and build meaningful relationships. As Goleman noted, "In a very real sense, we have two minds, one that thinks and one that feels." This underscores the idea that your emotional experiences play a crucial role in shaping your thoughts and actions. By becoming more aware of your emotions, you can better understand how they influence your behavior and decision-making processes.

One practical application of emotional intelligence is in managing stress and conflict. For instance, consider a scenario where you receive critical feedback at work. Your initial reaction might be defensive or anxious. However, by applying emotional intelligence, you can pause to recognize these feelings without judgment. Instead of reacting impulsively, you can choose to respond thoughtfully by seeking clarification on the feedback and viewing it as an opportunity for growth. This shift in perspective helps you manage your emotions and fosters a more constructive dialogue with your colleagues.

Research supports that higher emotional intelligence is linked to better mental health outcomes. A study published in the *Journal of Personality and Social Psychology* found that individuals with greater EI tend to experience lower levels of anxiety and depression. This correlation suggests that developing emotional intelligence can serve as a protective factor against mental health challenges. Emotional intelligence refers to your ability to recognize, understand, and manage your emotions while also empathizing with the emotions of others. This skill is foundational for emotional regulation, which involves the strategies and processes you use to influence your emotional experience and expression.

Reflecting on your experiences, think about moments when your emotional responses influenced your interactions with others. Have there been times when heightened awareness of your feelings helped you navigate a difficult conversation or resolve a conflict? For example, imagine a woman who struggles with her emotions after a breakup. Initially overwhelmed by sadness and anger, she practices mindfulness and journaling to process her feelings. Through this practice, she recognizes patterns in her emotional responses and learns to express her feelings constructively rather than reactively. This newfound awareness allows her to heal and ultimately leads her to healthier relationships in the future.

As you consider the role of emotional intelligence in your life, remember that it is not just about understanding your own emotions; it also involves recognizing the emotions of those around you.

Empathy is a key component of EI that fosters connection and understanding in relationships.

Developing emotional intelligence is an essential aspect of personal growth that empowers you to navigate life's challenges with resilience and clarity. By recognizing and managing your emotions while empathizing with others, you can cultivate deeper connections and foster a more fulfilling life. As you embark on this journey of self-discovery and emotional awareness, remember that enhancing your emotional intelligence is not only beneficial for you, but it also enriches the lives of those around you.

SEEKING PROFESSIONAL HELP AND SUPPORT

Earlier in my life, I knew I needed to talk to a professional counselor to help me with my prior traumas. I saw a counselor for a couple of years, which helped. It is nothing to be ashamed about. I cared enough about myself to seek help from another.

Seeking professional help and support is a courageous step, and it signifies personal growth and a willingness to change. Acknowledging that you may need assistance is not a sign of weakness. It reflects a profound understanding of your limitations and the recognition that managing life's challenges alone can feel overwhelming. As renowned expert Brené Brown said, "Vulnerability is the birthplace of innovation, creativity, and change." When you reach out for professional support, you demonstrate strength and commitment to your well-being. It takes courage to confront the stigma often associated with seeking help, as many people fear judgment or believe that asking for assistance indicates personal failure.

In reality, seeking help is a proactive choice. It shows how serious you are about improving your life and becoming the person you are meant to be. The journey toward self-improvement often requires guidance from those who are trained to help you navigate through emotional turmoil and mental health challenges.

For example, consider my life. In my mid-thirties I had been struggling with anxiety. Initially, I tried to cope with it on my own, believing I could handle it without external support. However, as my anxiety intensified, I realized my usual strategies were no longer effective. By choosing to seek therapy, it provided me with new perspectives and coping mechanisms. Through this process, I learned valuable tools for managing anxiety and understood the root causes of my feelings. I only saw a counselor for a couple of years, but this decision not only improved my mental health but also empowered me to face other life challenges with newfound resilience. I am sharing this personal story so you know it is perfectly alright and prudent to seek professional help if needed.

Seeking professional help is a significant step toward personal growth that embodies courage, vulnerability, and a commitment to change. By acknowledging your need for support, you are prioritizing your well-being and taking control of your journey toward healing and self-discovery. Remember that reaching out for help is a sign of strength, not weakness. It reflects your dedication to becoming the best version of yourself and living a fulfilling life.

GRATITUDE PRACTICE

Focusing on gratitude in life is a pivotal element of transforming and overcoming our suffering. An entire upcoming chapter will fully explore this necessary practice for extraordinary living. Focusing on what we are grateful for can shift our mindset from negativity to positivity. By regularly acknowledging what we are grateful for, we can cultivate a deeper appreciation for the good things in our lives and reduce the tendency to ruminate on the negative. Keeping a gratitude journal, for instance, allows you to document a variety of things you are thankful for each day, helping you notice how this simple practice can profoundly change your outlook. As you will discover in an upcoming chapter, embracing gratitude not only enhances your emotional well-being but also fosters resilience and a greater sense of fulfillment in your daily life. This short introduction into gratitude practices is a vital tool for transforming pain into purpose. We will explore more on this topic later.

THE INDOMITABLE SPIRIT OF NEW ORLEANS: A TESTAMENT TO HUMAN PERSEVERANCE

In the annals of human resilience, few stories shine as brightly as that of New Orleans in the wake of Hurricane Katrina. The devastating storm that struck in 2005 left an indelible mark on the city and its people, presenting challenges that would test the limits of human endurance and spirit. Yet from the depths of despair, the people of New Orleans emerged as a shining example of perseverance in the face of overwhelming adversity.

The losses endured by New Orleans residents were staggering. Homes were swept away, leaving only concrete steps where thousands of houses had been destroyed from the powerful storm surge and flooding. These could have remained as tombstones of neighborhoods lost, but the citizens of New Orleans refused to let this happen. Cherished possessions, family heirlooms, and irreplaceable mementos were lost to the floodwaters. Jobs disappeared overnight as businesses were destroyed or forced to relocate. Loved ones perished in the storm or its chaotic aftermath. The very fabric of the community was torn asunder, with families and friends scattered across the country.

In the immediate aftermath, many residents were in a state of profound shock and disorientation. The familiar landmarks of their lives had vanished, replaced by a landscape of destruction. As a New Orleanian, I can tell you we all faced an uncertain future, grappling with questions that had no easy answers: Where would we live? How would we rebuild? Could our beloved city ever recover?

Yet in the face of these daunting challenges, the people of New Orleans demonstrated remarkable courage and resilience. We drew strength from our deep-rooted culture, our sense of community, and our unwavering belief in the spirit of our city. Neighbors helped neighbors, strangers became friends, and a collective determination to rebuild took hold.

This resilience manifested in countless ways. Some residents returned to their damaged homes, living in FEMA trailers while slowly rebuilding their lives piece by piece. Others, unable to return immediately, worked tirelessly to maintain connections to their community from afar, planning for the day they could come home. Local musicians, even those who had lost everything, continued to play, using their art to heal and inspire. Entrepreneurs launched new businesses, seeing opportunity in the city's rebirth.

The story of New Orleans's recovery is not just about rebuilding structures; it's about rebuilding lives and preserving a unique cultural heritage. Residents faced each new challenge with a mix of pragmatism and creativity, finding innovative solutions to problems that seemed insurmountable. We advocated for better flood protection, reimagined our education system, and worked to create a more equitable and resilient city.

This spirit of perseverance is not unique to New Orleans, though the city's experience provides a particularly poignant example. Around the world, people face similar challenges in the wake of natural disasters such as fires, earthquakes, floods, and plagues; wars; and personal tragedies and suffering from disease, crime, hatred, discrimination, and other devastating personal events. Whether displayed in survivors of earthquakes in Haiti; refugees fleeing war, conflict, or terrorism; or individuals battling life-threatening circumstances, the human capacity to endure and overcome is a universal thread that binds us all.

What we can learn from New Orleans and other examples of resilience is that perseverance is not about avoiding pain or pretending that loss doesn't hurt. It's about acknowledging the pain, grieving what has been lost, and then finding the courage to take the next step forward, however small it may be. It's about holding on to hope, even when the future seems bleak, and drawing strength from community and shared purpose.

The journey of perseverance is rarely linear. There are setbacks, moments of doubt, and times when the challenges seem overwhelming. But as the people of New Orleans have shown, it is possible to rebuild, to heal, and to create something beautiful from the muddy murk of devastation. Their story reminds us that within each of us lies the strength to face our own "Katrinas"—whatever form they may take—and to emerge not just surviving but thriving.

After Hurricane Katrina, I was an invited guest on CNN's *The Situation Room with Wolf Blitzer*. Blitzer concluded our interview by asking me, "You are hopeful?" I said, "Yes, I'm from New Orleans. Yes, we will rebuild." We persevered, and we did.

As we face our challenges, whether personal or collective, we can draw inspiration from New Orleans's resilience. We can choose to persevere, support one another, and believe in the possibility of renewal. In doing so, we honor not just our own strength but the indomitable spirit of human perseverance that connects us all.

THE ONGOING ROLE OF SUFFERING IN PERSONAL GROWTH

Consider what our personal experiences would be like without any suffering. While it might seem appealing to live a life free of pain, suffering plays a crucial role in our growth and development. It shapes our character, builds resilience, and helps us develop empathy and compassion for others. A quote widely attributed to Kahlil Gibran, author of *The Prophet*, tells us, "Out of suffering have emerged the strongest souls; the most massive characters are seared with scars."

By understanding and embracing suffering, you tap into a wellspring of strength, resilience, and deeper connection—not only to yourself but also to others who walk a similar path. Your journey through suffering is not merely a tale of endurance but a powerful testament to your courage and capacity for transformation.

Embrace your suffering with empathy, strength, and radical candor. Acknowledge that you are not alone in this experience; countless others have faced similar trials and emerged stronger. The post-traumatic growth experienced by many, as described in positive psychology, shows that even in the aftermath of the most harrowing experiences, we can find meaning, purpose, and an enhanced appreciation for life. Viktor Frankl reminds us, "Those who have a 'why' to live, can bear with almost any 'how.'"

Your story of overcoming suffering is a beacon of hope, illuminating the path for others who may find themselves in similar darkness. Remember, even when suffering, there are blessings, grace, and abundance that coexist, enriching your life and providing a foundation for resilience and joy. These moments of grace are not just random occurrences. They are often the fruits of your ability to adapt and grow and a testament to the power of neuroplasticity and resilience in reshaping your response to suffering.

As we emerge from the depths of suffering, having explored its many facets and the profound ways it shapes our lives, we stand at a pivotal moment. The pain we've confronted, the wisdom we've gained, and the strength we've cultivated have all led us to this point. But this is not the end of our journey. It is from this very crucible of hardship that the seeds of perseverance and tenacity take root.

Just as the strongest steel is forged in the hottest fires, our greatest strengths are often born from our most challenging trials and through the realization that our lives continue to change. Don't forget what Margaret Mitchell's resilient character Scarlett O'Hara said in the closing line of the epic book and movie, *Gone with the Wind*: "After all, tomorrow is another day."

My mother always used to tell me that when I was sad and down. She was right.

CHAPTER 17

Blessings, Gratitude, and Grace

"And God said, Let there be light: and there was light."
—Genesis 1:3 (KJV)

As we journey through life, striving to become the person we are meant to be, we often focus on the challenges we must overcome, the goals we must achieve, and the growth we must undergo. However, there is a crucial element that ties all of these aspects together, one that is both a catalyst for personal transformation and a result of it: gratitude. In this chapter, we will explore why recognizing our blessings, cultivating gratitude, and embracing grace are not just beneficial practices, but essential *musts* in our quest for joy, peace, and self-actualization. By embracing gratitude, we not only enhance our own well-being but also create a ripple effect of positivity that touches the lives of those around us. We will learn to see that blessings are not just something we experience in moments of joy but are always present, even in the darkest times, waiting to be acknowledged and cherished.

Throughout this book, we've discussed the importance of identifying our core values, overcoming limiting beliefs, and aligning our actions with our deepest purpose. Gratitude is the thread that weaves through all these elements, enhancing their power and deepening their impact on our lives. It is both a practice we must develop and a state of being that becomes more accessible as we progress in our journey to the Must Zone.

My path to understanding the critical role of gratitude in personal development was not an easy one. For years, I focused solely on achievement, constantly pushing myself to overcome obstacles and reach new heights. While this drive led to professional success, I often felt a gnawing emptiness, a sense that something fundamental was missing. It wasn't until I faced a series of personal setbacks—including health challenges and the loss of loved ones—that I truly appreciated the power of gratitude.

I remember waking up one morning, feeling particularly low, and deciding to take a walk outside. The sun was shining, birds were singing, and the air was filled with the sweet scent of blooming flowers. But what struck me most was not just the beauty of the day. It was the realization that these blessings were not just present in moments of joy but also in the darkest moments of suffering. I realized when life seemed at its bleakest, threads of grace and goodness were always woven into the fabric of my existence.

This realization marked a turning point for me. I practiced gratitude daily, taking time to reflect on the blessings in my life, no matter how small they seemed. I journaled about the things I was thankful for, from the support of loved ones to the simple pleasures of life, like a good cup of coffee or a beautiful sunset. But I also made a conscious effort to recognize the blessings that were present even in the midst of hardship. I learned to see the resilience of my family, the kindness of strangers, and the strength that emerged from our collective struggles as blessings in their own right.

In those moments of vulnerability and reflection, I realized my relentless pursuit of goals had blinded me to the countless blessings already present in my life. The simple act of acknowledging these gifts—from the support of friends and family to the beauty of a sunrise—began to shift my perspective profoundly. I discovered that gratitude wasn't just a feel-good practice; it was a transformative force that allowed me to access deeper levels of joy, resilience, and purpose.

Challenges still arose, but I faced them with greater resilience and peace. Gratitude wasn't just about feeling good; it was about living a life of purpose and fulfillment. It allowed me to connect more deeply with my core values and to appreciate the grace that flowed through every aspect of my existence.

This realization led me to understand that gratitude is not just a by-product of reaching our goals or living in our Must Zone—it is a vital component in getting there. By cultivating gratitude, we open ourselves to new possibilities, enhance our resilience in the face of challenges, and deepen our connection to our core values and purpose. In essence, gratitude becomes a *must* practice that accelerates our journey toward becoming our best selves.

As we progress in aligning our lives with our Must Values and Actions, gratitude becomes more readily accessible. The more we live authentically and purposefully, the more we recognize the abundance of blessings in our lives. This creates a beautiful cycle: gratitude fuels our growth, and our growth enhances our capacity for gratitude.

In this chapter, we will explore practical strategies for developing a gratitude practice, examine the scientific evidence supporting its benefits, and share personal stories of transformation through thankfulness. We will also delve into the concept of grace—both giving and receiving it—and how it intertwines with gratitude to create a more compassionate, fulfilling life.

As we embark on this exploration of blessings, gratitude, and grace, I invite you to open your heart and mind to the transformative power of thankfulness. Whether you're just beginning your journey to the Must Zone or are well along your path, cultivating gratitude will undoubtedly enrich your experience and accelerate your growth. Let us discover together how this essential *must* can unlock new levels of joy, peace, and self-actualization in our lives.

Every life has its share of struggles, and yours and mine are no exception. We've all faced moments that seemed insurmountable, times when we questioned whether we had the strength to keep moving forward. But if we look back, we'll see that these moments often came with unexpected gifts of insight, resilience, or a deepened sense of empathy. It's as if the universe balances our burdens with blessings, ensuring we are never left completely in the dark.

What if we could see every experience—every high and every low—as a part of this grand design? What if, instead of giving in to our inherent negative bias of focusing solely on our pain or challenges, we also opened our hearts to the blessings that are always present, waiting to be recognized and cherished? This is the essence of living with a sense of abundance and a growth mindset: to not just see what is lacking, but to appreciate what is abundant in our lives truly.

This perspective of seeing every experience as part of a grand design aligns perfectly with both the growth mindset and the Must Mindset we explored earlier. The growth mindset encourages us to view challenges as opportunities for learning and development rather than insurmountable obstacles. Similarly, the Must Mindset compels us to approach our personal growth with unwavering commitment and urgency.

By cultivating an abundance mindset, we're not just passively accepting our circumstances; we're actively choosing to see the potential for growth and blessing in every situation. This aligns with the Must Mindset's emphasis on taking control of our personal development. When we choose to focus on abundance and gratitude, we're making a conscious decision to shape our reality that supports our growth and fulfillment. This shift in perspective becomes a *must*—an essential practice that propels us toward becoming the person we are meant to be. It transforms gratitude from a mere positive thinking exercise into a powerful tool for personal transformation, pushing us to continuously seek opportunities for growth and appreciation in every aspect of our lives.

A MOMENT OF PRESENT MINDFULNESS

Let's take a deep breath together, right here, right now. Let go of the worries that clutter your mind—the tasks that demand your attention, the anxieties that gnaw at the edges of your peace. For just this moment, release them all. Feel the tension in your shoulders melt away as you inhale deeply and exhale slowly. Allow yourself to be fully present, here in this moment.

Focus on your breathing. Notice the gentle rise and fall of your chest with each breath, the air filling your lungs and then releasing, carrying with it any lingering stress. As you breathe, begin to tune in to the world around you. Listen closely. Can you hear the birds chirping outside? Their songs are simple, yet they fill the air with a melody of life. Feel the breeze as it brushes against your face, cool and refreshing, carrying the subtle scent of the earth. Notice the warmth of the sun as it touches your forehead and cheeks, a gentle reminder of the life-giving energy that surrounds us.

Ah, yes, each of these is a blessing. In this moment, as we expand our awareness, we also expand our recognition of the countless blessings that are abundantly before us and within us. As we quiet the noise in our minds, our senses come alive, awakening to the beauty of the present. The sounds, the sensations, the very act of being—each is a gift, often overlooked in the rush of daily life.

How often do we rush through our days, not truly noticing the world around us? We become so absorbed in our thoughts, our worries, our to-do lists that we forget to really see, hear, and feel the life that is unfolding in each second of our existence. But when we pause, when we allow ourselves to simply be, we notice the extraordinary in the ordinary. We see that the breeze isn't just a breeze—it's a tender caress from the universe. The warmth of the sun isn't just warmth—it's a reminder we are alive, here, in this moment, part of something much greater than ourselves.

Even the very act of breathing, something we do thousands of times a day without a second thought, is a miracle. Each breath sustains us, connecting us to the world around us in the most intimate way. Our hearts, tirelessly beating, pump life through our arteries, a constant, rhythmic reminder of the miracle of our existence. We are not just passive observers of this life. We are active participants, interwoven with the fabric of the universe.

This is you. This is us. This is our place in the grand, expanding realm of life. We are part of something vast, something magnificent. And within this vastness, we are surrounded by an infinite number of blessings if only we take the time to notice them.

As you continue to breathe deeply, feel a sense of awe begin to fill your heart. The miracle of your existence, the sheer improbability of you being here, now, on this planet, is an extraordinary circumstance of unfathomable grace and goodness. Every element of your being, every heartbeat, every breath, is a testament to the incredible gift of life.

This moment of mindfulness is a doorway to deeper awareness—a way to step into the fullness of life with all your senses, with your entire being. It's a practice of expanding your vision, of seeing the world not just with your eyes, but with your heart and soul. And as your vision expands, so too does your realization of the blessings that surround you, that fill you, that make up the very essence of who you are.

So, my friend, let us embrace this moment for now. Let us cherish the simple, beautiful existence of each element we experience. Let us celebrate the miracle of our being, of being part of this vast, expanding universe of life. This is our journey, our shared experience, our collective embrace of the abundance that is always, always present.

COUNT YOUR BLESSINGS

Acknowledging our blessings involves consciously recognizing the positive aspects of our lives, both big and small. This awareness serves as a foundation for cultivating gratitude, which is an active practice of expressing appreciation for these blessings. Gratitude goes beyond mere recognition, involving a deeper emotional connection and a sense of thankfulness that can lead to positive changes in attitude and behavior. Grace, on the other hand, often refers to the unmerited favor or goodwill we receive, whether from a higher power, other people, or life circumstances. It encompasses the idea that we are given gifts or opportunities that we may not have earned or deserved. While acknowledging blessings and practicing gratitude are largely within our control, grace is often seen as something bestowed upon us. Together, these three elements create a powerful synergy that can enhance our perspective on life, foster resilience, and promote a more positive and fulfilling existence.

Nick Vujicic's life is a profound example of the transformative power of focusing on blessings, even when faced with unimaginable challenges. Born with tetra-amelia syndrome, a rare disorder that left him without arms or legs, Nick had an early life marked by physical and emotional struggles. As a child, he endured bullying, loneliness, and depression, even contemplating suicide at the age of ten. For Nick, simple acts that most take for granted seemed insurmountable, and he often questioned the value of his existence. Yet in the depths of his despair, Nick experienced a pivotal shift—a realization that his unique circumstances were not a curse but an opportunity to inspire others and live a life filled with purpose.

This transformation began when Nick embraced the belief that his life had meaning and his limitations did not define him. With unwavering determination, he learned to perform everyday tasks such as writing, swimming, and using a computer—actions that required extraordinary effort but symbolized his resilience. Nick's focus shifted from surviving to thriving, as he saw his challenges as blessings in disguise. He founded the nonprofit organization Life Without Limbs, authored bestselling books, and became a globally renowned motivational speaker. Through his work, Nick has touched millions of lives with his message of hope and perseverance.

Nick's ability to count blessings amidst adversity is evident in his words: "I'm ridiculously happy. And I think the reason why I'm happy is because I've seen many miracles in my life." By choosing to focus on what he could do rather than what he couldn't, Nick transformed his life from one of despair to one of joy and purpose. His story exemplifies how gratitude can serve as a powerful tool for overcoming challenges and finding fulfillment.

Nick's journey also highlights the importance of aligning one's actions with purpose—a concept central to this book's Must Framework. By living in alignment with his *musts*, Nick cultivated resilience and authenticity, using his challenges as a platform to empower others. His story reminds us that our circumstances do not define us; our response to them does. When we focus on blessings and live fully in our Must Zone, we can transcend even the most daunting obstacles and create lives of extraordinary impact.

Nick's life is a testament to the indomitable human spirit and the power of gratitude. As he says, "If you can't get a miracle, become one." His example encourages us all to embrace our blessings, align with our purpose, and transform adversity into opportunities for growth and connection.

Isn't it remarkable how life works? How, amid our deepest struggles, there are moments—sometimes small, almost imperceptible—that remind us of the good that still exists? It's as if life, in its infinite wisdom, knows just when to offer us a glimpse of light and a touch of grace to help us keep going. These blessings, whether grand or subtle, are always there, weaving their way through our experiences, waiting for us to acknowledge them.

Think about it: even when we are caught in the throes of sorrow or frustration, the sun still rises, the birds still sing, and the people who love us still offer their support. There is something gloriously comforting in knowing that our hardships do not erase the good in our lives. Instead, they coexist, intertwining to create the full spectrum of our human experience. It's this interplay between the challenges we face and the blessings we receive that makes our journey so rich and so uniquely ours.

The legendary country singer-songwriter Willie Nelson once said, "When I started counting my blessings, my whole life turned around."

Years ago, I began a simple yet profoundly impactful practice for my birthday—one that has reshaped my perspective on life in ways I never could have imagined. On that special day each year, I would sit quietly and reflect, pen in hand, as I wrote down a list of blessings I had encountered over the past year. The number of blessings on my list matched my age, and then, with a hopeful heart, I would add one more blessing for the year ahead. This ritual was more than just a moment of reflection. It was a celebration of the abundance in my life, a conscious acknowledgment of the gifts, both big and small, that had come my way.

But here's the thing I've realized: there really is no such thing as a small blessing. Each one, no matter how seemingly insignificant, carries infinite power in its existence. The smile of a stranger, the warmth of the morning sun, the sound of laughter echoing through the air—these moments, though they may appear small, are not small at all. They are integral in our lives, each one contributing to the joy, grace, and meaning that define our existence.

As this practice of listing my blessings deepened, it became more than just an annual tradition. Whenever my loved ones had birthdays, I created lists for them as well, capturing the ways in which they had brought light and love into the world. These lists became cherished gifts, reminders of the profound impact we have on one another and the gratitude we should hold for these connections.

Over the years, what started as a birthday ritual has evolved into a daily practice, an integral part of my life. Just as we diligently write down our Must Goals, I now take time each day to write down, read, and add to my list of blessings. In my personal Miracle Morning, this daily habit keeps me anchored in a mindset of appreciation and abundance, no matter what challenges the day may bring.

And here's the magic of this practice: by focusing on our blessings, we begin to understand that even in times of strife, those blessings simultaneously exist. They do not vanish in the face of adversity; rather, they stand firm, offering us comfort and strength. Our list of blessings becomes a beacon, guiding our focus toward the positive, even when life feels overwhelming.

It's often said that when we are genuinely thankful for our blessings and are filled with gratitude, there's little room left for the negative feelings that try to pull us down. Gratitude, much like a buoy, lifts us, helping us rise above the currents of negativity that seek to influence the story of our lives. By consciously focusing on our blessings, we allow that buoyancy to carry us, keeping our hearts light and our minds clear.

So I encourage you to embrace this practice of listing your blessings. Whether you do it daily, weekly, or just once a year, let it become a ritual that nurtures your spirit. As you sit quietly, pen in hand, reflecting on the blessings in your life, remember that each blessing holds infinite power, a force of grace that enriches your life in ways you may not always see.

Soon I will ask you to list your blessings. In the quiet moments of reflection, as you write down each blessing, your focus naturally shifts away from what's lacking or difficult in your life. Instead, you'll see the abundance that surrounds you, the richness of your experiences, and the love that fills your days. The smallest blessings—a kind word, the invigorating briskness of a breeze, the steady love you receive from others—each hold the power to transform your perspective, reminding you of the beauty and grace that are ever-present in your life.

Let your list of blessings be a living document, one that grows and evolves with you. As you continue to add to it, your perspective on life shifts in subtle but powerful ways. The more you focus on the good, the more you will attract it. And in those moments when life feels heavy, return to your list—let it remind you of the extraordinary power held within even the smallest blessings, of the beauty and grace that are always present, just waiting to be acknowledged.

THE SCIENCE OF ACKNOWLEDGING OUR BLESSINGS

The scientific findings on the importance of recognizing our blessings and the effects of this practice on our lives are both compelling and multifaceted. Research has consistently shown that practicing gratitude, which involves acknowledging and appreciating the positive aspects of life, can have profound impacts on mental and physical well-being. Studies have demonstrated that individuals who regularly practice gratitude experience more positive emotions, greater life satisfaction, and improved mood. A research study found that gratitude recognition leads to significantly lower symptoms of anxiety and depression. Furthermore, a large study conducted by Virginia Commonwealth University revealed that thankfulness predicted a substantially lower risk of major depression, generalized anxiety disorder, and other mental health issues.

The benefits of gratitude extend beyond psychological health. Research has linked increased gratitude with higher-quality sleep and fewer sleep disturbances, potentially due to falling asleep with a more positive outlook. Interestingly, studies have found that people who practice gratitude tend to exercise more than those who don't, possibly due to increased energy levels and a more positive outlook on life. Physical health improvements have also been observed, with research showing that individuals who focus on gratitude have fewer visits to physicians compared to those who focus on sources of aggravation. A recent study from the Nurses' Health Study even found that participants with higher gratitude scores had a 9 percent lower risk of dying over the following four years compared to those with lower scores, suggesting a potential link between gratitude and longevity.

Neurologically, acknowledging gratitude leads to the release of serotonin and dopamine, chemicals in the brain associated with happiness and pleasure. This can result in short-term reductions in anxiety and improvements in mood. Regular gratitude practice may lead to lasting changes in the brain, priming individuals to be more grateful. Socially, studies have found that giving thanks and counting blessings can help improve interpersonal relationships and increase positive social behavior.

The most common and scientifically studied gratitude interventions include gratitude journaling, the Three Good Things exercise, and writing gratitude letters. Gratitude journaling involves regularly writing down things you're grateful for, often on a daily or weekly basis. The Three Good Things exercise is a specific practice where you think of and write down three positive moments or things that happen each day. Writing gratitude letters entails composing letters expressing appreciation to others, which can be shared with the recipient or kept private. These practices, when done consistently, have been shown to yield benefits in as little as a few weeks.

Scientific research has consistently demonstrated that practicing gratitude and acknowledging our blessings can significantly enhance peak performance in sports and other fields. Studies have shown that grateful athletes experience reduced stress levels, improved sleep quality, and decreased burnout rates. This positive mindset leads to better emotional control, increased focus, and enhanced resilience in the face of challenges. Gratitude has been linked to higher levels of athlete engagement, improved coach-athlete relationships, and stronger team cohesion.

These physiological changes create an optimal internal environment for peak performance, not only in sports but across various areas of life. By fostering a sense of contentment and reducing negative emotions, gratitude allows individuals to approach their pursuits with greater clarity, motivation, and overall effectiveness.

By integrating this practice into your daily routine, you cultivate a mindset of abundance rather than scarcity. You train your mind to notice and appreciate the positive aspects of your life, which in turn creates a ripple effect of positivity and gratitude that touches every area of your existence. In this way, your list of blessings becomes more than just words on a page—it becomes a source of strength, a wellspring of joy, and a testament to the infinite power and abundance that define your life.

RELIGIOUS AND SPIRITUAL PERSPECTIVES ON BLESSINGS, GRATITUDE, AND GRACE

World religions offer diverse perspectives on blessings, gratitude, and grace, yet they share common threads that emphasize the importance of these concepts in spiritual life. These views provide insight into how different cultures and belief systems approach the recognition of divine favor and the appropriate human response.

In Christianity, gratitude is seen as a fundamental virtue and a proper response to God's grace. The apostle Paul emphasizes this in his writings, urging believers to "give thanks in all circumstances" (1 Thessalonians 5:18 NIV). Christian theology views grace as God's unmerited favor, with gratitude being the natural outcome of recognizing this gift. Martin Luther referred to gratitude as "the basic Christian attitude," highlighting its centrality in Christian faith. Brennan Manning, a renowned Christian author and speaker, says, "Gratitude is the echo of grace as it reverberates through the hollows of the human heart."

The concept of blessings in Christianity is often linked to both material and spiritual gifts from God, with an emphasis on the latter.

Islam similarly places great importance on gratitude, known as *shuk* in Arabic. The Quran states, "If you are grateful, I will surely increase you [in favor]" (Quran 14:7), suggesting that gratitude leads to further blessings.

Muslims are encouraged to express gratitude not only in times of abundance but also in adversity, viewing all circumstances as opportunities for spiritual growth. The Islamic perspective on blessings often emphasizes both worldly provisions and spiritual insights as gifts from Allah. Muslim author, speaker, and spiritual teacher Yasmin Mogahed says, "Gratitude is not only the greatest of virtues, but the parent of all others. The one who is not thankful for little will not be thankful for much. Alhamdulillah for everything—the good, the bad, and everything in between. For in every situation, there is always something to be grateful for."

In Judaism, gratitude is deeply ingrained in daily practice. The

Midrash teaches, "In pleasure or pain, give thanks!" This reflects the Jewish belief that one should acknowledge God's role in all aspects of life. The concept of *berakhah* (blessing) is central to Jewish prayer and ritual, with specific blessings prescribed for various occasions and experiences. Rabbi Jonathan Sacks noted, "Gratitude is the essence of faith and the heart of Judaism." Rabbi Sacks also proclaims that "gratitude is not only the greatest of virtues, but the parent of all others. The one who is not thankful for what he has received, then be thankful for what you have been spared."

Buddhism, while not theistic, also emphasizes gratitude as a virtue. The Buddha taught that gratitude is a quality of noble people, stating, "A person of integrity is grateful and thankful." In Buddhist thought, gratitude is often linked to mindfulness and the appreciation of interdependence. While the concept of grace is not prominent in Buddhism, the idea of blessings is often associated with good karma and the opportunity for spiritual advancement.

Hinduism views gratitude as a means of aligning oneself with the divine. The concept of *prasad*—seeing everything as a gift from God—encourages a constant state of thankfulness. The Bhagavad Gita teaches the importance of accepting both pleasant and unpleasant experiences with equanimity, a perspective that fosters gratitude in all circumstances. Blessings in Hinduism are often seen as manifestations of divine grace, known as *anugraha*.

Across these diverse traditions, we see a common recognition of gratitude as a transformative force in spiritual life. Whether expressed through formal prayer, daily rituals, or mindful awareness, gratitude is universally viewed as a pathway to deeper connection with the divine and greater contentment in life. The interplay of blessings, gratitude, and grace in these worldviews underscores their significance in human spiritual experience, offering rich approaches to cultivating a thankful heart and recognizing the sacred in everyday life.

CREATING OUR LIST OF BLESSINGS—TODAY

Having considered the vast benefits of the recognition of our blessings, of our gratitude, and of the grace bestowed on us, let's actively and intentionally move forward. There is no better time than now to start creating and writing down your list of blessings. Recognize that these blessings will have an instantaneous impact on your soul, spirit, and perspective on life. Your list of blessings should never be restricted by any limiting beliefs you once may have had. The world is indeed your oyster. To help you think about your blessings, I have provided you with categories of blessings so we can view them in an organized fashion.

As we journey through life, we are continuously receiving countless blessings—gifts that enrich our experiences, uplift our spirits, and provide us with the strength to navigate both the triumphs and challenges we encounter. These blessings are the threads that create a vibrant world of beauty, resilience, and joy in our lives. Let us explore the many blessings that grace our existence, from the divine and spiritual to the everyday comforts we often overlook. By thinking about these blessings through the lens of the Circle of Life, we can uncover blessings in unexpected places, recognizing how each aspect of our existence, from relationships and health to purpose and spirituality, contributes to a sense of fulfillment. The Circle of Life reminds us that even obstacles and challenges can be blessings in disguise, offering opportunities for growth, wisdom, and transformation. Beyond the traditional categories within the Circle of Life, we can also acknowledge additional blessings, such as the environment that nurtures us and the lessons embedded within adversity. As you read through each category, take a moment to pause, reflect, and perhaps begin your own list of blessings. By acknowledging each one, you'll uncover how abundantly blessed your life truly is and how gratitude can illuminate even the most hidden gifts in your journey.

HEALTH AND VITALITY

The blessings of health and vitality are foundational gifts we often take for granted until they are challenged or compromised. As we reflect on these profound blessings, we are reminded of their immeasurable impact on our lives and the lives of those around us. The miracle of birth marks the beginning of our journey in this world. Each new life is a testament to the intricate wonder of creation—a unique blend of genetic potential and infinite possibilities. The first cry of a newborn is a powerful reminder of the preciousness and fragility of life, awakening in us a sense of awe and gratitude for the gift of existence.

From our very first breath, we are recipients of an extraordinary biological legacy. Our bodies are marvels of complexity, with systems working in harmony to sustain life. Each breath we take is a miracle, bringing life-giving oxygen to every cell in our body. This simple act, repeated thousands of times a day without conscious thought, allows us to move, think, and engage with the world around us.

Our heartbeat, steady and strong, pumps life through our arteries. It's a rhythm that begins before birth and continues tirelessly throughout our lives. This incredible organ works ceaselessly, adapting to our needs whether we're at rest or exerting ourselves. The gift of a healthy heart enables us to experience the full range of human emotions and physical experiences.

The ability to move freely, without pain or limitation, is a blessing that allows us to embrace life fully. We can run, dance, hug our loved ones, and engage in activities that bring us joy and fulfillment. For those suffering from illness or injury, the longing for this freedom of movement can be profound, reminding us to cherish our health and mobility.

The process of healing is another profound blessing. Our bodies possess a remarkable capacity for regeneration and recovery, a testament to the resilience of life. Whether it's a small cut that heals or overcoming a serious illness, each instance of healing is a reminder of the precious gift of life and the strength within us.

In our appreciation for these blessings, we are called to be mindful of those who are suffering and to support them in whatever ways we can. This might include offering practical help or emotional support, or simply being present with them in their struggles. By recognizing life, birth, health, and healing as profound blessings, we cultivate compassion for others and a deeper appreciation for the gift of existence itself.

RELATIONSHIPS

The warmth of a loved one's embrace, the joy of shared laughter, and the comfort of knowing we are cherished and have relationships are among life's greatest blessings. These relationships offer us love, support, and a sense of belonging that enrich every aspect of our lives. As we receive these relational blessings, we are reminded of the importance of nurturing and valuing the connections we have.

Human connections form the fabric of our existence, providing rich experiences that shape our lives. The power of community extends beyond individual relationships. Being part of a community—whether it's family, friends, or a larger social group—provides us with a sense of identity and purpose. It offers a support system during challenging times and a shared joy during moments of celebration. Community involvement can also lead to personal growth as we learn from others' experiences and perspectives.

Nurturing these connections requires effort and intentionality. It involves active listening, empathy, and a willingness to be present for others. As we cultivate these relationships, we not only receive love and support but also have the opportunity to give it, creating a virtuous cycle of connection and belonging.

The blessing of love and community reminds us of our interconnectedness and the fundamental human need for belonging. It teaches us that we are not alone in our journey through life and that our experiences, both joyful and challenging, are shared by others. Our blessings of love, connection, and community are celebrated in Maya Angelou's belief that "love recognizes no barriers. It jumps hurdles, leaps fences, penetrates walls to arrive at its destination full of hope."

By recognizing and appreciating the blessings of love, connection, and community in our lives, we open ourselves to a deeper sense of fulfillment and purpose. We learn to value not just what we have, but who we have in our lives, fostering a gratitude that enhances our overall well-being and happiness.

CAREER

The realm of our career is a significant part of the Circle of Life, offering unique blessings that shape our sense of purpose, fulfillment, and contribution to the world. Our careers provide us with opportunities to express our talents, develop skills, and create value for others. Whether it's through meaningful work that aligns with our passions or the ability to support ourselves and our loved ones, careers often serve as a channel for personal growth and impact. Even in moments of challenge, such as navigating setbacks, workplace conflicts, or career transitions, there are blessings to be found. These experiences can teach us resilience, adaptability, and the importance of aligning our professional lives with our core values and *musts*.

When we examine the blessings within our careers through the lens of the Circle of Life, we gain a broader perspective on how this realm connects to other areas of fulfillment. A career can foster relationships through collaboration, contribute to financial stability that supports health and well-being, and even provide a platform for pursuing deeper life purposes. By recognizing these blessings, we can approach our work with gratitude and intention, seeing it not just as a means to an end but as an integral part of a balanced and meaningful life. Whether you are thriving in your current role or seeking a new path, reflecting on the blessings in your career can help you uncover opportunities for growth, align your professional pursuits with your *musts*, and help you find joy in the contributions you make each day.

FINANCIAL WELL-BEING

As we count our material blessings and financial well-being, it's important to recognize the abundance many of us enjoy in our daily lives. The comfort of a warm bed, the security of a roof over our heads, and the nourishment of regular meals are often taken for granted. These material comforts, from the clothes on our backs to the devices that connect us to the world, provide a foundation of stability and well-being that allows us to pursue our goals and dreams.

However, we must also acknowledge that countless individuals around the world struggle to meet even their most basic material needs. Many face the daily challenge of finding food, clean water, and shelter. As we express gratitude for our material blessings, let us also cultivate compassion for those who lack these essentials. May we be inspired to share our abundance, support organizations that provide aid, and work toward a world where everyone's basic needs are met. By recognizing our blessings and the struggles of others, we can foster a spirit of generosity and empathy, helping to alleviate the burdens of those in need and creating a more fruitful world for all.

PERSONAL GROWTH AND LEARNING

Our pursuit of knowledge is a blessing we receive through curiosity and education, expanding our minds and opening doors to endless possibilities. Each discovery and creative endeavor we undertake is a gift that fuels passion and innovation, allowing us to contribute uniquely to the world.

The thrill of discovering something new—whether it's a place, an idea, or a passion—is a blessing that keeps life vibrant and full of possibilities. As we receive the gifts of adventure and exploration, we push the boundaries of what we know and open doors to uncharted territories within and beyond ourselves.

The gift of curiosity and the ability to learn are fundamental intellectual blessings. As Albert Einstein said, "Imagination is more important than knowledge. Knowledge is limited. Imagination encircles the world." This highlights how our intellectual pursuits go beyond mere accumulation of facts to encompass the ability to imagine, question, and innovate.

Education, both formal and informal, is a powerful intellectual blessing. It opens doors to new opportunities, enhances our problem-solving skills, and broadens our perspectives. As we engage in lifelong learning, we continuously expand our mental horizons. This ongoing growth not only benefits us individually but also allows us to contribute more effectively to society.

Creativity is a unique blessing that allows us to express ourselves and bring new ideas into the world. Pablo Picasso captured this essence when he said, "The chief enemy of creativity is 'good' sense." This reminds us that creative blessings often involve thinking outside conventional boundaries. Our creative endeavors, whether in art, science, business, or any other field, are gifts that fuel passion and innovation. They allow us to leave our unique mark on the world.

Engaging with diverse cultures broadens our perspectives and fosters mutual understanding. These exchanges are blessings that enrich our lives with different viewpoints and experiences, adding layers of meaning to our journey. As we receive the blessings of diversity, we learn to appreciate the richness that comes from sharing and learning from others.

As Mikhail Gorbachev said, "Peace is not unity in similarity but unity in diversity, in the comparison and conciliation of differences." By embracing diversity, we learn to appreciate and respect differences rather than fear them. This understanding is crucial for fostering peace and tolerance in an increasingly interconnected world. We are blessed by being a part of this diverse, culturally abundant world.

The gift of diverse experiences enriches our lives in countless ways. Each new experience, whether it's traveling to a new place, trying a new skill, or meeting people from different backgrounds, expands our understanding of the world and ourselves. These experiential blessings foster personal growth, empathy, and adaptability. They challenge our preconceptions and broaden our worldview. As Mark Twain said,

"Travel is fatal to prejudice, bigotry, and narrow-mindedness." This highlights how our experiences can transform not just our knowledge, but our character.

The interplay of these blessings—intellectual, creative, and experiential—creates extraordinary personal growth and fulfillment. They enable us to continuously evolve, innovate, and contribute to the world in meaningful ways. By recognizing and cultivating these blessings, we open ourselves to a life of ongoing discovery, expression, and connection.

SPIRITUALITY, RELIGION, AND INNER PEACE

Our lives are enriched by divine, spiritual, and emotional blessings that provide comfort, guidance, and joy. These blessings manifest in various forms, offering us strength and support as we navigate life's journey.

For those with religious faith, divine blessings are seen as gifts from a higher power. These encompass grace, salvation, divine protection, answered prayers, and spiritual gifts. The Bible beautifully illustrates this from a Christian perspective in Ephesians 1:3, "Blessed be the God and Father of our Lord Jesus Christ, who has blessed us in Christ with every spiritual blessing in the heavenly places," reminding us of the spiritual blessings bestowed upon us. Other religions have very similar expressions. There is a serene peace that accompanies moments of deep prayer or meditation, a comforting assurance that we are never alone. The blessing of faith is a gift from a higher power, offering us guidance, comfort, and inner tranquility. We receive these spiritual blessings through our connection with the divine, helping us navigate life's storms with grace and resilience.

Even for those who don't adhere to a specific religion, spiritual blessings abound. These can be found in the form of inner peace, connection with nature, a sense of purpose, mindfulness, and personal growth. As Thich Nhat Hanh, the revered Buddhist monk, reminds us, "The present moment is filled with joy and happiness. If you are attentive, you will see it." This perspective encourages us to find spiritual fulfillment in the here and now regardless of our religious beliefs.

Emotional blessings play a crucial role in enriching our lives and relationships. These positive emotions include love, joy, gratitude, compassion, hope, contentment, excitement, serenity, pride, and awe. Psychologist Barbara Fredrickson underscores the significance of these emotional blessings, noting that "Positivity opens us. The first core truth about positive emotions is that they open our hearts and our minds, making us more receptive and more creative." By cultivating these positive emotions, we enhance our capacity for personal growth and meaningful connections with others.

Each of these blessings, whether divine, spiritual, or emotional, contributes to our overall well-being and equips us to face life's challenges with resilience and grace. By acknowledging and cherishing these blessings, we can foster a deeper sense of gratitude and fulfillment in our lives. This creates rich experiences that sustain and uplift us through both joyous and difficult times, reminding us of the abundant goodness that surrounds us, even in moments of hardship.

COMMUNITY AND LEGACY

The blessings of community and legacy, impact, and transformation shape our lives in profound ways, creating ripples that extend far beyond our immediate sphere. As we navigate life's journey, we receive the gift of knowing our actions have made a difference—whether through our work, relationships, or the values we uphold and pass on to others. This legacy becomes a blessing not just for us, but for generations to come, as we shape the future through mentorship and the lasting influence of our choices. Astrophysicist Neil deGrasse Tyson has expressed his sentiment about leaving a mark on the world, stating, "On my tombstone, I want the epitaph to read: 'Be ashamed to die until you have scored some victory for humanity.'"

The ability to grow and evolve through life's challenges is another transformative blessing we receive. As we face changes and obstacles, we are given the opportunity to shed old habits and beliefs, emerging stronger and wiser. This continuous process of renewal allows us to heal from past wounds and start anew with grace, embracing personal transformation as a lifelong journey of self-discovery and improvement.

Empowerment and autonomy stand as powerful blessings in our lives, granting us the freedom to chart our own course. Each day brings the opportunity to make choices that align with our values and aspirations, shaping our destiny with confidence. This blessing of self-determination allows us to take control of our lives, pursue our dreams, and live authentically.

The pursuit of work-life balance and inner harmony offers another dimension of blessing in our lives. As we strive to achieve equilibrium between our personal and professional spheres, we receive the gift of a fulfilling and well-rounded existence. This balance creates a sense of flow and alignment in our actions, beliefs, and goals, enhancing every aspect of our lives and contributing to our overall well-being.

Through these multifaceted blessings of legacy, transformation, empowerment, balance, and life's surprises, we are continually shaped and renewed. They remind us of the profound impact we can have on the world around us and the endless potential for growth and joy in our lives. By recognizing and embracing these blessings, we open ourselves to a richer, more meaningful existence, one that leaves a lasting positive imprint on the world.

RECEIVING NATURE'S BEAUTY AND SERENITY

The natural world offers us a continuous blessing of breathtaking beauty and serene environments. When we enter a lush forest, our senses come alive with the sights, sounds, and smells around us. The earthy scent of moss and pine needles creates a calming atmosphere. Sunlight filters through the leaves, creating patterns on the forest floor.

Leaves rustle gently in the breeze, accompanied by the calls of songbirds. A blue jay flies overhead, its bright wings contrasting with the green surroundings. A nearby stream flows over smooth stones, its clear water reflecting the sky.

In a sunny meadow, colorful wildflowers sway in the breeze. Bees buzz as they move from flower to flower, demonstrating nature's interconnectedness. A deer steps out from the trees, moving quietly and gracefully.

As the day goes on, we see nature's changing colors. The sunset paints the sky in warm golden tones. As night falls, new sounds emerge—an owl's call, crickets chirping, and the soft movements of nocturnal animals.

Experiencing nature's beauty soothes us and offers a break from busy modern life. It reminds us of the wonder around us and helps us feel connected to the natural world. John Muir, a famous naturalist, said, "Everybody needs beauty as well as bread, places to play in and pray in, where nature may heal and give strength to body and soul alike."

Rachel Carson, a marine biologist, wrote about nature's power: "Those who contemplate the beauty of the earth find reserves of strength that will endure as long as life lasts. There is something infinitely healing in the repeated refrains of nature—the assurance that dawn comes after night, and spring after winter." The beauty around us is not just for us to enjoy, but also for us to preserve. By spending time in nature, we reconnect with these blessings and find renewal.

THE BLESSINGS OF OBSTACLES, FAILURES, AND TRAGEDIES

Bestselling author and motivational speaker Lisa Nichols reminds us, "There are blessings everywhere, even in the rejections...even in the NOs...even in the breakups...even in the release of a job...even in the proposal or book deal I got turned down for...even in the things I thought I should have."

In our lives, we receive the blessings of obstacles, failures, and even tragedies—moments that challenge us deeply yet build our strength. As I shared my story of personal tragedies, I was able to ultimately understand the gifts of pain that lead to purpose. These experiences, though painful, are blessings in disguise. They forge our character, sharpen our resolve, and cultivate within us a resilience that is unbreakable. French philosopher Jean de La Bruyère urged, "Out of the fires of adversity, resilience and tenacity are forged, and it is through these crucibles that miracles grow."

As we face obstacles, we dig deeper into our reserves of courage and determination. These moments test our limits and push us to grow beyond them. Every setback, every failure is a lesson—a gift that guides us toward wisdom and deeper understanding. These experiences raise us, building a foundation of resilience and tenacity that supports every endeavor we undertake.

Tragedies, while leaving deep marks on our souls, bring the blessings of empathy and connection. Through our own pain, we learn to reach out to others, offering comfort and serving with grace. These experiences open our hearts and deepen our capacity for compassion, enabling us to serve others with understanding.

Reflect on the trials you have endured and recognize the strength, wisdom, and empathy that have emerged from these experiences. These are not just lessons; they are blessings. The obstacles, failures, and tragedies you've faced have forged you in adversity and raised you with resilience and tenacity. They have made you who you are—a person capable not only of surviving but thriving and, most importantly, serving others with the grace born from understanding. Your present recognition that these can be remarkable blessings is a testament to the growth you have experienced while on this book's journey.

THE RECOGNITION OF OUR CUMULATIVE BLESSINGS

Our lives are enriched by an abundance of blessings that span our past, present, and future. These divine gifts provide comfort, guidance, and joy, shaping our journey through life. From the grace and protection we've experienced in the past, to the love and opportunities surrounding us now, to the potential and hope that lie ahead, blessings permeate every aspect of our existence.

To fully harness the transformative power of these blessings, we must cultivate a conscious awareness of their presence. This mindful recognition is essential for maintaining a growth-oriented mindset and becoming our best selves. By acknowledging and cherishing these gifts, we foster a deeper sense of gratitude and fulfillment, creating experiences that sustain and uplift us through both joyous and challenging times.

Our blessings are not static; they evolve and multiply as we progress through life. The wisdom gained from past experiences becomes a blessing that guides our present decisions. The relationships we nurture today will be the support system of our future. Even our struggles can be reframed as blessings, offering opportunities for growth and resilience.

As we journey forward, it's crucial to remain attuned to the blessings that surround us, recognizing their transformative power in shaping our perspective and potential. This ongoing awareness serves as a foundation for personal growth, enabling us to approach each day with optimism and purpose regardless of the challenges we may face.

By consciously embracing our blessings—past, present, and future—and acknowledging our deep, sincere gratitude, we align ourselves with a mindset of abundance and possibility. This perspective fuels our perseverance, anchors us to our purpose, and propels us toward becoming the authentic selves we are meant to be in a state of grace. It is through this lens of gratitude and awareness that we can truly unlock our potential and live a life of meaning and fulfillment.

CHAPTER 18

On Love and Self-Love

"I love you without knowing how, or when, or from where. I love you simply, without problems or pride: I love you in this way because I do not know any other way of loving but this, in which there is no I or you, so intimate that your hand upon my chest is my hand, so intimate that when I fall asleep your eyes close."

—PABLO NERUDA, RENOWNED CHILEAN POET

As you know, my family's journey has been quite the catalyst for the forging of my purpose. I am eternally grateful for the love of my soulmate and the love of my family and friends. The expression of love is so very important. As my mother is quite frail at eighty-seven years old, and despite her indomitable positive spirit, I always have in the back of my mind that one day as I tell my mother I love her, that will turn out to be the last time I will be able to say it in her life. My story is also her story, so I asked her what the one thing was, above all, that she wanted you to know, that would be her lasting message to you. My mom told me to tell you this: "Please tell them that love is the most important thing in the world. It's love. Tell them to love."

As we have so intentionally delved into the hard, heavy topics, including suffering and the challenges of redefining ourselves, it's crucial to recognize that loving others and ourselves is not only a blessing but the enlightenment of life that allows everything to have glorious meaning. Love is the glue that ties all of our *musts* together, infusing our journey with purpose and significance.

Love, for both ourselves and others, illuminates our path through the darkest moments of suffering and self-doubt. It provides the strength to persevere when we face obstacles in our personal growth. As we navigate the complexities of our relationships, career aspirations, and financial goals, love serves as a guiding light, reminding us of our intrinsic worth and the value of human connection.

This profound force of love transforms our Must Journey from a solitary quest into a shared experience of growth and mutual support. It enhances our ability to embrace authenticity, fostering an environment where we can truly be ourselves while encouraging others to do the same. In essence, love becomes the catalyst that elevates our Must Mindset, Core Beliefs, and Values from abstract concepts to lived experiences that enrich every aspect of our lives.

By recognizing love as the unifying element of our *must* philosophy, we gain a deeper appreciation for the interconnectedness of our personal development journey. It reminds us that even as we strive for individual growth and achievement, we are part of a larger human experience, bound together by the transformative power of love and compassion.

As we delve further into the realm of love and self-love, it's crucial to recognize that we're now approaching these concepts from a more holistic perspective. Having already explored our mindset, core beliefs, limiting beliefs, and personal narratives, we've laid a foundation for understanding ourselves at a deeper level. This chapter builds upon that self-knowledge, inviting you to examine love and self-love through a broader lens that encompasses all aspects of your being.

Our journey thus far has equipped us with powerful insights into our thought patterns, fundamental beliefs, and the stories we tell ourselves. Now we'll use this self-awareness to cultivate a more comprehensive and nurturing relationship with ourselves and others. This holistic approach to love and self-love isn't just about positive thinking or affirmations. It's about integrating our newfound self-understanding into every facet of our lives.

By embracing this more expansive view of love and self-love, we can create a harmonious balance between our inner world and our external relationships. We'll explore how our enhanced self-awareness can deepen our capacity for love, both for ourselves and for others, leading to more authentic connections and a more fulfilling life. This chapter serves as a bridge, connecting our individual growth to our interactions with the world around us and demonstrating how true self-love can transform every aspect of our existence.

Love is the cornerstone of human existence, intricately woven into our well-being and happiness. It manifests in various forms—self-love, romantic love, familial love, platonic love, and compassionate love—each contributing uniquely to a fulfilling life. Here, we delve into the profound nature of love and the crucial role of self-love, offering insights, personal stories, and practical advice on nurturing these vital aspects of our existence.

WHAT IS LOVE, AFTER ALL?

Love, that elusive and powerful force that has captivated humanity since time immemorial, defies simple definition. From the ancient Greeks to modern philosophers, countless minds have grappled with the essence of love, attempting to unravel its mysteries.

The ancient Greeks, in their profound wisdom, dissected the intricate layers of love, unveiling its multifaceted nature with remarkable insight. Rather than confining this powerful emotion to a single monolithic concept, they recognized its diverse manifestations, each as distinct and vital as the vibrant hues in a Mediterranean sunset. Their understanding of love was as nuanced as the interplay of light and shadow on a classical sculpture, identifying four primary types that encompass the vast spectrum of human connection and emotion.

At the heart of this Greek philosophy of love lies *eros*, the passionate and intense force that ignites the soul with desire. Named after the mischievous god of love, *eros* embodies the all-consuming fire of romantic attraction. It's the love that makes poets wax lyrical and lovers lose sleep, a force so powerful that Plato described it as a "serious mental disease." Sappho, the renowned poet of ancient Greece, captured its essence beautifully: "Eros shook my mind like a mountain wind falling on oak trees."

Philia, in contrast, represents the deep, enduring bond of friendship and camaraderie. This is the love that forms the bedrock of lasting relationships, built on mutual respect, shared experiences, and genuine affection. Aristotle held *philia* in high regard, stating, "What is a friend? A single soul dwelling in two bodies." This form of love transcends mere companionship, creating connections that can withstand the tests of time and adversity.

Storge, the natural affection found in familial relationships, is perhaps the most instinctive form of love. It's the unconditional care a parent feels for a child, the protective bond between siblings, the deep-rooted connection to one's kin. This love is as fundamental as the earth itself, a foundation upon which much of human society is built. As Sophocles poignantly expressed, "One word frees us of all the weight and pain of life: That word is love."

Finally, there's *agape*, the highest and most encompassing form of love in Greek philosophy. This is the selfless, unconditional love for all humanity, a concept that transcends individual relationships to embrace the entire world. It's a love that asks for nothing in return, that gives without expectation. Plato touched on this universal love when he wrote, "Love is the name for our pursuit of wholeness, for our desire to be complete."

These distinctions remind us that love is not a singular emotion but a rich, varied spectrum of connections and feelings. Like the many facets of a finely cut diamond, each type of love reflects a different aspect of the human experience, contributing to the brilliant, complex whole. The Greeks' nuanced understanding of love continues to resonate through the ages, offering us a framework to comprehend and appreciate the diverse ways in which we connect, care, and cherish one another in this grand human existence.

As civilizations progressed, so did the understanding of love. In medieval times, courtly love emerged as a noble, often unrequited pursuit. The Renaissance brought a renewed focus on romantic love, with Shakespeare penning, in *A Midsummer Night's Dream*, "Love looks not with the eyes, but with the mind, And therefore is winged Cupid painted blind." In Shakespeare's Sonnet 116, he speaks of the nature of true love. Shakespeare offers, "Love is not love / Which alters when it alteration finds, / Or bends with the remover to remove. / O no! it is an ever-fixed mark / That looks on tempests and is never shaken." This period marked a shift toward viewing love as a personal, emotional experience rather than a purely social or religious construct.

The Enlightenment era saw love through the lens of reason and individual rights. Mary Wollstonecraft, an early feminist philosopher, argued for love based on equality and friendship: "The most holy bond of society is friendship." This perspective laid the groundwork for modern conceptions of romantic partnerships.

In the twentieth century, sociological and psychological insights further expanded our understanding of love. Erich Fromm's *The Art of Loving* posited that love is an art to be learned and practiced, stating, "Love is a decision, it is a judgment, it is a promise. If love were only a feeling, there would be no basis for the promise to love each other forever."

Contemporary views of love have become increasingly diverse and inclusive. The recognition of various sexual orientations and gender identities has broadened the definition of romantic love. Sociologist Anthony Giddens introduced the concept of "pure relationships" based on mutual satisfaction rather than traditional obligations.

Today, love is often seen as a complex interplay of biology, psychology, and culture. As Dr. Helen Fisher, a leading researcher on love, notes, "Romantic love is one of the most powerful sensations on Earth." This modern perspective acknowledges love's multifaceted nature, embracing its emotional, physical, and social dimensions in a way that ancient philosophers could only begin to imagine.

THE SCIENCE OF LOVE: UNDERSTANDING OUR MOST PROFOUND EMOTION

Love, that enigmatic force that has inspired poets, artists, and philosophers for millennia, is now under the microscope of modern science. Far from diminishing its magic, scientific inquiry has revealed love to be a complex interplay of biology, psychology, and social factors, each contributing to the profound experience that shapes our lives and drives our personal growth.

At its core, love is a neurobiological phenomenon. When we fall in love, our brains are flooded with a cocktail of chemicals—dopamine, norepinephrine, and serotonin—creating a natural high that rivals any artificial stimulant. This neurochemical surge creates the euphoric feelings associated with new love, affecting our mood, our energy levels, and even our perception of the world around us.

Dopamine, often called the "feel-good" hormone, is particularly active in the early stages of romantic love. It's responsible for the rush of pleasure we feel when thinking about or being with our loved ones. Norepinephrine, like adrenaline, contributes to the racing heart and sweaty palms characteristic of new love. Meanwhile, oxytocin, nicknamed the "cuddle hormone," promotes bonding and attachment between partners.

Dr. Helen Fisher, a renowned anthropologist and human behavior researcher, has extensively studied the brain in love. Her groundbreaking fMRI studies revealed that the brain regions associated with reward and motivation light up when individuals view photos of their beloved, mirroring the neural pathways activated by drug addiction. Dr. Fisher says that "romantic love is one of the most addictive substances on Earth." This explains the intense craving and withdrawal symptoms often associated with romantic love.

But love is more than just a biochemical reaction. It's a fundamental human need that plays a crucial role in our personal development and self-actualization. Psychologist Abraham Maslow placed love and belonging at the center of his hierarchy of needs, recognizing its essential role in human motivation and growth. As we navigate relationships, we learn about ourselves, develop empathy, and expand our capacity for emotional intelligence. Maslow said, "The needs for safety, belonging, love relations and for respect can be satisfied only by other people, i.e., only from outside the person. This means considerable dependence on the environment." This highlights Maslow's view that love and belonging are fundamental human needs that can only be fulfilled through relationships and connections with others. He saw these needs as essential for psychological health and growth, positioning them as a key level in his hierarchy of needs. Maslow believed that satisfying these needs for love, affection, and belongingness was crucial before individuals could fully address higher-level needs like self-esteem and self-actualization.

The journey of love begins in infancy with attachment. Psychologist John Bowlby's attachment theory suggests that the bonds we form with our primary caregivers in early childhood shape our ability to form secure relationships throughout life. At its core, this theory suggests that the bonds we forge with our primary caregivers in childhood create an "internal working model" that influences our perceptions of ourselves, others, and the world around us. This model serves as a blueprint for future relationships, affecting how we navigate intimacy, trust, and emotional closeness.

Bowlby eloquently captured the essence of this theory when he stated, "The propensity to make strong emotional bonds to particular individuals is a basic component of human nature." This fundamental human need for attachment forms the basis for our emotional and social development. Bowlby further emphasized the importance of love in human development, noting, "What cannot be communicated to the mother cannot be communicated to the self."

The theory identifies four primary attachment styles: secure, anxious, avoidant, and disorganized. Each style reflects different patterns of relating to others, shaped by early experiences with caregivers. Secure attachment, characterized by positive views of self and others, allows for comfortable intimacy and independence. Anxious attachment often manifests as fear of abandonment and a need for constant reassurance. Avoidant attachment typically involves struggles with intimacy and a tendency to prioritize independence. Disorganized attachment, often resulting from trauma or abuse, leads to inconsistent behavior in relationships.

These attachment styles profoundly impact not only romantic relationships but also friendships, family dynamics, and even professional interactions. They influence how we seek and give support, express emotions, and handle conflicts. However, Bowlby's theory also offers hope, emphasizing that these patterns are not set in stone. Through self-awareness, therapy, and positive relationship experiences, individuals can work toward developing more secure attachment patterns.

Understanding attachment theory provides valuable insights into our love relationship patterns and behaviors. It offers a framework for personal growth, helping us recognize how our past experiences shape our present interactions. By becoming aware of our attachment style and its origins, we can heal old wounds and develop healthier, more fulfilling connections across all areas of life. The quality of social relationships is a major determinant of mental health. This underscores the profound impact that understanding and improving our attachment patterns can have on our overall well-being and ability to form meaningful connections with others. This early template for love influences our core beliefs about ourselves and others, impacting our romantic relationships, friendships, and even our professional interactions.

As we mature, love evolves. Psychologist Robert Sternberg proposed the triangular theory of love, suggesting that love comprises three components: intimacy, passion, and commitment. The balance of these elements shifts as relationships progress, from the heady passion of new romance to the deep, companionate love of long-term partnerships. Understanding this evolution can help us navigate the changing landscape of our relationships and continue growing within them.

The science of love also sheds light on the transformative power of self-love. Neuroscientific research has shown that self-compassion activates the same brain regions as receiving compassion from others. By cultivating self-love, we literally rewire our brains, enhancing our resilience and capacity for personal growth. As the saying goes, "You can't pour from an empty cup"—learning to love ourselves is the foundation for loving others and reaching our full potential.

Love's impact on well-being extends beyond emotional benefits, influencing physiological responses to stress. A 2007 study found that women who embraced their romantic partners before a stressful event showed reduced cortisol responses compared to those who did not. More recent research has further supported this phenomenon, including a 2024 study where researchers observed that in older couples, partners' positive emotions were associated with lower cortisol levels, particularly for those reporting higher relationship satisfaction. Additionally, studies have shown that individuals in stable, satisfying relationships tend to have lower cortisol output across the day. This reduction in stress hormones may have significant implications for physical health, potentially lowering the risk of stress-related issues such as cardiovascular disease and compromised immune function.

It's important to note that the relationship between love and stress hormones is complex. During the initial stages of romantic love, cortisol levels may actually increase, possibly due to the excitement and novelty of the relationship.

However, as relationships stabilize, they often provide a buffer against stress. These findings underscore the importance of nurturing loving relationships as part of an overall health and well-being strategy. Healthy relationships can provide social and emotional support, potentially leading to better stress management and improved physical health outcomes.

A groundbreaking study conducted by researchers at Pennsylvania State University, led by Zita Oravecz, has shed new light on the concept of "felt love" and its profound impact on psychological well-being. Published in 2019, this research explored how brief experiences of love and connection in everyday life contribute to overall mental health and happiness.

The study defines "felt love" as the extent to which individuals feel loved and cared for in their daily lives, encompassing not just romantic relationships but also micro moments of connection with others, such as a neighbor's expression of concern. This broad approach aligns with growing research on the importance of social connections for overall health and well-being.

Key findings revealed a strong correlation between higher levels of felt love and increased psychological well-being, including enhanced feelings of purpose and optimism. Perhaps most intriguingly, the researchers observed that simply becoming more aware of moments of love and connection in daily life may itself serve as an intervention to boost overall feelings of being loved. The study emphasizes that "raising awareness of felt love in day-to-day life may itself be an intervention that could increase levels of felt love over time." This suggests that simply by paying attention to moments of love and connection in our daily lives, we may be able to increase our overall sense of being loved and cared for.

As we embrace the science of love, we gain powerful tools for self-discovery and personal growth. By understanding the neurochemical basis of attraction, we can make more-informed choices in our relationships. By recognizing the patterns set by our early attachments, we can work to heal old wounds and form healthier connections.

THE SPIRITUALITY OF LOVE

Love, in its most profound sense, transcends the boundaries of mere emotion and enters the realm of the spiritual. It is a force that has captivated the hearts and minds of spiritual leaders, philosophers, and seekers throughout history. While scientific, sociological, and psychological studies of love provide valuable insights, the spiritual dimension of love offers a more holistic understanding. It invites us to see love not just as an emotion or a relationship dynamic but as a fundamental aspect of existence itself, a transformative force that can lead us to profound self-realization and connection with the universe at large.

Indeed, love's essence extends far beyond the realms of understanding gleaned solely from emotional, sociological, physiological, or scientific perspectives. While these disciplines offer valuable insights into the mechanics and manifestations of love, they often fall short of capturing its ineffable, transcendent nature.

From a spiritual standpoint, love is often viewed as a cosmic force, an energy that permeates the universe and connects all beings. Many spiritual traditions speak of love as the fundamental fabric of existence, the divine essence that underlies all of creation. As Pierre Teilhard de Chardin, the French philosopher and Jesuit priest, eloquently stated, "Love is the affinity which links and draws together the elements of the world...Love, in fact, is the agent of universal synthesis." This perspective on love goes beyond the biochemical reactions in our brains or the societal constructs that shape our understanding of relationships. It suggests that love is a state of consciousness, a way of being that aligns us with the fundamental nature of reality. In this light, love becomes not just an emotion we experience, but a truth we embody.

The spiritual dimension of love also encompasses the concept of unconditional love—a love that is not based on merit, expectation, or reciprocation. This idea challenges our conventional understanding of love as a transaction or a response to specific stimuli. Instead, it suggests that love is an ever-present reality we can tap into regardless of external circumstances.

Many spiritual teachings suggest that love is not just something we give or receive, but our true nature. As we deepen our understanding and experience of love, we essentially uncover our authentic selves. This perspective transforms the journey of love from an outward search to an inward exploration.

CULTIVATING SELF-LOVE AND AUTHENTIC RELATIONSHIPS WITH VULNERABILITY

As discussed earlier, vulnerability is a powerful, yet often misunderstood, aspect of human experience. In the context of love, it's about having the courage to show up as our authentic selves, imperfections and all, even when the outcome is uncertain to be there for ourselves and others. This willingness to be seen in our truest form, without guarantees of acceptance or reciprocation, is the essence of vulnerability. C. S. Lewis profoundly reflected on the cost of being vulnerable. He said, "To love at all is to be vulnerable. Love anything and your heart will be wrung and possibly broken. If you want to make sure of keeping it intact you must give it to no one, not even an animal. Wrap it carefully round with hobbies and little luxuries; avoid all entanglements. Lock it up safe in the casket or coffin of your selfishness. But in that casket, safe, dark, motionless, airless, it will change. It will not be broken; it will become unbreakable, impenetrable, irredeemable."

The journey of embracing vulnerability is intrinsically linked to the development of self-love. As we learn to accept and love ourselves, flaws and all, we become more comfortable with showing our authentic selves to others. When we allow ourselves to be vulnerable with others and experience acceptance, it reinforces our own sense of self-worth. This beautiful cycle of vulnerability and self-love creates a foundation for deeper, more meaningful relationships.

In our connections with others, vulnerability plays a crucial role. It creates space for genuine intimacy and understanding. When we open up about our true thoughts, insecurities, feelings, and experiences, it often encourages others to do the same. This mutual vulnerability fosters empathy, deepens emotional bonds, and creates relationships built on authenticity and trust.

Embracing vulnerability requires courage, but it's a courage that's well worth cultivating. It's about recognizing that our imperfections and struggles don't diminish our worth—they make us human. As we practice vulnerability, we learn to treat ourselves with kindness and compassion, fostering a deeper sense of self-love.

Remember, vulnerability is not a weakness, but a strength. It's a valuable tool we must have the courage to access to experience the deepest levels of self-love and love for others. By allowing ourselves to be vulnerable, we open the door to genuine connection, personal growth, and a more authentic, fulfilling life.

Let's embrace vulnerability as a path to deeper self-understanding and more meaningful relationships. Junot Díaz, a renowned Dominican American writer and scholar, tells us, "You can't find intimacy—you can't find home—when you're always hiding behind masks. Intimacy requires a certain level of vulnerability. It requires a certain level of you exposing your fragmented, contradictory self to someone else. You running the risk of having your core self rejected and hurt and misunderstood."

It may feel uncomfortable at times, but it's through this discomfort that we grow, learn, and truly connect—both with ourselves and with others. In the words of Brené Brown, "Vulnerability is the birthplace of love, belonging, joy, courage, empathy, and creativity." By embracing vulnerability, we open ourselves to the full spectrum of human experience and connection, paving the way for a richer, more authentic life. Becoming vulnerable is necessary to truly experience the deepest sense of the many faces of love.

TYPES OF LOVE

Love is a multifaceted force that touches every aspect of our lives, and in this chapter, we will explore its various forms in greater depth. From self-love to romantic, familial, platonic, and universal love, each type plays a unique role in shaping who we are and how we connect with others. As we dive into these different expressions of love, we will focus on how to cultivate them more fully in alignment with our *musts*—our core values, beliefs, and purpose. By examining love through the lens of the Must Journey, we can deepen our understanding of how love enriches our lives while learning practical ways to nurture it in ways that reflect our authentic selves. Each form of love offers an opportunity for growth, connection, and fulfillment, and by embracing these opportunities, we move closer to living a life rooted in purpose and meaning.

SELF-LOVE

Finding self-love is a profound and transformative experience that lies at the heart of personal growth and fulfillment. It's a path that requires courage, vulnerability, and a willingness to challenge our deepest-held beliefs about ourselves.

Self-love is not merely a feel-good concept or a trendy phrase; it's the foundation upon which all other forms of love are built. It's not just a desirable goal—it's a *must*. We must prioritize self-love as a fundamental aspect of our personal growth and well-being. Just as we've discussed the Must Mindset in earlier chapters, we need to apply this same level of urgency and commitment to developing self-love as a *must*. It involves recognizing your inherent worth, taking care of your physical and emotional needs, and setting healthy boundaries. Self-love isn't a luxury or an indulgence; it's an essential foundation for a fulfilling life and healthy relationships. We must make a conscious, daily choice to treat ourselves with kindness, compassion, and respect. Remember, self-love is not selfish. By nurturing a strong sense of self-love, we become better equipped to love and support others. We must view self-love as a vital practice that enables us to show up fully in our lives and relationships. It's through this lens of self-love that we can truly become the person we are meant to be.

At the core of self-love is self-compassion, a critical component identified by psychologist Dr. Kristin Neff. She outlines three main elements: self-kindness, common humanity, and mindfulness. Neff explains, "Self-compassion involves acting the same way toward yourself when you are having a difficult time, fail, or notice something you don't like about yourself." Research consistently shows that cultivating self-compassion can lead to greater emotional resilience and overall well-being. Neff emphasizes the importance of self-compassion over self-esteem, arguing that self-compassion provides a more stable and healthier basis for self-worth.

As you evaluate and enhance your sense of self-love, remember that it's a deeply personal process. What works for one person may not work for another. Be patient with yourself and celebrate small victories along the way. Reflect on your self-talk: Are you kind to yourself? Do you offer yourself the same compassion you would a dear friend? How might practicing self-compassion change your life?

Self-love is a powerful force that can transform your life. It's about embracing your whole self—flaws, quirks, and all. Be patient and gentle with yourself. Every small step toward self-love is a victory worth celebrating. In the words of the poet Rupi Kaur, "How you love yourself is how you teach others to love you." By cultivating self-love, you not only enrich your own life but also enhance your capacity to love and connect with others. In loving yourself, you open the door to a more fulfilling and authentic life.

Cultivating self-love is not optional for true happiness. It is the foundation upon which we build our capacity to experience love in all its forms—romantic, platonic, familial, and spiritual. Without a deep sense of self-love, we limit our ability to fully give love to and receive love from others. By developing a strong foundation of self-love, we open ourselves to deeper, more authentic connections and a richer experience of life's joys.

So as you move forward on your journey of personal growth, make self-love a nonnegotiable part of your life. Embrace it as one of your *musts*. By doing so, you'll not only transform your relationship with yourself but also enhance your capacity to create meaningful connections and live a life of purpose and fulfillment. Remember, the depth of love you can experience with others is directly related to the love you cultivate for yourself. Make self-love your priority and watch as it unlocks new levels of happiness and fulfillment in every aspect of your life.

ROMANTIC LOVE

"You have bewitched me, body and soul, and I love, I love, I love you. I never wish to be parted from you from this day on."
—Mr. Darcy, in the 2005 film adaptation
of Jane Austen's *Pride and Prejudice*

Romantic love is perhaps the most celebrated form of love, marked by deep affection, passion, and a desire for intimacy. It has the power to elevate our spirits and provide profound joy, but it also requires effort, communication, and understanding to flourish.

While the terms are often used interchangeably, it's important to distinguish between romantic love and romantic relationships. Romantic love refers to the intense emotional and physical attraction between two people, often characterized by passion, idealization, and a sense of euphoria. It's the "falling in love" phase that poets and songwriters have celebrated for centuries.

Romantic relationships, on the other hand, encompass the broader long-term commitment between partners. They involve the day-to-day realities of sharing a life together, including communication, conflict resolution, and mutual support. While romantic love may be the initial spark, romantic relationships require ongoing effort, compromise, and growth to thrive.

Understanding this distinction is crucial because it helps set realistic expectations for love and relationships. The intense feelings of romantic love often fade over time, replaced by a deeper, more stable form of love. This transition can be challenging for couples who mistake the end of the "honeymoon phase" for the end of love itself.

Strong romantic relationships can exist even when the initial passionate love has cooled. These relationships are built on mutual respect, shared values, and a commitment to growing together. By discussing both romantic love and romantic relationships, we can provide a more comprehensive understanding of the complexities of human partnerships and help individuals navigate the different stages of their romantic journeys.

Science has identified several factors that contribute to romantic attraction between individuals. Physical attractiveness plays a significant role, with studies showing that people are initially drawn to those they find visually appealing. However, attraction goes beyond mere looks. Research has found that similarity in attitudes, values, and interests is a strong predictor of attraction. This phenomenon, known as the "similarity-attraction effect," suggests that we are more likely to be drawn to those who share our worldviews and experiences. Biological factors also play a crucial role in attraction. The release of neurotransmitters and hormones, such as dopamine, norepinephrine, and oxytocin, creates the euphoric feelings associated with falling in love.

Proximity, frequency of exposure, availability, and convenience are key factors in the formation of romantic relationships, as supported by several studies in social psychology. The "proximity effect" or "propinquity effect" suggests that physical and psychological closeness increases the likelihood of forming relationships. The mere exposure effect also plays a role. This psychological phenomenon suggests that people tend to develop a preference for things or people they encounter more frequently. In the context of relationships, increased exposure to someone can lead to increased liking and attraction. Availability and convenience are additional crucial factors in relationship formation. People are more likely to enter into and maintain relationships when they perceive a lack of better alternatives.

However, while these factors can facilitate initial attraction and relationship formation, they do not guarantee long-term relationship success or satisfaction. Proximity and availability may bring people together, but it's the ongoing investment and positive interactions that sustain a relationship.

Sex and intimacy play a crucial role in romantic relationships, serving as powerful bonding experiences that foster emotional closeness and physical connection. Research consistently shows that sexual satisfaction is strongly linked to overall relationship satisfaction and longevity. A study published in the *Journal of Sex & Marital Therapy* found that couples who reported higher levels of sexual satisfaction also experienced greater relationship stability and happiness.

However, intimacy extends beyond sexual activity. Emotional intimacy, characterized by vulnerability, trust, and deep understanding, is equally vital for relationship health. Couples who cultivate both physical and emotional intimacy tend to report higher levels of relationship satisfaction and stronger emotional bonds.

Reflect on your experiences: Have you felt the exhilaration of falling in love and the comfort of a long-term partnership? How have these relationships shaped your understanding of love?

Anthropologist Dr. Helen Fisher's research across 170 societies found evidence of romantic love in all of them, suggesting it's a universal human experience. However, the way it's expressed and valued differs greatly. This cultural perspective reminds us that there's no one "right" way to experience or express romantic love.

It's crucial to emphasize the importance of self-actualization in romantic relationships. As Abraham Maslow posited in his hierarchy of needs, self-actualization is the highest level of psychological development. Being a self-actualized individual can lead to healthier, more fulfilling relationships. Dr. Scott Barry Kaufman's research on self-actualization suggests that individuals who are more self-actualized, as we are here, working on personal development, tend to have more satisfying romantic relationships. Similarly, Brené Brown's research shows that individuals who are more self-aware and vulnerable tend to have stronger relationships, emphasizing the importance of personal growth and self-awareness.

Having high Must Standards and not settling is crucial for long-term relationship satisfaction. Dr. Ty Tashiro's research suggests that being selective about three to five nonnegotiable traits in a partner leads to more satisfying relationships than having a long list of preferences.

One of the biggest misconceptions in relationships is the belief that one can change their partner. Research by Dr. Diane Felmlee shows that the very qualities that attract us to our partners are often the same ones that later become sources of conflict. It's essential to accept your partner as they are rather than hoping for fundamental changes.

Maintaining realistic expectations is equally important. Dr. Eli Finkel suggests "recalibrating" relationship expectations to align with reality, focusing on core needs rather than an exhaustive list of desires. Consistent investment in the relationship is key, as illustrated by Dr. Gary Chapman's concept of love languages, which emphasizes showing love in ways that resonate with your partner. The five love languages offer valuable insight into how individuals express and receive love. The five love languages are words of affirmation, acts of service, receiving gifts, quality time, and physical touch.

Chapman suggests that understanding and speaking your partner's primary love language can significantly enhance relationship satisfaction and emotional connection. By recognizing and adapting to each other's preferred love language, couples can more effectively communicate their affection and meet each other's emotional needs.

Dr. Arthur Aron's research on self-expansion in relationships demonstrates that couples who continually have new experiences together maintain stronger bonds, underscoring the importance of embracing growth as a couple.

Forgiveness and repair are crucial elements of long-term satisfaction, as evidenced by Dr. Everett Worthington's research on forgiveness in relationships. Worthington identifies two types of forgiveness: decisional and emotional forgiveness. He states, "Decisional forgiveness involves deciding to forgive a personal offense and letting go of angry and resentful thoughts and feelings toward the person who has wronged you." Additionally, Dr. Elaine Hatfield's work on passionate love versus companionate love emphasizes the importance of balancing closeness with individual autonomy, highlighting the need to maintain individual identities within the relationship. Hatfield defines passionate love as "a state of intense longing for union with another" and companionate love as "the affection and tenderness we feel for those with whom our lives are deeply entwined."

By approaching romantic relationships with intention, self-awareness, and a commitment to growth, individuals can cultivate lasting, fulfilling partnerships, even in a culture that often prioritizes short-term gratification. Remember, a truly great relationship is not about finding your "other half," but about two whole individuals choosing to build a life together.

In cultivating and maintaining a healthy, thriving romantic love and relationship, embracing our *musts* is essential. We must prioritize open communication, mutual respect, and continuous growth both as individuals and as a couple. We must be willing to be vulnerable, to forgive, and to consistently choose love, even when it's challenging. We must recognize that a great relationship requires ongoing effort and intentionality, not just during difficult times but in everyday moments.

From a personal development standpoint, there are several key takeaways to keep in mind as you seek to establish and enhance your romantic loving relationship. Self-love and self-awareness are foundational; you must cultivate a strong sense of self before you can truly connect with another. Growth is a shared journey, and both partners must be committed to personal and mutual growth for the relationship to thrive. Compatibility in core values and life goals is crucial for long-term success. Effective communication, including active listening and expressing needs clearly, is vital. Maintaining individuality within the relationship is as important as fostering togetherness. Challenges should be viewed as opportunities for strengthening the bond, not threats to it. Continuous effort and intentionality are required, as love alone is not enough to sustain a healthy relationship.

A thriving, romantic, loving relationship is not about finding your "other half," but about two whole individuals choosing to build a life together. By embracing these principles and committing yourself to your *musts*, you can create a relationship that not only endures but flourishes over time.

FAMILIAL LOVE

Familial love forms the bedrock of human relationships, shaping our earliest experiences and influencing our connections throughout life. This profound bond encompasses the deep affection, loyalty, and support shared among family members, whether related by blood, marriage, or choice. Familial love is not confined to a single definition or structure. It thrives in diverse family units, from traditional nuclear families to single-parent households, blended families, and chosen families formed through deep friendships or shared experiences.

The foundation of familial love is often laid in our earliest moments through attachment and bonding. Picture a newborn nestled in their mother's arms, their tiny hand grasping a father's finger. This early bonding creates a sense of security and trust that can shape a person's ability to form relationships throughout their life. As psychologist John Bowlby noted, "The propensity to make strong emotional bonds to particular individuals is a basic component of human nature."

Unconditional love plays a pivotal role in family dynamics. It's the unwavering support a parent offers their child regardless of achievements or mistakes. Imagine a teenager coming home with a failed test, dreading their parents' reaction, only to be met with understanding and encouragement to do better next time. This unconditional acceptance creates a safe haven where family members can be their authentic selves, fostering emotional growth and self-esteem.

In *The Art of Loving,* Erich Fromm explains that familial love is vital for developing one's personality and emotional health. He notes, "The mother-child relationship is paradoxical and, in a sense, tragic. It requires the most intense love on the mother's side, yet this very love must help the child grow away from the mother and become fully independent." This highlights the complex nature of familial love, which must nurture while also fostering independence.

Consider your own family: How have these relationships provided support or posed challenges? How do you show love to your family members, and how do they show love to you? Reflecting on these questions can deepen our appreciation for the unique dynamics within our families and help us nurture these vital connections.

As we navigate the complexities of familial love, let us remember the words of Elizabeth Berg: "You are born into your family and your family is born into you. No returns. No exchanges." This profound truth underscores the enduring nature of familial bonds and the importance of nurturing these relationships throughout our lives.

Familial love profoundly influences self-esteem and identity formation. A child's love for a supportive parent is often characterized by deep attachment, trust, and a sense of security. Research has shown that children with supportive parents tend to develop stronger emotional regulation skills and healthier relationships later in life. In contrast, when a parent is absent or less present due to divorce or separation, a child's love can become more complex. They may experience conflicting emotions of love, longing, and resentment.

In cases where parents have been unsupportive or have abandoned the child, the child's love can become entangled with feelings of unworthiness and self-blame. This can impact their ability to form healthy relationships in adulthood. However, it's important to note that children often maintain a deep, complicated love for absent or unsupportive parents.

The impact of divorce, separation, or absent parents on familial love cannot be overstated. A study published in the *Journal of Marriage and Family* found that adult children of divorce often struggle with trust and intimacy in their relationships. However, with awareness and effort, these challenges can be overcome.

Familial sibling love is a unique and powerful bond that often lasts a lifetime. Research has shown that positive sibling relationships can have significant benefits for emotional well-being and social development. A study published in the journal *Child Development* found that siblings who had warm, supportive relationships were more likely to develop strong social skills and emotional regulation abilities. This highlights the importance of nurturing these bonds from an early age.

As psychologist Laurie Kramer notes, "Sibling relationships are a training ground for life outside the family." These relationships provide opportunities to learn crucial social skills like conflict resolution, empathy, and cooperation. The shared experiences and history between siblings create a deep connection that can be a source of comfort and support throughout life.

Nurturing familial love requires intentional effort and strategies. Effective communication is crucial; establishing and maintaining boundaries is equally vital. Forgiveness and reconciliation play a critical role in sustaining familial love through inevitable conflicts. However, forgiveness doesn't always mean reconciliation, and in some cases, maintaining distance may be necessary for individual well-being. Positive family relationships can provide a secure base from which individuals can explore their identity and develop a strong sense of self-worth.

Emotional intelligence and relationship skills are often first learned within the family context. A study published in the *Journal of Family Psychology* found that children who experienced warm, supportive family relationships were more likely to develop strong emotional regulation skills and form healthy relationships outside the family.

Familial love can be a powerful source of resilience and coping mechanisms. The concept of family resilience, developed by Dr. Froma Walsh, suggests that strong family bonds can help individuals navigate life's challenges more effectively. Research has shown that individuals with strong family support systems tend to cope better with stress, recover more quickly from trauma, and maintain better overall mental health.

Familial love, while often a source of great comfort and support, can also present unique challenges. Generational differences and conflicts are increasingly common in our rapidly changing world. As psychologist Dr. Mary Pipher notes, "The world has changed more in the last 50 years than in the previous 500." This rapid change can create a significant gap in values, beliefs, and communication styles between generations.

Sibling rivalry is another perennial challenge in family dynamics. A study published in the journal *Child Development* found that sibling conflict in childhood was associated with increased risk of depression and anxiety in adulthood. However, the same study also noted that positive sibling relationships could serve as a protective factor against these mental health issues, highlighting the complex nature of sibling bonds.

Research by sociologist Karl Pillemer found that about 27 percent of Americans report being estranged from a family member. This statistic highlights the prevalence of family conflicts and the need for better understanding and communication across generations.

Maintaining familial love in the face of deep disagreements or vastly different life views can be challenging, yet it remains a vital aspect of family relationships. Despite our differences, the bonds of family often run deeper than our disagreements. As author Anne Lamott wisely notes, "You can either practice being right or practice being kind." This sentiment reminds us that preserving love and kindness in our family relationships often requires us to look beyond our differences and focus on our shared humanity and history. Loving someone doesn't always mean agreeing with them. By cultivating empathy, practicing active listening, and setting healthy boundaries, we can maintain connections with family members whose views differ from our own. In doing so, we not only preserve our familial bonds but also create opportunities for growth, understanding, and even reconciliation over time.

Balancing individual needs with family obligations is another significant challenge. In many cultures, there's an expectation to prioritize family needs over personal desires. However, psychologist Dr. Harriet Lerner argues, "Defining yourself and choosing your own goals is the ultimate task of growing up, and it never stops."

Reflect on your family dynamics. How have generational differences affected your relationships? Have you struggled to balance your individual needs with family obligations? If you've experienced family separation, how has it impacted your understanding of familial love?

Expressions of familial love vary widely across cultures. For instance, in many Asian cultures, love is often expressed through acts of service rather than verbal affirmations. Anthropologist Ruth Benedict's work highlights how cultural norms shape family dynamics and expressions of love. Despite these variations, research suggests there are universal aspects of familial love. Anthropologist Dr. Helen Fisher's cross-cultural studies found that family bonds and the desire to protect and nurture offspring are universal human traits.

The enduring power of familial love lies in its ability to shape us, support us, and provide a sense of belonging. As author Mitch Albom writes, "This is part of what a family is about, not just love. It's knowing that your family will be there watching out for you."

As you reflect on your own family relationships, consider where improvements could be made. Are there estranged relationships that could be mended? How might strengthening your familial bonds improve your overall well-being?

Remember, nurturing familial love is not just about maintaining relationships; it's about creating a supportive environment where each family member can thrive and become their best self. As you continue on your journey of personal growth, make nurturing your family relationships a *must*. The love, support, and understanding you cultivate within your family can become a powerful foundation for your continued personal development and success in all areas of life.

PLATONIC LOVE

Aristotle famously said, "Friendship is a single soul dwelling in two bodies." This ancient wisdom highlights the deep connection and mutual understanding that characterize true friendship. Platonic love, often overshadowed by its romantic counterpart, is a profound and enriching form of human connection that deserves our attention and cultivation. At its core, platonic love is a deep, nonromantic affection and respect between individuals. It's a love that transcends physical attraction, instead rooted in mutual understanding, shared values, and emotional intimacy.

The concept of platonic love traces its origins to the ancient Greek philosopher Plato, who explored the idea in his work the *Symposium*. Plato posited that the highest form of love was not physical, but intellectual and spiritual. This notion challenged the prevailing views of his time and continues to offer a powerful alternative to our often romance-obsessed culture. A study published in the *Journal of Social and Personal Relationships* found that strong friendships in adulthood were a better predictor of health and happiness than family relationships. This underscores the often-overlooked value of platonic bonds in our lives.

"Friendship is unnecessary, like philosophy, like art...It has no survival value; rather it is one of those things which give value to survival," stated C. S. Lewis. He beautifully captures the essence of platonic love. It's not just about survival or practicality; it's about enriching our lives and giving them deeper meaning.

As we delve deeper into the concept of platonic love, challenge yourself to examine your own beliefs and experiences. Remember, platonic love manifests in various forms, each offering unique benefits and challenges.

How might cultivating stronger platonic bonds enhance your life? What barriers might you need to overcome to fully embrace and nurture these relationships? Consider your friendships: Which relationships have stood the test of time? How have your friends supported you through life's ups and downs, and how have you supported them?

Friendships, the most common form of platonic relationships, come in myriad forms. From childhood buddies to work colleagues, these bonds can range from casual to deeply intimate. Research by Robin Dunbar, an evolutionary psychologist, suggests that humans can maintain about 150 meaningful relationships, with an inner circle of about five close friends. This "Dunbar number" highlights the hierarchical nature of our social connections. Sociologist Mark Granovetter's work on "the strength of weak ties" further emphasizes the importance of a diverse network of relationships for personal and professional growth. French fabulist and poet Jean de La Fontaine said, "Rare as is true love, true friendship is rarer."

Mentorship, another powerful form of platonic love, involves guidance, support, and wisdom-sharing. A study in the *Journal of Vocational Behavior* found that individuals with mentors reported higher job satisfaction and career advancement. This aligns with social learning theory, developed by psychologist Albert Bandura, which emphasizes the importance of observational learning and modeling in personal development.

Temporary and long-term friendships present an interesting dichotomy in platonic relationships. Sociologist Gerald Mollenhorst's research on friendship networks found that people replace about half of their close network members every seven years, highlighting the dynamic nature of social connections. Long-term friendships, on the other hand, weather the tests of time and change. A study in the journal *Personal Relationships* found that long-term friendships were associated with better health outcomes and increased life satisfaction. This aligns with the socioemotional selectivity theory proposed by psychologist Laura Carstensen, which suggests that as people age, they prioritize emotionally meaningful relationships.

As you reflect on your platonic relationships, consider the diverse forms they take and the unique value each brings to your life. How might you nurture these connections more intentionally? Remember, as philosopher Alain de Botton notes, "The best friendships are those in which we learn about ourselves through others."

Becoming a proactive friend involves taking initiative in forming and nurturing relationships. Research by psychologist Jeffrey Hall suggests it takes about fifty hours of interaction to move from acquaintance to casual friend, and about two hundred hours to become a close friend. This underscores the importance of consistently investing time and effort in friendships.

Active listening and empathy are crucial skills in deepening friendships. Dr. John Gottman's research, though primarily focused on romantic relationships, applies to platonic ones as well. He emphasizes the importance of "turning toward" instead of "turning away" from our friends' bids for connection. This involves being fully present, offering support, and showing genuine interest in our friends' lives. As Ralph Waldo Emerson said, "The only way to have a friend is to be one." Offering support and being reliable are cornerstones of strong platonic relationships. Cultivating shared interests can also strengthen bonds.

Navigating challenges in platonic relationships requires skill and patience. Conflict is inevitable, but how we handle it can make or break a friendship. Dr. Gottman's research on "repair attempts" in relationships applies here—successful friends are able to de-escalate tension and resolve conflicts constructively.

The impact of platonic love on personal growth cannot be overstated. Through deep friendships and meaningful connections, we expand our perspectives and learn from others in profound ways. Platonic relationships provide a safe space to practice empathy, active listening, and conflict resolution. These skills not only enhance our friendships but also translate to other areas of life, including professional relationships. Building a strong support network of platonic relationships can be instrumental in both personal and professional growth.

In the digital age, platonic love has taken on new dimensions. Online friendships have become increasingly common, allowing us to connect with like-minded individuals across geographical boundaries. However, balancing virtual and in-person interactions presents new challenges. As Sherry Turkle notes in her book *Alone Together*, "We expect more from technology and less from each other." It's crucial to nurture both online and offline connections for a well-rounded social life.

Applying the Must Mindset to platonic love involves identifying what we truly value in friendships. We must commit to being the friend we want to have, embodying the qualities we seek in others. This requires applying personal development principles to strengthen our platonic bonds. As we cultivate a growth mindset in friendships, we open ourselves to continuous learning and improvement in our relationships. The transformative power of platonic love lies in its ability to enrich our lives in countless ways. By nurturing and valuing these relationships, we create a support system that sustains us through life's challenges and celebrates our successes.

AGAPE: UNIVERSAL LOVE FOR OTHERS

Agape love, the pinnacle of human compassion and connection, stands as a beacon of hope in our often self-centered world. This profound form of love transcends the boundaries of personal relationships, extending its warm embrace to all of humanity. At its core, agape is characterized by unconditional care and concern for others, a selfless and altruistic nature that goes beyond the confines of our immediate circle.

The concept of agape has deep roots in both Greek philosophy and Christian theology, offering valuable meaning that has evolved over centuries. In ancient Greek thought, agape initially described a deep love for a spouse or close family member.

However, its meaning expanded over time, particularly through its use in the Septuagint, the Greek translation of the Hebrew Bible. In Christian contexts, agape took on a more profound significance, becoming synonymous with God's love for humanity and the ideal love that Christians should strive to embody.

To fully appreciate agape, it's helpful to contrast it with other forms of love recognized by the ancient Greeks: *eros* (romantic or sexual love), *philia* (deep friendship or brotherly love), and *storge* (familial love). While these forms of love are often conditional or based on personal connections, agape stands apart in its universal and unconditional nature.

Author and motivational speaker Wayne Dyer wisely noted, "Love is my gift to the world. I fill myself with love, and I send that love out into the world. How others treat me is their path; how I react is mine." This sentiment captures the essence of agape's selfless and all-encompassing nature. It's a love that asks for nothing in return, freely given to all without discrimination or expectation.

Author and speaker Leo Buscaglia beautifully expressed the transformative power of agape when he said, "Too often we underestimate the power of a touch, a smile, a kind word, a listening ear, an honest compliment, or the smallest act of caring, all of which have the potential to turn a life around." These simple acts of kindness and compassion are the building blocks of agape love, capable of creating ripples of positive change in the world.

In our journey of personal development, cultivating agape love can be profoundly transformative. It challenges us to expand our circle of compassion beyond our immediate relationships, fostering a sense of connection with all of humanity. By embracing agape, we not only enrich our own lives but also contribute to a more compassionate and understanding world.

The psychological and social implications of agape love are profound and far-reaching. Research has shown that individuals who practice agape love experience higher levels of personal well-being and happiness. This selfless, unconditional love promotes positive emotions and life satisfaction, boosting self-esteem and confidence. Studies have linked agape love to better physical health outcomes, including lower blood pressure and reduced risk of heart disease.

Beyond individual benefits, agape love plays a crucial role in fostering social cohesion. Encouraging acts of kindness, compassion, and generosity creates a ripple effect of positivity throughout society. This form of love strengthens social relationships and builds more resilient communities. As Dr. Martin Luther King Jr. eloquently stated, "Love is the only force capable of transforming an enemy into a friend," highlighting the transformative power of agape in social contexts.

However, practicing agape love is not without its challenges. It requires overcoming selfishness, letting go of personal desires, and often going against societal norms that prioritize individual gain. The sacrificial nature of agape love can be difficult to maintain, especially when faced with rejection or lack of reciprocation. As C. S. Lewis noted, "Love is not affectionate feeling, but a steady wish for the loved person's ultimate good as far as it can be obtained."

Cultivating agape love involves developing empathy and compassion. This process often begins with active listening and seeking to understand others' perspectives. As Wayne Dyer wisely observed, "When you change the way you look at things, the things you look at change." This shift in perspective is crucial for developing the kind of universal love that agape represents.

Overcoming barriers to universal love requires consistent practice and self-reflection. It involves examining our biases, confronting our fears, and expanding our capacity for empathy. The concept of *ubuntu*, an African philosophy emphasizing the interconnectedness of humanity, aligns closely with agape love. As Archbishop Desmond Tutu explained, "My humanity is caught up, is inextricably bound up, in yours."

Another significant concern is the potential for burnout or self-neglect. The selfless nature of agape love can sometimes lead individuals to prioritize others' needs to the detriment of their own well-being. It's crucial to find a balance between caring for others and maintaining self-care. As the saying goes, "You can't pour from an empty cup." Practicing self-compassion and maintaining healthy boundaries are essential for sustaining the ability to love others unconditionally.

Addressing skepticism and cynicism toward the concept of agape love is another hurdle. In a world often characterized by self-interest and competition, the idea of unconditional love for all can seem naive or impractical. Critics may argue that such love is impossible to sustain or that it leaves individuals vulnerable to exploitation.

Despite these challenges, proponents of agape love argue that its practice can lead to profound personal growth and social transformation. By cultivating empathy, compassion, and unconditional regard for others, individuals can contribute to creating a more caring and harmonious world.

Community service and humanitarian efforts are powerful expressions of agape love. Volunteering at local food banks, participating in community cleanup efforts, or supporting global humanitarian causes all reflect the selfless nature of agape. These actions not only benefit the recipients but also enrich the lives of those who serve, creating a cycle of positive impact.

In daily life, agape love manifests in small acts of kindness. From offering a smile to a stranger to helping a neighbor with groceries, these seemingly insignificant actions can have a profound impact. As the Dalai Lama said, "Be kind whenever possible. It is always possible." By consistently choosing kindness and compassion in our everyday interactions, we cultivate a habit of agape love that can transform our relationships and communities.

Agape love finds expression in various spiritual traditions across the world. In Christianity, it is often associated with God's unconditional love for humanity and the ideal love that followers should strive to embody. In Buddhism, the concept of *metta*, or loving-kindness, bears similarities to agape, emphasizing unconditional goodwill toward all beings.

Modern interpretations and applications of agape love extend beyond religious contexts. In contemporary psychology and personal development, agape is seen as a powerful tool for fostering empathy, building stronger relationships, and contributing to social harmony. It is increasingly recognized as a valuable approach in fields such as education, healthcare, and conflict resolution.

Research on altruism and prosocial behavior has provided valuable insights into the nature of agape love. Studies have shown that engaging in altruistic behaviors not only benefits others but also has profound positive effects on the physical and psychological well-being of the person performing the act. For instance, volunteerism has been positively correlated with self-reported happiness, health, and well-being.

Studies on the benefits of practicing unconditional love have yielded promising results. Research has shown that cultivating compassion can lead to increased parasympathetic nervous system response, as measured by heart rate variability (HRV). Higher HRV is associated with states of contentment, calmness, and safety. Compassion training has been found to reduce neural activity in networks associated with threat when individuals practice compassion, while increasing activity in these same networks when they are being self-critical.

Embracing agape love as a cornerstone of personal development can lead to profound transformation and growth. This journey begins with self-reflection, a process that requires honest introspection and a willingness to confront our own limitations and biases. As we delve deeper into understanding ourselves, we create space for growth and the expansion of our capacity to love unconditionally. Self-reflection in the context of agape love involves examining our thoughts, actions, and motivations through the lens of universal compassion. It challenges us to question our judgments and preconceptions, asking ourselves, "Am I approaching this situation with unconditional love? How can I extend more compassion to myself and others?" This ongoing process of self-examination fosters personal growth and a deeper understanding of our interconnectedness with others.

Expanding one's circle of compassion is a natural progression in the practice of agape love. It involves consciously extending our care and concern beyond our immediate circle to encompass a wider range of individuals, including those we may find challenging to love. Integrating agape principles into daily life requires intentional practice and commitment. It might involve starting each day with a meditation on universal love, practicing random acts of kindness, cultivating empathy in challenging interactions, and seeking to understand before being understood. These practices, when consistently applied, can transform our relationships and our approach to life's challenges.

In our increasingly connected world, the relevance of agape love has never been more apparent. As global communication brings us closer together, it also exposes us to diverse perspectives and challenges. Agape love offers a framework for navigating these complexities with compassion and understanding. The potential role of agape love in addressing global challenges is significant. From climate change to social inequality, many of our most pressing issues require collective action and mutual understanding. By fostering a sense of universal love and interconnectedness, we can build the empathy and cooperation necessary to tackle these challenges effectively.

Fostering a culture of universal love and understanding is perhaps the most ambitious and transformative application of agape love. This involves not only individual practice but also systemic changes in education, policy, and social norms. By prioritizing empathy, compassion, and unconditional love in our institutions and interactions, we can create a more harmonious and just world. As we conclude this exploration of agape love, it's crucial to consider how you can apply these principles in your own life. Embracing agape as a *must* in your personal growth journey aligns perfectly with the Must Mindset we discussed earlier in this book. It challenges you to view unconditional love not as an option but as a necessity for your development and fulfillment.

Consider making a commitment to yourself: "I must cultivate agape love in my life." This might involve daily reflection on how you can extend more compassion to yourself and others; actively seeking opportunities to practice unconditional love, especially in challenging situations; expanding your circle of concern to include those outside your immediate community; and integrating agape principles into your decision-making process. Remember, the journey of personal growth through agape love is ongoing. It requires patience, practice, and perseverance. As you continue this path, you'll likely find that your capacity for love and compassion grows, leading to deeper connections, greater fulfillment, and a more profound sense of purpose.

By making agape love a *must* in your life, you're not only investing in your growth but also contributing to a more loving and understanding world. This aligns perfectly with our ongoing journey of becoming the best version of ourselves. Embrace this challenge with an open heart and mind, knowing that each step toward unconditional love is a step toward your highest potential.

LOVE IS THE FOUNDATIONAL AND PINNACLE BUILDING BLOCK OF YOUR *MUST*

In your journey of becoming the person you are meant to be, we arrive at a profound truth: love is both the foundation and the pinnacle of your *must*. It is the essential element that infuses meaning, purpose, and fulfillment into every aspect of your life.

Love, in its purest form, is not just an emotion but a transformative force that shapes our actions, decisions, and relationships. It is the bedrock upon which we build our most authentic selves and the highest peak we aspire to reach in our personal growth. When we embrace love as our core value, it becomes the guiding principle that aligns all other aspects of our Must Journey.

Consider how love intersects with every area of the Circle of Life we've explored:

In health and vitality, love manifests as self-care and respect for our bodies and minds. It drives us to nurture ourselves with the same compassion we would offer to a loved one.

In relationships, love is the essence of connection, fostering trust, empathy, and understanding. It enables us to form deep, meaningful bonds that enrich our lives and support our growth.

In career and professional achievement, love fuels our passion and dedication. It inspires us to pursue work that aligns with our values and contributes positively to the world.

In financial well-being, love guides us to use our resources wisely, not just for personal gain, but to create security for ourselves and others and to contribute to causes we care about.

In personal growth and learning, love opens our hearts and minds to new experiences, fostering curiosity and a desire for continuous improvement.

In spirituality, religion, and inner peace, love connects us to something greater than ourselves—whether through faith, meditation, or reflection—and provides a sense of purpose and serenity that grounds us in times of uncertainty. Love fosters inner harmony by aligning our values with our spiritual practices, helping us cultivate peace within ourselves and with the world around us.

In community and legacy, love inspires us to contribute meaningfully to the lives of others and leave a lasting impact on the world. It drives us to build communities rooted in compassion, support causes that align with our values, and create a legacy defined by kindness, generosity, and purpose.

By recognizing love as the core of your *must*, you create a powerful synergy within your values, beliefs, and actions. This alignment leads to a life of greater authenticity, purpose, and fulfillment. As you continue on your journey of becoming, let love be your compass, guiding you toward your highest potential and the extraordinary life you are meant to live.

Remember, love is not just an emotion, but a powerful force that propels you toward self-actualization and becoming the best version of yourself. By focusing on love and self-love, you unlock the key to overcoming obstacles, fostering deeper connections, and realizing your true potential in life as a glorious human being.

Conclusion

THE JOURNEY OF BECOMING

"Life isn't about finding yourself. Life is about creating yourself."
—Attributed to George Bernard Shaw,
Irish playwright and philosopher

As we reach the final pages of this book, I want to take a moment to acknowledge and congratulate you. The journey you've undertaken is not a small one—it's monumental. The person who first opened these pages is not the same person who sits here now. You have evolved, transformed, and grown into a vibrant, flourishing human being, filled with energy, insight, and intentional direction. You have stepped into your own Must Life, and that, my dear friend, is a powerful and extraordinary accomplishment.

Take a moment to reflect on the extraordinary journey you've undertaken. When you first opened these pages, you were seeking ways to grow. Now, as you reach the end, you've blossomed into a vibrant, purposeful being, ready to embrace the world with newfound strength and clarity.

Your transformation began with the recognition that within you lay dormant greatness, waiting to be awakened. You courageously chose to embark on this path of self-discovery, facing your fears and confronting the shadows that once held you back. With each chapter, you peeled away layers of doubt, misconception, and limitation, revealing the radiant core of your true self.

Through the exploration of the Must Mindset, you've learned to view challenges not as obstacles, but as opportunities for growth. You've embraced the power of *must*—that unwavering inner voice that propels you toward your highest potential. This shift in perspective has been nothing short of revolutionary, transforming how you approach every aspect of your life.

You've delved deep into your core beliefs, examining the very foundation of your worldview. With courage and introspection, you've dismantled limiting beliefs that once confined you, replacing them with empowering truths that align with your authentic self. This process of belief reconstruction has been both challenging and liberating, setting the stage for profound personal growth.

The journey through your values and personal narrative has been equally transformative. You've learned to author your own story, no longer allowing external circumstances or past experiences to dictate your path. Instead, you've become the conscious creator of your life, aligning your actions with your deepest values and crafting a narrative of purpose and fulfillment.

In exploring the Must Zone, you've discovered a realm of continuous, purposeful action. You've learned to dance with your fears, embracing discomfort as a sign of growth rather than a signal to retreat. This shift has propelled you from a place of stagnation to one of constant evolution, where each day brings new opportunities for self-improvement and achievement.

STEPPING INTO YOUR MUST LIFE

Now you stand as a testament to the power of intentional living. You've discovered your authentic purpose, aligned your goals with that purpose, and taken decisive Must Actions to create a life of meaning, fulfillment, and joy. You've learned to embrace your vulnerabilities, to face the dark moments of your life not as defining failures but as essential experiences that have contributed to your growth and resilience.

You've cultivated habits that support your purpose-driven goals, and you've committed to living in alignment with your Must Core Values and Standards. You've understood the importance of perseverance, of having the tenacity to keep moving forward even when the path is difficult. You've grounded yourself in a mindset of abundance, recognizing that you are blessed with grace, love, and the capacity to give and receive these gifts freely.

You have successfully evaluated the precious elements of your Circle of Life. You've explored your health and vitality, relationships, career and professional achievements, financial well-being, personal growth and learning, spirituality and peace of mind, and contributions and legacy. These elements are now constructed from a thorough examination of your newly found appreciation for your Must Mindset, Must Core Beliefs, Must Values, and Must Standards.

You've discovered your Must Purpose and learned to execute it in your Must Zone through Must Actions aligned with your purpose-driven goals. You've honed your time management and productivity skills, shedding the heavy aspects of suffering and embracing the brilliant light of life's blessings. Through gratitude and grace, you've cultivated a state of love and self-love that permeates every aspect of your being.

This journey has empowered you to live authentically, with a deep understanding of your true self and a clear vision of the extraordinary life you are meant to live. As you move forward, remember that becoming the person you are meant to be is an ongoing process, one that requires continuous reflection, growth, and alignment. Embrace this journey with open arms, for it is through this conscious evolution that you will continue to unlock your full potential and create a life of profound meaning and fulfillment.

You have stepped into your power, embraced your unique journey, and become the architect of your destiny. The life you are creating is one of vibrancy, authenticity, and profound meaning. You are living your Must Life—boldly, unapologetically, and with unwavering commitment to your highest self.

As you stand at the threshold of this new chapter in your life, you are no longer the person who first picked up this book. You have become the master of your mindset, and the author of your story. You've not just read about transformation; you've lived it, breathed it, and embodied it.

EMBRACING THE JOURNEY OF BECOMING

As you continue this journey, remember that becoming is a lifelong process. It's not about reaching a final destination but about continuously evolving, growing, and stepping closer to the person you've always dreamed of being. It's about living each day with intention, guided by your purpose, values, and the deep knowledge that you are worthy of every blessing, every success, and every moment of joy that life has to offer.

Success is not just about the external markers of achievement. It's about the internal alignment with your true self, the deep sense of fulfillment that comes from knowing you are living a life that is authentically yours. It's about waking up each day with a sense of purpose, energized by the knowledge that you are on the path of your choosing, becoming the person you were always meant to be.

Know that the journey is far from over. The insights you've gained, the changes you've made, and the growth you've experienced are just the beginning. Your Must Life will continue to unfold, offering new challenges, new opportunities, and new heights of personal and spiritual fulfillment.

Remember, the journey of becoming is endless, and that is its greatest gift. Each day offers a new chance to grow, to learn, to serve, and to live in even greater alignment with all aspects of yourself. Embrace it with open arms, with the vibrant energy that now flows through you, and with the confidence that you are exactly where you need to be—on the path of your Must Life.

A FINAL WORD

As we move forward, I encourage you to carry with you the lessons you've learned, the habits you've cultivated, and the spirit of perseverance that has brought you to this point. Trust in yourself, in your journey, and in the process of becoming. You are a powerful, capable, and extraordinary individual, and the world is better because you are living your Must Life.

I leave you with two requests. First, let's stay in touch. I am here for you in every way possible, whether you're in search of additional resources and programs, a personal development community, or just periodic words of encouragement.

Second, if you have gained knowledge and wisdom from this book, please share it and recommend it to others. My purpose is to make a profound difference in your life and the lives of those you love.

May you continue to thrive, flourish, and inspire others with your example. May your life be filled with the richness of purpose, the joy of alignment, and the deep satisfaction of knowing you are living fully, authentically, and in accordance with your truest self.

As we reach the end of our journey together, remember, your *must* is not just a concept, but a calling from the depths of your soul. It is the whisper of your true self, urging you to become who you were always meant to be. Through the valleys of despair and the peaks of triumph, your *must* has been your constant companion, your guiding light. Now, as you stand on the threshold of your transformed life, let your *must* be the force that propels you forward. Embrace it with every fiber of your being, for in doing so, you embrace your destiny.

The world awaits the unique gift only you can give—the gift of your authentic, fully realized self.

With my deepest admiration and encouragement,

Your Friend,

Stephen Rue

Acknowledgments

Before all else, I wish to acknowledge and thank my personal Lord and Savior, Jesus Christ. He is my guiding light, my source of strength, and the foundation upon which all my growth and hope are built. Without His grace and love, none of this would have been possible.

My deepest gratitude goes to my family. To my mother, Jeannie Rue Pearson, whose unwavering love and resilience have been the paramount inspiration for this book and my life. To my younger sister, Elizabeth Rue Brennan, who has walked alongside me through our family's suffering and her own and who continues to be a glowing example of overcoming adversity and being an exceptional mother to her daughters, my nieces, Brooke and Ashley Brennan.

This book is also dedicated to my dear Uncle Bob, J. Robert Ates. Without being asked, you became the closest father figure I have ever known. Your brilliance as a lawyer, a professor, a mentor, and the best wordsmith I have ever met guided and supported me through the long and important editing process. Your wisdom and encouragement have been invaluable.

To the love of my life, Elizabeth Herberg, thank you for your steadfast support and love through every emotional high and low of this writing journey. Your belief in me and this work has been a constant source of strength and inspiration.

My heartfelt appreciation goes to my professional editor, Holly Gorman, whose mastery and dedication helped bring together a massive amount of information into an organized, cohesive, and impactful book. Holly, your skill, insight, and encouragement ensured that the content and message of this book will truly benefit every reader.

I am deeply grateful to my educational and inspirational mentors—all my teachers and professors, beginning in grade school, through high school, college, my MBA, law school, post-law-school leadership training, and during my doctorate studies. Each of you played a vital role in shaping my mind and spirit.

To the many teachers and mentors in my personal development journey outside formal education, including the hundreds of luminaries mentioned in this book, I am honored to forward your enduring wisdom. Your teachings and examples have profoundly moved me and enriched my life.

A special thank-you to all who have shared their personal stories of suffering and triumph over adversity. Your courage and openness have given this book its heart.

I am grateful to Tony Robbins, Les Brown, Brian Tracy, Loren Lahav, and Jack Canfield for your words of encouragement, friendship, and mentorship throughout the years. Knowing you all has been an honor and a blessing.

Thank you to my friend, Bruce Silver, for your constant encouragement and friendship throughout this endeavor. You are a great friend.

I cannot forget to thank my ever-loving Cavapoo, Evie. Each night as I wrote and rewrote this book, Evie was by my side, relaxing or sleeping on her doggie bed next to me. Her companionship and love were a constant comfort and joy.

Finally, and most importantly, I acknowledge you—the reader. We are kindred spirits, striving for personal development and improvement. I appreciate your heart, your spirit, and your willingness to share the message of this book with your friends and family. The words "thank you" are not enough. By reading and living these principles, you have become a part of my legacy. Thank you.

With all my gratitude,

Stephen Rue

About the Author

STEPHEN RUE is a multifaceted individual whose diverse life experiences and professional achievements have shaped his mission to inspire and uplift others. Stephen, a renowned lawyer and counselor-at-law licensed in multiple states, has academic credentials that include a BBA from Southern Methodist University, a law degree and MBA from Loyola University, Harvard Law School leadership training, and ongoing doctoral work at National University. Voted "Best Attorney" in New Orleans, his true passion lies in personal growth and helping others overcome adversity.

Certified as a trauma recovery life coach, Stephen draws from his own triumphs over family tragedies and personal challenges. Through law and personal development, he has helped thousands to flourish and thrive in their lives. His zest for life extends to being a Mardi Gras king, author, motivational speaker, artist, sculptor, and marathon runner.

For over three decades, Stephen has immersed himself in various endeavors, studies, and deep research, culminating in this masterpiece book—*Must*. Synthesizing insights from luminaries in psychology, neuroscience, philosophy, and personal development, he offers a practical and effective roadmap for personal transformation. His unique approach combines academic rigor with real-world application, making complex concepts accessible and actionable.

Through this book, Stephen shares wisdom gained from overcoming adversity, providing readers with tools to navigate life's challenges and emerge stronger, more resilient, and aligned with their true selves as the person they are meant to be.

How to Stay in Touch with Me

StephenRue.Live
StephenRue.com
Instagram @SouthernFriedLawyer
Facebook: Stephen Rue Official Facebook Page
YouTube @TheStephenRue
X @StephenRue
Mail: 416 N. Vermont Street, Covington, LA 70433
Stephen@StephenRue.com

Bibliography

ABC News. "2015 FIFA Women's World Cup: Carli Lloyd Visualized Record-Breaking Goals in May." July 6, 2015. https://abcnews.go.com/Entertainment/2015-fifa-womens-world-cup-carli-lloyd-visualized/story?id=32249479.

Adams, Patch, and Maureen Mylander. *Gesundheit! Bringing Good Health to You, the Medical System, and Society Through Physician Service, Complementary Therapies, Humor, and Joy*. Healing Arts Press, 1998.

Ainsworth, Mary D. Salter, Mary C. Blehar, Everett Waters, and Sally N. Wall. *Patterns of Attachment: A Psychological Study of the Strange Situation*. Lawrence Erlbaum Associates, 1978.

Ainsworth, Mary S., and John Bowlby. "An Ethological Approach to Personality Development." *American Psychologist* 46, no. 4 (1991): 333–41. https://doi.org/10.1037/0003-066X.46.4.333.

Albahari, Miri. "Against No-Ātman Theories of Anattā." *Asian Philosophy* 16, no. 1 (2006): 5–20. https://doi.org/10.1080/09552360220142225.

Albom, Mitch. *For One More Day*. Hyperion, 2006.

Allen, James P. *The Ancient Egyptian Pyramid Texts*. Society of Biblical Literature Press, 2015.

Amato, Paul R., and Tamara D. Afifi. "Feeling Caught Between Parents: Adult Children's Relations with Parents and Subjective Well-Being." *Journal of Marriage and Family* 68, no. 1 (2006): 222–35. https://doi.org/10.1111/j.1741-3737.2006.00243.x.

American Psychiatric Association. *Diagnostic and Statistical Manual of Mental Disorders.* 5th ed. American Psychiatric Publishing, 2013.

American Psychological Association. "Anger." Accessed January 15, 2025. https://apa.org/topics/anger.

American Psychological Association. "Growth After Trauma." *Monitor on Psychology* 47, no. 10 (2016): 48. https://apa.org/monitor/2016/11/growth-trauma.

American Psychological Association. "Resilience." In *APA Dictionary of Psychology.* Last modified April 19, 2018. https://dictionary.apa.org/resilience.

Angelou, Maya. *All God's Children Need Traveling Shoes.* Random House, 1986.

Angelou, Maya. *Gather Together in My Name.* Random House, 1974.

Angelou, Maya. *The Heart of a Woman.* Random House, 1981.

Angelou, Maya. *I Know Why the Caged Bird Sings.* Random House, 1969.

Angelou, Maya. *Mom & Me & Mom.* Random House, 2013.

Angelou, Maya. *Singin' and Swingin' and Gettin' Merry like Christmas.* Random House, 1976.

Angelou, Maya. *A Song Flung up to Heaven.* Random House, 2002.

Aron, Arthur, Christina C. Norman, Elaine N. Aron, Colin McKenna, and Richard E. Heyman. "Couples' Shared Participation in Novel and Arousing Activities and Experienced Relationship Quality." *Journal of Personality and Social Psychology* 78, no. 2 (2000): 273–84. https://doi.org/10.1037/0022-3514.78.2.273.

Asgharnia, Shayan, dir. "How Tyler Perry Made a Fortune from Nothing." AARP Studios, August 5, 2022. YouTube, 3:58. https://youtube.com/watch?v=7knT83CJ3NM.

Ashford, Susan J., and L. L. Cummings. "Feedback as an Individual Resource: Personal Strategies of Creating Information." *Organizational Behavior and Human Performance* 32, no. 3 (1983): 370–98. https://doi.org/10.1016/0030-5073(83)90156-3.

Aurelius, Marcus. *Meditations.* Translated by Gregory Hays. Modern Library, 2002.

Austen, Jane. *Pride and Prejudice.* Edited by Vivien Jones. Penguin Classics, 2003.

Bach, Richard. *Illusions: The Adventures of a Reluctant Messiah.* Dell Publishing, 1977.

Baldwin, James. *Nobody Knows My Name: More Notes of a Native Son.* Dial Press, 1961.

Bandura, Albert. *Social Learning Theory.* Prentice Hall, 1977.

Bardwick, Judith M. *Danger in the Comfort Zone: From Boardroom to Mailroom—How to Break the Entitlement Habit That's Killing American Business.* AMACOM, 1995.

Bartell, Patricia. *From Crutches to Crushing It: A Journey from Pain to Power.* Published by the author, 2024.

Barton, Katheryn. "Seeing Ourselves, Understanding Others: The Dynamic Duo of Self-Awareness and Empathy." Uplift and Connect Counseling. February 1, 2024. https://upliftcounselingandmediation.com/building-bridges-of-understanding-the-transformative-role-of-self-awareness-in-relationships.

Cerf, Bennett. *Shake Well Before Using: A New Collection of Impressions and Anecdotes Mostly Humorous.* Simon and Schuster, 1948, 249.

BBC. "Ruth Bader Ginsburg in Pictures and Her Own Words." September 19, 2020. https://bbc.com/news/world-us-canada-54218139.

Beck, Aaron T. *Cognitive Therapy and the Emotional Disorders.* Penguin, 1979.

Beck, Aaron T. "Thinking and Depression: II. Theory and Therapy." *Archives of General Psychiatry* 10, no. 6 (1964): 561–71. https://doi.org/10.1001/archpsyc.1964.01720240015003.

Bennett, Roy T. *The Light in the Heart.* Published by the author, 2016.

Berg, Elizabeth. *The Art of Mending.* Random House, 2004.

Berscheid, Ellen, and Harry T. Reis. "Attraction and Close Relationships." In *The Handbook of Social Psychology*, edited by Daniel T. Gilbert, Susan T. Fiske, and Gardner Lindzey. McGraw-Hill, 1998.

Bezos, Jeff. "Amazon & Customer Experience: 13 Quotes from Jeff Bezos." SuiteFeedback. Accessed June 1, 2025. https://suitefeedback.com/amazon-customer-experience-13-quotes-from-jeff-bezos/.

Biggs, Michael. "Self-Fulfilling Prophecies." In *The Oxford Handbook of Analytical Sociology*, edited by Peter Bearman and Peter Hedström. Oxford University Press, 2011.

Bird, Matthew D., Christian Swann, and Patricia C. Jackman. "The What, Why, and How of Goal Setting: A Review of the Goal-Setting Process in Applied Sport Psychology Practice." *Journal of Applied Sport Psychology* 36, no. 1 (2024): 75–97. https://doi.org/10.1080/10413200.2023.2185699.

Black History Month. "Harriet Tubman's Impact on American History." March 16, 2023. https://blackhistorymonth.org.uk/article/section/history-of-slavery/harriet-tubmans-impact-on-american-history-from-the-underground-railroad-to-womens-suffrage/.

Blackmon, Kelly. "The Science Behind Getting Out of Our Comfort Zones." LinkedIn. March 13, 2023. https://linkedin.com/pulse/science-behind-getting-out-our-comfort-zones-kelly-blackmon.

Blitzer, Wolf, host. *The Situation Room*. Aired February 18, 2006, on CNN.

Boston, Patricia, Anne Bruce, and Rita Schreiber. "Existential Suffering in the Palliative Care Setting: An Integrated Literature Review." *Journal of Pain and Symptom Management* 41, no. 3 (2011): 604–18. https://doi.org/10.1016/j.jpainsymman.2010.05.010.

Bowlby, John. *Attachment and Loss*, vol. 1, *Attachment*. Basic Books, 1969.

Bowlby, John. *A Secure Base: Parent-Child Attachment and Healthy Human Development*. Basic Books, 1988.

Brach, T. *Radical Acceptance: Embracing Your Life with the Heart of a Buddha*. Bantam, 2003.

Brooks, Arthur C., and Oprah Winfrey. *Build the Life You Want: The Art and Science of Getting Happier*. Portfolio, 2023.

Brown, Brené. *Atlas of the Heart: Mapping Meaningful Connection and the Language of Human Experience*. Random House, 2021.

Brown, Brené. *Braving the Wilderness: The Quest for True Belonging and the Courage to Stand Alone*. Random House, 2017.

Brown, Brené. "Brene Brown: How Vulnerability Can Make Our Lives Better." Interview by Dan Schawbel. *Forbes*, April 21, 2013. https://www.forbes.com/sites/danschawbel/2013/04/21/brene-brown-how-vulnerability-can-make-our-lives-better/.

Brown, Brené. *Dare to Lead: Brave Work. Tough Conversations. Whole Hearts*. Random House, 2018.

Brown, Brené. *Daring Greatly: How the Courage to Be Vulnerable Transforms the Way We Live, Love, Parent, and Lead*. Gotham Books, 2012.

Brown, Brené. *The Gifts of Imperfection: Let Go of Who You Think You're Supposed to Be and Embrace Who You Are*. Hazelden Publishing, 2010.

Brown, Brené. *I Thought It Was Just Me: Women Reclaiming Power and Courage in a Culture of Shame.* Gotham Books, 2007.

Brown, Brené. *I Thought It Was Just Me (but It Isn't): Making the Journey from "What Will People Think?" to "I Am Enough."* Gotham Books, 2007.

Brown, Brené. "The Power of Vulnerability." Presentation at TEDxHouston, Houston, TX, June 2010.

Brown, Brené. *Rising Strong: How the Ability to Reset Transforms the Way We Live, Love, Parent, and Lead.* Random House, 2015.

Brown, Les. *It's Not Over Until You Win: How to Become the Person You Always Wanted to Be No Matter What the Obstacle.* Simon & Schuster, 1997.

Brown, Les. "This One Thing Determines Whether You Will Be Successful or Not!" Goalcast, April 28, 2018. YouTube, 6:35. https://youtube.com/watch?v=xFroFKnaLDk.

Brown, Les. *Live Your Dreams.* William Morrow, 1992.

Brown, Les. *The Power of Purpose: How to Create the Life You Always Wanted.* Nightingale-Conant, 2014.

Brown, Les. *Up Thoughts for Down Times: Encouraging Words for Getting Through Life.* Thomas Nelson, 2004.

Brown, Les. *You've Got to Be HUNGRY: The Greatness Within to Win.* Hay House, 2020.

Brown, Les, and Stephen Rue. *Rise Above: Overcoming Setbacks with Les Brown's Wisdom.* You Have Greatness LLC, 2024.

Bryant, Kobe. *The Mamba Mentality: How I Play.* MCD, 2018.

Budge, E. A. Wallis, trans. *The Egyptian Book of the Dead: (The Papyrus of Ani) Egyptian Text Transliteration and Translation.* Dover Publications, 1967.

Buist, Kirsten L., Maja Deković, and Peter Prinzie. "Sibling Relationship Quality and Psychopathology of Children and Adolescents: A Meta-Analysis." *Clinical Psychology Review* 33, no. 1 (2013): 97–106. https://doi.org/10.1016/j.cpr.2012.10.007.

Buscaglia, Leo. *Bus 9 to Paradise: A Loving Voyage.* Slack Incorporated, 1986.

Buscaglia, Leo. *The Fall of Freddie the Leaf: A Story of Life for All Ages.* Slack Incorporated, 1982.

Buscaglia, Leo. *Living, Loving & Learning.* Ballantine Books, 1982.

Buscaglia, Leo. *Love: What Life Is All About.* Fawcett, 1972.

Buscaglia, Leo. *Loving Each Other: The Challenge of Human Relationships.* Slack Incorporated, 1984.

Byrne, Donn. *The Attraction Paradigm.* Academic Press, 1971.

Cacioppo, John T. "Loneliness Is a Major Health Risk for Older Adults." Presentation at American Association for the Advancement of Science (AAAS) Annual Meeting, Chicago, IL, February 2014.

Canfield, Jack, and Mark Victor Hansen. *Chicken Soup for the Soul: 101 Stories to Open the Heart and Rekindle the Spirit.* Health Communications, 1993.

Canfield, Jack, Mark Victor Hansen, and Lisa Nichols. *Chicken Soup for the African American Woman's Soul: Laughter, Love and Memories to Honor the Legacy of Sisterhood.* Health Communications, 2006.

Canfield, Jack, Mark Victor Hansen, Lisa Nichols, and Tom Joyner. *Chicken Soup for the African American Soul: Celebrating and Sharing Our Culture, One Story at a Time.* Health Communications, 2004.

Canfield, Jack, and Janet Switzer. *The Success Principles: How to Get from Where You Are to Where You Want to Be.* HarperCollins, 2005.

Cardenas, Bianca. "Transformative Leadership: Unveiling Satya Nadella's Three Revolutionary Strategies at Microsoft." Leadership Worth Following. Accessed June 15, 2025. https://worthyleadership.com/transformative-leadership-unveiling-satya-nadellas-three-revolutionary-strategies-at-microsoft/.

Carstensen, Laura L. "Social and Emotional Patterns in Adulthood: Support for Socioemotional Selectivity Theory." *Psychology and Aging* 7, no. 3 (1992): 331–38. https://doi.org/10.1037/0882-7974.7.3.331.

Carter, C. Sue. "The Role of Oxytocin and Vasopressin in Attachment." *Psychodynamic Psychiatry* 45, no. 4 (2017): 499–517. https://doi.org/10.1521/pdps.2017.45.4.499.

CBS Sports. "The Most Dangerous Mind in the NFL: How Drew Brees Continues to Defy the Odds." August 7, 2017. https://cbssports.com/nfl/news/the-most-dangerous-mind-in-the-nfl-how-drew-brees-continues-to-defy-the-odds/.

Chapman, Gary. *The 5 Love Languages: The Secret to Love That Lasts*. Northfield Publishing, 2015.

Chen, Lung Hung, and Ying Hwa Kee. "Gratitude and Adolescent Athletes' Well-Being." *Social Indicators Research* 89, no. 2 (2008): 361–73. https://doi.org/10.1007/s11205-012-0145-2.

Chopik, William J. "Associations Among Relational Values, Support, Health, and Well-Being Across the Adult Lifespan." *Personal Relationships* 24, no. 2 (2017): 408–22. https://doi.org/10.1111/pere.12187.

Churchill, Winston S. *Never Give In! The Best of Winston Churchill's Speeches*. Pimlico, 1941.

Cirillo, Francesco. "Pomodoro Technique." Accessed June 15, 2025. https://pomodorotechnique.com.

Cirillo, Francesco. *The Pomodoro Technique*. FC Garage GmbH, 2006.

Clear, James. *Atomic Habits: An Easy & Proven Way to Build Good Habits & Break Bad Ones*. Penguin Random House, 2018.

Cloud, Henry, and John Townsend. *Boundaries: When to Say Yes, How to Say No to Take Control of Your Life*. Zondervan, 2017.

Clow, Angela, Frank Hucklebridge, and Lisa Thorn. "The Cortisol Awakening Response in Context." *International Review of Neurobiology* 93 (2010): 153–75. https://doi.org/10.1016/S0074-7742(10)93007-9.

Collins, Jim C. *Good to Great: Why Some Companies Make the Leap—and Others Don't*. HarperBusiness, 2001.

Confucius. "Chinese Text Project." Accessed January 7, 2025. https://ctext.org/liji/li-yun.

Cordes, Liane. *The Reflecting Pond: Meditations for Self-Discovery*. Hazelden Publishing, 1981.

Covey, Stephen R. *The 7 Habits of Highly Effective People: Powerful Lessons in Personal Change*. Simon & Schuster, 2013.

Craft, Lynette L., and Frank M. Perna. "The Benefits of Exercise for the Clinically Depressed." *Primary Care Companion to the Journal of Clinical Psychiatry* 6, no. 3 (2004): 104–11. https://doi.org/10.4088/pcc.v06n0301.

Csikszentmihalyi, Mihaly. *Flow: The Psychology of Optimal Experience*. Harper & Row, 1990.

Currey, Mason. *Daily Rituals: How Artists Work*. Knopf, 2013.

Dalai Lama [XIV]. *The Art of Happiness: A Handbook for Living*. Riverhead Books, 2019.

Dalai Lama [XIV]. *The Compassionate Life*. Wisdom Publications, 2002.

Dalio, Ray. *Principles: Life and Work*. Simon & Schuster, 2017.

Davidson, Richard J., and William Irwin. "The Functional Neuroanatomy of Emotion and Affective Style." *Trends in Cognitive Sciences* 3, no. 1 (1999): 11–21. https://doi.org/10.1016/s1364-6613(98)01265-0.

Davidson, Richard J., and Antoine Lutz. "Buddha's Brain: Neuroplasticity and Meditation." *IEEE Signal Processing Magazine* 25, no. 1 (2008): 176–74. https://doi.org/10.1109/msp.2008.4431873.

Davidson, Richard J., and Bruce S. McEwen. "Social Influences on Neuroplasticity: Stress and Interventions to Promote Well-Being." *Nature Neuroscience* 15, no. 5 (2012): 689–95. https://doi.org/10.1038/nn.3093.

de La Bruyère, Jean. "The Ancient Greeks' 6 Words for Love (and Why Knowing Them Can Change Your Life)." YES! Magazine. December 28, 2013. https://yesmagazine.org/health-happiness/2013/12/28/the-ancient-greeks-6-words-for-love-and-why-knowing-them-can-change-your-life.

De Neve, Jan-Emmanuel. "Functional Polymorphism (5-HTTLPR) in the Serotonin Transporter Gene Is Associated with Subjective Well-Being: Evidence from a US Nationally Representative Sample." *Journal of Human Genetics* 56, no. 6 (2011): 456–59. https://doi.org/10.1038/jhg.2011.39.

Devine, Megan. *It's OK That You're Not OK: Meeting Grief and Loss in a Culture That Doesn't Understand*. Sounds True, 2017.

Diamond, Jared. *The World Until Yesterday: What Can We Learn from Traditional Societies?* Viking, 2012.

Ditzen, Beate., Inga D. Neumann, Guy Bodenmann, Bernadette von Dawans, Rebecca A. Turner, Ulrike Ehlert, and Markus Heinrichs. "Effects of Different Kinds of Couple Interaction on Cortisol and Heart Rate Responses to Stress in Women." *Psychoneuroendocrinology* 32, no. 5 (2007): 565–74. https://doi.org/10.1016/j.psyneuen.2007.03.011.

Dohnavur Fellowship. "Amy Carmichael (1867–1951)." March 1, 2018. https://dohnavurfellowship.org/amycarmichael/.

Doidge, Norman. *The Brain That Changes Itself: Stories of Personal Triumph from the Frontiers of Brain Science.* Penguin Books, 2007.

Doran, George T. "There's a S.M.A.R.T. Way to Write Management's Goals and Objectives." *Management Review* 70, no. 11 (1981): 35–36. https://community.mis.temple.edu/mis0855002fall2015/files/2015/10/S.M.A.R.T-Way-Management-Review.pdf.

Dostoevsky, Fyodor. *The Brothers Karamazov.* Translated by Andrew MacAndrew. Bantam Books, 1981.

Drucker, Peter F. *The Practice of Management.* Harper & Brothers, 1954.

Duckworth, Angela. *Grit: The Power of Passion and Perseverance.* Scribner, 2016.

Duckworth, Angela L., Betty Kim, and Eli Tsukayama. "Life Stress Impairs Self-Control in Early Adolescence." *Frontiers in Psychology* 3 (2013): 608. https://doi.org/10.3389/fpsyg.2012.00608.

Duckworth, Angela L., Christopher Peterson, Michael D. Matthews, and Dennis R. Kelly. "Grit: Perseverance and Passion for Long-Term Goals." *Journal of Personality and Social Psychology* 92, no. 6 (2007): 1087–101. https://doi.org/10.1037/0022-3514.92.6.1087.

Duhigg, Charles. *The Power of Habit: Why We Do What We Do in Life and Business.* Random House, 2012.

Dunbar, R. I. M. "Neocortex Size as a Constraint on Group Size in Primates." *Journal of Human Evolution* 22, no. 6 (1992): 469–93. https://doi.org/10.1016/0047-2484(92)90081-J.

Dunbar, Robin. *How Many Friends Does One Person Need? Dunbar's Number and Other Evolutionary Quirks.* Harvard University Press, 2010.

Durant, Will. *The Story of Philosophy: The Lives and Opinions of the World's Greatest Philosophers.* Simon & Schuster, 1926.

Dweck, Carol S. *Mindset: Changing the Way You Think to Fulfil Your Potential.* Rev. and updated ed. Penguin UK, 2017.

Dweck, Carol S. *Mindset: The New Psychology of Success.* Updated ed. Ballantine Books, 2016.

Dweck, Carol S. *Self-Theories: Their Role in Motivation, Personality, and Development.* Psychology Press, 2000.

Dyer, Wayne. *Everyday Wisdom*. Hay House, 2005.

East-West Ministries. "Missionary Mindset: Amy Carmichael." March 3, 2015. https://eastwest.org/blog/missionary-mindset-amy-carmichael/.

The Economic Times. "10 Executives Who Wake Up Really Early." August 30, 2014. https://economictimes.indiatimes.com/people/10-executives-who-wake-up-really-early/slideshow/41267260.cms.

Eisenhower, Dwight D. "Address at the Second Assembly of the World Council of Churches, Evanston, Illinois." The American Presidency Project. August 19, 1954. https://www.presidency.ucsb.edu/documents/address-the-second-assembly-the-world-council-churches-evanston-illinois.

Elrod, Hal. *The Miracle Morning: The Not-So-Obvious Secret Guaranteed to Transform Your Life (Before 8AM)*. Hal Elrod International, 2012.

Emerson, Ralph Waldo. *Essays: First Series*. James Munroe and Company, 1841.

Emerson, Ralph Waldo. *Self-Reliance and Other Essays*. Dover Publications, 2015.

Emmons, Robert A. "Gratitude and Well-Being." Gratitude Works. Accessed June 15, 2025. https://emmons.faculty.ucdavis.edu/gratitude-and-well-being/.

Emmons, Robert A. "Ten Ways to Become More Grateful." *Greater Good Magazine*. November 17, 2010. https://greatergood.berkeley.edu/article/item/ten_ways_to_become_more_grateful1.

Emmons, Robert A. *Thanks! How the New Science of Gratitude Can Make You Happier*. Houghton Mifflin, 2007.

Emmons, Robert A., and Teresa T. Kneezel. "Giving Thanks: Spiritual and Religious Correlates of Gratitude." *Journal of Psychology and Christianity* 24, no. 2 (2005): 140–48. https://www.psychology.hku.hk/ftbcstudies/refbase/docs/emmons/2005/57_Emmons+Kneezel2005.pdf.

Emmons, Robert A., and Michael E. McCullough. "Counting Blessings Versus Burdens: An Experimental Investigation of Gratitude and Subjective Well-Being in Daily Life." *Journal of Personality and Social Psychology* 84, no. 2 (2003): 377–89. https://doi.org/10.1037/0022-3514.84.2.377.

The Emmy Awards. "Fred Rogers Acceptance Speech." September 14, 1997. YouTube, 3:22. https://youtube.com/watch?v=Upm9LnuCBUM.

Enright, Robert D. *Forgiveness Is a Choice: A Step-by-Step Process for Resolving Anger and Restoring Hope.* American Psychological Association, 2001.

Enright, Robert D., and Richard P. Fitzgibbons. *Helping Clients Forgive: An Empirical Guide for Resolving Anger and Restoring Hope.* American Psychological Association, 2000.

Ericsson, Karl A., Ralf T. Krampe, and Clemens Tesch-Römer. "The Role of Deliberate Practice in the Acquisition of Expert Performance." *Psychological Review* 100, no. 3 (1993): 363–406. https://doi.org/10.1037/0033-295X.100.3.363.

Erikson, Erik. *Childhood and Society.* Norton & Company, 1950.

Eugenides, Jeffrey. *Middlesex.* Farrar, Straus and Giroux, 2002.

Felmlee, Diane H. "From Appealing to Appalling: Disenchantment with a Romantic Partner." *Sociological Perspectives* 44, no. 3 (2001): 263–80. https://doi.org/10.1525/sop.2001.44.3.263.

Ferriss, Tim. *The 4-Hour Workweek: Escape the 9–5, Live Anywhere and Join the New Rich.* Crown Publishers, 2007.

Festinger, Leon, Stanley Schachter, and Kurt Back. *Social Pressures in Informal Groups: A Study of Human Factors in Housing.* Stanford University Press, 1950.

Finkel, Eli J. *The All-or-Nothing Marriage: How the Best Marriages Work.* Dutton, 2017.

Fisher, Helen E. *Anatomy of Love: A Natural History of Mating, Marriage, and Why We Stray.* 2nd ed. Norton & Company, 2016.

Fisher, Helen E. "The Brain in Love." TED. February 2008. Video, 16:46. https://ted.com/talks/helen_fisher_the_brain_in_love.

Fisher, Helen E. "The Nature of Romantic Love." *The Journal of NIH Research* 6, no. 4 (1994): 59–64. https://helenfisher.com/downloads/articles/04natofrl.pdf.

Fisher, Helen E., Arthur Aron, and Lucy L. Brown. "Romantic Love: A Mammalian Brain System for Mate Choice." *Philosophical Transactions of the Royal Society B: Biological Sciences* 361, no. 1476 (2006): 2173–86. https://doi.org/10.1098/rstb.2006.1938.

Fisher, Helen E., Xiaomeng Xu, Arthur Aron, and Lucy L. Brown. "Intense, Passionate, Romantic Love: A Natural Addiction? How the Fields That Investigate Romance and Substance Abuse Can Inform Each Other." *Frontiers in Psychology* 7 (2016): 687. https://doi.org/10.3389/fpsyg.2016.00687.

Flood, Gavin. *An Introduction to Hinduism.* Cambridge University Press, 1996.

Flown. "In the Zone: The Science Behind Flow States and How to Spark Productivity." Accessed June 15, 2025. https://flown.com/blog/deep-work/in-the-zone-the-science-behind-flow-states-and-how-to-spark-productivity.

Floyd, Kory. *Communicating Affection: Interpersonal Behavior and Social Context.* Cambridge University Press, 2006.

Floyd, Kory, Colin Hesse, and Mark T. Haynes. "Human Affection Exchange: XV. Metabolic and Cardiovascular Correlates of Trait Expressed Affection." *Communication Quarterly* 55, no. 1 (2007): 79–94. https://doi.org/10.1080/01463370600998715.

Fowler, James, and Nicholas A. Christakis. "Cooperative Behavior Cascades in Human Social Networks." *Proceedings of the National Academy of Sciences* 107, no. 12 (2010): 5334–38. https://doi.org/10.1073/pnas.0913149107.

Frank, Anne. *The Diary of a Young Girl: The Definitive Edition.* Doubleday, 1995.

Frankl, Viktor E. *Man's Search for Meaning.* Beacon Press, 2006.

Franklin, Benjamin. *Poor Richard's Almanack.* 1735.

Fredrickson, Barbara L. *Positivity.* Crown Publishers, 2009.

Fredrickson, Barbara L. "The Role of Positive Emotions in Positive Psychology: The Broaden-and-Build Theory of Positive Emotions." *American Psychologist* 56, no. 3 (2001): 218–26. https://doi.org/10.1037/0003-066X.56.3.218.

Fromm, Erich. *The Art of Loving.* Harper & Row, 1956.

Gandhi, Mahatma. "General Knowledge About Health [-XXXII]: More About Mosquitoes." *The Collected Works of Mahatma Gandhi.* Indian Opinion, 1913.

Gardner, Chris. *The Pursuit of Happyness.* Amistad Press, 2006.

Gethin, Rupert. *The Foundations of Buddhism.* Oxford University Press, 1998.

Ghaemi, Nassir. *A First-Rate Madness: Uncovering the Links Between Leadership and Mental Illness.* Penguin, 2011.

Ghosh, Rajashi, and Thomas G. Reio Jr. "Career Benefits Associated with Mentoring for Mentors: A Meta-Analysis." *Journal of Vocational Behavior* 83, no. 1 (2013): 106–16. https://doi.org/10.1016/j.jvb.2013.03.011.

Gibran, Kahlil. *The Prophet*. Alfred A. Knopf, 1923.

Giddens, Anthony. *The Transformation of Intimacy: Sexuality, Love and Eroticism in Modern Societies*. Stanford University Press, 1992.

Gilbert, Elizabeth. *Eat, Pray, Love: One Woman's Search for Everything Across Italy, India and Indonesia*. Viking Press, 2006.

Girma, Haben. *Haben: The Deafblind Woman Who Conquered Harvard Law*. Twelve, 2019.

Gizzi, Chiara. "10 Howard Schultz Quotes on the Journey to Success." Fearless Motivation. March 18, 2016. https://fearlessmotivation.com/2016/03/18/howard-schultz-quotes/.

Gladwell, Malcolm. *Outliers: The Story of Success*. Little, Brown and Company, 2008.

Gleason, Steve, and Jeff Duncan. *A Life Impossible: Living with ALS: Finding Peace and Wisdom Within a Fragile Existence*. Penguin Random House, 2024.

Goggins, David. *Can't Hurt Me: Master Your Mind and Defy the Odds*. Lioncrest Publishing, 2018.

Goldin, Philippe R., Michael Ziv, Hooria Jazaieri, Kevin Hahn, Richard Heimberg, and James J. Gross. "Impact of Cognitive Behavioral Therapy for Social Anxiety Disorder on the Neural Dynamics of Cognitive Reappraisal of Negative Self-Beliefs: Randomized Clinical Trial." *JAMA Psychiatry* 70, no. 10 (2013): 1048–56. https://doi.org/10.1001/jamapsychiatry.2013.234.

Goleman, Daniel. *Emotional Intelligence*. Bantam Books, 1995.

Gollwitzer, Peter M., and Paschal Sheeran. "Implementation Intentions and Goal Achievement: A Meta-Analysis of Effects and Processes." *Advances in Experimental Social Psychology* 38 (2006): 69–119. https://doi.org/10.1016/S0065-2601(06)38002-1.

Goodall, Jane. *My Life with the Chimpanzees*. Pocket Books, 1996.

Goodell, Jeff. "Steve Jobs in 1994: The Rolling Stone Interview." *Rolling Stone*, June 16, 1994.

Gottman, John M. *The Marriage Clinic: A Scientifically Based Marital Therapy*. Norton & Company, 1999.

Gottman, John M., and Nan Silver. *The Seven Principles for Making Marriage Work*. Crown Publishers, 1999.

Granovetter, Mark S. "The Strength of Weak Ties." *American Journal of Sociology* 78, no. 6 (1973): 1360–80. https://doi.org/10.1086/225469.

Grant, Bridget F., Deborah S. Hasin, Frederick S. Stinson, Deborah A. Dawson, S. Patricia Chou, W. June Ruan, and Roger P. Pickering. "Prevalence, Correlates, and Disability of Personality Disorders in the United States: Results from the National Epidemiologic Survey on Alcohol and Related Conditions." *Journal of Clinical Psychiatry* 65, no. 7 (2004): 948–58. https://doi.org/10.4088/jcp.v65n0711.

Graybiel, Ann M. "Habits, Rituals, and the Evaluative Brain." *Annual Review of Neuroscience* 31 (2008): 359–87. https://doi.org/10.1146/annurev.neuro.29.051605.112851.

Greater New Orleans Foundation. "Greater New Orleans Foundation, Gayle and Tom Benson Charitable Foundation Announce $1.5 Million Gift to Create Disaster Relief Fund." June 12, 2024. https://gnof.org/benson-fund-announcement-pr/.

Grover, Tim S. *Relentless: From Good to Great to Unstoppable.* Scribner, 2013.

Hall, Brandon. "Drew Brees Took Mental Reps in Empty Practice Facility Day Before Record-Breaking Performance." Stack. December 18, 2019. https://stack.com/a/drew-brees-mental-reps/.

Hall, Jeffrey A. "How Many Hours Does It Take to Make a Friend?" *Journal of Social and Personal Relationships* 36, no. 4 (2018): 1278–96. https://doi.org/10.1177/0265407518761225.

Hanh, Thich Nhat. *Anger: Wisdom for Cooling the Flames.* Riverhead Books, 2001.

Hanh, Thich Nhat. *The Miracle of Mindfulness: An Introduction to the Practice of Meditation.* Beacon Press, 1987.

Hanh, Thich Nhat. *No Mud, No Lotus: The Art of Transforming Suffering.* Parallax Press, 2014.

Hanh, Thich Nhat. *Peace Is Every Step: The Path of Mindfulness in Everyday Life.* Bantam Books, 1991.

Hanh, Thich Nhat. *True Love: A Practice for Awakening the Heart.* Shambhala Publications, 2004.

Hare, Todd A., Colin F. Camerer, and Antonio Rangel. "Self-Control in Decision-Making Involves Modulation of the vmPFC Valuation System." *Science* 324, no. 5927 (2009): 646–48. https://doi.org/10.1126/science.1168450.

Harkin, Benjamin, Thomas L. Webb, Betty P. I. Chang, Andrew Prestwich, Mark Conner, Ian Kellar, Yael Benn, and Paschal Sheeran. "Does Monitoring Goal Progress Promote Goal Attainment? A Meta-Analysis of the Experimental Evidence." *Psychological Bulletin* 142, no. 2 (2016): 198–229. https://doi.org/10.1037/bul0000025.

Harvey, Peter. *An Introduction to Buddhism: Teachings, History and Practices.* 2nd ed. Cambridge University Press, 2013.

Harvey, Steve. "Make a Vision Board." The Official Steve Harvey, November 26, 2018. YouTube, 2:57. https://youtube.com/watch?v=_LBJdqTYj24.

Harvey, Steve. "Write Your Vision | Motivated +." The Official Steve Harvey, September 15, 2019. YouTube, 8:44. https://youtube.com/watch?v=DlMAIYd7-J4.

Haskins, Henry Stanley. *Meditations in Wall Street.* William Morrow & Co, 1940.

Hatfield, Elaine, and Richard L. Rapson. *Love, Sex, and Intimacy: Their Psychology, Biology, and History.* HarperCollins College Publishers, 1993.

Hayes, Stephen C., Kirk D. Strosahl, and Kelly G. Wilson. *Acceptance and Commitment Therapy: The Process and Practice of Mindful Change.* 2nd ed. Guilford Press, 2011.

Hazlitt, William. "On Prejudice." In *Sketches and Essays.* Richards, 1903.

Heckhausen, Jutta, and Carol S. Dweck, eds. *Motivation and Self-Regulation Across the Life Span.* Cambridge University Press, 1998.

Hempel, Jessi. "Satya Nadella on Growth Mindsets: 'The Learn-It-All Does Better than the Know-It-All.'" LinkedIn. December 9, 2019. https://linkedin.com/pulse/satya-nadella-growth-mindsets-learn-it-all-does-better-jessi-hempel.

Herrmann, Dorothy. *Helen Keller: A Life.* University of Chicago Press, 1998.

Hill, Napoleon. *Think and Grow Rich.* The Ralston Society, 1937.

Hiroto, Donald S., and Martin E. P. Seligman. "Generality of Learned Helplessness in Man." *Journal of Personality and Social Psychology* 31, no. 2 (1975): 311–27. https://doi.org/10.1037/h0076270.

Holt-Lunstad, Julianne, Timothy B. Smith, Mark Baker, Tyler Harris, and David Stephenson. "Loneliness and Social Isolation as Risk Factors for Mortality: A Meta-Analytic Review." *Perspectives on Psychological Science* 10, no. 2 (2015): 227–37. https://doi.org/10.1177/1745691614568352.

Holt-Lunstad, Julianne, Timothy B. Smith, and J. Bradley Layton. "Social Relationships and Mortality Risk: A Meta-Analytic Review." *PLOS Medicine* 7, no. 7 (2010): e1000316. https://doi.org/10.1371/journal.pmed.1000316.

Hölzel, Britta K., James Carmody, Mark Vangel, Christina Congleton, Sita M. Yerramsetti, Tim Gard, and Sara W. Lazar. "Mindfulness Practice Leads to Increases in Regional Brain Gray Matter Density." *Psychiatry Research: Neuroimaging* 191, no. 1 (2011): 36–43. https://doi.org/10.1016/j.pscychresns.2010.08.006.

@ariannahuff, Twitter, May 20, 2019. "Fearlessness is like a muscle. I know from my own life that the more I exercise it the more natural it becomes to not let my fears run me."

Huffington, Arianna. *Thrive: The Third Metric to Redefining Success and Creating a Life of Well-Being, Wisdom, and Wonder.* Harmony Books, 2014.

Hunt, Melissa G., Richard Marx, Courtney Lipson, and Jordyn Young. "No More FOMO: Limiting Social Media Decreases Loneliness and Depression." *Journal of Social and Clinical Psychology* 37, no. 10 (2018): 751–68. https://doi.org/10.1521/jscp.2018.37.10.751.

Hutton, Laurence. *A Boy I Knew and Four Dogs.* Harper & Brothers, 1897.

Huxley, Aldous. *Brave New World.* Doubleday, Doran & Co, 1932.

Huxley, Aldous. *Proper Studies.* Chatto & Windus, 1927.

Hyatt, Michael. *Your Best Year Ever: A 5-Step Plan for Achieving Your Most Important Goals.* Baker Publishing Group, 2018.

Integration Academy. "Surgeon General Advisory on Epidemic of Loneliness and Isolation." Agency for Healthcare Research and Quality. May 15, 2023. https://integrationacademy.ahrq.gov/news-and-events/news/surgeon-general-advisory-epidemic-loneliness-and-isolation.

Investopedia. "What Is Batch Processing? How It Works, Examples, and History." Last updated August 4, 2021. https://investopedia.com/terms/b/batch-processing.asp.

James, William. *The Principles of Psychology.* Henry Holt and Company, 1890.

Jensen, Mike. "Mental Toughness Key to Carli Lloyd's Success." *The Philadelphia Inquirer.* July 1, 2015. https://inquirer.com/philly/sports/soccer/worldcup/20150702_Carli_Lloyd_tells_The_Inquirer_how_she_stays_focused.html.

Joseph, Stephen. *What Doesn't Kill Us: The New Psychology of Posttraumatic Growth.* Basic Books, 2011.

Juran, Joseph M. *Architect of Quality: The Autobiography of Dr. Joseph M. Juran.* McGraw-Hill Education, 2004.

Juran, Joseph M. *Quality Control Handbook.* McGraw-Hill, 1951.

Kabat-Zinn, Jon. "Mindfulness-Based Interventions in Context: Past, Present, and Future." *Clinical Psychology: Science and Practice* 10, no. 2 (2003): 144–56. https://doi.org/10.1093/clipsy.bpg016.

Kaufman, Scott Barry. "Self-Actualizing People in the 21st Century: Integration with Contemporary Theory and Research on Personality and Well-Being." *Journal of Humanistic Psychology* 58, no. 4 (2018): 400–19. https://doi.org/10.1177/0022167818809187.

Kaur, Rupi. *Milk and Honey.* Andrews McMeel Publishing, 2015.

Kaur, Rupi. *The Sun and Her Flowers.* Andrews McMeel Publishing, 2017.

Keller, Helen. *Optimism: An Essay.* T. Crowell and Company, 1903.

Kendler, Kenneth S., Xiao-Qing Liu, Charles O. Gardner, Michael E. McCullough, David Larson, and Carol A. Prescott. "Dimensions of Religiosity and Their Relationship to Lifetime Psychiatric and Substance Use Disorders." *American Journal of Psychiatry* 160, no. 3 (2003): 496–503. https://doi.org/10.1176/appi.ajp.160.3.496.

Keng, Shian-Ling, Maria J. Smoski, and Clive J. Robins. "Effects of Mindfulness on Psychological Health: A Review of Empirical Studies." *Clinical Psychology Review* 31, no. 6 (2011): 1041–56. https://doi.org/10.1016/j.cpr.2011.04.006.

Kierkegaard, Søren. *Concluding Unscientific Postscript to Philosophical Fragments.* Translated by Howard V. Hong and Edna H. Hong. Princeton University Press, 1992.

King, Charlie. "Yvon Chouinard: The Founder of Patagonia." *Sustainability Magazine.* October 4, 2024. https://sustainabilitymag.com/articles/yvon-chouinard-the-founder-of-patagonia.

King, Martin Luther, Jr. "Remaining Awake Through a Great Revolution." Commencement address at Oberlin College, June 14, 1965.

King, Martin Luther, Jr. *Strength to Love.* Harper & Row, 1963.

Kini, Prathik, Joel Wong, Sydney McInnis, Nicole Gabana, and Joshua W. Brown. "The Effects of Gratitude Expression on Neural Activity." *NeuroImage* 128 (2017): 1–10. https://doi.org/10.1016/j.neuroimage.2015.12.040.

Kipchoge, Eliud. *No Human Is Limited: A Memoir by the Fastest Marathoner of All Time*. Gallery Books, 2020.

Kirby, James N., James R. Doty, Nicola Petrocchi, and Paul Gilbert. "The Current and Future Role of Heart Rate Variability for Assessing and Training Compassion." *Frontiers in Public Health* 5 (2017): 40. https://doi.org/10.3389/fpubh.2017.00040.

Klimecki, Olga M., Susanne Leiberg, Matthieu Ricard, and Tania Singer. "Differential Pattern of Functional Brain Plasticity After Compassion and Empathy Training." *Social Cognitive and Affective Neuroscience* 9, no. 6 (2014): 873–79. https://doi.org/10.1093/scan/nst060.

Kluger, Jeffrey. *The Sibling Effect: What the Bonds Among Brothers and Sisters Reveal About Us*. Riverhead Books, 2011.

Koenig, Harold G. "Research on Religion, Spirituality, and Mental Health: A Review." *The Canadian Journal of Psychiatry* 54, no. 5 (2009): 283–91. https://doi.org/10.1177/070674370905400502.

Kramer, Laurie. "The Essential Ingredients of Successful Sibling Relationships: An Emerging Framework for Advancing Theory and Practice." *Child Development Perspectives* 4, no. 2 (2010): 80–86. https://doi.org/10.1111/j.1750-8606.2010.00122.x.

Kübler-Ross, Elisabeth. *On Death and Dying*. Macmillan, 1969.

Kübler-Ross, Elisabeth, and David Kessler. *On Grief and Grieving: Finding the Meaning of Grief Through the Five Stages of Loss*. Scribner, 2005.

Kulu, Hill. "Marriage Duration and Divorce: The Seven-Year Itch or a Lifelong Itch?" *Demography* 51, no. 3 (2014): 881–93. https://doi.org/10.1007/s13524-013-0278-1.

Kundera, Milan. *The Unbearable Lightness of Being*. Harper & Row, 1984.

La Fontaine, Jean de. *The Complete Fables of Jean de La Fontaine*. Translated by Norman R. Shapiro. University of Illinois Press, 2007.

Lally, Phillippa, Cornelia H. M. van Jaarsveld, Henry W. W. Potts, and Jane Wardle. "How Are Habits Formed: Modelling Habit Formation in the Real World." *European Journal of Social Psychology* 40, no. 6 (2010): 998–1009. https://doi.org/10.1002/ejsp.674.

Lamott, Anne. *Hallelujah Anyway: Rediscovering Mercy*. Riverhead Books, 2017.

Lerner, Harriet Goldhor. *The Dance of Anger: A Woman's Guide to Changing the Patterns of Intimate Relationships*. Harper Perennial, 1998.

Lewis, C. S. *The Four Loves*. Harcourt, 1960.

Lewis, C. S. *A Grief Observed*. Faber and Faber, 1961.

Lewis, C. S. *The Problem of Pain*. HarperOne, 1940.

Li, Chenyang. *The Confucian Philosophy of Harmony*. Routledge, 2014.

Li, Qing. *Forest Bathing: How Trees Can Help You Find Health and Happiness*. Viking, 2018.

Ligonier Ministries. "Who Was Amy Carmichael?" January 30, 2023. https://learn.ligonier.org/articles/missionary-amy-carmichael.

Litman, Laken. "Carli Lloyd Had a Vision She'd Score Four Goals in the World Cup Final." *USA Today*. July 6, 2015. https://ftw.usatoday.com/2015/07/carli-lloyd-had-a-vision-shed-score-four-goals-in-the-world-cup-final.

Locke, Edwin A., and Gary P. Latham. *New Developments in Goal Setting and Task Performance*. Routledge, 2013. https://doi.org/10.4324/9780203082744.

Locke, Edwin A., and Gary P. Latham. "Building a Practically Useful Theory of Goal Setting and Task Motivation: A 35-Year Odyssey." *American Psychologist* 57, no. 9 (2002): 705–17. https://doi.org/10.1037/0003-066X.57.9.705.

Locke, John. *Some Thoughts Concerning Education*. London, 1693.

Lorde, Audre. *Sister Outsider: Essays and Speeches*. Crossing Press, 1984.

Lustig, Robert. *The Hacking of the American Mind: The Science Behind the Corporate Takeover of Our Bodies and Brains*. Avery, 2017.

Lyubomirsky, Sonja. *The How of Happiness: A Scientific Approach to Getting the Life You Want*. Penguin Press, 2007.

Lyubomirsky, Sonja, Kennon M. Sheldon, and David Schkade. "Pursuing Happiness: The Architecture of Sustainable Change." *Review of General Psychology* 9, no. 2 (2005): 111–31. https://doi.org/10.1037/1089-2680.9.2.111.

Maathai, Wangari. *Unbowed: A Memoir*. William Heinemann, 2007.

Maestripieri, Dario, Nicole M. Baran, Paola Sapienza, and Luigi Zingales. "Between- and Within-Sex Variations in Hormonal Responses to Psychological Stress in a Large Sample of College Students." *Stress* 13, no. 5 (2010): 413–24. https://doi.org/10.3109/10253891003681137.

Manning, Brennan. *All Is Grace: A Ragamuffin Memoir*. David C Cook, 2011.

Månsson, Kristoffer N. T., Alireza Salami, Andreas Frick, Per Carlbring, Gerhard Andersson, Tomas Furmark, and C. J. Boraxbekk. "Neuroplasticity in Response to Cognitive Behavior Therapy for Social Anxiety Disorder." *Translational Psychiatry* 6, no. 2 (2016): e727. https://doi.org/10.1038/tp.2015.218.

The Marketing Society. "Habit Formation—an Inside Out Understanding." Accessed June 15, 2025. https://marketingsociety.com/the-gym/habit-formation-inside-out-understanding.

Martins, Alexandra, Nelson Ramalho, and Estelle Morin. "A Comprehensive Meta-Analysis of the Relationship Between Emotional Intelligence and Health." *Personality and Individual Differences* 49, no. 6 (2010): 554–64. https://doi.org/10.1016/j.paid.2010.05.029.

Maslow, Abraham. "A Theory of Human Motivation." *Psychological Review* 50, no. 4 (1943): 370–96. https://doi.org/10.1037/h0054346.

Maslow, Abraham. *Toward a Psychology of Being*. 2nd ed. Van Nostrand Reinhold, 1968.

Matthews, Gail. "Goals Research Summary." Presentation at the Ninth Annual International Conference of the Psychology Research Unit of Athens Institute for Education and Research (ATINER), San Rafael, CA, May 2015. https://dominican.edu/sites/default/files/2020-02/gailmatthews-harvard-goals-researchsummary.pdf.

Mauss, Iris B., Maya Tamir, Craig L. Anderson, and Nicole S. Savino. "Can Seeking Happiness Make People Unhappy? Paradoxical Effects of Valuing Happiness." *Emotion* 11, no. 4 (2011): 807–15. https://doi.org/10.1037/a0022010.

Mayer, John D., Peter Salovey, and David R. Caruso. "Emotional Intelligence: Theory, Findings, and Implications." *Psychological Inquiry* 15, no. 3 (2004): 197–215. https://doi.org/10.1207/s15327965pli1503_02.

McAdams, Dan P. "The Psychology of Life Stories." *Review of General Psychology* 5, no. 2 (2001): 100–22. https://doi.org/10.1037/1089-2680.5.2.100.

McAdams, Dan P., Ed de St. Aubin, and Regina L. Logan. "Generativity Among Young, Midlife, and Older Adults." *Psychology and Aging* 8, no. 2 (1993): 221–30. https://doi.org/10.1037/0882-7974.8.2.221.

McConaughey, Matthew. *Greenlights*. Crown Publishing Group, 2020.

McGonigal, Kelly. *The Upside of Stress: Why Stress Is Good for You, and How to Get Good at It*. Avery, 2015.

McAdams, Dan P. "The Psychology of Life Stories." *Review of General Psychology* 5, no. 2 (2001): 100–22. https://doi.org/10.1037/1089-2680.5.2.100.

Miraglia, Mariella, and Gary Johns. "Going to Work Ill: A Meta-Analysis of the Correlates of Presenteeism and a Dual-Path Model." *Journal of Occupational Health Psychology* 21, no. 3 (2016): 261–83. https://doi.org/10.1037/ocp0000015.

Mitchell, Margaret. *Gone with the Wind*. Pan Books, 2014.

Möhler, Hanns. "The GABA System in Anxiety and Depression and Its Therapeutic Potential." *Neuropharmacology* 62, no. 1 (2012): 42–53. https://doi.org/10.1016/j.neuropharm.2011.08.040.

Mollenhorst, Gerald, Beate Völker, and Henk Flap. "Changes in Personal Relationships: How Social Contexts Affect the Emergence and Discontinuation of Relationships." *Social Networks* 37 (2014): 65–80. https://doi.org/10.1016/j.socnet.2013.12.003.

Mother Teresa. *A Simple Path*. Ballantine Books, 1995.

Muennig, Peter A., Megan Reynolds, David S. Fink, Zafar Zafari, and Arline T. Geronimus. "America's Declining Well-Being, Health, and Life Expectancy: Not Just a White Problem." *American Journal of Public Health* 108, no. 12 (2018): 1626–31. https://doi.org/10.2105/AJPH.2018.304585.

Muir, John. *Nature Writings*. Edited by William Cronon. Library of America, 1998.

Mundy, Liza. "Q & A." Accessed June 15, 2025. https://lizamundy.com/michelle/q-a/.

Murray, J. "Carmichael, Amy Beatrice." In *Biographical Dictionary of Christian Missions*, edited by Gerald H. Anderson. Macmillan Reference USA, 1998.

Murthy, Vivek. *Together: The Healing Power of Human Connection in a Sometimes Lonely World*. Harper Wave, 2020.

Mylett, Ed. *#Maxout Your Life: Strategies for Becoming an Elite Performer*. Published by the author, 2020.

Mylett, Ed. *The Power of One More: The Ultimate Guide to Happiness and Success*. Wiley, 2022.

Nadella, Satya. *Hit Refresh: The Quest to Rediscover Microsoft's Soul and Imagine a Better Future for Everyone*. HarperBusiness, 2017.

Nakamura, Jeanne, and Mihaly Csikszentmihalyi. "Flow Theory and Research." In *Oxford Handbook of Positive Psychology*, edited by C. R. Snyder and Shane J. Lopez. Oxford University Press, 2009.

Nasr, Seyyed. *Islam: Religion, History, and Civilization*. HarperOne, 2003.

National Institute of Mental Health. "Depression." Last reviewed December 2024. https://nimh.nih.gov/health/topics/depression.

National Park Service. "Harriet Tubman and the Underground Railroad." March 11, 2017. https://nps.gov/articles/harriet-tubman-and-the-underground-railroad.htm.

National Science Foundation. "Exploring the Brain's Relationship to Habits." January 14, 2013. https://new.nsf.gov/news/exploring-brains-relationship-habits.

Neff, Kristin D. "The Development and Validation of a Scale to Measure Self-Compassion." *Self and Identity* 2, no. 3 (2003): 223–50. https://doi.org/10.1080/15298860309027.

Neff, Kristin. *Self-Compassion: The Proven Power of Being Kind to Yourself*. William Morrow, 2011.

Nelson, Shasta. *Frientimacy: How to Deepen Friendships for Lifelong Health and Happiness*. Seal Press, 2016.

Neruda, Pablo. "One Hundred Love Sonnets: XVII." In *The Essential Neruda: Selected Poems*, edited by Mark Eisner. City Lights Books, 2004.

Newport, Cal. *Deep Work: Rules for Focused Success in a Distracted World*. Grand Central Publishing, 2016.

Nichols, Lisa. *Abundance Now: Amplify Your Life & Achieve Prosperity Today*. HarperCollins, 2016.

Nichols, Lisa. "Everything Happens for a Reason." Motivating the Masses. July 17, 2020. https://motivatingthemasses.com/everything-happens-for-a-reason/.

Nichols, Lisa. *Living Proof: Celebrating the Gifts That Came Wrapped in Sandpaper*. Amber Books Publishing, 2004.

Nichols, Lisa. *No Matter What! 9 Steps to Living the Life You Love*. Grand Central Publishing, 2009.

Nietzsche, Friedrich. *On the Genealogy of Morals*. Translated by Walter Kaufmann. 1967.

Nightingale, Earl. *The Strangest Secret*. Merchant Books, 2013.

Nooyi, Indra. *My Life in Full: Work, Family and Our Future*. Portfolio/Penguin, 2021.

Nyad, Diana. *Find a Way: The Inspiring Story of One Woman's Pursuit of a Lifelong Dream*. Knopf, 2015.

Obama, Michelle. *Becoming*. Crown Publishing Group, 2018.

Obama White House Archives. "International Women's Day: Women Who Inspire Our Work." March 8, 2016. https://obamawhitehouse.archives.gov/blog/2016/03/08/international-womens-day-3-women-who-inspire-us.

Office of the Surgeon General. *Our Epidemic of Loneliness and Isolation: The U.S. Surgeon General's Advisory on the Healing Effects of Social Connection and Community*. US Department of Health and Human Services, 2023.

Online Etymology Dictionary. "Must." Accessed June 15, 2025. https://etymonline.com/word/must.

Oracle. "Global Study: 70% of Business Leaders Would Prefer a Robot to Make Their Decisions." News release, April 19, 2023. https://prnewswire.com/news-releases/global-study-70-of-business-leaders-would-prefer-a-robot-to-make-their-decisions-301799591.html.

Oravecz, Zita, Jessica Dirsmith, Saeideh Heshmati, Joachim Vandekerckhove, and Timothy R. Brick. "Psychological Well-Being and Personality Traits Are Associated with Experiencing Love in Everyday Life." *Personality and Individual Differences* 153 (2020): 109620. https://doi.org/10.1016/j.paid.2019.109620.

Pangambam, Sendash. "Full Transcript: Esther Perel on Modern Love and Relationships at SXSW 2018." January 28, 2019. https://singjupost.com/full-transcript-esther-perel-on-modern-love-and-relationships-at-sxsw-2018/.

Pareto, Vilfredo. *Cours d'économie politique*. Droz, Geneva, 1896.

Park, Irene J. K., Lijuan Wang, David R. Williams, and Margarita Alegría. "Coping with Racism: Moderators of the Discrimination—Adjustment Link Among Mexican-Origin Adolescents." *Child Development* 88, no. 3 (2017): 854–70. https://doi.org/10.1111/cdev.12856.

Parkinson, C. Northcote. "Parkinson's Law." *The Economist*, November 19, 1955. https://www.economist.com/news/1955/11/19/parkinsons-law.

Touroutoglou, A., Andreano, J., Dickerson, B. C., & Barrett, L. F. "The Tenacious Brain: How the Anterior Mid-Cingulate Contributes to Achieving Goals." Cortex 123 (2020): 12–29. https://doi.org/10.1016/j.cortex.2019.09.011

Patzelt, Edward H., Wouter Kool, Alexander J. Millner, and Samuel J. Gershman. "The Transdiagnostic Structure of Mental Effort Avoidance." *Scientific Reports* 9, no. 1 (2019): 1689. https://doi.org/10.1038/s41598-018-37802-1.

Peale, Norman Vincent. *The Power of Positive Thinking*. Prentice-Hall, 1952.

Peña, Michael. "Steve Jobs to 2005 Graduates: 'Stay Hungry, Stay Foolish.'" Stanford Report. June 12, 2005. https://news.stanford.edu/2005/06/14/jobs-061505/.

Perry, Bruce D., and Oprah Winfrey. *What Happened to You? Conversations on Trauma, Resilience, and Healing*. Flatiron Books, 2021.

Perry, Ralph Barton, ed. *The Thought and Character of William James*. Little, Brown and Company, 1935.

Pew Research Center. "Religion in Marriages and Families." October 26, 2016. https://pewresearch.org/religion/2016/10/26/religion-in-marriages-and-families/.

Pichère, Pierre, and Anne-Christine Cadiat. *Maslow's Hierarchy of Needs*. Lemaitre, 2015.

Pierce, Wendell. "Interview with Wendell Pierce, Part Two: Treme, New Orleans, and Chef Culture." Interview by Maggie Borden. James Beard Foundation, October 7, 2014. http://jamesbeard.org/stories/interview-with-wendell-pierce-part-two-treme-new-orleans-and-chef-culture.

Pike, Alison, Joanne Coldwell, and Judith F. Dunn. "Sibling Relationships in Early/Middle Childhood: Links with Individual Adjustment." *Journal of Family Psychology* 19, no. 4 (2005): 523–32. https://doi.org/10.1037/0893-3200.19.4.523.

Pillemer, Karl, J. Jill Suitor, Seth Pardo, and Charles Henderson Jr. "Mothers' Differentiation and Depressive Symptoms Among Adult Children." *Journal of Marriage and Family* 82, no. 3 (2020): 957–70. https://doi.org/10.1111/j.1741-3737.2010.00703.x.

Pipher, Mary. *Another Country: Navigating the Emotional Terrain of Our Elders*. Riverhead Books, 1999.

Poirier-Leroy, Olivier. "How Michael Phelps Used Visualization to Stay Calm Under Pressure." YourSwimLog. Accessed June 15, 2025. https://yourswimlog.com/michael-phelps-visualization/.

Pollack, Pam, and Meg Belviso. *Who Is J. K. Rowling?* Grosset & Dunlap, 2012.

Pooley, Eric. "Grins, Gore, and Videotape: The Trouble with Local TV News." *New York Magazine*, October 9, 1989.

Porto, Patricia Ribeiro, Leticia Oliveira, Jair Mari, Elaine Volchan, Ivan Figueira, and Paula Ventura. "Does Cognitive Behavioral Therapy Change the Brain? A Systematic Review of Neuroimaging in Anxiety Disorders." *The Journal of Neuropsychiatry and Clinical Neurosciences* 21, no. 2 (2009): 114–25. https://doi.org/10.1176/jnp.2009.21.2.114.

Post, Stephen G. "Altruism, Happiness, and Health: It's Good to Be Good." *International Journal of Behavioral Medicine* 12, no. 2 (2005): 66–77. https://doi.org/10.1207/s15327558ijbm1202_4.

Prevailing Intercessory Prayer. "Amy Carmichael: Missionary in India." Accessed June 15, 2025. https://path2prayer.com/famous-missionaries/amy-carmichael-missionary-in-india.

Raeburn, Paul. *Do Fathers Matter? What Science Is Telling Us About the Parent We've Overlooked.* Scientific American/Farrar, Straus and Giroux, 2014.

Randler, Christoph. "Defend Your Research: The Early Bird Really Does Get the Worm." *Harvard Business Review* 88, nos. 7–8 (2010): 30–31. https://hbr.org/2010/07/defend-your-research-the-early-bird-really-does-get-the-worm.

Ricard, Matthieu. *Happiness: A Guide to Developing Life's Most Important Skill.* Little, Brown and Company, 2007.

Robbins, Mel. *The 5 Second Rule: Transform Your Life, Work, and Confidence with Everyday Courage.* Savio Republic, 2017.

Robbins, Mel. *The High 5 Habit: Take Control of Your Life with One Simple Habit.* Hay House, 2021.

Robbins, Mel. *The Let Them Theory: A Life-Changing Tool That Millions of People Can't Stop Talking About.* Hay House, 2024.

Robbins, Mel. *Stop Saying You're Fine: Discover a More Powerful You.* Harmony, 2011.

Robbins, Tony. *Awaken the Giant Within: How to Take Immediate Control of Your Mental, Emotional, Physical & Financial Destiny!* Simon & Schuster, 1992.

@TonyRobbins, Twitter, October 2, 2023. "The quality of your life is in direct proportion to the amount of uncertainty you can comfortably live with." https://twitter.com/TonyRobbins/status/1708894288988532816.

@TonyRobbins, Twitter, June 13, 2022. "Where focus goes, energy flows. And where energy flows, whatever you're focusing on grows. In other words, your life is controlled by what you focus on. That's why you need to focus on where you want to go, not on what you fear." https://twitter.com/TonyRobbins/status/1536370847555809281.

Robbins, Tony. *Unlimited Power: The New Science of Personal Achievement.* Free Press, 1997.

@TonyRobbins, Twitter, August 28, 2015. "Whatever you hold in your mind on a consistent basis is exactly what you will experience in your life." Twitter, August 28, 2015. https://x.com/TonyRobbins/status/637266065391681536.

Robinson, Ken. *The Element.* Viking, 2009.

Rogers, Carl R. *Freedom to Learn.* Charles E. Merrill Publishing Company, 1969.

Rogers, Carl R. *On Becoming a Person: A Therapist's View of Psychotherapy.* Houghton Mifflin, 1995.

Rogers, Fred. *The World According to Mister Rogers: Important Things to Remember.* Hyperion, 2003.

Rohner, Ronald P. "The Parental 'Acceptance-Rejection Syndrome': Universal Correlates of Perceived Rejection." *American Psychologist* 59, no. 8 (2004): 830–40. https://doi.org/10.1037/0003-066X.59.8.830.

Rohr, Richard. *The Universal Christ: How a Forgotten Reality Can Change Everything We See, Hope for, and Believe.* Convergent Books, 2019.

Roosevelt, Theodore. "Address at the Sorbonne in Paris, France: 'Citizenship in a Republic.'" The American Presidency Project. April 23, 1910. https://www.presidency.ucsb.edu/documents/address-the-sorbonne-paris-france-citizenship-republic.

Rowling, J. K. *Harry Potter and the Philosopher's Stone.* Bloomsbury Publishing, 1997.

Rowling, J. K. "The Fringe Benefits of Failure, and the Importance of Imagination." Commencement speech, Harvard University, 2008.

Rusbult, Caryl E. "Commitment and Satisfaction in Romantic Associations: A Test of the Investment Model." *Journal of Experimental Social Psychology* 16, no. 2 (1980): 172–86. https://doi.org/10.1016/0022-1031(80)90007-4.

Rushton, Cynda. *Moral Resilience: Transforming Moral Suffering in Healthcare.* Oxford University Press, 2018.

Ryan, Richard M., and Edward L. Deci. "Self-Determination Theory and the Facilitation of Intrinsic Motivation, Social Development, and Well-Being." *American Psychologist* 55, no. 1 (2000): 68–78. https://doi.org/10.1037/0003-066X.55.1.68.

Sacks, Jonathan. *The Koren Siddur*. Koren Publishers Jerusalem, 2009.

Salovey, Peter, and John D. Mayer. "Emotional Intelligence." *Imagination, Cognition and Personality* 9, no. 3 (1990): 185–211. https://doi.org/10.2190/DUGG-P24E-52WK-6CDG.

San Diego Air & Space Museum. "The Wright Brothers." Accessed June 15, 2025. https://sandiegoairandspace.org/hall-of-fame/honoree/the-wright-brothers.

Satir, Virginia. *The New Peoplemaking*. Science and Behavior Books, 1988.

Schwartz, Allan. "The Psychological Importance of Gratitude and Gratefulness." Mental Health. November 26, 2013. https://mentalhealth.com/library/the-psychological-importance-of-gratitude-and-gratefulness.

Seligman, Martin E. P. *Flourish: A Visionary New Understanding of Happiness and Well-Being*. Free Press, 2011.

Seligman, Martin E. P., and Steven F. Maier. "Failure to Escape Traumatic Shock." *Journal of Experimental Psychology* 74, no. 1 (1967): 1–9. https://doi.org/10.1037/h0024514.

Seligman, Martin E., Tracy A. Steen, Nansook Park, and Christopher Peterson. "Positive Psychology Progress: Empirical Validation of Interventions." *American Psychologist* 60, no. 5 (2005): 410–21. https://doi.org/10.1037/0003-066X.60.5.410.

Semmelweis, Ignaz. *The Etiology, Concept, and Prophylaxis of Childbed Fever*. Translated by K. Codell Carter. University of Wisconsin Press, 1983.

Shetty, Jay. *8 Rules of Love: How to Find It, Keep It, and Let It Go*. Simon & Schuster, 2023.

Shetty, Jay. *Think like a Monk: Train Your Mind for Peace and Purpose Every Day*. Simon & Schuster, 2020.

Sinek, Simon. *Start with Why: How Great Leaders Inspire Everyone to Take Action*. Portfolio, 2009.

Singer, Michael Alan. *The Untethered Soul: The Journey Beyond Yourself*. New Harbinger Publications, 2007.

Singer, Tania, and Olga M. Klimecki. "Empathy and Compassion." *Current Biology* 24, no. 18 (2014): R875–78. https://doi.org/10.1016/j.cub.2014.06.054.

Shakespeare, William. *Measure for Measure.* Arden Shakespeare. 2006.

Shakespeare, William. *A Midsummer Night's Dream.* Dover Publications, 1994.

Shakespeare, William. "Sonnet 116." In *Shakespeare's Sonnets.* Washington Square Press, 1997.

Skinner, B. F. *The Behavior of Organisms: An Experimental Analysis.* Appleton-Century, 1938.

Soble, Alan. *Eros, Agape, and Philia: Readings in the Philosophy of Love.* Paragon House, 1989.

Soccer Psychology Tips. "How Carli Lloyd's Pregame Preparation Leads to Success." Accessed March 5, 2024. https://soccerpsychologytips.com/2020/how-carli-lloyds-pregame-preparation-leads-to-success/.

Song, Mengli, Michael S. Garet, Rui Yang, and Drew Atchison. "Did States' Adoption of More Rigorous Standards Lead to Improved Student Achievement? Evidence from a Comparative Interrupted Time Series Study of Standards-Based Reform." *American Educational Research Journal* 59, no. 3 (2024): 610–47. https://doi.org/10.3102/00028312211058460

Southwick, Steven M., and Dennis S. Charney. "The Science of Resilience: Implications for the Prevention and Treatment of Depression." *Science* 338, no. 6103 (2012): 79–82. https://doi.org/10.1126/science.1222942.

Corliss, Richard. "Show Business: I Dream for a Living: Steven Spielberg, the Prince of Hollywood, Is Still a Little Boy at Heart." *Time.* July 15, 1985. https://time.com/archive/6704465/show-business-i-dream-for-a-living/.

Sprecher, Susan. "Sexual Satisfaction in Premarital Relationships: Associations with Satisfaction, Love, Commitment, and Stability." *Journal of Sex Research* 39, no. 3 (2002): 190–96. https://doi.org/10.1080/00224490209552141.

Sprecher, Susan, Stanislav Treger, and Joshua D. Wondra. "Effects of Self-Disclosure Role on Liking, Closeness, and Other Impressions in Get-Acquainted Interactions." *Journal of Social and Personal Relationships* 30, no. 4 (2013): 497–514. https://doi.org/10.1177/0265407512459033.

Steptoe, Andrew, Aparna Shankar, Panayotes Demakakos, and Jane Wardle. "Social Isolation, Loneliness, and All-Cause Mortality in Older Men and Women." *Proceedings of the National Academy of Sciences* 110, no. 15 (2013): 5797–801. https://doi.org/10.1073/pnas.1219686110.

Sternberg, Robert J. *The Triangle of Love: Intimacy, Passion, Commitment.* Basic Books, 1988.

Sternberg, Robert J. "A Triangular Theory of Love." *Psychological Review* 93, no. 2 (1986): 119–35. https://doi.org/10.1037/0033-295X.93.2.119.

Stoker, Bram. *Dracula*. Archibald Constable and Company, 1897.

Strategies for Influence. "Stephen Covey—Habits of Highly Effective People." Accessed June 15, 2025. https://strategiesforinfluence.com/stephen-covey-coaching-tips/.

Szyf, Moshe. "The Early Life Environment and the Epigenome." *Biochimica et Biophysica Acta (BBA)—General Subjects* 1790, no. 9 (2009): 878–85. https://doi.org/10.1016/j.bbagen.2009.01.009.

Tang, Yi-Yuan, Britta K. Hölzel, and Michael I. Posner. "The Neuroscience of Mindfulness Meditation." *Nature Reviews Neuroscience* 16, no. 4 (2015): 213–25. https://doi.org/10.1038/nrn3916.

Tashiro, Ty. *The Science of Happily Ever After: What Really Matters in the Quest for Enduring Love*. Harlequin, 2014.

Tedeschi, Richard G., and Lawrence G. Calhoun. "Posttraumatic Growth: Conceptual Foundations and Empirical Evidence." *Psychological Inquiry* 15, no. 1 (2004): 1–18. https://doi.org/10.1207/s15327965pli1501_01.

Tedeschi, Richard G., and Lawrence G. Calhoun. "The Posttraumatic Growth Inventory: Measuring the Positive Legacy of Trauma." *Journal of Traumatic Stress* 9, no. 3 (1996): 455–71. https://doi.org/10.1002/jts.2490090305.

Teilhard de Chardin, Pierre. *Activation of Energy: Enlightening Reflections on Spiritual Energy*. Harcourt, 1968.

Teilhard de Chardin, Pierre. *The Phenomenon of Man*. Harper & Row, 1959.

Tolle, Eckhart. *A New Earth: Awakening to Your Life's Purpose*. Dutton, 2005.

Tracy, Brian. *Eat That Frog! 21 Great Ways to Stop Procrastinating and Get More Done in Less Time*. 3rd ed. Berrett-Koehler Publishers, 2017.

Tracy, Brian. *Goals! How to Get Everything You Want—Faster than You Ever Thought Possible*. 3rd ed. Berrett-Koehler Publishers, 2024.

Tracy, Brian. *Maximum Achievement: Strategies and Skills That Will Unlock Your Hidden Powers to Succeed*. Simon & Schuster, 1993.

Tracy, Brian. *No Excuses! The Power of Self-Discipline*. Vanguard Press, 2010.

Tracy, Brian. *The Psychology of Selling: Increase Your Sales Faster and Easier than You Ever Thought Possible.* Thomas Nelson, 2004.

Trafecante, Kate. "Patagonia's Founder Transfers Ownership into Two Entities to Help Fight the Climate Crisis." CNN Business. September 14, 2022. https://cnn.com/2022/09/14/business/patagonia-ownership/index.html.

Treadway, Michael T., Joshua W. Buckholtz, Ronald L. Cowan, Neil D. Woodward, Rui Li, M. Sib Ansari, Ronald M. Baldwin, Ashley N. Schwartzman, Robert M. Kessler, and David H. Zald. "Dopaminergic Mechanisms of Individual Differences in Human Effort-Based Decision-Making." *Journal of Neuroscience* 32, no. 18 (2012): 6170–76. https://doi.org/10.1523/JNEUROSCI.6459-11.2012.

Tremaine, Leigh. "A Meditation to Find Your True Self." Accessed January 4, 2025. https://leightremaine.com/meditation-to-find-your-true-self/.

Turkle, Sherry. *Alone Together: Why We Expect More from Technology and Less from Each Other.* Basic Books, 2011.

Tutu, Desmond. *No Future Without Forgiveness.* Doubleday, 1999.

Underwood, Lynn G. "Compassionate Love: A Framework for Research." In *The Science of Compassionate Love: Theory, Research, and Applications*, edited by Beverley Fehr, Susan Sprecher, and Lynn G. Underwood. Wiley-Blackwell, 2009.

University of New Orleans. "In Memoriam: Ellis Marsalis, New Orleans Musical Patriarch and UNO Emeritus." April 2, 2020. https://uno.edu/news/2020-04-02/in-memoriam-ellis-marsalis-new-orleans-musical-patriarch-and-uno-emeritus-0.

University of West Alabama. "Why We Physically Feel Fear." UWA Online. June 21, 2019. https://online.uwa.edu/news/what-causes-fear/.

Vermont Business Magazine. "Award-Winning CEO Todd Graves' Message to Business Owners: Find Your 'One Love' and Stay True to It." September 8, 2021. https://vermontbiz.com/news/2021/september/08/award-winning-ceo-todd-graves-message-business-owners-find-your-one-love-and.

Vujicic, Nick. *Life Without Limits: Inspiration for a Ridiculously Good Life.* Doubleday, 2010.

Wahl, Grant. "Carli Lloyd Turns in Women's World Cup Final Performance for the Ages." *Sports Illustrated.* July 6, 2015. https://si.com/soccer/2015/07/06/carli-lloyd-usa-japan-womens-world-cup-final.

Waldinger, Robert J., and Marc S. Schulz. *The Good Life: Lessons from the World's Longest Scientific Study of Happiness.* Simon & Schuster, 2023.

Waldinger, Robert J., and Marc S. Schulz. "What's Love Got to Do with It? Social Functioning, Perceived Health, and Daily Happiness in Married Octogenarians." *Psychology and Aging* 25, no. 2 (2010): 422–31. https://doi.org/10.1037/a0019087.

Walsch, Neale Donald. *Conversations with God*. G. P. Putnam's Sons, 1995.

Walsh, Froma. *Strengthening Family Resilience*. 3rd ed. Guilford Press, 2015.

Walster, Elaine, Vera Aronson, Darcy Abrahams, and Leon Rottman. "Importance of Physical Attractiveness in Dating Behavior." *Journal of Personality and Social Psychology* 4, no. 5 (1966): 508–16. https://doi.org/10.1037/h0021188.

Walther, Joseph B. "Computer-Mediated Communication: Impersonal, Interpersonal, and Hyperpersonal Interaction." *Communication Research* 23, no. 1 (1996): 3–43. https://doi.org/10.1177/009365096023001001.

Watkinson, W. L. *The Supreme Conquest, and Other Sermons Preached in America*. Fleming Revell Company, 1907.

Weiner, Aaron S. B., and James W. Hannum. "Differences in the Quantity of Social Support Between Geographically Close and Long-Distance Friendships." *Journal of Social and Personal Relationships* 30, no. 5 (2013): 662–72. https://doi.org/10.1177/0265407512465997.

Werner, Emmy E. "Risk, Resilience, and Recovery: Perspectives from the Kauai Longitudinal Study." *Development and Psychopathology* 5, no. 4 (1993): 503–15. https://doi.org/10.1017/S095457940000612X.

White, Alasdair. *From Comfort Zone to Performance Management*. White & MacLean Publishing, 2009.

White, Timothy. *Catch a Fire: The Life of Bob Marley*. Holt Paperbacks, 1992.

Williamson, Marianne. *A Return to Love: Reflections on the Principles of "A Course in Miracles."* HarperCollins, 1992.

Willink, Jocko, and Leif Babin. *Extreme Ownership: How U.S. Navy SEALs Lead and Win*. St. Martin's Press, 2015.

"Daily Affirmations with Stuart Smalley." *Saturday Night Live*. Aired February 9, 1991, on NBC.

Winfrey, Oprah. *Food, Health, and Happiness: 115 On-Point Recipes for Great Meals and a Better Life*. Macmillan, 2017.

Winfrey, Oprah. *Journey to Beloved*. Hyperion, 1998.

Winfrey, Oprah. "Oprah Winfrey's Commencement Address." Wellesley College, May 30, 1997. https://www1.wellesley.edu/events/commencement/archives/1997commencement/commencementaddress.

Winfrey, Oprah. *The Path Made Clear: Discovering Your Life's Direction and Purpose*. Flatiron Books, 2019.

Winfrey, Oprah. *The Uncommon Wisdom of Oprah Winfrey: A Portrait in Her Own Words*. Carol Publishing Group, 1997.

Winfrey, Oprah. *What I Know for Sure*. Flatiron Books, 2014.

Winfrey, Oprah. *The Wisdom of Sundays: Life-Changing Insights from Super Soul Conversations*. Flatiron Books, 2017.

Wollstonecraft, Mary. *A Vindication of the Rights of Woman*. Yale University Press, 2014.

Wong, Paul T. P., and Victoria Bowers. "Mature Happiness and Global Wellbeing in Difficult Times." In *Scientific Concepts Behind Happiness, Kindness, and Empathy in Contemporary Society*, edited by Nava R. Silton. IGI Global, 2018.

Wood, Alex M., Jeffrey J. Froh, and Adam W. A. Geraghty. "Gratitude and Well-Being: A Review and Theoretical Integration." *Clinical Psychology Review* 30, no. 7 (2010): 890–905. https://doi.org/10.1016/j.cpr.2010.03.005.

Wood, Alex M., Stephen Joseph, Joanna Lloyd, and Samuel Atkins. "Gratitude Influences Sleep Through the Mechanism of Pre-Sleep Cognitions." *Journal of Psychosomatic Research* 66, no. 1 (2009): 43–48. https://doi.org/10.1016/j.jpsychores.2008.09.002.

Wood, Wendy, and David T. Neal. "A New Look at Habits and the Habit-Goal Interface." *Psychological Review* 114, no. 4 (2007): 843–63. https://doi.org/10.1037/0033-295X.114.4.843.

Woods, Earl. *Training a Tiger: A Father's Guide to Raising a Winner in Both Golf and Life*. HarperCollins, 1997.

Woods, Earl. *Playing Through: Straight Talk on Hard Work, Big Dreams and Adventures with Tiger*. HarperCollins, 1998.

Woods, Randall B. *John Quincy Adams: A Man for the Whole People*. Dutton, 2024.

Woods, Tiger. *How I Play Golf*. Warner Books, 2001.

Woods, Tiger. *The 1997 Masters: My Story*. Grand Central Publishing, 2017.

Wordsworth, William. "My Heart Leaps Up." In *Poems, in Two Volumes*. 1802.

World Health Organization. "Depression." Accessed June 15, 2025. https://who.int/health-topics/depression.

Worthington, Everett L., Jr. *Handbook of Forgiveness*. Routledge, 2007.

Yahoo Health. "Steal Carli Lloyd's Mental Trick That Helped the US Win the World Cup." Yahoo!Life. July 6, 2015. https://yahoo.com/lifestyle/steal-carli-lloyds-mental-trick-that-helped-the-123378222937.html.

Yerkes, Robert M., and John D. Dodson. "The Relation of Strength of Stimulus to Rapidity of Habit-Formation." *Journal of Comparative Neurology and Psychology* 18, no. 5 (1908): 459–82. https://doi.org/10.1002/cne.920180503.

Yin, Henry H., and Barbara J. Knowlton. "The Role of the Basal Ganglia in Habit Formation." *Nature Reviews Neuroscience* 7, no. 6 (2006): 464–76. https://doi.org/10.1038/nrn1919.

Yogananda, Paramahansa. *Autobiography of a Yogi*. Self-Realization Fellowship, 1946.

Young, Simon N. "How to Increase Serotonin in the Human Brain Without Drugs." *Journal of Psychiatry & Neuroscience* 32, no. 6 (2007): 394–99. https://pmc.ncbi.nlm.nih.gov/articles/PMC2077351/.

Yousafzai, Malala. "Malala Yousafzai Speech at United Nations Youth Assembly 2013 Transcript." United Nations. July 12, 2013. https://www.rev.com/transcripts/malala-yousafzai-speech-at-united-nations-youth-assembly-2013-transcript.

Yousafzai, Malala, and Christina Lamb. *I Am Malala: The Girl Who Stood Up for Education and Was Shot by the Taliban*. Little, Brown and Company, 2013.

Zahn, Roland, Jorge Moll, Mirella Paiva, Griselda Garrido, Frank Krueger, Edward D. Huey, and Jordan Grafman. "The Neural Basis of Human Social Values: Evidence from Functional MRI." *Cerebral Cortex* 19, no. 2 (2009): 276–83. https://doi.org/10.1093/cercor/bhn080.

Zajonc, Robert B. "Attitudinal Effects of Mere Exposure." *Journal of Personality and Social Psychology* 9, no. 2, pt. 2 (1968): 1–27. https://doi.org/10.1037/h0025848.

Zak, Paul J. *The Moral Molecule: The Source of Love and Prosperity*. Dutton, 2012.

Ziglar, Zig. *GOALS with Zig Ziglar*. Nightingale-Conant Corporation, 1986.

www.ingramcontent.com/pod-product-compliance
Lightning Source LLC
Chambersburg PA
CBHW030508080526
44586CB00011B/113